The Author

John Richard Alden has already gained the attention of historians with an earlier work, *John Stuart and the Southern Colonial Frontier, 1754-1775*, for which he was awarded the American Historical Association's Beveridge Prize in 1945.

He is also the author of *General Gage in America* and has had several articles published in leading professional magazines. At present he is working on *The American Revolution*, a volume to be included in the new *Rise of the American Nation* series edited by Henry Steele Commager.

Dr. Alden is professor of history at the University of Nebraska. He received his bachelor's and advanced degrees at the University of Michigan, where he held the Alfred H. Lloyd Memorial Research fellowship for one year.

"Old things need not be therefore true."
O brother men, nor yet the new;
Ah! still awhile the old thought retain,
And yet consider it again!

ARTHUR HUGH CLOUGH

Charles Lee Esq.
Major General of the American Forces

Contemporary engraving (No accurate likeness of Lee is known
to exist)

GENERAL
CHARLES LEE

Traitor or Patriot?

By John Richard Alden

LOUISIANA STATE UNIVERSITY PRESS

Baton Rouge

COPYRIGHT, 1951

LOUISIANA STATE UNIVERSITY PRESS

PRINTED IN THE UNITED STATES OF AMERICA
BY THE WILLIAM BYRD PRESS, INC., RICHMOND, VA.

TO MY MOTHER

PREFACE

THIS IS an attempt to tell the history of an extraordinary individual, of an Englishman who played a major role as an American leader in the drama of the American Revolution. It is not the first book to be devoted to a study of the career of Charles Lee. Four works concerning Lee, by Edward Langworthy, Sir Henry Bunbury, Jared Sparks, and George H. Moore, were published between 1792 and 1860. Of these, the biography written by Sparks is the only one of any considerable value. The others are brief, and that by Moore is permeated by strong prejudice against its subject. Although large quantities of data concerning the American Revolution—and Lee—have become available since 1860, no full-length study of Lee has hitherto appeared. This circumstance is probably explained in part by the fact that Lee became a bitter enemy of George Washington and *ipso facto* a sinister figure in the minds of many persons, including even historians; and it undoubtedly proceeds in part from a suspicion that Lee was a traitor to the American cause. Nevertheless, Lee was one of the fathers of the American Republic, and his career obviously deserves serious examination. The present writer has tried to set aside national, partisan, and personal prejudices and to relate objectively his story upon the basis of the evidence now available. The Lee who appears herein is, in all likelihood, not the Lee the reader has known, but it is hoped that he bears strong resemblance to the original. If the writer's judgments of Lee seem too favorable, they do not proceed from a desire to set up an idol nor from a wish to destroy one, but from the bias which the author of a biographical study commonly develops toward his subject.

The writer gratefully acknowledges the courtesies and assistance of the staffs of the Don Love Memorial Library, University of Nebraska; the Nebraska Historical Society; the General Library, University of Michigan; the William L. Clements Library, University of Michigan; the Library of Congress; the Archives of the United States of America; the New York Public

Library; the Harvard College Library; the American Antiquarian Society; the Sterling Library, Yale University; the Philadelphia Library Company, Ridgeway Branch; the Historical Society of Pennsylvania; the American Philosophical Society; the John Carter Brown Library; the Rhode Island State Historical Society; the British Museum; and the British Public Record Office. Dr. Randolph G. Adams, Librarian of the William L. Clements Library, and Colton Storm, Curator of Manuscripts in the same institution, gave very useful advice and help. For gracious responses to requests for information, thanks are due to Miss Sarah Corwin, Miss Norma Cuthbert, Mlle. Yvonne Fernillot, Lord Herbert, Mrs. Katherine Leighley, Dean C. H. Oldfather, Mr. Harry Ammon, Sir Charles Bunbury, Bart., Sir William Ll. Davies, Mr. Warren A. McCullough, Mr. Henry Marceau, Mr. Paul E. Miller, Mr. Stephen T. Riley, Dr. Reuben I. Seime, and Dr. Louis B. Wright. Professors Boyd Carter, Donald Dysinger, G. W. Gray, and James L. Sellers, Mr. Frederick Kirkland, and Mr. Bernhard Knollenberg generously gave advice and encouragement. Miss Dorothy C. Barck, Librarian, and Dr. Donald Sheehan, Curator of Manuscripts, of the New-York Historical Society, and Mr. Wilmer Leach and Mr. Edward B. Morrison of the Division of Manuscripts, New York Public Library, rendered services above and beyond the call of duty. Mr. P. H. Lawson, of Chester, England, and Mr. Gustave Lanctot, Deputy Minister, Public Archives of Canada, were exceedingly kind in supplying copies of much needed documents to the author. The writer wishes to acknowledge with much gratitude the helpful and generous services of Dr. John Powell, and the kindness of Robert R. Logan, Esq., who graciously permitted the use of some of his valuable family papers.

The writer is heavily indebted to the University of Nebraska for financial aid, especially in the form of the Franklin E. and Orinda M. Johnson Faculty Research Fellowship, which he held during the second semester of the academic year 1947-48, and for release from teaching duties during the period February–September, 1948. He also owes to that institution the efficient secretarial services of Mrs. Elnora Hazelrigg. For their careful editing of the manuscript the author wishes to express his thanks to Mrs. Ann Riley and Mrs. Patricia Smylie of the Louisiana State University Press.

The maps for this volume were prepared by his wife, Pearl Wells Alden.

A word regarding citations. The writer, largely because of greater accessibility, has in general preferred, when possible, to cite printed documents rather than manuscripts. However, to avoid errors, he has consulted the manuscript sources when feasible and seemingly desirable. The personal papers of Charles Lee, except for a few items, have been lost or destroyed. Fortunately, a large part of them were published, with other Lee items, in four volumes over seventy years ago, by the New-York Historical Society. Reference is very frequently made to these very valuable volumes. Although the printed Lee Papers are not without minor deviations from the manuscripts upon which they are based, they may generally be used with confidence. Deletions in some of the letters in the first volume of this collection arose from a belief that passages considered obscene should not be printed. Passages in certain letters from Charles Lee to Miss Sidney Lee are omitted because the heirs of Miss Lee considered them to be concerned only with minor family matters.

Old-style dates have not been altered to conform with the modern calendar.

UNIVERSITY OF NEBRASKA   JOHN RICHARD ALDEN

CONTENTS

ILLUSTRATIONS

CHAPTER ONE

YOUNG REDCOAT IN AMERICA

Forc'd from their homes, a melancholy train,
To traverse climes beyond the western main;
Where wild Oswego spreads her swamps around,
And Niagara stuns with thund'ring sound.
GOLDSMITH, *The Traveller*

O N JANUARY 26, 1732, Charles, son of Colonel John Lee and Isabella Bunbury Lee, was baptized in St. Martin's Church in the beautiful old fortress town of Chester in northwestern England.[1] Sixteen days later in far-off Virginia was born George Washington. As fate would have it, these two men, so nearly the same age, eventually became intimately associated in the American Revolution. There was a day when the American people had greater faith in Charles Lee, second ranking officer in the Continental army, than they had in Washington, the commander in chief. In the fall and early winter of 1776, when the main American army threatened to disintegrate under the assaults of the British forces under Sir William Howe, it was the Englishman Lee to whom many Americans looked for salvation. Two years later, after a bitter quarrel with Washington, Lee was disgraced. He was finally dismissed from the American service, and he died almost in obscurity in Philadelphia in 1782. Three-quarters of a century after his death the publication of evidence suggesting that Lee attempted to betray the American cause in 1777 excited great public interest. Then gradually he became almost a forgotten man, now remembered principally as the officer at whom Washington swore on Monmouth battlefield. It is ironic that he is so remembered, since Washington did *not* curse Lee at Monmouth. It is an even more remarkable fact that the Englishman has been neglected by the historians for almost a century, for in his time he was a figure of world importance; and this remarkable personality should not be denied a place among the leaders of the American Revolutionary generation.

Charles Lee came from a distinguished ancestry. On his father's side he was descended from Lees who had appeared in the vicinity of Chester as early as the thirteenth century and who had acquired an estate at Dernhall in the time of James I. Distantly connected with the Lees who held the earldom of Litchfield, those of Dernhall were not without honor in their own county. Thomas Lee, Charles's great-grandfather, was once high sheriff of Cheshire. Although Colonel Lee had sold Dernhall and had removed to Chester before Charles's birth, he and his family continued to enjoy high social rank in the county. Colonel Lee never became a great figure in England or even in the British army, but he was looked upon as a respectable gentleman. Through his mother Charles was descended from more famous stock, for the Bunbury family had produced and has continued to produce persons of talent and repute. His mother was a niece of Sir Thomas Hanmer, who won fame in the first half of the eighteenth century as both a politician and a scholar, serving as speaker of the House of Commons and as an editor of Shakespeare. With the blood of Lees, Hanmers, and Bunburys in his veins Charles Lee was born into the English gentry and needed to bend the knee socially before no man.[2]

Although Lee possessed from the day of his birth the extremely important social advantage of gentle ancestry—in eighteenth-century Britain almost indispensable for a public career—he was the youngest of seven children, and his parents, although not poor, were by no means rich. His father's income was probably little more than his salary and perquisites; his mother, however, had inherited fairly considerable wealth. As the youngest child, with four older brothers and two older sisters, Charles's opportunities for education and a professional career might have been seriously limited, but all of his brothers and one of his sisters died long before he reached maturity. Death took an amazingly heavy toll in his family, for William and Thomas, twins born in 1718, a second Thomas, born in 1721, Henry, born about 1722, and Elizabeth, born in 1728,[3] all died in childhood or youth. One might infer that the family was physically frail, yet such was probably not the case. As an adult Charles spoke of inheriting a strong constitution from his parents. In any event, Charles and his sister Sidney, born in 1726 or 1727, were the only children who lived beyond youth.[4]

Lee's education was not neglected. He was apparently sent to school somewhere in Britain, probably near Chester, at an early age.[5] After he had acquired a rudimentary training, he was placed in an academy in Switzerland.[6] Precisely when he was put in school in Switzerland cannot be learned, but it is to be supposed that Colonel Lee desired his son to become familiar with languages and peoples other than English. Returning to England, Lee was admitted on June 25, 1746, as a student at the King Edward VI Free Grammar School at Bury St. Edmunds in Suffolk,[7] probably at the instance of his uncle, the Reverend Sir William Bunbury, a man of very great wealth, who resided near Bury St. Edmunds. How long he remained at this school is not known, but it is clear that it played an important part in his life, for several boys who attended the school were his life-long friends and companions. Among these was William Butler of Cornist in Flintshire, who had been a schoolmate since Lee was eight or nine years of age.[8] Others included the four Davers brothers—Robert, Henry, Charles, and Thomas, sons of Sir Jermyn Davers, Bart., of Rushbrooke in Suffolk. Charles, who inherited the baronetcy in 1763, served as a member of the House of Commons for Bury St. Edmunds for over thirty years, and fathered eight illegitimate children, was especially intimate with Lee. Also notable among the boys at the school was Thomas Charles Bunbury, Lee's first cousin, about nine years younger than Lee and the inheritor of his father's title and wealth in 1764.[9] Sir Charles, as he was later known, continued to be Lee's friend, or at least to own his kinship, through thick and thin.

Twentieth-century readers may be somewhat startled to learn that Lee was an ensign in the British army before he entered school in Suffolk. But in eighteenth-century England it was common practice to issue a commission to a boy still occupied with his studies. Probably he had been destined for a military career from an early age, since his father and several relatives were army officers. Lee's commission was dated April 9, 1746,[10] and he was enrolled in the regiment commanded by his father—the Fifty-fifth, then in Scotland helping to put down the rebellion of '45 led by Bonnie Prince Charlie. That his father, relatives, and friends had used influence to secure the ensigncy is not to be questioned, for ensigncies were highly prized and were issued as a matter of patronage. While Lee conned his lessons at Bury St. Edmunds, he was carried on the regimental roll as engaged in "recruiting."[11]

Lee is said to have been a student also at Reims, France, in a college maintained by the Jesuits for the sons of English gentlemen,[12] although no record can now be found connecting him with such an institution.[13] According to another report Lee was a student both at Westminster School and at Oxford University, but this report is almost certainly incorrect.[14] It is likely, however, that Lee had the advantages of advanced intellectual training, for even as a young man he was familiar with the classics, history, and languages.

Whatever his academic training, Lee early acquired the habits of a thorough scholar. He came to use French with ease, to read Greek and Latin, and to read and write Italian. It is even said that he learned to speak an Indian dialect with facility during his service in America in the French and Indian War.[15] Throughout his mature years he read constantly and discriminatingly, carrying with him whenever possible a store of good books. He perused Machiavelli's studies in politics and warfare, Montaigne's essays, Homer, Vergil, Henry Fielding, Milton, Oliver Goldsmith, Rabelais, Xenophon, Seneca, Montesquieu, Thucydides, Swift, the memoirs of Cardinal de Retz, Terence, Addison, John Locke, Horace, Pope, Cicero, and a host of other authors. Among those whom he loved best was the "divine Shakespeare."[16] Lee's own writings are studded with allusions to and quotations from the great Elizabethan dramatist. He was profoundly affected also by his studies in the classics, especially, perhaps, the biographies of Plutarch, which inspired in him a romantic love of republican and antique virtues that endured almost to the end of his life.[17] That love was no doubt nourished by his readings in Shakespeare. He seems also to have been greatly influenced by the now-forgótten Paul de Rapin, a French Huguenot, whose strongly pro-Whig history of England supported Whig principles planted in Lee by his father.[18] It is therefore not altogether surprising that in maturity he found in Jean Jacques Rousseau "my divine and incomparable master."[19] Lee's tastes were catholic, with emphasis on the humanities and the science of war. Except that he seems to have displayed no interest in science and mathematics, he was truly a child of the eighteenth-century Enlightenment.

Not long after Lee completed his formal education, death struck again in his family: Colonel Lee died on August 5, 1750.[20] Lee seems to have admired his father—perhaps loved him—and his passing must have been a shock. By his father's will, the widow received the income from £1,000 placed in trust, the principal to go to Charles after his mother's death. Another £1,000 was given to Sidney Lee. Charles received his father's books, pictures, and plate, and the residue of the estate after his father's debts had been paid. The widow possessed substantial property in her own right, and provision had previously been made for Sidney.[21] Charles, who was sole executor, seems to have inherited little directly from his father.

Still further family distress came to Lee some time before 1754. Nothing can be learned regarding his attitude as a child and as a youth toward his mother. By 1754, however, the mother and son were on very bad terms. The fundamental causes of the enmity between them cannot even be conjectured. In any case, Lee gave up a project to go recruiting for his regiment in Chester in 1754 because his mother did not wish to see him.[22] The breach between them was never thoroughly healed. After that time the only member of his immediate family who held his affection was his sister Sidney, a well-bred, amiable, and kindly woman, who never married. Charles and Sidney exhibited a lifelong fondness for each other.

Although the bases of dislike between Charles Lee and his mother cannot surely be discovered, it seems that there was a strain of eccentricity in the Bunbury family, which both inherited. This eccentricity was noted in Sir William Bunbury,[23] in Sir Charles Bunbury,[24] and in Lee himself. Indeed, Lee admitted on various occasions that he possessed a peculiar mentality and once ascribed it, at least in part, to heredity. In Lee this eccentricity manifested itself, among other ways, in moodiness and a choleric temper. Both of these characteristics appeared early in life and continued through the passing years.[25] They were apparently associated with a family tendency toward that physical imbalance which produced the disorder known as the gout, that painful affliction so fashionable in the eighteenth century.

The Charles Lee who finally reported for active duty in the Fifty-fifth regiment, soon renamed the Forty-fourth, was obviously a remarkable individual. Slender, fairly tall,[26] and possessing unusually small hands and feet, he was not especially imposing in physique, although his body was sturdy enough to carry him through a succession of illnesses and wounds sufficient to kill several ordinary men. But the true quality of the man was evident in his lean, dark, bony face and in his long aquiline nose—a nose so startling and so impressive that it won for him at a later time the sobriquet "Naso." If Lee could be, and was, described as ugly, none of his fellow officers in the regiment could doubt that a most extraordinary person had entered their fellowship. They discovered him to be a scholar, in a day when scholars were uncommon in the British army. What could one think of a man who begged that a copy of Thucydides be sent to him while he was campaigning in the wilds of America? To be sure, James Wolfe placed the glory of composing the *Elegy Written in a Country Churchyard* above all military fame, but Wolfe was also a freak. They noted that Lee read omnivorously even in military literature, as if one could learn about war in books. The more observant ones discerned in him a brain that was quick and not without depth. All recognized in him vanity, soaring ambition, strength of will, and utter fearlessness.

In the Forty-fourth regiment Lee met Major Thomas Gage, who, like himself, was to play a great role in world affairs. While Sir Peter Halkett, the colonel who succeeded Lee's father, was perhaps no more than a brave soldier, Gage, lieutenant colonel after 1751, was a gentleman of superior quality. A second son

of Viscount Gage of Firle, Gage was a tall, handsome, courteous, and kindly officer. Educated at Westminster and in
France, Gage was a polished man of the world without major
vices or viciousness. Benevolent, he was also a courageous and
faithful soldier. It is evident that Lee admired him. Years later,
when Gage, as commander in chief of the British army in
America and as governor of Massachusetts, was bitterly attacked
by Americans in their newspapers, Lee printed a letter defending Gage's character, even though Lee had then given his allegiance to the American cause. Eventually Lee was to censure
bitterly Gage's behavior with reference to public affairs and to
blame him profanely for the outbreak of the War of Independence, but for many years Lee saw in Gage only a friend and
a generous-hearted superior. Lee formed enduring friendships
with several other officers in the regiment. He found only one
who was seriously objectionable—Major John Beckwith.

The Forty-fourth was a splendid regiment and had already
won laurels upon several battlefields. When Lee joined it in
1748 or soon afterward, too late to take part in the War of the
Austrian Succession,[27] it was stationed in Ireland on inactive
garrison duty. Opportunities for promotion were therefore not
very great for some years. Nevertheless, Lee was able to purchase a lieutenancy which fell vacant, thus securing his first promotion on May 1, 1751. Not until the fall of 1754 was the regiment again called up for field service. Then it was ordered to
America. Earlier in the year, Virginians led by George Washington had exchanged shots with French regulars near the junc-
tion of the Monongahela and Allegheny rivers. The French
had been the victors and had built a fort at the confluence of
the two rivers. On the assumption that the French were ag-
gressors and that they had invaded British territory the British
cabinet decided to drive them back beyond the Great Lakes,
and the Forty-fourth and Forty-eighth regiments under Major
General Edward Braddock were sent out to do the job, with
the assistance of American colonial troops. The Seven Years'
War, called in America the French and Indian War, had begun.

Lee was enjoying himself at the health and social resort at
Bath when the news came. He prudently made his will, leaving

most or all of his property to his sister.[28] Passing over to Ireland, he joined the regiment at Cork, from which place the troops sailed in transports at the beginning of 1755. How the redcoats reached Virginia, how they marched against the French at Fort Duquesne, and how they suffered a disastrous defeat is well known. What adventures befell Lee cannot be ascertained. He served throughout the campaign, but the various contemporary accounts of it and of Braddock's defeat do not mention him.[29] If he was with his regiment on the battlefield, he escaped without a wound. Possibly Lee was unable because of illness to take part in the march through the wilderness which ended so fatally.[30] He was with the regiment in Philadelphia, to which place the British regiments retreated after the battle; and he accompanied the Forty-fourth from Philadelphia to the neighborhood of Albany, where it went into winter quarters in the fall of 1755.

Lee's early impressions of America were highly favorable. He told his sister, " . . . there is a magnificence and greatness . . . not equal'd in any part of Europe; our rivers and lakes (even the greatest) are to these little rivulets and brooks; indeed Nature in every article seems to be in great here what on your side the waters, she is in small." He found some of the American towns "very good," and Philadelphia, which was to be a scene of both triumph and disaster for him, he described as "charming." He noted that the ladies of that place were "extremely pretty and most passionately fond of red coats, which is for us a most fortunate piece of absurdity."[31]

With the regiment in winter quarters Lee had time on his hands. Never one to be idle, he struck up an acquaintance with Sir William Johnson, who lived in the grand manner at near-by Johnson Hall and handled British diplomacy with respect to the Indians of the Six Nations. Johnson, a trader in Indian goods in his youth, had learned to speak the dialects of the Iroquois and had contracted several marriage alliances among them. Lee emulated Johnson. He read Cadwallader Colden's famous history of the Indian confederacy, lived among the Mohawks, and learned at least a little of their language. Although he found the Indian habits of slaying captives and of scalping somewhat disturbing, he was soon rhapsodizing to his sister about the grace, manners, and handsome appearance of the Mohawk warriors. He romanticized also about the Indian women and actually married one, a daughter of White Thunder (otherwise known as Silver Heels), a Seneca chief. "She is a very great beauty," he slyly wrote to Sidney, "and is more like your friend Mrs. Griffith than anybody I know. I shall say nothing of her accomplishments for you must be certain that a woman of her fashion cannot be without many." As the result of this alliance Lee was inducted into the tribe of the Bear, under the appropriate name, as he gave it, of Ounewaterika, signifying "boiling water, or one whose spirits are never asleep." For many years Lee was known among his English friends as "Boiling Water." There were other results of this alliance, for Lee's Indian wife bore him copper-skinned twins, a boy and a girl. The boy had Lee's imposing aquiline nose, which he is reported to have lost as the result of disease acquired "in the arms of a harlot."[32] It is not unlikely that Lee's Indian wife was living at Quebec in 1774, that she still retained her fondness for him, and that he kept in touch with her for many years after their marriage.[33] However, Lee eventually turned completely against the Indians, coming to the conclusion that they deserved extirpation.[34]

"Boiling Water" purchased his captaincy in the Forty-fourth in June, 1756, and served through the following campaign, which brought to British arms a new disaster, the fall of Fort Oswego on Lake Ontario to the intrepid Marquis de Montcalm. The Forty-fourth was sent to strengthen Oswego, but it was too late and turned back toward Albany. In the spring of 1757 Lee and the Forty-fourth took part in an expedition against the French fort of Louisburg on Cape Breton Island, which guards the mouth of the St. Lawrence River. The Earl of Loudoun, a Scottish peer who had become commander in chief of the British forces in America just before the fall of Oswego, personally directed this venture. Because of the lack of naval power, it achieved nothing. Lee, with others, became disgusted with Loudoun's leadership when Montcalm took advantage of Loudoun's absence to capture the weakly defended Fort William Henry in northern New York. Lee justly observed that

Loudoun could not be censured for his failure to take Louisburg, but he charged him with poor judgment and dawdling.[35]
In the winter of 1757-58 at New York, Lee openly made fun of
the Louisburg operation. Loudoun had ordered his men to plant
cabbages at Halifax so as to obtain fresh vegetables. It may have
been Lee who coined the witty sobriquet "cabbage-planting expedition" for Loudoun's venture, a term which became famous
in its day and is not yet forgotten.[36] After the end of the campaign, at a dinner attended by many English officers who entertained anti-Scottish sentiments and who were opposed to Loudoun, Lee gave a toast, "A Head to the Army."[37] Considering
the company present, the toast was just as effective as if it had
been given in a public address. Loudoun's management of the
army was something less than praiseworthy, and Lee's attack
upon him was somewhat justified. But Lee displayed in his
criticisms of Loudoun the intemperate spirit for which he later
became famous.

Loudoun was removed from the supreme command and was
replaced by Major General James Abercromby in the spring of
1758. Abercromby's main effort was an attack upon Fort Ticonderoga, held by the Marquis de Montcalm. Lee led a British detachment northward from Albany, and he took part in an unsuccessful grand assault made against the French entrenchments.
He was badly wounded by a musket shot which shattered two
ribs and passed through his body. He was carried from the field
by his servant, and it seemed for a time that he was mortally injured. But he was conveyed back to the Schuyler estate near
Albany, where his wound slowly mended. When leading forward his detachment Lee is said to have requisitioned horses,
grain, and other supplies from the Schuyler estate without the
customary warrants and to have rejected truculently the protests of the family; but he was graciously cared for by Madam
Schuyler, the matriarch of the family, whom he lavishly thanked
for her assistance.[38]

Lee did not fully recover from his wound for several months,
but he was sufficiently well in mid-September to send home to
England a slashing attack upon Abercromby, whom he called a
"damn'd beastly poltroon" and "our booby in chief," charac-

terizing Abercromby's conduct as stupid, ridiculous, dishonorable, and infamous. These were strong terms, even though Abercromby had indeed been a miserable failure, wasting the lives of many brave men and accomplishing less than nothing. It is perhaps significant that, on the other hand, Lee lavished praise upon Viscount Howe, who was among the slain at Ticonderoga.[39] In more moderate language, historians have agreed with Lee that Abercromby was a blunderer and that Howe was a man of great merit. Lee's judgment of his superiors was recklessly asserted, but not unsound. The fact that he defended Braddock's reputation after that general's death is also interesting,[40] since most historians have come to the conclusion that Braddock was by no means incapable.

Although Lee had scarcely recovered from his wound, his life was again threatened in the fall of 1758 after he had gone into winter quarters on Long Island. An army surgeon had written a paper attacking Lee which he read publicly before the commander in chief and others, and Lee thrashed him. As Lee tells the story, the surgeon obtained two pistols from Major Beckwith and waited in ambush for him as he rode along a road in company with Captain William Dunbar, a friend and fellow officer in the Forty-fourth. The surgeon leapt from his hiding place, grasped the bridle of Lee's horse, and fired at Lee's heart. Fortunately for Lee, his horse shied away, and the bullet glanced off his ribs. The surgeon attempted to fire his second pistol, but Dunbar struck it from his hand. The surgeon was permitted to resign his commission to escape a court-martial. Learning that he had obtained his weapons from Beckwith, Lee suspected the attack had been inspired by Beckwith and publicly tongue-lashed him in the hope of forcing him into a duel, to no avail. In the spring of 1760 Lee determined to drive his superior officer from the regiment or to leave it himself at the end of the campaign.[41] As it happened, Lee did quit the regiment some months later, but apparently not because of Beckwith.

The tide of war, except for Abercromby's dismal failure at Ticonderoga, had turned in favor of the British in 1758. Both Fort Duquesne (promptly renamed Fort Pitt) and Louisburg had fallen into English hands. The prospects of the army in

America were excellent as the campaign of 1759 opened, particularly since Sir Jeffrey Amherst and Major General James
Wolfe had been placed in command in New York and on the
lower St. Lawrence, respectively. Lee came to admire the military abilities of both men, giving the palm to the "hero" Wolfe,[42]
as have almost all students of the two generals. While Amherst
pushed forward to capture Ticonderoga and Crown Point and
Wolfe captured Quebec, Lee served in the western wilderness.
As part of the military plan for 1759 Amherst sent the Forty-
fourth and other troops up the Mohawk Valley under Brigadier
General John Prideaux to take Fort Niagara and to reoccupy
Fort Oswego. Niagara fell to the arms of the English, and a
French force which attempted to relieve its garrison was driven
off. In an assault upon Niagara, Lee's hair was creased by two
bullets simultaneously, but he was uninjured and able to do
further duty. Reporting enthusiastically these successes to his
sister and to his uncle, Sir William Bunbury, Lee wrote almost
ecstatically of Niagara, "quite a paradise," and of the great falls,
"the most stupendous cataract in the world." "I believe I shall
settle, marry and trade here," he told Sidney.[43] He was romanc-
ing, and he certainly had no immediate opportunity either to
marry properly in the English style or to settle at Niagara, for
Gage found other occupation for him. Prideaux had been killed
during the siege of the French fort. Gage, then a brigadier
general and Prideaux's successor, was concerned about the non-
arrival of reinforcements scheduled to come to his aid from
Fort Pitt and especially about the French relieving force, which
had vanished into the woods. He ordered Lee to lead a party of
soldiers to Fort Pitt and to collect information.

With another officer and fourteen men, Lee left Niagara on
September 19 and made his way to Lake Erie. The party—the
first Englishmen to sail on that lake—crossed to Presque Isle and
then moved on southward past the French Forts Le Bœuf and
Venango toward Fort Pitt. The detachment saw many Indians,
individuals and small groups, but no trace of the French, and
arrived without loss at Fort Pitt on October 4.[44] From that
place Lee was sent to Crown Point to report to Amherst. Amherst ordered him to return to his regiment at Niagara, and Lee

made another long journey to Oswego. As it happened, transportation from Oswego to Niagara was lacking—possibly because he did not try too hard to find it, since he could not have enjoyed the prospect of winter quarters at Niagara, no matter how much he admired the place in summer. Lee turned back to Albany, where he reported to Gage at Christmas time. Since there was nothing else Lee could do, Gage sent him to Philadelphia,[45] on recruiting service, an assignment which Lee must have welcomed.

In Philadelphia, however, Lee became involved in another of those fracases into which circumstances and his violent temper so frequently involved him. In April, 1760, he recruited there a young man who turned out to be an apprentice, bound by Pennsylvania law to serve his master. As Lee tells the story, the master agreed to release the youth, provided that he received a small sum of money in compensation for lost services. The master, the apprentice, and Lee were conferring about the situation, when they were interrupted by a "fellow" who seized the apprentice by the shoulder and declared him to be a prisoner, giving no authority for his action. Lee undertook to release the boy, and the "fellow" grasped him by the collar, ripped his shirt, and pushed him about. Lee then struck the "fellow," with results which were disastrous, if for no other reason than that he turned out to be James Rowan, a constable. The British officer was promptly arrested on the charge of resisting the policeman in the execution of his duty. On April 28 he was bonded to keep the peace for a period of one year; as guarantees he put up £500, and David Franks and Robert Morris each paid £250. The same day Lee, Franks, and Morris gave bonds of £100, £50, and £50, respectively, to ensure that Lee would appear to answer a charge of assault and battery before the mayor, recorder, and aldermen at the next court of quarter sessions. At the trial he was found guilty, was fined £50, and was informed by the court that he had been "let off easy." Lee appealed the case to the supreme court of Pennsylvania and also asked Amherst to use his influence with the governor of the colony to secure a remission of the fine. The results of this request are unknown.[46] Whatever the physical sufferings of Rowan and the injured feelings of Lee, Lee had apparently acquired the acquaintance of Robert Morris, who was much later to be his intimate and loyal friend.

By 1760 Lee had obtained his reputation for pugnacity and hotheadedness. Many years afterward Thomas Jones, the Tory historian of New York, who disliked him and who is notoriously unreliable, described him as "quarrelsome, satirical, and abusive." "He was under more arrests, had more court martials held upon him, and more courts of inquiry into his conduct, than all the officers of the [British] army put together. He was thought by many to be insane, and was known by the name of 'Mad Lee.' "[47] Jones's statements cannot be directly supported by much evidence and must be discounted. Nevertheless, it is apparent that there is some truth in them. It is also clear that Lee possessed the courage signified by his name and by the three lions upon his family's coat of arms.

In the spring of 1760, Lee traveled by way of New York to Albany, where he reported to Amherst and was sent back to Niagara.[48] Joining his regiment at that place, he took part in the successful attack which Amherst made upon Montreal and which destroyed the French grip upon Canada. Lee served in an army that Amherst personally led down the St. Lawrence River to Montreal. Montreal surrendered early in September, and Lee promptly sailed for England on leave of absence.

Lee had more than one reason for hurrying off to England. Sir William Bunbury, who had enjoyed his nephew's lively letters from America and who had sent him chocolates and books, was fond of him and eager to help him in his profession. In the winter of 1759 he urged his nephew to come to England, indicating he could doubtless obtain a promotion by doing so. He informed Lee that Lord Ligonier, who was commander in chief of the British army and hostile to Lee, was in very poor health, and that the Marquis of Granby, who was a friend of the Bunbury family, would succeed Ligonier.[49] The Earl of Pembroke, a fellow officer, almost simultaneously offered his support to Lee.[50] He could hardly fail to grasp his opportunity, especially since the war was virtually over in America, and future opportunities for winning promotion in the field would be few. Besides, Sidney soon afterward sent him a warning that money which he had invested was in danger of being lost, and begged him to come home.[51]

Lee reached England some time before the end of 1760. He did not return to America until thirteen years had passed. When he again crossed the Atlantic, he came as General Lee, major general in the army of Poland.

CHAPTER TWO

EUROPEAN ADVENTURES

And o'er him many changing scenes must roll,
Ere toil his thirst for travel can assuage,
Or he shall calm his breast, or learn experience sage.
BYRON, *Childe Harold's Pilgrimage*

IN ENGLAND, Lee soon discovered that his property was not endangered and that his hoped-for promotion would be delayed. Some of his friends promised to secure for him an interview with the elder William Pitt, who as principal secretary of state and the leading member of the cabinet had led Britain to staggering victories over France. Lee hoped to give Pitt useful information about America and to gain some advantage for himself.[1] However, if he obtained the interview, it brought him nothing discernible in the way of favors from the great man. In any case, he promptly gave to the public both information about North America and recommendations regarding the policy that should be pursued with reference to that continent. Before the end of 1760 he published an extraordinary pamphlet, apparently his first major venture into the field of governmental affairs.

Even before the capture of Montreal—before the conquest of Canada was assured—literary warfare developed in England regarding the advisability of keeping Canada. It was cogently argued by some students of public policy that Canada should be given back to France when peace was made, because the presence of the French on America's northern frontiers would tend to prevent Britain's American colonists from seeking independence. It was likewise urged that Britain, having conquered both Canada and the French sugar island of Guadeloupe in the West Indies, could not and perhaps should not keep both, and that Guadeloupe was far more valuable to Britain in an economic way than Canada. Benjamin Franklin, agent for Pennsylvania in London, had written very effectively in favor of the retention of Canada. Lee, leaping into the fray, ably supported Franklin in an anonymously published pamphlet entitled *The Importance of Canada Considered In Two Letters to a Noble Lord.*[2]

Never much interested in economic policy, Lee said little about Canada in that respect; but he vigorously insisted that it should be retained in British hands—especially the Niagara communication, the military key to the interior of America and also the key to the fur trade, as he saw it. It was true that the French might no longer be able to attack the English colonies from Canada, were they allowed to retain it; but, Lee pointed out, the Indians in the region of the Great Lakes and in the Ohio Valley were formidable and they might be stirred up by the French to attack the English. The Shawnee and Delaware tribes in the Ohio Valley, he observed, were already uneasy and disposed to be hostile to the English; and an Indian uprising would be disastrous, especially if many small garrisons were maintained in the western wilderness. His arguments were briefly, lucidly, and even charmingly presented. That they exercised much influence is doubtful, although Franklin is reputed to have welcomed Lee as an ally and to have praised his work.[3] Nevertheless, Lee displayed an almost prophetic vision. Canada was kept; Amherst established many small posts in the Indian country; no effort was made to conciliate the Indians. Lee's predictions came true. The Delawares and Shawnees were largely instrumental in organizing the savage assaults upon the English which culminated in the great Indian war of 1763, and several of the garrisons set up by Amherst were destroyed by the redskins. No one ever had greater right to say "I warned you" than Lee when the news of the uprising led by Pontiac came to England in the summer of 1763.

In London in February, 1761, Lee's fortunes were at a low ebb. He was desperately ill of a pulmonary disorder, recovering but slowly. Moreover, his efforts to obtain a promotion were running into snags. In the eighteenth century, appointments in the British army were secured in large part through influence rather than merit, and Lee had made an enemy of Lord Ligonier, possibly because he had recklessly condemned a friend or friends of Ligonier. The commander in chief refused to support Lee for a majority and perhaps actively used his power against him. The Earl of Pembroke and the Earl of Thanet, a rich peer of liberal views who had contracted an enduring admiration for Lee,[4] energetically pushed his claims, but without result for some months. Lee secured a promise from the Scottish Earl of Bute, formerly the mentor of George III, who had great influence with the king, to speak in his favor. He also presented his desires in a formal petition to the king on February 18, without any immediate consequence.[5] The solicitations of Lee and his friends had no effect until the following summer.

In the meantime Lee visited Chester with his sister, sojourned for a brief time with Lord Thanet, and became intimate with John Hall-Stevenson, who was to be his lifelong friend. How Lee made the latter's acquaintance is not known; apparently they met through the medium of Colonel George Lawson Hall, a brother of Hall-Stevenson who had served in America and who accompanied Lee to Hall-Stevenson's home in Yorkshire.

Hall-Stevenson's residence was a strangely jumbled architectural curiosity known as "Crazy Castle," and he himself was known as "Crazy Hall." He was about thirteen years older than Lee and had been handsome in his youth. He had become somewhat eccentric, one of his oddities being that he always went to bed when the wind blew from the east. Since he relied upon a weather vane to indicate the direction of the wind, friends gleefully sent him to bed upon occasion by manipulating the vane. A well-educated and accomplished man of the world, generous-minded and kindly, he was addicted to the pursuit of pleasure and was apparently one of the twelve Monks of Medmenham, that secret society of rakes who mildly surprised even eighteenth-century London by their revels. In 1765 he was to publish *Crazy Tales*, a collection of droll stories modeled after Chaucer's *Canterbury Tales* and Queen Margaret of Navarre's *Heptameron*. His stories were often witty, uniformly broad, and frequently pornographic. At Crazy Castle, more formally known as "Skelton," Hall-Stevenson led a gay and unconventional life. He was, of course, fond of lively company, and he organized there a drinking society called the "Demoniacs," consisting of several scholars, professional men, and gentlemen in the neighborhood. One of his best friends was Laurence Sterne, whom he had met as a student at Cambridge. Sterne frequently visited Hall-Stevenson, wrote part of his famous *Tristram Shandy* at Skelton, and used his host as the model for the character Eugenius.

It was a brilliant, gay, and perhaps dissolute society into which Lee plunged at Crazy Hall; and it is evident that he enjoyed it. He became very intimate with Hall-Stevenson and friendly with Sterne. In June, 1761, Sterne was teasingly urging Lee to marry before peace was made.[6] Many years later Lee declared that he was coauthor of a song which was published with one of Sterne's poems.[7] Through his connection with Hall-Stevenson, Lee seems to have met a number of other public figures, men prominent in literature, the theater, and politics. Among those who were later Lee's acquaintances or friends and who frequented Crazy Castle were Constantine Phipps (afterward Lord Mulgrave), the son of Lady Lascelles, a courteous and witty young naval captain, who lived near-by in Yorkshire; and the Irish peer James Caulfeild, Earl of Charlemont, a distant relative of Phipps and a lover of liberty who was instrumental in obtaining the virtual separation of Ireland from England in 1783.[8] Perhaps through Lee, Charles Davers and Major Horatio Gates, an associate of Lee afterward famous as the victor of Saratoga, also became intimate with Hall-Stevenson and visited Crazy Castle.

Learning that his prospects for promotion had greatly improved, Lee returned to London in the early summer of 1761. His friends had been active in his behalf. Lord Pembroke had taken Ligonier to task for opposing Lee's ambitions, and Thanet had brought great pressure upon Thomas Townshend, the secretary at war, demanding Townshend go to the king immediately to recommend Lee and to obtain his decision. The secretary at war yielded, and George III promised Lee the first vacant majority.[9] Shortly afterward, because of increased tension between Britain and Spain, a new regiment, the One Hundred and Third, was added to the army; and Lee was made major in that regiment on August 10. He was still not satisfied, although he had done fairly well to obtain his majority at the age of thirty. He soon drew up a proposal for raising a new regiment in America, which he himself would command, and he persuaded his friend Clotworthy Upton[10] to present it to Lord Bute. Bute at first refused to commit himself on the scheme. After open war had broken out between Britain and Spain in the following winter, Bute, who had in the meantime become prime minister, displayed some interest in Lee's plan. Bute indicated that he might give his approval, if the scheme received Amherst's blessing. Unwilling to wait for action on the part of Amherst—and possibly doubting that Sir Jeffrey would give his consent—Lee tried early in 1762 to bring further influence upon Bute. He had become in some degree a favorite of the Earl of Shelburne, later Marquis of Lansdowne, a rising young man in politics. Although Shelburne was a stout Whig and entertained principles incompatible with those of Bute, he was on very good terms with the Scottish politician at this time. Lee asked Shelburne to push his project. Whether Shelburne took up the cudgel for it is not known, but it came to nothing.[11]

At this point in his career the first certain evidence appears regarding Lee's political opinions. Although he was constantly—and necessarily, if he wished to succeed in his career—soliciting preferment from George III and those who had influence in the ministry, his political views were definitely of a liberal, not to say radical, complexion. He was on friendly terms not only with Shelburne but also, and more particularly, with Colonel Isaac Barré, Shelburne's associate and a passionate liberal. Moreover, in London in 1761, Lee was expressing his views with his customary vigor, so forcefully and so heedlessly that Shelburne kindly undertook to caution him to guard against his temper and his tongue. Exactly what his opinions then were cannot be said, but there is no doubt that he was arguing energetically and quite openly against the authority of the crown, which he believed was increasing as the result of the efforts of George III.[12]

Early in 1762 the One Hundred and Third regiment was placed on the alert for active service, and with it, Lee. In August, 1761, the Bourbon kings Charles III of Spain and Louis XV had entered into a Family Compact, and the entrance of Spain into the Seven Years' War as an ally of France had become almost inevitable. Bute had tried to stave off war with Spain, but without success. Spain entered the conflict and even demanded that Portugal do likewise, under threat of a Spanish invasion. The Portuguese government refused, whereupon Spanish armies prepared to march on Lisbon. Portugal had long been a British ally, and British troops and fleets had more than once come to her assistance. In 1762, Britain again sent the redcoats across the Bay of Biscay to join the Portuguese army. Among them was the One Hundred and Third regiment. On this expedition Lee held the rank of lieutenant colonel, a purely local rank.

Anxious to learn the business of soldiering and to rise in the army, Lee undoubtedly looked upon this venture with favor, especially because he would serve under a master of the art of warfare, Count William La Lippe,[13] a German princeling and the grandson of George I and his mistress the Duchess of Kendall. La Lippe, the teacher of Gneisenau and Scharnhorst, and one of the great generals of modern times, is now forgotten. In his day he was looked upon with awe, and he had been given the post of commander in chief of the Portuguese army with the heavy task of checking the Spanish invasion. Lee was the more anxious to go to Portugal because he carried a letter of recommendation from Shelburne, who had served with La Lippe in Germany. Lee hoped to secure a post as the German's aide-de-camp and thus to improve himself and his opportunities.

The British expedition to Portugal, at first under the command of the Earl of Tyrawley, later succeeded by the Earl of Loudoun, was off Cape Finisterre on July 10 and landed at Lisbon on July 21. On board ship Lee wrote to Shelburne promising he would try to mend his faults and sending his love to Barré.[14] From Lisbon he reported to his sponsor that he had met La Lippe, who was civil, but gave no sign of offering him an appointment on his staff. Lee also reported that the Portuguese army contained no more than fifteen thousand men, poorly trained and ill equipped, concluding with the charge, "Remember me to all that audacious faction who dare to think for themselves, particularly to Barré."[15] La Lippe continued to treat Lee with reserve for some time, but Lee controlled his tongue and behaved prudently. Ironically he declared to his patron that "an excommunicated miscreant" could hardly expect to be welcomed. "I am only surprised that any civiliz'd community will even suffer me to shew my treason hatching head amongst them."[16]

Strangely enough, this expedition which began so disappointingly for Lee brought him both opportunity and glory. Large Spanish forces had crossed the frontier and were steadily advancing toward Lisbon. La Lippe's task was to hold them off only until the coming of the rainy season, for a general peace was about to be made. However, his army, including both Portuguese and English, was small, and the Portuguese were hardly more than a mob. Fortunately for La Lippe, the Spanish exhibited neither skill nor energy, and he was eventually able to force them to halt. In part his success was due to the gallantry and enterprise of Lee. Brigadier General John Burgoyne, Lee's immediate superior officer, who commanded a force on the south side of the Tagus River which was trying to checkmate a Spanish thrust, learned that a Spanish camp upon some hills north of the river near Villa Velha was not too strongly defended. Knowing that the camp contained munitions and supplies, Burgoyne sent Lee with 250 British grenadiers and 50 light horsemen to make a surprise attack upon it. Lee managed to ford the river in the night of October 5, marched around the Spanish, and struck them from the rear at two o'clock in the morning. The grenadiers broke into the camp with bayonets fixed, completely surprising the enemy, who put up a brave but ineffective resistance. Some Spanish cavalry managed to form, but were effectively dispersed by Lee's horsemen. The enemy was routed, and his magazines were destroyed. The Spanish losses, which included a brigadier general, were heavy, and Lee was able to carry off several prisoners and much booty.

This brilliant little victory over superior forces, even though Burgoyne received much of the credit, was a bright feather in Lee's cap. La Lippe publicly thanked him in an order of the day and secured for him a colonelcy in the Portuguese army. The commander in chief and Loudoun sent to the British cabinet glowing accounts of Lee's achievement, and La Lippe recommended him for promotion in the British army. Lee himself joyfully sent a report on the raid to Shelburne, ecstatically referring to the "noble" and "honest" La Lippe and urging him to give what support he could to the German's recommendation.[17] There was only one flat note in Lee's song. After he had received his colonelcy in the Portuguese army Loudoun issued an order declaring that an English officer could not accept a rank in that army which would make him senior to an officer superior to him in the British contingent. Applied to Lee, the rule would have deprived him of his colonelcy. Since bad feeling already existed between Lee and Loudoun, Lee hotly resented his action and refused to accept his ruling, given after the campaign was over and after the Portuguese commission had been offered to him. La Lippe heartily approved of Lee's stand, and Lee did not abandon his Portuguese rank.[18]

Back in England in 1763 Lee met with disappointment. The war came to a close, and the British army reverted to a peacetime footing, with the result that opportunities for promotion were limited. Nevertheless, he had a real claim to preferment, for his services in Portugal deserved recognition, and he had a right to expect it. Lord Thanet secured a promise from George III that something would be done for him,[19] but nothing was done. Instead, he was retired from active service as a major and placed on half-pay in November, 1763. Although he did not know it, he would never again command in the British army.

Possibly Lee had enemies, not now known, who prevented him from securing promotion in 1763. Certainly, by 1764 he had acquired the hostility of Sir Jeffrey Amherst, a powerful figure in English politics. After his return from Portugal he became president of a club of officers who had served in America and interested himself seriously in affairs relating to the American colonies. In the fall of 1763 and the following winter Amherst was bitterly criticized both in America and in England because of his mismanagement of military and Indian problems after the fall of Canada. Amherst had failed to recognize the importance of conciliating the red men in the western wilderness; he had scoffed at their military prowess; and he had made no preparation for an Indian uprising. His army was scattered all over America when the red men struck most effectively in the spring of 1763. Amherst had followed policies directly contrary to those urged by Lee in his Canada pamphlet, and with disastrous results. Lee could hardly fail to take pleasure in his own prescience and to point out to his friends the folly of Amherst's behavior. But he spoke intemperately against his former commander, and he wrote at least two attacks upon him which appeared in print in London.[20] These and other assaults on Amherst did the general no major harm. His earlier achievements were so great and his friends were so influential that he continued to play a most important part both in the army and in public affairs. There can be no question, however, that he resented Lee's criticisms and that he bore ill will toward him. Apparently, Bute also turned strongly against Lee at this time, probably because he declaimed too vigorously against the policies of the king and of the king's favorite.[21]

Lee was unhappy professionally in 1763 and 1764, and he seems to have been somewhat embarrassed financially after he was placed on half-pay. Nevertheless, he made a jaunt to Yorkshire late in the summer of 1764 and sojourned with Hall-Stevenson for some time at Harrogate, which had become a fashionable watering place. Laurence Sterne regretted his inability to join them because he enjoyed their "jolly" company,[22] but it does not appear that the two friends were overly gay there. Alexander Carlyle of Inveresk, who visited Harrogate at the same time and who resided at the Granby, as they did, had previously known both men. Carlyle reports that Lee had become known as "Savage" Lee and that he spent much time arguing and quarreling with another guest, a contentious General Clerk. He also describes the brief stay at Harrogate of the Scottish Laird McLeod of McLeod and his beautiful daughter, a girl just over sixteen. The McLeods gave a concert one evening, at which Carlyle, Hall-Stevenson, and Lee were guests. The young lady sang a Scottish song, and Lee was delighted; she sang an Italian song, and he was transported. He appeared to be greatly impressed by her charms. He refused to speak for several days after the McLeods departed for a resort where there were better opportunities for the laird to gamble, and did not even object to the pleasantries of his companions regarding his "grand passion."[23] It would seem that a fit of melancholy had come upon a lonely and rather unhappy man who could appreciate charm and beauty, but who had neither comeliness nor wealth to attract the feminine sex.

In the summer of 1764 Lee hit upon speculation in American lands as a method of making his fortune. While he was in Portugal his cousin Charles Bunbury had married the famous beauty Lady Sarah Lennox. Bunbury, who became Sir Charles before the end of the year, had grown into a handsome, elegant, languid, easygoing, and somewhat eccentric man. His great passion was horses. Later he won the Derby, but no laurels in the House of Commons, where he sat for some years—a wag once declared that he would have been a great politician, had his constituents each possessed four legs and a tail. Lady Sarah was an even more striking personality, and George III himself had been her serious admirer. She was the sister of the Duke of Richmond and the sister-in-law of Henry Fox, Lord Holland. Through her and her husband, Lee became intimate with Lord Holland and also with the latter's brother-in-law, the Earl of Ilchester. Holland and Ilchester asked Lee's help in providing for Ilchester's daughter, Lady Susan Strangway, who had eloped with an Irish actor named William O'Brien. They wished to obtain a comfortable living for the young couple in America, not in England, and decided to try to secure for them a grant of land in America. Since Lee was familiar with America, they asked his advice. He urged the superior merits of the colony of New York, and the two noblemen accepted his counsel. They obtained a salaried post for O'Brien in that colony and formed with Lee, Clotworthy Upton, and Walter Patterson (like Upton, a friend of Lee's) a combination to petition for a grant of 100,000 acres there. Lady Susan, Mr. O'Brien, Lee, Upton, and Patterson were each to have 20,000 acres. Holland and Ilchester managed to get a royal order for the grant, and Lee began to entertain visions of future wealth, which continued for about three years. Eventually, however, it proved to be impossible for the group to secure lands that would have any great value in

the foreseeable future, because other speculators who had greater
influence pushed them aside. In the end Lee actually lost money
in this enterprise.[24]

In November, 1764, Lee and Patterson also asked for grants
of lands on Prince Edward Island,[25] and were eventually successful in obtaining them. But Lee knew that these American
speculations would bring no return immediately, if ever; and he
could not afford to wait for them to bear fruit. Without prospects of military advancement at home, with social inclinations
above his means, and with ambitions unsatisfied, he decided to
secure employment abroad, at least until his mother's death,
when he would come into a valuable inheritance.[26] He left
England for Poland.

How Lee came to seek his fortune in Poland is largely explained by the remarkable career of Stanislaus Poniatowski. As
a handsome, witty, and fascinating young man, this Polish nobleman had caught the fancy of Catherine the Great. After ceasing to be his mistress, Catherine became his friend and his em-
ployer. In September, 1764, for her own purposes, she compelled the Diet of Poland to elect him king of that unhappy
country. As it happened, Stanislaus had visited England a decade
earlier and had contracted friendships there. It seemed likely
that he would raise an army. Lee therefore sought letters of
recommendation to Stanislaus in the hope of obtaining employment in his service. Fortunately for him, he managed to obtain
one from Charles Yorke, son of the Earl of Hardwicke and formerly an intimate of the new king. Carrying a mass of recommendations, Lee sailed in December, 1764, from Harwich to
Holland.

At The Hague, Lee met Sir Joseph Yorke, brother of
Charles and for many years the British ambassador to Holland,
and Sir Joseph graciously gave him a warm letter of introduction to Sir Thomas Wroughton, the British representative at
Warsaw.[27] With this additional equipment he traveled on to
Brunswick. There he presented a letter from his former commander La Lippe to the Hereditary Prince of Brunswick, who
treated him very kindly and gave him papers of introduction to

both Stanislaus and Frederick the Great of Prussia. In Berlin, Brunswick's sponsorship brought him the entree to Frederick and to his nephew and heir Prince Frederick William. The warrior king was cordial and held at least two conversations of some length with him, mostly on American affairs.[28] Frederick was sufficiently impressed by Lee to remember him more than a decade later.[29]

Reaching Warsaw about the middle of March, 1765, Lee was quickly introduced to Stanislaus. The new monarch was not raising an army, but to please Charles Yorke he gave Lee an appointment as his personal aide-de-camp.[30] Lee was soon comfortably located at Warsaw, where he lived in an apartment supplied by Prince Adam Casimir Czartoryski and dined with the king. His first contacts with Stanislaus and Prince Czartoryski, head of a leading Polish family and a relative of Stanislaus, were happy ones. The king and the prince knew English and were liberally educated, and Lee derived great pleasure from their companionship.[31] He found the king, strangely enough, a friend of liberty and a kindred soul. Before long he developed an enduring affection for Stanislaus, who seems at least to have admired Lee. Like a true courtier Lee arranged to present to the king a sword which had once apparently belonged to Oliver Cromwell. He would later find fault with the king's political behavior. Lee also discovered a pleasant companion in Sir Thomas Wroughton; and he was reasonably contented for a time. But Warsaw was really a dull place; his restless spirit longed for action, and he soon began to yearn for more active employment. Stanislaus humored him and considered sending him to Prussia and to England on royal errands. Finally the king suggested that he accompany the Polish ambassador to the Sultan on a journey to Constantinople.

Lee eagerly accepted his new master's suggestion and promptly hurried off with the ambassador. However, finding that the emissary traveled too slowly, he finally joined a Turkish detachment convoying treasure from Moldavia to the Turkish capital. Crossing the Balkans in winter, the troops suffered terribly, and Lee contracted "rheumatism," which crippled him for some days after his arrival on the Golden Horn in February, 1766.[32] He remained at Constantinople for at least three months and survived "a dreadful earthquake."

At the Turkish capital Lee received from his sister the news of the death of his mother. The brief comment on this event which he sent to Sidney in a lengthy letter ran: "I have this instant rec'd yours with the melancholy account of my mother's death; had it happen'd some years before, I shou'd not have been so shocked as I really find myself; for I confess in the latter part of her life that my affection for her was much stronger than in the former. . . ." It is evident that he was not sorely grieved.[33]

From Warsaw and Constantinople Lee wrote not only to Sidney but also to his friends in Britain, including Lord Thanet, the Earl of Charlemont, and Charles Yorke. In these letters his political views appear for the first time in some detail. He censured George III for attempting to increase the royal authority in England and politicians like Bute and the Earl of Sandwich who supported him; he referred to the ministry headed by George Grenville—the ministry responsible for the Stamp Act— as "our damnable administration"; and he condemned indignantly David Hume and other "Tory" writers whose pens failed to attack the royal prerogative. He pictured the miseries of the Germans and the subjects of the Turkish Empire under absolute monarchical rule and begged his friends to do what they could to forestall the setting up of a similar political tyranny in Britain. Under absolutism the British would be even more unhappy than the Christians under the rule of the Sultan, for they would suffer more because of their superior education. He saw the "enlightened slave" as the most wretched of human beings. He would have liked to force Hume to see personally the effects of arbitrary government in eastern Europe. He did not hesitate to describe his own doctrines as "not the most favorable to monarchy." It is to be suspected that he was dreaming (and had been dreaming) of ideal republics nurturing the "natural rights of mankind," but that he was willing to settle for a true, but limited, monarchical system in England. Significantly, in view of his later career, he joyfully greeted the opposition of the American colonists to the Stamp Act pushed through Parliament by George Grenville: "May God prosper the Americans in their resolutions, that there may be one asylum at least on the earth for men, who prefer their natural rights to the fantastical prerogative of a foolish perverted head because it wears a crown."[34] It is hardly surprising that he had made enemies among persons in power in Britain.

From Constantinople, Lee planned to return to Warsaw and to solicit permission from Stanislaus to pass on to England in the winter of 1766-67, for Thanet had given him reason to believe that the road to preferment was again open to him at home.[35] Besides, it was no doubt necessary for him to go to England in order to take advantage of the property which became his at his mother's death. While it is not certain that he carried out his plan in full, he did secure the approval of Stanislaus. But he may have returned to England by way of the Mediterranean.[36] In any case, he reached London toward the end of 1766 and immediately placed himself under Thanet's wing.[37] It may safely be inferred that the earl considered Lee's chances to be enhanced by the downfall of the Grenville ministry and the coming to power of Lord Rockingham and his liberal Whig faction in the summer of 1765. While Lee was still on the Continent, however, the Rockingham cabinet also fell and was replaced by a ministry of "all the talents" headed by William Pitt, in August, 1766. This change in the political scene was a blow to Lee, most of whose associates were aligned with Rockingham. Shelburne, perhaps still Lee's friend, had thrown in his lot with Pitt and had become secretary of state for the southern department, but Amherst was also high in the councils of the Pitt government.

Soon after reaching England, Lee delivered a letter of recommendation from Stanislaus to George III and reminded the British king that long before he went to Poland Thanet had received a promise that something would be done for his friend. Henry Conway, an army officer and a Whig attached to Rockingham, gave his support to Lee's pretensions, but the king refused to redeem the pledge he had made three years earlier. When Lee sought to bring further pressure on George III through Prince

Ferdinand of Brunswick, who was about to visit England, the
prince refused to intervene in Lee's behalf. He told Lee the
king had paid little heed to earlier recommendations which he
had made for other officers. Lee at the time ascribed his failure
to secure promotion to powerful enemies who disliked his
political opinions.[38] There can be little doubt that his disappointment strengthened Lee's dislike of the king's policies. It
was afterward commonly asserted, and no doubt with some justice, that the treatment which he received from the king at this
juncture led Lee to join the American army in 1775. Horace
Walpole was not utterly in error in 1779 when he asserted that
"Lee was a galant adventurer whom George 3ᵈ disgusted by an
absolute breach of promise, and drove into the service of the
colonies."[39]

That Lee was vexed because of the continuing neglect which
was his lot is undoubtedly true, but his disappointment must
have been somewhat alleviated by the change in his financial
situation brought about by the death of his mother. With his
inheritance he had an income approaching £1,000 per annum;
thus he could satisfy his comparatively frugal tastes and live
like a gentleman. Since he was not fond of gambling, nor of
dress, nor of society in general, his income was now really more
than ample. Indeed, his fortune seems to have increased steadily
after 1766, partly because he suffered from fits of parsimony—
probably a relic of the days when his tastes surpassed his funds—
and in spite of the fact that he was extremely careless about his
business affairs.

Unable to set aside without bitterness his disappointed military ambitions in England,[40] Lee became more and more violent
in his politics during the period 1766-68. He was at first not
seriously displeased with Pitt's ministry. He deprecated Pitt's
acceptance of the earldom of Chatham and was inclined to believe that Pitt had abandoned his principles to satisfy his vanity
and his lust for power. He found merit, however, in two members of the cabinet, Shelburne and the young Duke of Grafton.
Nevertheless, his sympathies lay with Lord Rockingham, and
he was praising both Rockingham and his follower Edmund
Burke, who had recently acquired influence. When Pitt tem-

porarily disappeared from the political arena and the King's Friends began to assume more and more complete control of administration, Lee was sorely vexed. When Grafton became virtually an ally of the king, Lee denounced him as a disgrace to the human race. On the other hand, Lee enthusiastically praised the radical John Wilkes for challenging the king and his supporters. At the end of 1768 he declared, "If we can but see one of these state rascals brought to the block my soul shall rest satisfy'd"; and he expressed a belief that he himself might be able to bring about "a glorious revolution" in national affairs could he but secure election to the House of Commons from Cheshire.[41] His anger against the king and the King's Friends was so great that he might have gotten into "some cursed scrape," as he himself later declared, had it not been that he soon afterward left England.[42]

During the period 1766-68 Lee continued to display great interest in America for both political and economic reasons. In 1766 he was given a grant of 20,000 acres in the new colony of East Florida, with the stipulation that he develop the soil; and in the following year he obtained possession of ten thousand acres of choice lands on Prince Edward Island.[43] The East Florida speculation proved to be no more profitable than his New York venture. It seems likely that Lee's lands on Prince Edward Island eventually brought some return.

Lee's interest in British handling of American problems had no connection with his land speculations, but it was an absorbing one. He continued to look upon the British colonies in North America as the last "asylum" of freedom and to be a passionate defender of American "rights," not only for the sake of the Americans but also, as he thought, in behalf of the British themselves. He rejoiced in the repeal of the Stamp Act, contending that the successful execution of that measure would have led to the passage of other laws taxing the Americans and reducing them to a state of virtual slavery. In October, 1767, he predicted that all would be well between England and America if the Mother Country possessed sufficient wisdom not to enact another law similar to the Stamp Act, " . . . but if another attempt of the same nature should be made upon them, by a wicked blundering minister, I will venture to prophecy, that this country will be shaken to its foundation in its wealth, credit, naval force, and interior population, even without the supposition of a civil war."⁴⁴ The second "attempt" on the Americans which Lee inveighed against, embodied principally in the Townshend Acts, was already in progress. It did not have quite the disastrous effects which Lee predicted, because the British government finally backed down before American opposition in 1770, repealing the Townshend taxes, except for the import tax on tea, which was retained on the statute books as an indication that Britain still claimed the power to levy external duties in America for revenue. When a third "attempt" on America was made in 1773, Lee's prophecy came true; and he personally helped to carry it out.

By 1768 Lee was fairly well known to be a defender of American liberty. By March of that year, if not before, he had made the acquaintance of Benjamin Franklin, the leading representative of the American colonists in London. On March 12 Lee, General Robert Monckton, Major Horatio Gates, and other British officers who had served in the New World and who were advocates of the colonists dined with Franklin.⁴⁵ A year later Lee was denouncing as vigorously as any American the ineffective attempts of "a blundering knavish" secretary of state, the Earl of Hillsborough, and a "scoundrel attorney," Governor Francis Bernard of Massachusetts, to bring America to heel.⁴⁶

Socially, the years 1766-68 were characterized for Lee by an increased intimacy with Sir Charles and Lady Sarah Bunbury and by efforts on the part of his sister to persuade him to marry and settle down in England, preferably at Chester. The French Duc de Lauzun, who had met the Bunburys in Paris and who had contracted a passion for Lady Sarah, relates a curious anecdote of Lee. Lauzun followed the Bunburys to London and met Lee at their town house in February, 1767. He looked like "a great [h]ostler," the Frenchman afterward recalled. Both Lauzun and Lee were invited to visit Barton, the Bunbury home in Suffolk, and they set out with their hosts for that place. During the first part of the journey Lee rode in a post chaise with Lady Sarah, and Lauzun in a carriage with Sir Charles. Soon Lee complained that his fair companion bored him, and the travelers exchanged partners, Lee and the French nobleman riding together. Before long Lee protested that Lauzun was even more boring than the lady. Again there was an exchange, and he was paired off with Bunbury. Shortly afterward, seeing some friends engaged in fox hunting, he rode off, deserting his hosts and their guest entirely.[47]

In the summer of 1767 Lee was back in London, uncertain whether to pay a visit to Hall-Stevenson at Crazy Castle or to go to Compiègne in France. Apparently he remained in or near the capital until the following winter.[48] In April, 1768, he was again, with Sir Charles Davers, a guest at Barton, recuperating from an illness and considering a sojourn at Harwich or Boulogne for his health. He was in London in November and December, attending the theater and rhapsodizing about the charms of a Miss Morris, who had made a hit in the character of Juliet. He was more than mildly interested in her, and he was seriously considering marriage; but he was not quite ready to assume its responsibilities, because he doubted his own temper and constancy. At that time he thought it would be "not only rash but dishonest" to marry. However, he told Sidney that he might be ready to do so after another campaign. A war had just broken out between Russia and Turkey, and he had made up his mind to return to eastern Europe and to take a post in the Russian army. Sidney urged him to remain in England in the hope that the Rockingham faction would come again into power and would promote him in the British army, but to no avail. He desired more experience in the business of warfare; and his experience would enhance his claims in England. In any event, service in eastern Europe would give him something more to talk about over the kitchen fire in his old age.[49]

CHAPTER THREE

MORE EUROPEAN ADVENTURES

"He ever warr'd with freedom and the free:
Nations as men, home subjects, foreign foes,
So that they utter'd the word 'Liberty!'
Found George the Third their first opponent. Whose
History was ever stain'd as his will be
With national and individual woes?"

BYRON, *The Vision of Judgment*

WHEN HE RETURNED to England in 1766 Lee had King Stanislaus' blessing, and the king and his aide continued their friendship by correspondence. Lee sent a vivid description of the British political scene to his master, and the king gave him a miniature containing his royal likeness. Because of their common interest in Lee the Earl of Thanet and Stanislaus also entered into communication, exchanging gifts; and Lee kept in touch with his friends Prince Czartoryski and Sir Thomas Wroughton.[1] In 1768 Stanislaus promised to use his influence with the Russians to secure for him a command in the armies of Catherine the Great, and Lee determined to take advantage of the opportunity.

After drawing up his will and settling his business affairs, Lee set out for Paris in December with Captain Constantine Phipps, who was traveling to the French capital for diversion. Lee intended to go on to Marseille and if possible to Corsica, hoping to see something of the Corsican struggle for independence from France before the campaign opened in eastern Europe. In Paris, however, he met Prince Czartoryski, who informed him that there would not be time to visit the troubled Mediterranean island. In January, 1769, the prince and Lee made their way to Vienna. Poland was in a state of wild disorder because many more or less patriotic Poles, organized in the Confederation of Bar, had taken up arms against Stanislaus and Russian domination. The travelers were compelled to wait for an escort in order to proceed safely to Warsaw, and did not reach that place until about the beginning of March. Lee expected to proceed promptly to the Turkish frontier and to assume command of a body of Cossacks and Walachian horsemen—he would as lief be a "church warden" as to serve in the line[2]—but he was held up in the Polish capital for almost four months. Warsaw was loosely besieged by the Confederates, and it was impossible for him to advance further without armed protection.

In Warsaw, Lee had leisure to undertake the education of a certain Louisa C——, who seems to have been a bit of a coquette. Apparently he tried to guide her reading and also teach her English. He was sufficiently attracted to her in the course of their studies to beg her hand and was firmly rejected. He protested her decision in dignified and moving language, but to no purpose.[3] His determination to marry was as strong as his affection for her, for he expressed a desire to marry Miss Morris only four days later.[4] Other idle hours he occupied by writing to relatives and friends in England, largely on English politics. Bewailing the lack of attention paid to educating females concerning public affairs, he urged his cousin, Lady Arabella Bunbury Blake, to exert her intelligence and charms in behalf of liberty.[5] Characterizing Poland as a country with a noble ruler and a vicious people and Britain as one with a wicked monarch and a virtuous people, he wittily suggested that the two kings exchange posts. Stanislaus as a person was worth more, he argued, than the whole British royal family—a judgment not utterly indefensible. Even in far-off Poland, Lee was able to work up a rage against George III and his political allies. He declared his intention not to return to England until "the virtue which I believe to exist in the body of the people can be put in motion," and he hinted that he was seeking military knowledge and experience which might be useful in England. Informed that Lady Sarah Bunbury had deserted her husband for one of her lovers, he wrote savagely to Sidney: "I am not surprised at Lady Sarah's flight. I knew the woman. Nor can be grieved at it. My soul is so sick of publick griefs it has no room for private ones. I think it right the corporal prostitution of our women sh^d go hand in hand with the political prostitution of our men. . . ."[6]

In Warsaw, Lee also had time to refresh his friendship with Stanislaus, who generously gave him a commission as major general in the Polish army, a much-prized honor which made Lee extremely happy.[7] It might be argued that in view of his political principles Lee should have supported the Confederates of Bar against Stanislaus and the Russians, on the ground that the Confederates were defenders of Polish liberty. However, Lee appears at the time to have thought of them as "banditti";[8] and he was bound to Stanislaus by ties of affection and gratitude. He did not serve against the Confederates, for his Polish commission was really honorary. He departed from Warsaw as soon as possible to join the Russians on their southwestern frontier. On June 20, Prince Repnin, Russian ambassador to Poland, left his post to take service in the Russian army. He had an escort of twelve hundred men, and Lee accompanied him. After a wild march through enemy-infested country they succeeded in finding that army before Chotin, a Turkish fortress south of the Dniester River in Bessarabia.[9]

The Russian army encountered difficulties at Chotin. The Russians did not have sufficiently heavy artillery to batter down its walls, nor did they have enough men to carry it by assault. An attempt to blockade it failed dismally. When the Grand Vizier of Turkey appeared with a large relieving force, it became clear that nothing could be accomplished; and after both sides had suffered rather heavy casualties, the Russians withdrew north of the Dniester to the powerful fortress of Kamenets Podolsk. Lee—who actually was an observer rather than a commander, for his hoped-for appointment was not granted— watched these operations from the back of a "cart-horse." He had not expected genius in the Russian and Turkish commanders, and he did not find it.[10] Nor did he remain with the army until the close of the campaign. He was vexed by "rheumatism" and a slow fever before joining it; his condition was aggravated by the hardships of the field; and he was advised to hurry to Budapest for treatment before it was too late.

A caricature of Charles Lee by Barham Rushbrooke (contemporary engraving)

Lee made his way with extreme difficulty from Kamenets Podolsk across the Carpathian Mountains to the little village of Munkács in eastern Hungary. There he was desperately ill— delirious for eight days and given up for lost for three weeks, as he tells us. Finally, toward the end of September, he gained sufficient strength to move on to the town of Košice, where he obtained better care and regained his health in some degree. After a month's stay there, he obtained a passport to travel to Budapest and thence to Vienna. By using funds obtained from the sale of his horses he managed to reach the Austrian capital in December.[11]

Before Lee joined the Russian army he was planning to spend the winter of 1769-70 in southern Italy, Sicily, or in the islands of the Aegean Sea. At Munkács he made up his mind to winter somewhere in the Bourbon kingdom of Naples. It was his intention to live "cooly and regularly" in some small town and to ride constantly in order to regain his health.[12] However, he was delayed in Vienna for three months, partly because he had difficulty in obtaining funds from England but more because his physical condition remained uncertain. At times he thought himself well; again he felt very low. During his slow recuperation he went into society in the old capital and enjoyed himself rather thoroughly. Even Joseph II, the Holy Roman Emperor, who was eager to learn about the Russo-Turkish War, sent for him. The emperor and the Polish general talked not only about the war but also about Britain and America. Lee reported that Joseph knew more about American problems than a monarch who was "more concerned in the subject." He accurately predicted that the emperor would "make a figure" when he came into control of the Austrian hereditary possessions, "at least comparatively with the sad automata of [the] sceptered herd."[13]

From Vienna, Lee traveled through Venice to Florence and Leghorn in the spring of 1770. At that time he was seriously considering trying to join the Russian fleet in the Mediterranean in search of further adventures, but his health would not permit him to do so.[14] He lingered for some time in Tuscany and Lucca.[15] On June 30, Sir Charles Davers humorously and affectionately reported the progress of their mutual friend to Horatio Gates and said that "the rambler" was thinking of an early return to England. Lee was "so well recover'd, that he stiles himself a widow's man, a province so little assign'd him, that I think you or I should never have dream'd of it, for him, he is grown a great Gascoon, & vaunts wonderfully . . . it would make the heart of so callous a bouger as I am to jump if I could meet you and boiling water, & Hall somewhere or other."[16] Lee traveled southward, however, to Sicily and Malta, partly to indulge in sea-bathing in the warm waters of the Mediterranean in order to recover his health and spirits, partly to satisfy his insatiable curiosity. He did not return to northern Italy until almost a year later.

Although his physical condition remained variable, it is reported that during his stay in Italy he became involved in a duel with a foreign officer. According to the report, the opponents fought first with swords, and Lee lost the use of two fingers. The duel being continued with pistols, he killed his opponent and was forced to flee for his life.[17] About the end of March, 1771, still in dubious health, Lee embarked at Leghorn on a merchant vessel going to Minorca and Gibraltar. It was his intention to travel from Gibraltar directly to Spa in order to take the waters there, but for some unknown reason he journeyed instead from Gibraltar to England, arriving in London in June, 1771.[18]

The gout, "rheumatism," and similar disorders are commonly accompanied by irritability, morbid reflections, and psychic imbalance; and it would appear that Lee became increasingly irritable, moody, and more extreme in the expression of his opinions after the onset of his illness in the spring of 1769. The denunciations of George III and of his supporters which he sent to England before joining the Russian army were vigorous, but they were relatively mild when compared to his later effusions. From Vienna he savagely attacked the Duke of Grafton, then prime minister, describing him as a man without conscience, without honor, and without even a sense of decorum:[19] " . . . if the axe is not applied to his neck, it is laid to the root of our liberties, national honor, and importance;

there is no medium. . . ." For himself, he would rather go into exile to be free than submit to the domination of the king and his associates. He hoped the American colonists would be successful in their opposition to the Townshend Acts and related measures, and that their victory would inspire the people of Britain to emulate them.[20] In May, 1770, he expressed a longing to be in England, but also a "dread" of "the agitations I should be thrown into by the too slow progress of public virtue." Wildly he continued: "Let the hallowed Sir George Savile, honour, and the genius of England, triumph over tyranny, corruption, Grafton, North, and the devil; and I will hasten to participate the joy; or should the sword of our good angel be unsheathed, my puny dagger shall contribute its mite of annoyance to the breast of despotism and wickedness. You will excuse my not delivering myself like a man of this world; I never can on so heating a subject."[21]

From Florence in the spring of 1770 Lee sent what he himself termed an "enthusiastical rant" to his former schoolmate and old friend, Davers. Davers, a man of liberal thought, was a member of the House of Commons and was considering a withdrawal from politics, on the ground that he could accomplish nothing. Lee inveighed against

> this indolent or despairing method of reasoning . . . which has reduced us to the dreadful situation we are in at present. . . . I conjure you therefore my dear friend not in despair to quit the deck and get under the hatches—hand a rope, work at the pump, do everything with good will and firmness, encourage others to do the same, and with so intrepid a pilot as Sir George Saville, the vessel may perhaps work into the harbour, notwithstanding the hellish treason of the major part of the crew. . . . I must therefore my dear school fellow and fellow soldier, my friend, entreat you over and over again, I must conjure you by the spirits of Cato, Brutus, Hampden, and Sidney, by every thing that is divine and sacred, not to desert your post, but to give to the world as convincing testimonies as you have to me, of your virtue to persevere in your opposition until we are all buried in the last dyke of liberty.[22]

Lee's language is far more drastic than his sentiment. To support Savile was to follow the leadership of a public-spirited and generous-minded leader who was no revolutionary, but an honest and independent Whig and a steady opponent of George III and his friends in the House of Commons.

The "rhapsody into which this subject always hurries me" appears again in a letter which Lee wrote about the same time to a friend in Vienna. He had been urged to pay another visit to the beautiful city on the banks of the Danube. If, he replied, he were assured that his friends and acquaintances there had not already seen too much of him and if his American affairs did not take him to the New World, he would certainly make a second visit, and that a long one; " . . . as to England, I have forsworn it—if it is my fate to live in a country govern'd not by establish'd laws but by the will of men—I will certainly chuse a master who hits my fancy. . . ." He would rather live under the sway of the emperor, a "respectable sensible virtuous master," than under George III, a "despicable and tho stupid at the same time not innoxious dolt." The Romans who were forced to kneel to Julius Caesar and the English who were compelled to bow before Cromwell had at least the consolation that they bent before genius; " . . . but that a reptile, who has no pretension to be suppos'd endued with animation unless from some symptoms of dissimulation obstinacy and vindictiveness shou'd be able to encompass the ruin of a sensible and spirited nation is too much to bear. . . ." He could only hope that in spite of the "accursed profligacy of those dens of thieves the Lds and Commons" the virtue of the British people would eventually triumph.[23]

Once again in London, Lee promptly began to write against the king and the existing administration. In the *Public Advertiser* of July 27, 1770, he struck hard at the king in an essay ostensibly devoted to a description of "The Character of the PRESENT EMPEROR of GERMANY." Publishing anonymously but without much effort to hide his authorship—Lee told his sister and at least one friend that he was responsible for the essay— he drew a most flattering portrait of Joseph II and a very unfavorable one of George III. The British monarch's name was not mentioned, but no one could mistake Lee's meaning. Joseph, said Lee, was neither specially imposing in stature nor particularly graceful in figure, but he was nevertheless physically attractive. He did not possess "a heavy, inert, lethargick disposition." His eyes were remarkably fair, but they did not have "that unmeaning, vacant glare which we so frequently observe in eyes of this colour. . . ." Joseph's mother, the Empress Maria Theresa, had seen to it that he had a broad liberal education. She had not "laboured to narrow his mind, contract his ideas, and darken his understanding to render him timid, forward and obstinate, to instill into him all disregard for the opinion of his people, and make him deaf to their calls, to extinguish in him every honest ambition . . . to disqualify him totally for the commonest offices of his station, only that she might throw the reins of government into the hands of some arrogant, arbitrary minion and his creatures. . . ." Joseph had imbibed "very generous notions of the rights of mankind"; had fortune "placed him at the head of a free people, so far from making any attacks on the privileges of his subjects, directly by open force, or indirectly by cabal and the arts of corruption, he would have laboured to secure them against the attempts of any of his successors. . . ." The emperor had highest confidence in "the people," and the "greatest diffidence of courtiers." He did not "provoke the indignation of his own subjects in seeing the fruits of their toil and industry pensioned away on dull prostitute scribblers in exchange for fulsome praise, or lavished to feed the vanity and avarice of titled drones and ribbon'd sycophants. . . ." He traveled throughout the empire, not confining himself to Vienna and Schönbrunn (London and Windsor Castle); his reviews of troops and his activities at military maneuvers were not "childish puppet shews" (in Hyde Park). "Though the domestic life of a prince whose government is inglorious, contemptible and ruinous, is of little importance to the public, whether he is insipidly regular, a solemn-water-drinker, or a pragmatical bibbering Gotlip, like James the First; whether he is chaste to the marriage bed (as it is eternally run in our ears of Charles the First,) or diffusely gallant like Charles the Second, it matters naught to the people if their interest is neglected, their glory tarnished, their treisure dissipated, un-accounted for, and their most sacred laws violated or bafiled."[24] Lee would not even admit that George's domestic virtues were anything much in his favor—and Joseph possessed the same virtues with other great qualities.

After his return to England, Lee also wrote a lengthy essay as an introduction to a proposed critique on David Hume's history of England. Hume's extenuation of the faults of the Stuart monarchs, especially Charles I, had long irritated him; and he was convinced that the Scotsman's kindly treatment of the Stuarts created an atmosphere favorable to the increase of the power of George III because Hume's reputation as a philosopher and a skeptic gave authority to his historical writings. The proposed critique was largely completed, but it was never published and has been lost; nor has the introductory essay been found, except in draft. Certainly the essay would have aroused public interest, for it contained a singularly persuasive attack upon George III. Lee roundly scored the tyranny, corruption, extravagance, and inefficiency of government under the king's leadership. He contended that the Hanoverians had been brought from their trifling principality in Germany to the throne of Britain by the will of the British people, and he insisted that the king was subverting the British constitution. He singled out the pecuniary influence of the crown, septennial parliaments, and the large standing army as specially effective instruments of misrule. Lee argued energetically that kings should be the servants of their people, and that they should suffer death whenever they threatened popular liberty. Agreeing with the contention of the great Italian reformer, the Marquis di Beccaria, that capital punishment should seldom be used, Lee asserted that it should be retained with respect to monarchs and their families. The extirpation of a royal house was preferable to the loss of public freedom. He preached the contract theory of government in an extreme form. Incidentally, Lee hit savagely at several of the king's supporters. He accused George, Viscount Townshend, then master of Ireland, of trying to cheat Wolfe out of the glory of the capture of Quebec; the third Earl of Albemarle of robbing his men of their share of the spoils derived from the capture of Havana in 1762; and Viscount Barrington, secretary at war, for pushing the promotion of favorites rather than the deserving in the army.[25] Since the essay verged upon sedition, it is possible that Lee could find no publisher bold enough to print this assault on the king and his friends.

Hume's history likewise inspired Lee to plan a history of the Roman Emperors Claudius and Nero. Imitating Hume, he would by "decent softenings and coloring" remove "the ill humour and prejudice of mankind with regard to those injur'd characters." He wrote a stinging dedication to Hume, and he sought to interest Hall-Stevenson in the project, probably vainly. No trace of such an ironical history of the two emperors has been found.[26]

With these productions and plans the formal writings of Lee in England on public questions apparently ceased. Since the period 1760-71, in which he was more or less active, was approximately the same as that in which the renowned "Junius" published his famous attacks upon the king and his associates, Lee almost inevitably has been identified with that mysterious personage. The views of Junius and Lee were in general similar; and Lee's ability with the pen was not completely incommensurate with that of this great unknown. Conceivably, Lee could have written the Junius letters, had he taken care to give greater polish to his writings. Indeed, in 1803 Thomas Rodney of Delaware, no doubt a trustworthy person, reported a conversation between himself and Lee which supposedly took place in 1773 and which at first reading indicates that Lee himself claimed to be Junius.

General Lee said there was not a man in the world, no, not even Woodfall the publisher, that knew who the author was; that the secret rested wholly with himself, and forever would remain with him. Feeling in some degree surprised at this unexpected declaration, after pausing a little, I replied, "No, General Lee, if you certainly know what you have affirmed, it can no longer remain solely with him; for certainly no one could know what you have affirmed but the author himself." Recollecting himself, he replied, "I have unguardedly committed myself, and it would be but folly to deny to you that I am the author; but I must request you will not reveal it during my life; for it never was nor ever will be revealed by me to any other." He then proceeded to mention several circumstances to verify his being the author, and, among them, that of his going over to the continent, and absenting himself from England the most of the time in which these letters were published in London. This he thought necessary, lest by some accident the author should become known, or at least suspected, which might have been his ruin.[27]

At first sight Rodney's statement is impressive; and no less a critic than Walter Savage Landor was inclined, after a casual examination, to believe that Lee was Junius.[28] But it is impossible that he should have written all, if any, of the letters. Marked stylistic dissimilarities exist between the known writings of Lee and those of Junius; moreover, Junius expresses minor opinions which conflict with those of Lee. But conclusive proof appears in the fact that Junius was responding in London in 1769 to hostile writings within a few days of their appearance, while Lee was at a great distance on the Continent. It may well be that Lee knew something about Junius. If the letters were the product of several men, as has been contended, Lee might have been one of those men. But this hypothesis also seems unlikely. As to the Rodney-Lee conversation, it is probable that Rodney did not recall the exact substance of it after thirty years. It is also probable that Lee was having a little fun at the expense of his young acquaintance. Significantly, he coupled his supposed admission with remarks tending to indicate that he could have been Junius even while he was on the Dniester. Lee knew it was really impossible for him to have written many of the letters, and he tried to prevent Rodney from realizing the fact.[29]

It was, then, Lee, but not Junius, who spent a few weeks in London in the early summer of 1771 and then went to visit Davers at Rushbrooke in Suffolk. From Rushbrooke he traveled to Hothfield, Lord Thanet's home, near Ashford in Kent. He spent about a month at each place and apparently enjoyed himself thoroughly at both—he was not always in a black mood. In August he was planning to go to Spa for the baths because his physical disorders were still troubling him seriously.[30] It is not clear that he actually went to the watering place in Liège. He may have gone instead with Davers to visit Hall-Stevenson at Crazy Castle, for both were invited there in the late summer.[31] He spent the following winter in France in search of health and recreation. With William Butler, his old schoolmate and fellow army officer, and another officer, possibly Lieutenant Primrose Kennedy, who had served with Lee in the Forty-fourth and in the Braddock expedition, he went in early winter to Dijon. Because of sickness among Butler's horses and bad weather they stayed longer than they desired to at that place, eventually parting to go their respective ways. Lee's physical condition had changed for the worse, although he was leading an active life, even playing tennis. "I must have some advice . . . ," he wrote to Clotworthy Upton; "I am in a strange way—I have an unnatural insatiable appetite, grow very weak, my eyes glassy, my complexion yellow, and am universally relaxed—the great quantities I eat turn not to nutrition—in short if I was much attach'd to this beldam planet, the earth—I should think myself in a wofull condition—but I would willingly gather health to look out for a more honorable exit than that in a stinking winding sheet. . . ."[32]

Lee was suffering at Dijon from distemper of the brain as well as of the body, and he quarreled with Butler.[33] He confessed to his sister that the fault was his.

> I begin in my cooler candid moments to be sensible that my temper is alter'd for the worse, whether it is to disappointed ambition, too high an opinion of my own merit I cannot tell; but sometimes I am apt to flatter myself that the alteration which I am conscious of, may be attributed to . . . the declension of publick virtue, and the giant strides which tyranny is taking. . . . But whatever the causes may be, I feel the effects, and I wish I only felt 'em myself, but I am afraid that those who by accident are much connected with me must feel 'em still more sensibly. I have just merit enough to condemn and detest myself, and wish to throw myself at

the feet of those whom my deportment must disgust and shock.[34]

It is a strange fact that Lee has been characterized by one student of the American War of Independence as a "charlatan" and by another as a "mountebank." Both of these words imply that he deceived others and was perhaps self-deceived. The fact is, as this passage abundantly indicates, that he could be desperately honest about his own motives and that he could bitterly condemn his own conduct. It is almost equally astonishing that the motives and behavior of other men of Lee's generation who smugly ascribed their actions to love of God, country, and mankind have frequently escaped searching analysis.

From Dijon, Lee moved on to Lyon, where he remained for some time, and thence apparently to Switzerland, where he hoped to be able to consult Dr. Samuel Auguste Tissot of Lausanne, who had achieved international fame for the treatment of disorders similar to those from which Lee suffered. He was also eager to see the democratic institutions of the smaller Swiss cantons in operation.[35] Whether Dr. Tissot was able to assist him is not known. He returned to England in the summer of 1772 and apparently went to visit Davers at Rushbrooke.[36] Toward the end of the year he was again in London and was planning to meet Hall-Stevenson at Manchester and likewise to see Primrose Kennedy.[37] It is likely that Lee made another visit to Crazy Castle in 1773, but no record of such a visit has been found. In the summer of that year he was once more in London, and in August he sailed for America, never to return.

Before his final departure from England, Lee came into contact with the great painter Sir Joshua Reynolds and his friend Edmund Burke, the sturdy champion in England of the American colonists.[38] He was also in touch with Mrs. Catharine Macaulay, a well-known republican who was engaged in writing a popular history of England from the beginning of the reign of James I—a history from the republican viewpoint; and he was likewise on very friendly terms with Captain Constantine Phipps and George Dempster, a Scottish member of Parliament, both of whom were members of a little coterie formed about Mrs. Macaulay in London.[39] Dempster and Phipps were apparently not republicans, nor can it be said that Lee had become one, but it is not to be doubted that he sympathized with the views of Mrs. Macaulay. He was to become something more of a republican later. Phipps became a famous Arctic explorer, one of the King's Friends, and Lord Mulgrave.

Whatever the exact state of his political views, the feelings of disgust and despair which obviously were aroused in Lee by the English political situation and which led him to consider exile as early as 1769 continued without abatement until his final departure from England. A general raising of rank in the army which took place in 1772 and which carried him up to a lieutenant colonelcy had no effect on his opinions. Consoling Davers on the loss of a Parliamentary election in that year, he profanely urged him to abandon England: " . . . pack up your penates, and transfer them along with me to some climate and soil more friendly to the spirit of liberty. North America stretches forth her capacious arms, Switzerland, or even the little state of Lucca has room to admit a generous few. . . ."[40] Lee was thinking more and more of visiting America, not only to find refuge from England, but also to look into his land speculations.[41] In addition to his lands on Prince Edward Island and his claim in East Florida, he had been given a grant in West Florida and was considering an application to the colony of Virginia for another in the Ohio Valley. He had not reached a decision to settle on the American continent—he was considering Bermuda as a possible residence in 1773[42]—and there is no special reason to think that he was motivated by a desire to meddle in America in relations between the colonists and the Mother Country, although another crisis in those relations was approaching at the time of his embarkation.

Seeking companionship for the voyage, Lee urged a French gentleman in London, the Comte de Lauraguais, to join him. The count—who was a French spy, though Lee was probably unaware of the fact—finally decided not to go.[43] However, Lee found safer company in Major William Butler and Major William Dunbar, his former comrade in the Forty-fourth. They

sailed about the middle of August in Captain James Chambers'
London and arrived at New York on Friday night, October
8.[44] The three men soon separated, Butler and Dunbar presumably going to their respective duties. Without occupation,
Lee began a plunge into politics which took him ever deeper
and deeper.

CHAPTER FOUR

PROPAGANDIST FOR FREEDOM

Hear him but reason in divinity,
And all-admiring with an inward wish
You would desire the king were made a prelate:
Hear him debate of commonwealth affairs,
You would say it hath been all in all his study:
List his discourse of war, and you shall hear
A fearful battle render'd you in music. . . .
SHAKESPEARE, *King Henry V*

ON NOVEMBER 2, 1773, General Frederick Haldimand, Swiss soldier of fortune who had become a British citizen and who was temporarily in command of the British army in America, wrote from headquarters at New York to the commander in chief, General Thomas Gage, who was in England on leave of absence. Since the two men were good friends, Haldimand wrote about both business and private matters. He reported that Governor William Tryon of New York was trying to obtain a decision from the Heralds' College in London which would give him social precedence over Gage and that Tryon was very uneasy about ships carrying tea which were momentarily expected in the harbor. When Parliament repealed most of the Townshend duties in 1770, that on tea carried into America had been retained on the statute books in order to assert British authority to levy such taxes. In 1773 Parliament had made it possible for the East India Company to sell tea in America cheaper than smuggled Dutch tea. This new legislation was designed to help the hard-pressed company out of financial straits. For Lord North it had another advantage: the Americans would surely buy the company's tea in preference to the more expensive Dutch product and would pay the Townshend duty, thus aiding the treasury and paying a tax against which they had vehemently protested. Many Americans also believed that the company's tea would be purchased and the tax paid, should the tea ever reach American merchants. Tryon feared that New Yorkers, determined to prevent the collection of the duty, would even resort to violence in order to stop the landing of the tea. Haldimand also reported to his superior that Gage's old acquaintance Lee was in New York. Lee had intended to travel by way of the Ohio and the Mississippi rivers to West Florida, but the gout had seized upon him and he had been forced to postpone his journey until spring.[1] Responding, Gage described Lee as "a most extraordinary character" and predicted that "the effusions of his tongue" would be acceptable in America and that he would acquire there "the reputation of an honest patriot."[2] Gage's prophecy was accurate.

Residing in New York with an old acquaintance of the Forty-fourth, Captain Thomas Gamble, Lee nursed his gout and talked fluently and brilliantly about European affairs. He sang the praises of Joseph II and spoke critically of Frederick the Great.[3] He extolled his former master Stanislaus for his personal qualities and condemned him for serving as Catherine's tool in the impending destruction of Polish independence; and he was responsible for a sketch of Stanislaus which appeared in the New York *Gazetteer* on November 25.[4] It is significant that he gave the palm to Joseph, who was liberal in thought and who would later attempt to be benevolent in practice. Lee was championing the cause of freedom in Europe, speaking against the British ministry and its attempt to persuade the Americans to buy taxed tea, and lauding the Bostonians for their spirited resistance.[5] He was soon intimate with James Rivington, the long-nosed, competent, and jolly printer of the New York *Gazetteer*. Later Rivington became a Tory and a bitter enemy of Lee, but he described him in his paper on December 2 as "a sincere friend to liberty in general, and an able advocate for the freedom and rights of the colonies in particular."[6]

On November 29, 1773, Lee was sufficiently recovered from the gout to set out on a tour of the "southern" colonies.[7] He went first to Philadelphia, where he spent more than a month. There he came into touch with several American leaders, in part probably because he carried a letter of recommendation from Benjamin Franklin. In Philadelphia he was on friendly terms with Charles Thomson, a trusted correspondent of Franklin and afterward famous as the secretary of the Continental Congress;[8] Richard Bache, Franklin's son-in-law;[9] Stephen Moylan, a popular young Irishman; and no doubt others of equal and greater fame. On December 17, Lee was a guest with Anthony Benezet of the Friendly Sons of St. Patrick, a society which had been organized by Moylan.[10]

After consulting Charles Thomson about routes from Philadelphia to Virginia, Lee traveled southward through Delaware and the eastern shore of Maryland. Ferrying across Chesapeake Bay, he reached Hampton, Virginia, toward the middle of February, 1774.[11] He spent the following three months in Virginia visiting the celebrities of that colony and taking a minor part in the politics of the Old Dominion. It is certain that he associated with Colonel William Byrd of Westover, George Mason, Thomas Jefferson, and Richard Henry Lee; it is probable that he met many others who played great roles in Virginia affairs. He was well received, partly no doubt because of his distinguished ancestry and partly because of his own gifts and opinions. As a guest of Byrd at Westover, he was on such good terms with the Byrd family that he played with the children.[12] Later Byrd's son Otway was his aide-de-camp in the Continental army. He became especially intimate with Richard Henry Lee, in whom he found a faithful friend. Although the two men were not related by blood,[13] there was an enduring bond of sympathy between them which lasted until the Englishman's death. Richard Henry, a recognized leader of the small farmers against the planter aristocracy and later a potent figure in the Second Continental Congress, remains a somewhat mysterious person in American history, perhaps because he has lacked a competent biographer; however, there can be no question but he was most important in the life of Charles Lee.

In Virginia in the spring of 1774, Lee began to play an active part in Anglo-American politics, if he had not already done so. He was at Williamsburg, the capital of Virginia, when the news came of the passage by Parliament of the Boston Port Bill, which closed the harbor of Boston to commerce after June

1, the law being one of the Coercive Acts, the series of measures calculated to punish the Bostonians for their Tea Party and to establish British power on a firmer basis in Massachusetts. The Virginia assembly was in session, and some of its leaders were eager to display their sympathy for their brethren in Massachusetts. Lee the Englishman worked together with those American leaders. Lee and Thomas Jefferson, then beginning his great career, talked over the situation. Although both men were unorthodox in their religious views, they came to the conclusion that a fast on June 1 proclaimed by the clergy was the most effective way to express Virginia's sympathy and that the burgesses should be persuaded to pass a resolution calling on the clergy to announce it. Such a resolution could hardly be put forward by Jefferson, and the two men decided to persuade John Carter Nicholas, a man known for his piety, to introduce it. This strategy was approved by Richard Henry Lee, his brother Francis Lightfoot Lee, and Patrick Henry; the resolution was carried on May 24 before the Earl of Dunmore, the royal governor, could prevent its passage by dissolving the legislature.[14]

On June 1 the fast was observed in Williamsburg, but Lee observed it, if he did observe it, elsewhere. Early in May he was making arrangements for a journey northward to pay a visit to Boston in order to meet Samuel Adams and then, if war did not intervene, to make his journey to West Florida. At that time he received a letter from his old friend and fellow officer Horatio Gates, who had resigned from the British service and settled on a plantation he called "Traveller's Rest" in the Shenandoah Valley, in Berkeley County, Virginia (now West Virginia). The jolly, kindly Gates was eager to see him. Lee promised to pay a brief call on Gates as he went northward and confided to him that he believed it "incumbent on every man of liberality or even common honor to contribute his mite to the cause of mankind and of liberty, which is now attacked in her last and only asylum . . . for my own part I am determin'd (at least I think I am) not to be slack in whatever mode my service is required. . . ."[15]

For some unknown reason Lee failed to go to Traveller's

Rest. He went directly to Philadelphia. He was in Philadelphia in early June and in New York a month later. Gates was keenly disappointed because Lee did not visit him, and sent after him a warning to temper his "zeal in the noble cause . . . be careful how you act. . . ." For his own part, Gates was "ready to risque my life to preserve the liberty of the western world." Amiable and perhaps lonely, he coupled with his warning a generous invitation to Traveller's Rest. "I wish therefore most anxiously you would come to my retreat, and let us philosophize on the vices and virtues of this busy world, the follies and the vanities of the great vulgar and the small." He would furnish two or three Negro slaves "to supply all your wants and whimsies, and space enough about us for you to exercise away all your spleen and gloomy moods. . . . " Indeed, there was a fine estate near by which could be purchased at a reasonable price. Why did not Lee buy it and settle down? [16]

Eventually Lee was to follow Gates's advice to purchase the estate, but he paid little heed to his counsel to be cautious. Indeed, Gates's warning did not reach him until after he had plunged deeply into the boiling caldron of public affairs. In Philadelphia, Lee found the citizenry preparing to elect delegates to the First Continental Congress and discussing passionately what measures should be taken in response to the Boston Port Bill and the other Intolerable Acts which Parliament was passing to bring Massachusetts to heel. Many citizens were urging "moderate" measures so as not to inflame an already dangerous situation. Lee boldly joined in the fray, publicly calling for energetic action and the election to Congress of persons who would push for such action. In a lengthy address "To the Citizens of Philadelphia" published in the *Pennsylvania Journal*[17] and signed "Anglus Americanus," he characterized moderation as the equivalent of submission to Britain and urged that the strongest civil measures be taken. Only through such measures, which might force the king and Parliament to retreat, could internecine war be avoided and American rights be preserved. In order to put extreme pressure on London the Congress should arrange a boycott on British goods and place an embargo on American goods going to England. In exalted and moving language he begged his readers to act decisively to protect their own freedom and with it the freedom of Britain and of mankind generally.

The liberties of Great Britain are so involved in those of America, that the instant the latter is enslaved, that instant absolute despotism is established in the former; and the generous and liberal of all nations turn their eyes to this continent as the last asylum of liberty, which by a black conspiracy of the tyrants of the earth has been rooted out from the other hemisphere; hither they pursue her with inexpiable rage; here, if their machinations prevail, not only the substance but the name and every vestige of liberty will be obliterated from the face of the globe.[18]

This effusion, of which the authorship was barely hidden, cannot be shown to have exercised great influence in Philadelphia, although it nettled the moderates;[19] but a similar production which Lee had distributed by handbills in New York in July had some effect upon public opinion,[20] especially since it was reprinted in most of the influential newspapers of New England. The New Yorkers were in the same situation as the Philadelphians, and the address of Anglus Americanus "to the citizens of New York" used the same arguments, with minor changes, as his earlier pronunciamento. Action was indispensable. Lord North was a tyrant, even by heredity. He and the king had attacked freedom everywhere, not even neglecting the little islands of Jersey, Guernsey, and Minorca. Upon the Americans rested the cause of human freedom. They could defend their liberty without civil war if they moved decisively and supported nonimportation of British goods and nonexportation of American products.[21] This bit of propaganda was undoubtedly much to the liking of Alexander McDougall, the leading opponent of Britain among the Americans in New York. Lee and McDougall joined forces; and when it became apparent to McDougall that his adherents had won out over more conservative elements in Manhattan, he entrusted to Lee's care an exulting letter to Samuel Adams in which he described the victory.[22]

Reporting on July 21 to Gage, who had recently returned to America in the double capacity of commander in chief and governor of Massachusetts and who was faced with the unpleasant task of enforcing the Intolerable Acts in Massachusetts, Haldimand mentioned Lee's departure from New York on the preceding day for Boston. He slyly suggested that his superior would be forced to use his "civil" authority to bring Lee to reason, unless the latter behaved more moderately in Boston than he had in New York.[23] Gage, already suffering from the activities of the Massachusetts patriots, wryly replied that he hoped the gout would seize upon Lee and prevent him from reaching Boston.[24] But Gage found no ally in the gout. On July 30 the Providence *Gazette* announced the arrival "last week" in Newport of General "Leigh," and he reached Providence the same day. He set out for Boston on August 1[25] and reached that place without any known difficulties. His passing through the coastal towns of Connecticut and Rhode Island aroused great interest, and the scholarly Ezra Stiles, afterward president of Yale College, but then living at Newport, soberly and suspiciously noted in his diary that Lee "talks high for American liberty, and seems to endeavor to enspirit the people to take arms. He says the king is a fool & his ministers rogues & villains. . . . General Gage was advanced over his head—he is chagrined and disappointed—he published a bold sensible well written address to the citizens of New York. Whether he is a pimp of the ministry or a sincere friend to public liberty, is to me uncertain."[26] Shortly afterward, on being told that Lee had been educated in a Jesuit school in France, Stiles again expressed a typical Yankee suspicion: "His having had a popish education is a disagreeable circumstance. . . ."[27] Eventually Stiles became profoundly convinced of Lee's loyalty to American liberty. Then, again like a true Yankee, he refused to abandon his conviction, although many others turned against Lee.[28]

From Newport, Lee wrote to Samuel Adams to notify that most redoubtable propagandist and politician of his coming and to ask that Adams try to find him quarters in some airy spot at Boston where he could be comfortable. Rhapsodizing again about America as the "last asylum of liberty" and again casti-

gating "the scepter'd monsters" of Europe, he reported Mc-
Dougall's recent success in New York.[29]

In Boston, American patriots, unlike Stiles, had little fear
of Lee's secret intentions. On August 9 the Essex *Gazette* proclaimed the coming of General "Leigh," "a great friend to
American liberty." Lee took quarters at the Cromwell's Head,
a hostelry operated by Joshua Brackett, an admirer of Samuel
Adams. He immediately inquired where he could find Adams,
the acknowledged leader of the Massachusetts patriots, and
refused to accept food until Brackett led him to Adams' house.
Not finding him at home, they returned to the tavern. Adams
soon appeared there and was closeted for two or three hours
with Lee, who was able to produce credentials, including a letter of introduction from Richard Henry Lee, which convinced
the shrewd Yankee of his trustworthiness. Richard Henry had
written that the general was "a most true and worthy friend
to the rights of human nature in general, and a warm, spirited
foe to American oppression. This gentleman's principles do
him honor, and I am sure his acquaintance will give you much
pleasure." This interview was the beginning of a lifelong friendship between such different characters. Moreover, Adams introduced Lee to Dr. Joseph Warren, John Hancock, Dr.
Thomas Young, and others who were foremost in the struggle
Massachusetts was waging against Britain. Lee was hardly ever
out of the company of these gentlemen while he was in Boston.[30]

Lionized by the Boston patriots, Lee carefully avoided going
to see Governor Gage, of whom he had long been fond. Amherst, watching Lee's progress from England, hopefully predicted that his affection for Gage and his hatred of the British
government would lead Lee into inconsistencies in Boston.[31]
But Lee was well aware that a call upon Gage would create dis-
trust among his new friends. Instead he wrote a letter to his
old comrade, a letter which may have been approved in advance
by Adams. In this curious document he avowed a great affection for Gage as a man, an affection which could "never be
wean'd," at the same time denouncing violently Gage's employers and their measures. He warned Gage against the
trickery of the Court of Britain, more hostile to the rights of

man than that of Tiberius or of Philip II. The cabinet will cheat and destroy you, he argued, a prediction which proved to be all too well grounded. "May God Almighty extricate you with honour safely from their clutches." Descanting upon the strength and devotion of the patriots to their cause, he declared: ". . . they must be victorious—I most devoutly wish they may—for if the machinations of their enemies prevail, the bright goddess Liberty must like her sister Astrea[32] utterly abandon the earth, and leave not a wreck behind—she has by a damn'd conspiracy of kings and ministers been totally driven from the other hemisphere—here is her last asylum—here I hope she may fix her abode."[33]

In Boston, Lee also wrote to Earl Percy, heir of the great Percy family and son of the Duke of Northumberland, who had come from England to join the army that Gage was collecting to defend royal authority in Massachusetts. Lee eloquently explained his views, tried to justify his conduct, and expressed a faint hope that Percy would embrace his principles and use his influence in their behalf. It is evident that Lee was concerned lest he would be regarded in the British army and at home as an opponent of government merely because of personal vexations.

I flatter myself that some time or other, your Lordship will not simply approve my conduct, but become a friend to the same cause. My Lord, I will venture to say that it is the cause of Great Britain as well as of America; it is the cause of mankind. Were the principle of taxing America admitted Great Britain would that instant be ruined, the pecuniary influence of the crown, and the army of placemen and pensioners would be so increased that all opposition to the most iniquitous measures would be forever borne down.

. . . I act not from any pique and disappointment . . . but from principle . . . an English soldier owes a very great degree of reverence to the king as first magistrate . . . but I think he owes still a greater degree of reverence to the rights and liberties of his country. I think his country is every part of the empire; that in whatever part of the empire a flagitious minister manifestly invades these rights and privileges, whether in Great Britain, Ireland or America, every

Englishman (soldier or not soldier) ought to consider their cause as his own: and that the rights and liberties of this country are invaded every man must see who has eyes, and is not determined to keep them shut. These my Lord, are my principles; from these, I swear by all that is sacred and tremendous, I purely and solely act. . . .[34]

It should be emphasized that Lee expressed in this letter—as he did in his addresses to the citizens of Philadelphia and New York —the sentiments of an English Whig (those of a lover of universal liberty, rather), not those of an American. At the moment there was no clash between his opinions and those of the dominant Americans. When the ruling American sentiment later embraced the idea of permanent separation from Britain, he was torn by conflicting loyalties.

Lee doubtless talked about more than politics to Adams and his cohorts. The shadow of warfare between Britain and the colonists was already hovering over Boston, and the military power of the colonists must have been balanced against that of the Mother Country. A veteran redcoat, Captain John Brown, according to his later recollection, was actually asked in October by Moses Gill, one of Adams' followers—in the presence of Hancock—whether he would be willing to serve under Lee against the British.[35] As it happened, the conversations between Lee and Adams were cut short by Adams' departure for Philadelphia to attend the First Continental Congress. Lee remained in Boston, however, until August 17. On the fifteenth Israel Putnam, New England's own military hero, came to town. Putnam had brought a flock of sheep from Connecticut to help feed the poor of Boston, who were suffering as the result of unemployment caused by the closing of the harbor. Lee and Putnam made a visit to the Common, where many British troops were camped. There they met British officers with whom they had served in the French and Indian War. These bantered Putnam and Lee, inquiring facetiously whether they had come to Boston to fight. Neither man, Dr. Young gleefully reported to Adams, gave "the strongest assurances to the contrary,"[36] On August 22, announcing the departure of Lee on the seventeenth and of Putnam on the twenty-second, the Boston *Evening-Post* and the Boston *Gazette* issued identical statements, including the pregnant words: "Amidst all our calamities this town has had the satisfaction to be visited by two of the greatest military characters of the present age. . . ."

Whatever was secretly said or done concerning military arrangements in the event of an Anglo-American war, Lee's visit to Boston was a great personal victory. Dr. Young informed Adams that Lee bore with him on his departure "the regards of as many citizens as any stranger ever did since I was acquainted here"[37] and that "Never man parted from us with a more general regret than General Lee."[38]

Leaving Boston in triumph, Lee retraced his steps to Philadelphia in order to observe the proceedings of the First Continental Congress, for he had abandoned his projected journey to West Florida and was becoming more and more heavily involved in public affairs. Though not a member of the Congress, he became intimate with many personages who were and with prominent Pennsylvanians generally. Among these were Richard Penn, a former governor of Pennsylvania and a liberal-minded man; John Dickinson, the author of the famous *Letters of a Farmer in Pennsylvania;* Dr. Benjamin Rush, the renowned physician, who had become an ardent republican before completing his medical education in Scotland; Thomas Mifflin, the handsome and charming Quaker who was later to serve three terms as governor of Pennsylvania; Silas Deane, soon to be an important American diplomat; John Adams; and George Washington. Some of these men he had probably met earlier. Indeed his acquaintance with Washington may have extended back to the Braddock expedition. At Philadelphia he also renewed his contacts with Richard Henry Lee, Samuel Adams, Patrick Henry, Alexander McDougall, and Robert Morris, before long the great financier of the War of Independence. He supped at Mifflin's home with the Adamses, Washington, Rush, and others;[39] he dined at Richard Penn's magnificent house with a large company, including John Adams, Dickinson, and Stephen Moylan;[40] he had dinner at Dr. Cadwalader's with John Adams, Henry, and Edmund Pendleton;[41] and he was a guest at a similar party given by Dickinson, the roll of guests including Samuel Chase, Mifflin, John Adams, and William Paca.[42]

Never shy, Lee no doubt exerted every possible effort at Philadelphia to make acquaintances and friends. Certain it is that his fluent, witty, and often brilliant conversation, his broad knowledge, his travels, his military experience, and his self-assurance greatly impressed almost everyone he met. Long afterward John Adams, who was perhaps as much impressed as any, recalled that Lee exerted the same fascination as Francisco de Miranda, the South American patriot, whose powerful personality on several occasions almost persuaded the British government to assist in freeing the South Americans from Spanish rule. There can be no doubt that Lee was happy at Philadelphia. A letter which Paul Revere brought from Boston to Newport at the beginning of October accurately portrays Lee's feelings. "G—— L—— is there, battening beneath the rays of the assembled Gods; he rejoices unmeasurably at the bright'ning prospect."[43]

Strangely enough, Lee's activities at Philadelphia seem to have included even the authorship, or part authorship, of one of the official papers of the Congress, an address to the people of Canada asking for their support in the struggle against Britain. Lee was carrying around and displaying a draft of this paper two weeks before the Congress directed it to be prepared.[44] That it was possible for this Englishman to participate in such an important activity, in view of the lofty level of ability among the delegates, is further testimony to the extraordinary effect which his personality had upon them.

After his arrival in America, Lee had written twice to Edmund Burke, who had cautioned him against going to extremes; to Sir William Baker, a wealthy London merchant deeply interested in American affairs;[45] and to Sir Charles Davers. From Philadelphia he wrote again to Davers, solemnly and exultingly warning that the empire was lost, "unless everything [done] lately with respect to this country, is speedily and totally reversed." Gage, he pointed out, had been virtually besieged in Boston since September 1 and had "perhaps the most able and determined men of the world to deal with. In short he stands on such damned ground that he slips every instant." He argued that the Americans—including the New Englanders, who had acquired an undeserved reputation for military ineptitude in the French and Indian War—would if necessary fight, and fight well. "You will ask, where they will find generals? But I ask, what generals have their tyrants? In fact the match in this respect will be pretty equal."[46] To much the same effect Lee wrote a month later, but in more dignified and more cautious language, to the Duke of Richmond, long a defender of America in Parliament.[47]

As Lee hinted to Davers, he himself was ready to accept a command in an American army, should one be raised. Indeed, before the Congress adjourned, he began to draw up a plan for the formation and organization of American battalions. On October 24, Mifflin and Lee called upon John Adams, and Lee expatiated upon the plan.[48] He completed it, and finally had it almost ready for the printer in February, 1775. If it was printed, it was circulated secretly, for no contemporary printed copy of it can now be found. Certainly there was much interest in it among American leaders. In January and February, 1775, Thomas Johnson, member of the Congress from Maryland, was earnestly promising Washington that he would send him a copy, in manuscript, if necessary.[49] It is not certain that the great Virginian ever saw the plan, nor is it clear that Lee's proposals had any great influence upon the structure of the American army as it was later formed. Lee's battalion called for a total of about eight hundred men organized in five companies, including one of light infantry.[50]

In addition to his activities with respect to the Congress and the formation of American battalions, Lee was busy with the pen in the fall of 1774. An article signed "Junius Americanus" and written by Arthur Lee, brother of Richard Henry and an American agent in London, was appearing everywhere in American newspapers. Lee did not know the identity of the author,[51] and he was moved to write a rebuttal, curiously enough, to defend Gage. Junius Americanus, without much regard for fact, flayed Gage, describing him as a willing and contemptible tool of the British government. This performance was too much for Lee, who may have resented the injustice of the attack and who doubtless looked upon Gage as his own exclusive subject. He accordingly produced an attractive essay, "Of General Gage," which appeared in the Philadelphia *Pennsylvania Packet* on November 7 and which was widely reprinted in the American newspapers.[52] In this striking little piece he described Gage's career, abilities, and character with almost startling accuracy, making it clear that whatever Gage's politics and public actions might be, he was a just, benevolent, and lovable man.[53] Quite characteristically, Lee himself in the heat of political and military conflict later passionately denounced his old friend as a contributor to the secession of America from the empire.[54]

Lee's most important production in Philadelphia, however— and no doubt the most important of all his writings—was his *Strictures upon A "Friendly Address to All Reasonable Americans."* This pamphlet, first published in Philadelphia in November, 1774,[55] was reprinted no less than five times during the following winter—twice in Boston, and once each in New York, Newport, and New London. The essay was also republished in American newspapers,[56] and even appeared in John Almon's *Remembrancer* in London itself. Although it has received very little attention from historians of the American Revolution, the *Strictures* was probably one of the most influential pieces of propaganda in the Revolutionary period.

The *Friendly Address to All Reasonable Americans*, written anonymously by the Reverend Dr. Myles Cooper, president of King's College (now Columbia University), and published by James Rivington, who had already become a Tory, was a persuasive pamphlet urging the impropriety, foolishness, and hopelessness of American opposition to the will of Britain. Cooper ridiculed charges of British tyranny, pointed out that no one was required to pay the tax on tea unless he consumed it, and solemnly declared it was the duty of every citizen to obey his rulers. He asserted that the unrest existing in America was largely produced by a few fanatical agitators, principally of Boston. Many colonists, he suggested, were being misled by a factious few. But his most potent argument was that resistance to Britain was useless, for Britain could put an end to the quarrel by the use of the army. The regulars, even so small a force as seven thousand men, would be irresistible. Moreover, Britain could call upon large bodies of men, including German mercenaries, and many Tories would rally to the royal standard. It was absurd, Cooper contended, for the undisciplined and unorganized Americans even to think of opposing them, especially since these superior forces would be led by veteran and experienced commanders. Because the power of the regular army—particularly in view of the fact that it had gloriously done the major part of the fighting in America in the French and Indian War—was greatly respected in the colonies, Cooper's argument was a telling one. It is not too much to say that it daunted many waverers and cast disquiet upon the most zealous American hearts.

With his broad learning and his abilities as a writer, Lee had the military knowledge and reputation which peculiarly fitted him for the task of answering Cooper. There was no other man in America who had equal military prestige, save possibly Gage and Haldimand, and Lee could therefore pose as *the* authority on warfare. Writing anonymously but without any attempt to conceal his identity, so that he was soon known to be the author of the *Strictures*, Lee fluently, tartly, wittily, and brilliantly demolished Cooper's contentions.

He began by ridiculing Cooper as the author of the *Friendly Address*. The author must be an "ecclesiastick," he asserted, since "he has the want of candour and truth, the apparent spirit of persecution, the unforgivingness, the deadly hatred to dissenters, and the zeal for arbitrary power which has distinguished churchmen in all ages, and more particularly the *high* part of the Church of England." Moreover, insinuated Lee, Cooper's head was itching for a bishop's miter. Countering most of Cooper's arguments rather casually but successfully, he devoted himself largely to destroying the fear which Cooper strove to induce. He pooh-poohed the achievements of the redcoats in the French and Indian War, pointing out that they had had to spend several years learning how to fight under American conditions and that the colonials had performed brilliantly on several occasions. He cast doubt upon the assertion Britain could employ large numbers of Hessians and Hanoverians—it was likely for various reasons that Britain would not be able to secure their services. He argued that the parade maneuvers in which the redcoats were so thoroughly trained were of little or no military importance and declared, with some truth, that the victories of Frederick the Great were largely won by the Prussian militia. The skills really needed to fight effectively in large formations could be easily and quickly acquired. The Americans were brave and numerous; they would fight in a good cause. Only a few dozen Tories would join the British. As for generalship, the British had no James Wolfe to lead them, and the Americans would have no difficulty in finding military leaders equal to those of the regulars. Did not the nonprofessional officers of the armies of Parliament far excel those of the forces of Charles I in the English Civil War? The best way to avoid another civil war, he wrote, was to prepare for one; "to keep the swords of your enemies in their scabbards, you must whet your own." Remonstrances, petitions, prayers, and supplications will make no impression upon "our callous Court . . . fear alone can operate; there are symptoms that it already begins to operate. The monster Tyranny already begins to pant; press her now with ardor, and she is down." Urging that American liberties were threatened so long as military camps, forts, and barracks remained in the colonies, he begged his readers to ponder the danger arising from them. "It is worth your consideration, Americans, whether these badges [of slavery] should remain or no. I shall now conclude, brave citizens, with invoking the Almighty God, from whom all virtues flow, to continue you in that spirit of unanimity and vigor which must ensure your success, and immortalize you through all ages, as the champions and patrons of the human race."[57]

The *Strictures*, as the publisher of the Salem *Essex Gazette* declared,[58] removed the terror the people had for redcoats, and they were very popular, though not with the clergy.[59] There was no one in America who could make an effective rebuttal; and a Captain Henry Barry of the British Fifty-second regiment, "an awkward sappy looking chap" who attempted it, produced a "performance . . . pretty much like himself."[60] It is to be suspected that the *Strictures*, together with the reputation of their author, greatly encouraged American opponents of British authority and that Lee's pamphlet in some degree persuaded the American patriots to insist, even at the risk of armed hostilities, upon British acceptance of their views of a satisfactory relationship between the Mother Country and the colonies. Of course, it would be saying too much to suggest that they would have bent before British authority had it not been for Lee's *Strictures*.

It is apparent that during the fourteen months after his arrival in New York from England, Lee played an important role in Anglo-American relations; and it is not to be doubted that his writings, his conversation, and his very presence in America contributed to the rising tide of anti-British sentiment in the Old Thirteen colonies. By November, 1774, this exotic Englishman had already become one of the architects of the American Revolution. Conspicuous even from the moment of his landing, he was marked for further distinction in the troubled days to come.

CHAPTER FIVE

THE BREAKING OF THE STORM

When a man hath no freedom to fight for at home,
Let him combat for that of his neighbours;
Let him think of the glories of Greece and of Rome,
And get knock'd on the head for his labours.

To do good to mankind is the chivalrous plan,
And is always as nobly requited;
Then battle for freedom wherever you can,
And, if not shot or hang'd, you'll get knighted.

BYRON, *Stanzas*

FROM THE DAY he stepped ashore in New York in the fall of 1773 Lee was a man upon whom British officials cast an inquiring eye; and as months passed, they watched him more and more carefully. Indeed, so dangerous did he appear that in September, 1774, the Earl of Dartmouth, secretary of state for the colonies, sent a "secret" letter to Gage, instructing the general to take every possible legal step to prevent mischief on Lee's part.[1] Nor were British officials the only persons in England who saw Lee as a dangerous enemy to George III and his regime. The London *General Evening Post* on October 29 printed a note which explained to the public that Lee was giving support to the American cause not only from principle but also because of personal resentment against the king and his cohorts. "Take care, ye tools of m[inistry]," the note warned, "that he does not prove a second Coriolanus."[2] In November it was even whispered about in London that the cabinet had sent out an order for his arrest,[3] but there was no legal way in which the cabinet could act effectively against him.

There was one man, however, who could hurt Lee—James Rivington, the gifted printer of the New York *Gazetteer.* Turning Tory in the course of 1774, Rivington began to attack Lee in December, reprinting a savage assault upon him which had earlier appeared in the London *General Evening Post*. This item described him as a factious, disappointed, and malignant man who had distinguished himself in the Forty-fourth regiment only by volubility, superficial knowledge, vanity, and turbulence, and asserted that his regiment was remarkable for arrests and dueling until Lee was "removed" from it.[4] In January, 1775, after the *Strictures* had been spread about in New York, Rivington struck again by publishing an epigram which was poor in its poetical quality, rather feeble in its humor, but biting nevertheless.

May a halter bind him, whom honor and honesty cannot!
Overstock'd with ambition and high-mettled spirit,
Without either wisdom, or prudence or merit;
Poor Lubin a regiment strove to obtain,
Till his coffers he empty'd, and addl'd his brain.
Thro' various nations he publish'd his mind,
But in vain—for still *all* to his merits were blind.
Then swelling with anger, quoth Lubin, "I swear,
"To America—I strait will repair:
"I'll head their bold sons, and the sound of my name
"Shall lead them to victory, freedom and fame."
Jack Catch, who stood by, with significant leer,
Cries, "Courage, my hero, push on, never fear,
"Your reward you shan't lose, I'll be d——n'd if you do,
"See here!" and a halter presents to his view.
"Hands off, (bellows *Lubin*,) away with your string:
"If these are your tricks, you shan't catch me to *fight*,
"But in spite of your slip-noose, by G——, I will *write*."[5]

In February, Rivington struck again, using a half-column to paint "The Portrait of an Imposter."[6] Admitting that Lee had great gifts and that these had been improved by extensive reading, the author of this sketch, probably the publisher himself, accused him of quarrelsomeness and likewise of tyranny when he held command. The author declared that Lee had come to America in order to meddle and to gratify his ambition by stirring up discord; and he slyly and deceitfully reported that "Adamisius" (Samuel Adams) had seen a rival in him, and that "Adamisius," "Cooperensis" (Dr. Samuel Cooper), and "Handesetius" (John Hancock) had made sure that he acquired no influence in Massachusetts.

That Rivington succeeded in scorching Lee is certain. Indeed, Lee was sufficiently exasperated to prepare a squib on the printer which he planned to publish in John Holt's New York *Journal*, a rival newspaper. His essay, "A Breakfast for Rivington," for some unknown reason was withheld from the public.[7] Fortunately a copy of it was preserved in Lee's papers. The meal which Lee would have presented to the publisher would not have pleased Rivington's palate, for the essay cleverly, effectively, and rather indelicately accused Rivington of ignorance.[8]

If Lee suffered in a minor degree from Rivington's attacks, he had the consolation of knowing that he was not the only patriot leader who received the unwanted attentions of the printer. In any case, he pursued his way without undue concern for "Jack Catch."

Leaving Philadelphia late in the fall of 1774, he set out for Annapolis, Maryland, the home of Daniel Dulany, a famous pamphleteer whose acquaintance he had long desired to make.[9] In Maryland he made the acquaintance not only of Dulany but also of Charles Carroll of Carrollton, if indeed he had not met Carroll earlier. Likewise at Annapolis he was attracted to a Miss Robinson, whose charms led him once more to entertain thoughts of marriage. But his tempestuous personality, his ugliness, and even his age were against his wishes, and he had to accept from Miss Robinson friendship instead of love. When she wrote to him a year later, he begged to be her preceptor, since he could not be her lover.[10]

Again disappointed in the field of the tender emotions, Lee engaged more successfully in public affairs. When the Maryland Provincial Congress voted to raise and train troops, his plan for organizing battalions was adopted.[11] Governor Josiah Martin of North Carolina, a British brother officer who passed through Annapolis in December on his way from New York to his province, was astonished to see Lee actually drilling some of these troops.[12]

Before the end of 1774, Lee traveled to Mount Vernon, where he appeared on December 30 with John Balendine. He spent five days as George Washington's guest, riding to Alexandria with his host on January 2 and leaving after breakfast on January 4. During this visit he borrowed from Washington £15,[13] which with his customary carelessness about money he seems never to have repaid. The two men were renewing an acquaintance which may have begun in 1755, but Washington's diary, which is the only record of this visit, gives only the facts mentioned above. The two men undoubtedly talked about public questions, since Lee was seldom silent about them; and it may reasonably be inferred that they discussed Lee's plan for organizing colonial troops.[14] Probably they exchanged ideas on the formation and leadership of an American army, should it be necessary to raise one in order to oppose Britain effectively. Certainly their conversations were part of an increasing intimacy which was to lead to astonishing results, including final catastrophe for Lee. But neither man could penetrate the veil of the future. If they had been able to see what was to come, both men might have forsworn their association forever.

From Mount Vernon, Lee passed on to Williamsburg, from which place he meditated a journey to South Carolina.[15] This plan, however, was for some reason abandoned, and he remained in Virginia until about the beginning of May. Instead he seems to have paid a visit to Horatio Gates at Traveller's Rest and to have inspected Hopewell, a near-by plantation which belonged to Jacob Hite and which was for sale. He probably made a tentative decision to buy the property. It may be that the two Englishmen told each other they would offer their services to Congress should an American army be formed.[16]

After leaving Philadelphia, Lee continued to be active with his pen. In the winter of 1774-75 he produced at least three pieces of formal propaganda, including two which appeared in the newspapers. On January 18, 1775, the Philadelphia *Pennsylvania Journal* published some pointed "Queries proposed to General GAGE, and which if he does not think it consistent with prudence publicly to answer, he is earnestly requested to revolve in his own breast." These queries, reprinted in the *Essex Gazette* of February 14, where Gage could easily have seen them, may have given him some uneasiness. The theses persuasively and eloquently put forth in them were that Gage as a former Whig could only be unhappy in his present situation, that he would be a scapegoat in the event of an American triumph, and that he would be a tyrant in case of a British victory. Such was Gage's predicament, and he knew it. The implication of Lee's queries was that Gage should abandon the cause of the ministry, perhaps resign.[17] If Gage saw them, he paid no heed to them, continuing to do his duty as he saw it.

In February, 1775, Lee also published a remarkable essay, "On a Famous Trial in the Court of Common Pleas, between General Mostyn, Governor of Minorca, and an Inhabitant of That Island," which appeared in Purdie's *Virginia Gazette* at Williamsburg on the twenty-fourth of the month. The purpose of this little piece, not apparent in its title, was to convince the Virginians who read it that George III was an enemy to liberty everywhere in his dominions. In it Lee cogently argued that the king and his advisers firmly supported tyrannical and corrupt governors in all parts of the empire. He pointed out that the "infamous" Francis Bernard, who had been an unpopular and possibly dishonorable governor of Massachusetts, had been made a baronet for his services, and that George, Viscount Townshend, as viceroy of Ireland had "oppressed, beggared, and insulted" the Irish people and had been rewarded by the smiles and caresses of the king. But there was "a still more comfortable prospect" for "our fellow subjects who are not of British extraction." Consider, Lee asked his readers, what has happened to Mr. Fabrigas in the British island possession of Minorca. Mr. Fabrigas, not an Englishman, presumed to petition Governor John Mostyn, and was promptly thrown into a dungeon and later banished from the island for his pains. And when the Court of Common Pleas in London gave Fabrigas a verdict of damages against Mostyn, the British treasury paid for him! The implication was obvious. Townshend and Mostyn were military men. Soon, if America did not resist, her people would lie beneath the heels of brutal military oppressors.

George III had iniquities in store which the Americans had not yet experienced.[18]

Another Lee production of this period, which apparently was not published, was an address to the Provincial Congress of Virginia. That it had any effect upon that body, that it was even seen by any of its members, is uncertain. It is an enlightening document because it displays Lee's penchant for extreme measures. The council of New York and the lower house, by a vote of eleven to ten, had expressed a wish for reconciliation with Britain; and there was powerful sentiment in that colony against the nonimportation and nonexportation program adopted by the First Continental Congress. Lee's paper urged the Virginians to boycott New York merchants; to make arrangements to ostracize the eleven erring assemblymen; and to call upon the New Yorkers generally for united support of the common cause.[19] An essay which he began, but did not complete, is even more startling in content. Noting the prosperity of Switzerland in contrast to the comparative poverty of France and the economic well-being of the republics of Genoa and Venice as opposed to the backwardness of the other Italian states, he asked the reason and gave the answer: "They have no king—they have no court."[20] It may properly be inferred that he was not utterly averse to the destruction of the British monarchy in favor of republican institutions.

In his private letters Lee was far more outspoken. In December he wrote in a curiously romantic strain to Edmund Burke, denying reports current in England that he was the leader of the Americans in their resistance to Britain[21] and asserting the Americans' firm resolution to persevere in their opposition. They could not be subdued, he assured Burke; Britain would be wise to meet their demands.[22] Almost simultaneously he declared meaningfully to Dr. Benjamin Rush, " . . . I was in hopes before this to have heard of a certain conflagration. I am sorry to have been disappointed. Every time I think upon the subject, it appears more and more requisite that the step should be taken." In other words, he regretted that the Massachusetts militia had not attacked Gage's army in Boston.[23] He urged Rush and Robert Morris to stir

the Pennsylvania patriots to action, particularly in the matter
of raising and training troops. To Morris he expressed himself
with typical vigor: " . . . that damn'd slow heavy quakering
nag your province is mounted upon ought [to] be flogg'd and
spurr'd though she kicks and plunges."[24]

Certainly Lee was ready to mount his war horse, and a
second visit which he paid to Washington at Mount Vernon
in April therefore arouses questions which cannot be answered,
since it is mentioned only briefly in Washington's diary. From
April 16 to April 20 he was Washington's guest. On the sixteenth, George Mason and young Henry Lee (soon to be
famous as "Light-Horse Harry" and always to be his name-
sake's great admirer), among others, also partook of Washington's hospitality.[25] Less than three months later, learning that
the Englishman had accepted a commission in the Continental
army, Henry Lee wrote to him, asking to be allowed to serve
under him so as to learn the art of war. As it happened, Light-
Horse Harry's letter was intercepted by the British and therefore had no results.[26] Nor was Henry Lee the only person at
Mount Vernon in April who was impressed by talents of
Charles Lee. His host, as commander in chief of the American
army, eagerly sought his assistance two months afterward.
Probably Washington and Lee again conversed at length about
things military, in the event of a British-American clash.[27] Although they did not know it, the shooting had begun at Lexington and Concord even before Lee left the plantation on the
lofty banks of the Potomac.

Washington was preparing, while Lee was his guest, to go
to Philadelphia as a Virginia delegate to the Second Continental
Congress, and he set out for William Penn's city a few days
later. Lee likewise, but separately, made his way to Philadelphia,
appearing there on Saturday evening, May 6. The *Pennsylvania
Journal* of May 10, inserting the announcement of his arrival
among similar statements concerning members of the Congress,
made it clear that he had now become a personage in America,
referring to him as "a gentleman whose steady attachment to
the rights of human nature, and to the principles of the British
constitution in particular, hath endeared him to all the colonies."

When Gage, under instructions from the cabinet to take the initiative, sent his famous expedition to Concord, and the redcoats fought a series of bloody skirmishes with the Massachusetts minutemen and militia on April 19, the die was cast; and upon the Second Continental Congress inevitably fell the task of organizing the colonies as a whole for war. It was immediately apparent that an American army rather than a number of local forces was needed, and the Congress promptly began to plan its establishment. From the first, Lee and Gates were seriously considered for important commands in that army. As early as December, 1774, it had been suggested by "a gentleman of Philadelphia" that Washington, Israel Putnam, and Lee would hold rank in the order named, if the patriots created a continental military organization.[28] At Philadelphia, if John Adams' recollection long afterward is to be trusted, the leading candidates for the post of commander in chief were Washington; Artemas Ward, a New Englander in command of the American troops about Boston; and Lee. John Hancock also aspired to the honor; at least, he desired the refusal of the post. According to Adams, whose estimate is perhaps not too reliable, the candidates in ascending order of popularity were Hancock, Lee, Washington, and Ward.[29]

That Lee, an Englishman by birth, with his moods and tempers, was a principal candidate for the supreme command is remarkable. His manners had deteriorated, although he could be the perfect gentleman when he chose; he had, in general, become slovenly about his person; and he had developed a strange passion for dogs, a train of which now followed him wherever he went. (Perhaps he was aping Frederick the Great— there was something of the poseur in him.) On the other hand, Lee had cultivated the acquaintance of American leaders for many months before the Second Continental Congress met, and he was assiduous, as Adams later remembered, in calling on its members. His abilities were evident. He was seen as "a classical and universal scholar," "one of the greatest generals in the world," a hero covered with wounds; and he excited "much such an enthusiasm, and made as many proselytes and partisans" as Francisco de Miranda did some years later.[30] Above all, he was a regular army officer, and it was assumed, correctly, that he knew more about the business of warfare than any American. Certainly there was no real doubt of Lee's availability. If Washington indicated he was ready to serve by wearing the uniform of a Virginia colonel at a meeting of the Congress, Lee gave an even more effective hint, for he was soon organizing and drilling three regiments of militia recently raised in the city.[31]

Although Lee was seriously weighed and proposed for the supreme command, he could hardly have hoped, in view of his birthplace, to obtain it. Washington desired the post, and he was the logical man for it. There were political considerations which pointed strongly toward him, he had had some military experience, he was highly respected, he came from the fundamentally important colony of Virginia, and he was a member of the Congress. Thus far the American Revolution had been characterized in considerable degree by leadership on the part of New England; and it was advisable for the sake of unity that the post of commander in chief go to some person from one of the middle or southern colonies. Moreover, the choice of an aristocrat would please the more conservative element in the American population. Recognizing the need for sacrificing the claims of Ward, Elbridge Gerry, speaking for himself and Dr. Joseph Warren and, in effect, for the Massachusetts Provincial Congress, which had assumed governmental authority outside of Boston, informed the Massachusetts delegates at Philadelphia in a letter of June 4 that New England would accept Washington. At the same time he declared that a "regular" general would be badly needed for a period of one year, during which time the untrained American officers and troops might learn to stand against the redcoats; and he suggested that the presence and services of Lee at the American headquarters would be of the greatest value.[32]

Assured of some support from Massachusetts, John and Samuel Adams vigorously pushed for Washington's appointment,[33] and he was unanimously chosen. Then came up the question of the major general who would be second in command. Lee was endorsed for this post by many members and was ardently sponsored by Thomas Mifflin, who asserted that he could hardly be expected, in view of his existing rank and experience, to serve under any man but Washington. Mifflin, as John Adams expressed his opinion, insisted Lee must be *aut secundus aut nullus*—second in command or nothing.[34] According to a later report, Thomas Johnson of Maryland made a long speech against choosing Lee, on the ground that he was merely a disappointed Englishman and was not to be trusted. It was claimed that the whole New York delegation supported Johnson.[35] In any event, a New England man was politically the logical choice, and Ward was finally, though not unanimously, selected. Lee was then proposed as the second ranking major general. Again there was opposition to him, and all sorts of objections were raised. However, Washington wanted Lee's assistance—and Gates's also—and urged that Lee be given the appointment.[36] His request seems to have had some influence upon the Adamses. Having secured the first major general's position for New England, they were in a position to back Lee, and they fought vigorously for him, Samuel somewhat more enthusiastically than his cousin. John, after "the most mature deliberation . . . judged him the best qualified for the service and the most likely to connect the colonies," gave him his support, and was "willing to abide the consequences,"[37] John Hancock, Robert Treat Paine, and Thomas Cushing, the other members of the Massachusetts delegation, were strongly against Lee's appointment.[38] When it was approved by a heavy, though not a unanimous, vote,[39] Hancock remarked disappointedly, "I hope it will turn out well."[40]

Other major appointments in the Continental army, including that of Gates as adjutant general with the rank of brigadier, were all quickly approved. On June 19 a committee consisting of Patrick Henry, John Adams, and Thomas Lynch of South Carolina was sent to notify Lee of his selection and to obtain his acceptance or refusal. Lee declared he had the "highest sense of the honor conferred upon him by Congress," and that no effort in his power would "be wanting in the American cause." On the other hand, before finally accepting he wished to talk about his private fortune to a committee of Congress consisting of one member from each colony. The committee was immediately chosen. In conference with it Lee gave information to its members which placed his fortune at about £11,000. Suggesting that the British government might confiscate his property, he asked Congress to undertake, if it should become necessary, to indemnify him. The committee considered his request to be reasonable and so reported to Congress, and it was resolved before the day was over that he was to be reimbursed for any losses which he might suffer.[41]

Although he was very careless about business matters, Lee was fond of money; rather, he had occasional fits of avarice;[42] and his behavior at this juncture has subjected him to heavy criticism. His request for indemnification has been contrasted with Washington's refusal to accept more than his expenses as commander in chief. Admittedly there was something mercenary in Lee's attitude, and admittedly he was not prepared to throw away all his property in order to bring into practice the ideals which he had so fervently preached. On the other hand, it is evident that Congress in the main hired him as a professional soldier, that he was not looked upon as an American, and, indeed, that his services might not be required for any long period. Nor should it be forgotten that by accepting an American commission Lee exposed his property to confiscation whether the Americans won or lost in the struggle which had begun. Very few American patriots, if any, had property in England to lose. Washington's wealth was at least reasonably safe in the event of an American victory. It should be added that Lee was already negotiating for the purchase of Hopewell, partly in order to identify himself economically with the Americans and perhaps to further his military ambitions.[43] It seems fair to say he was trying to become an American without making what some "realists" might describe as an unnecessary and quixotic economic sacrifice. In defense of Lee's behavior, it should be recalled that the records do not show him refusing to serve without a promise of indemnification and that a Congress containing many gifted men promised reimbursement with remarkable celerity. It should also be noted that he made a very real immediate sacrifice such as no other high officer in

the American army made, for he gave up his lieutenant colonelcy in the British army, potentially worth £4,000, and his half-
pay, more than £130 per annum.

Whatever one's opinion may be concerning his conduct
with respect to indemnification, Lee's appointment was unsatisfactory, not only to some members of Congress, but also for a
short time in certain quarters in Massachusetts. Samuel Adams
therefore found it necessary to assure his friends at home of
Lee's integrity and devotion to the American cause. He suggested that Lee would fight as earnestly against George III as
Prince Eugene, though presumably a Frenchman, had struggled
against Louis XIV. Informing James Warren of the promise
of Congress to reimburse Lee if his property in England should
be confiscated, Adams requested that this transaction not be
made public, at least for a time.[44] Before long, however, Lee
won an enduring popularity in Massachusetts, and he gained
the firm friendship of the Adamses. One reason that John
Adams developed a soft spot for Lee probably was the general's behavior with respect to the former's indiscreet letter to
James Warren of July 24, 1775, made famous when it was intercepted and gleefully published by the British. Adams referred to John Dickinson as "a piddling genius," and made
somewhat more complimentary remarks about Lee. "You observe in your letter the oddity of a great man. He is a queer
creature. But you must love his dogs if you love him, and forgive a thousand whims for the sake of the soldier and the
scholar."[45] The Pennsylvania Farmer was much annoyed, but
Lee was amused by Adams' description of his character and
abilities; at least, he wisely pretended to be amused. He wrote
a humorous commentary letter "in the language of doggism,"
signing it with the name of Spada, his pet dog.[46] Confessing to
Rush that he *was* whimsical and that he loved dogs, he declared
that he considered Adams' description complimentary—which
indeed it was, in a New England way. So far as his love of
dogs was concerned, he was proud of it, for they were to be
preferred "to some other animals who are pleas'd to think their
convenience, pleasures, and dignity . . . the only objects of the
great Creator of all things." Besides, it was typical of a lover

of general liberty that he should be cynical regarding individual persons and fond of dogs. The high value which he placed upon dogs was evidence that he loved the principle of liberty.[47] To Adams himself Lee wrote in similar vein, thanking him for the flattering reference to his attainments as a soldier and a scholar and expressing warm admiration.[48] It is not surprising, therefore, to find Adams soon afterward adding to his description of Lee:

> I frankly confess . . . that a little whim and eccentricity so far from being an objection to anyone in my mind, is rather a recommendation, at first blush, and my reasons are, because few persons in the world, within my experience or little reading, who have been possessed of virtues or abilities, have been entirely without them, and because few persons have been remarkable for them, without having something at the same time, truly remarkable in them.
>
> I confess farther that a fondness for dogs, by no means depreciates any character in my estimation because many of the greatest men have been remarkable for it; and because I think it evidence of an honest mind and an heart capable of friendship, fidelity and strong attachments being the characteristicks of that animal.[49]

In the fall of 1775, Adams amicably accompanied Lee and his dogs on a tour of the American lines at Boston. Indeed, Adams and Lee, so different in personality, never quarreled.[50]

Lee is to be praised not only for refusing to permit himself to be insulted by Adams' indiscreet remarks but also for attempting to reconcile Dickinson and Adams. The two members of Congress differed sharply—even before the appearance of the letter—on the subject of a declaration of independence, the New Englander being warmly for separation from Britain and the Pennsylvanian being strongly opposed. A bitter quarrel between the two men could have created very serious dissension in the Continental Congress and among the supporters of the American cause generally. Lee, apparently when Adams visited the American camp, asked the Massachusetts leader "what devil" inspired him to write so caustically regarding his colleague. Adams offered an explanation and an apology which Lee relayed to Dickinson and which probably soothed his hurt feelings. Adams "honestly confess'd that he had wrote in a pet just after a warm squabble he had with you, and that in such a humour a man was apt to run into gross misrepresentations, that he really thought he had incurr'd the guilt, for that you were indisputably a man of genius and integrity, tho he must still continue to think you deficient in that vigor of mind, so much more requisite, than parts, in civil contests." Lee was all the more convincing as a peacemaker because he frankly told Dickinson that he was in full agreement with Adams in the New Englander's condemnation of Dickinson's attitude toward the question of independence.[51]

Before actually serving in the Continental army, Lee finally and definitely severed his connection with the British army, so far as it was within his power, renouncing his half-pay, and in effect his commission, in a letter of June 22 to Viscount Barrington, British secretary at war. He would be glad, he asserted, to fight for England against her hereditary enemies or in defense of the king's "just rights and dignity," but he felt himself "obliged in conscience, as a citizen, *Englishman*, and soldier of a free state" now to oppose the king.[52] On August 3, possibly before his resignation reached London, Lee's name, together with those of two other British officers assisting the Americans in their "unnatural rebellion," was stricken from the half-pay list.[53] Lee's letter and this action on the part of London officials may have saved his life in 1777.

Early in the morning of June 23, Washington, Lee, Philip Schuyler, and other Continental officers set out for American headquarters at Boston. They were escorted for some distance by a troop of light horse and many militia officers; they were also accompanied by the envy of John Adams, who ruefully coveted the laurels he believed they would win. Two days later they reached New York and were given a tumultuous welcome, while Governor William Tryon, who returned from England the same evening, received rather less attention. From New York they passed on through New Haven, where they reviewed Yale College students drilling on the green, and thence to Hartford and Cambridge, reaching the latter place at the beginning of July. In Massachusetts they were joyfully received, both Washington and Lee being offered welcoming addresses by the Provincial Congress. The circumstances considered, there was nothing remarkable in the greeting extended to the commander in chief, but the address which was presented to Lee was a startling effusion, particularly in view of its source. It is striking testimony that many persons then placed their hopes of victory in Lee as much as in Washington.

> From your character, from your great abilities and military experience, united with those of the commander in chief, under the smiles of Providence, we flatter ourselves with the prospect of discipline and order, success and victory.
>
> Be assured, sir, that it will give us great pleasure to be able to contribute to your happiness. May the favours and blessings of heaven attend you. May Divine Providence guard and protect you, grant you the reward of the brave and virtuous hero, the applauses of mankind, and the approbation of your own conscience, and eternal happiness hereafter.[54]

Lee responded briefly but in the heroic style:

> Nothing can be so flattering to me as the good opinion and approbation as the delegates of a free and uncorrupt people. I was educated in the highest reverence for the rights of mankind, and have acquired by long acquaintance, a most particular regard for the people of America.
> You may depend, therefore, gentlemen, on my zeal and integrity. I can promise you nothing from my abilities. God Almighty grant us success equal to the righteousness of the cause . . . .[55]

Promptly assuming command of a wing of the army under Washington, Lee soon established himself in a comfortable two-story farmhouse near the foot of Prospect Hill, quarters to which he gave the name "Hobgoblin Hall." He had command of the left wing, Artemas Ward of the right, and Israel Putnam of the center. He was immediately plunged into army business and was fairly well occupied by it, but he did not take part in any serious fighting for a whole year. The British army, much smaller than the American forces, was strongly entrenched behind Boston Neck and could not be dislodged except by heavy artillery, which Washington did not have in quantity until the following winter. On the other hand, Gage could not hope to acquire any valuable advantage, even if he could successfully assail Washington. The result was a stalemate and the continuance of the siege which had begun on April 19.

Although there was little fighting at Boston after Lee's arrival, there was plenty of work to do, such as building entrenchments, drilling men, laying plans for the creation of a more effective American army, and carrying on military correspondence. Lee labored strenuously and lent a vigorous hand to Washington, who badly needed support. His very presence lifted morale in the army; his knowledge of military affairs was of great value; and he was a tower of strength to the American cause.[56] Typical of the wide range of his efforts was a warm letter he wrote to General John Thomas in an endeavor to persuade him not to resign because he was dissatisfied with his rank.[57] Most interesting of all Lee's official activities was his participation in the famous exchange of correspondence between Washington and Gage on the treatment of prisoners. His part in this well-known episode, peculiarly enough, has never been mentioned before by any historian.

Gage had created a serious problem because he refused to recognize the ranks of American officers, treating them as if they were privates. Moreover, Gage mistakenly entrusted the care of prisoners to a rascal, Provost Cunningham, who abused them. The result was deep resentment in the American army. As early as July 11 Lee was planning to write a letter to him to demand better treatment for the prisoners in his hands, threatening reprisals if Gage's reply should prove unsatisfactory.[58] Presumably this letter would have been sent in Washington's name. A month later, when the problem had become urgent, the commander in chief did send such a message to the British general.[59] It is likely that Lee's reputation as a scholar and writer led Washington to call on him to help compose it.[60] In any case, Gage's reply, written in large part by Lee's old comrade John Burgoyne, flamboyantly denied the American

charges and accused the Americans of mistreating *their* prisoners. In the language of an exalted, righteous, and heroic
patriot, Lee composed a rejoinder which Washington, soften-
ing its terms, used as the basis of a letter to Gage of August 20.[61]
The British commander did not even respond. Washington prudently refrained from taking stern measures against the redcoats in his hands. Conceivably, however, his protests had
some effect upon Gage's conduct.

In September, 1775, Lee also helped to prepare a proclamation addressed to the French Canadians by Washington which
called upon them to assist American troops who were about
to invade Canada. In this connection Lee's command of the
French language was most valuable.[62]

In spite of his many official duties with the besieging army,
Lee had time for propaganda on Anglo-American relations, for
an extensive correspondence, and for social activities. Socially
he was not an unqualified success, but he played a role of some
importance in politics, as will later appear.

Civilians in Massachusetts hardly knew what to think of the
English general. Among those with whom Lee associated was
Abigail Adams, John's wife, a remarkable person in her own
right. She reported dryly to John, "General Lee looks like a
careless, hardy veteran, and by his appearance brought to my
mind his namesake, Charles the Twelfth, of Sweden. The ele-
gance of his pen far exceeds that of his person."[63] Abigail did
not know quite how to take Lee. In December at a party given
by Thomas Mifflin and his wife, he ordered his dog Spada to
mount a chair and to present his paw to her. With some reluctance she finally shook his "hand," whereupon Lee slyly exclaimed, "That, madame, is the dog which Mr. [Adams] has
rendered famous."[64] James Warren also was puzzled by Lee.
Informing John Adams that both Washington and Lee were
considered in Massachusetts as excellent men in their respective
positions, he declared that Lee seemed "a genius in his way; he
had the marks about him of having been in the trenches." Later
he reported what appeared to be an instance of bad manners
on Lee's part; and he finally concluded that the general was indeed an odd personality. Fortunately his wife, Mercy Warren,

also had opportunities to inspect Lee, including one occasion on which he was a dinner guest at the Warren home. Later, in her history of the American Revolution, she wrote one of the most discerning analyses of Lee's complex character penned by any of his contemporaries. Dr. Jeremy Belknap was another civilian who had an opportunity to observe Lee. After having had dinner at the American camp on October 21 in a company including the general, he noted in his diary that Lee was "a perfect original, a good scholar and soldier, and an odd genius; full of fire and passion, and but little good manners; a great sloven, wretchedly profane, and a great admirer of dogs,—of which he had two at dinner with him, one of them a native of Pomerania, which I should have taken for a bear had I seen him in the woods." Belknap also gives another instance of the wit for which Lee had already become famous in America. Two days before, Lee had written a letter of introduction for a Mr. Page to Israel Putnam and had advised Putnam to don full military regalia and pistols, and even to blacken one side of his face, so that Page would be properly impressed.[65]

CHAPTER SIX

TOWARD INDEPENDENCE

... for what peace will be giv'n
To us enslav'd, but custody severe,
And stripes, and arbitrary punishment
Inflicted?

MILTON, *Paradise Lost*

LEE THE LETTER WRITER was as active as ever at Boston and New York during the last half of the year 1775 and the first two months of 1776; and he was soon embarked upon a tide of political discussion which swept him on until he came to demand the complete separation of America from Britain. Indeed, he was one of the first openly to set the American goal as nothing less than independence.

The best-known part of Lee's correspondence of this period is the bizarre exchange of letters between him and handsome John Burgoyne, who had been sent out from England in the spring as a junior major general with William Howe and Henry Clinton to join and to bolster Gage.[1] Burgoyne was a courageous soldier, possessed some literary talent—he wrote one really good play—and he was not without liberal sentiment. He was also grandiloquent and pompous. Lee was on friendly, though not cordial, terms with him after their association in Portugal in 1762 and addressed a letter to him from Philadelphia on June 7, even before it was definitely known that Burgoyne had reached American shores. This letter in essence was a piece of propaganda, not a personal message, for it was printed by Lee before Burgoyne received it. Again Lee defended the justice of the American cause, arguing that the king and the "felonious" North were inveterate enemies of liberty and that the Americans were struggling in behalf of universal human freedom. He assured Burgoyne—and the public—that Britain could not conquer America, and he hinted that Burgoyne and Howe, whose views were not unfriendly to America, should refuse to serve under the British banner.[2]

It is not certain that Lee had any real hope of detaching Burgoyne and Howe from the British army at Boston, but Burgoyne fancied that he could play upon Lee's vanity and British sentiments and wean him away from the Americans![3] After consulting Gage, he dispatched a friendly note to Lee on July 5, to which Lee promptly replied, forwarding his compliments to Howe and Clinton, with whom he was acquainted.[4] Three days later Burgoyne sent across the lines a long letter in which he described himself as a lover of liberty and as an active participant from conviction in the Anglo-American struggle. He contended, without too great respect for truth, that Britain had given up all thought of collecting taxes in America and that the Americans could no longer harbor resentment on that score. Therefore they could be striving only for independence. The whole British nation, including Burgoyne, would enthusiastically fight to prevent a separation, and the Americans would inevitably be defeated. He had some letters in his hands for Lee from Lord Thanet and Sir Charles Davers, both of whom were against America, Burgoyne subtly averred. Would not Lee meet him at the battle lines on Boston Neck to receive the letters and to renew their ancient friendship? Gage would give Lee safe-conduct.[5]

This invitation was a trap, and Burgoyne hoped to enlist Lee's services as a British agent by bribing him and by holding up as an example General George Monck, who had won renown by deserting the Commonwealth and engineering the return to the throne of the Stuarts in the person of Charles II.[6] If so much could not be accomplished, even an unsuccessful interview could be of some use because the very fact that it was held might cast doubt in American minds upon Lee's loyalty. Lee almost fell into the trap. Presenting Burgoyne's letter to the Provincial Congress of Massachusetts, he indicated that he would accept or refuse Burgoyne's invitation in accordance with the opinion of that body. If its opinion was in the affirmative, he desired one of its members to accompany him, so that there could be no suspicion of treachery on his part.[7] The Congress pointed out that such an interview, no matter what was said, might cast a shadow upon Lee's fidelity to the American cause. It appointed Elbridge Gerry to accompany him if he went to meet Burgoyne, but suggested that he should not do so except with the approval of a council of war.[8] Lee then wrote, on July 11, to the British general that minds had been made up, that no good could come from an interview, and that he must therefore "defer the happiness of embracing a man whom he most sincerely loves."[9] This letter was read by several persons before it was dispatched. But Lee sent simultaneously and secretly a second letter in which he tried to persuade the British, by working on their fears, to abandon the contest, asserting on his honor that France and Spain were prepared to assist the colonists against the Mother Country.[10] Later the British government used the letter to put a pointed question to the French ambassador at London, which received an evasive answer. The French government would only commit itself *orally* that no promises had been made.[11]

In this exchange of letters the attempts of the parties to seduce each other failed. Burgoyne won a minor victory, since the very existence of the correspondence inevitably led some Americans to question Lee's devotion to their cause, particularly because Lee's letter of June 7 and his public letter of July 11, together with that of Burgoyne of July 8, were published throughout the thirteen colonies and in England as well.[12] Lee, however, had the final word. Learning that Burgoyne was about to sail for home, he addressed him once more at the beginning of December, begging him in moving language to do what he would to save the empire from disruption.

> The whole British empire stands tottering on the brink of ruin, and you have it in your power to prevent the fatal catastrophe. . . . For heaven's sake . . . tell the people at home, that they must immediately rescind all their impolitic, iniquitous, tyrannical, murderous acts; that they must overthrow the whole frantic system, or that they are undone.

The Americans had never wanted independence; they did not

yet want it; but they soon would insist upon it, unless their demands were promptly met. As for himself, wrote Lee:

> I swear by all that's sacred . . . that I most earnestly and devoutly love my native country; that I wish the same happy relation to subsist for ages betwixt her and her children, which has raised the wide arch of her empire[13] to so stupendous a height; but at the same time I avow, that if the parliament and people should . . . support any longer the present ministry in their infernal scheme, my zeal and reverence for the rights of humanity are so much greater than my fondness for . . . the place of my nativity, that, had I any influence in the councils of America, I would advise not to hesitate a single instant, but decisively to cut the Gordian knot, now besmeared with civil blood.[14]

It might reasonably be concluded from this extraordinary outpouring that Lee was ready, though with many pangs, to plump for an American declaration of independence on December 1, 1775, since he could not have entertained any substantial hope that Burgoyne or any British friend of America would be able to achieve an about-face in British policy. Such was the fact; and indeed, Lee had privately announced his allegiance to an independent American republic as early as October. He was one of the very first American leaders to commit himself in writing; and it is to be suspected that he had looked upon an independent American republic as an ideal long before the fall of 1775. With Samuel Adams, John Adams, and Benjamin Franklin, he was among the first major American leaders to be converted to that ideal. However, his conversion, although it was expressed in passionate language, was intellectual and romantic rather than thoroughly and practically considered, and therefore had a shaky foundation. While he detested the king and his friends, and their policies too, there cannot be much doubt that he retained a love for England. That love he expressed—paradoxical as it might seem—in denunciations of British rulers and British policy and even of Britain herself. His denunciations were to a degree motivated by a desire to convince himself that the ideal to which he had committed himself was utterly right. His brain gave a superficial devotion to an

American republic; his viscera yearned for the continuance of the empire.

All through the latter part of 1775 Lee was advocating more vigorous measures and swifter action. In July and later he censured sharply the Olive Branch Petition, sent by Congress to London in a last effort to persuade the British government peacefully to meet American demands. "What the devil posses'd the Congress to send another petition to the callous tyrant . . . ? . . . it implies that some dregs of fear still remain among us. . . . We must work on theirs, by talking high & acting decisively. . . ." Instead, wrote Lee to Richard Henry Lee, Congress should have said to the king: "Sir, if you do not withdraw your troops upon the receipt of this, we will absolve ourselves from all allegiance to you, and we will divorce ourselves forever from Britain, whose abject patience in suffering such tyranny as that she has experienced through your whole reign, renders her totally unworthy to be the presiding power of a great empire."[15] As early as July, Lee was also urging that Congress order the arrest of William Tryon, who as governor of New York could do much damage to the American cause in and about Manhattan, where he remained unmolested. Why in the name of Satan was Tryon not seized, he asked Robert Morris.[16] On October 10 he again impatiently insisted in a letter to Rush that something be done about Tryon. It was no time, he asserted, to be too delicate in conduct.[17] Congress, however, hesitated to act because it feared that the arrest of the governor would cause commotion in New York and possibly drive some waverers into the British camp. Moreover, it was believed that British warships in New York harbor would bombard the town in reprisal; and the local patriots insisted that Congress should not place their homes and their families in jeopardy. On October 26 Lee took an extreme step in this matter, writing to Alexander McDougall and vehemently urging the New York patriots to apprehend Tryon and the leading Tories who supported him. Many in the camp at Boston were murmuring because of the inactivity of their brethren at New York, he told McDougall. The local patriot committee of safety should do the job, and then assure the senior British captain in the harbor that if he cannonaded the town "the first house he sets on fire shall be the funeral pile of His Excellency." What is more, declared Lee, unless the British leave the town unmolested, execute your threat! If the local committee would not adopt this strategy, McDougall should secretly send some young and enthusiastic patriots after Tryon. Once the governor was a prisoner, all would applaud, predicted Lee.[18] But Lee's advice was too strong a medicine for even McDougall, not a remarkably cautious man. McDougall had planned to go after the Tories, but his superiors had restrained him.[19]

Lee advocated the same forthright measures for the Earl of Dunmore, the last royal governor of Virginia, whom he saw as another danger to the American cause.[20] Dunmore soon proved to be a sharp thorn in the sides of the Virginia patriots, and Lee was no doubt wise in urging that steps be taken to deal with him and Tryon. Although the extremist appears in his suggestion to McDougall that a British cannonade of New York should spell execution for Tryon, it seems likely that the attitude adopted by him was much the same as that taken by Washington and many other officers in the camp at Boston.[21]

In October, Lee proposed to John Adams two more drastic steps: that the property of Tories be partly or wholly confiscated, and that the American ports be thrown open to European commerce.[22] In November he descanted upon the "impudence and cant" of the Quakers, who wished to "enjoy all the blessings of liberty without contributing a single mite towards the acquiring or preservation of that blessing. . . ."[23] Early in December he proposed to Benjamin Franklin a thoroughgoing plan for waging the war.[24] He urged that every American be required to join in "A Solemn League and Covenant" binding its members to common action, both defensive and offensive, against the enemy; and that any persons near the seacoast refusing to subscribe be removed inland and placed on small pensions, their property being confiscated in whole or in part. The army should be completely reorganized, with militia formed on a continental basis and regulars drafted from the militia or from "substitutes."[25] Lands should be promised to regular soldiers for their services. New York ought to be strongly fortified and

garrisoned, or destroyed; Charleston should be effectively protected; and mobile "flying camps" were needed in Maryland
and Virginia. In addition everything possible should be done to
win the good will of the Indians, so that the western frontiers
of the colonies would not be too seriously exposed. These measures were far too vigorous for Congress, although Franklin did
not find them entirely distasteful.[26]

The very vigor of Lee's language and the nature of his proposals on public affairs seem to suggest that he was well on the
road to championing American independence long before the
end of 1775. As early as September he confided to Rush that he
shared with him a republican aversion to titles. Referring to
those which the patriots of Massachusetts had concocted for
Washington and himself, "His Excellency" and "His Honor"
respectively, Lee declared they made him "spew," and that even
to refer to the "Honorable" Continental Congress created a
"wambling" in his stomach. "What cou'd add dignity to the
simple title of the Continental Congress of America . . . ?" he
rhetorically asked his friend. To that confirmed republican he
was also writing meaningfully at the same time about reaping
in Congress "the full harvest which we have sown with such
infinite pains and labor."[27] Was the "harvest" an independent
American republic? Certainly Rush was already voicing his sentiments to Lee without restraint, which fact suggests that he
believed him to be sympathetic. On October 10 Lee was warning the physician to be a bit careful in declaring his principles—
Virginians and Carolinians were not yet prepared for republican
doctrines.[28] But Lee *was* sympathetic. Ten days later he told
Rush that both he and Gates had been preaching republicanism
in camp—Gates so openly and enthusiastically that he aroused
astonishment. But Rush must be a little patient—another year,
and those who were condemning the cabinet and reverencing
the king would lump them together as tyrants. "I am even
sanguine enough to flatter myself that nurses will soon frighten
their naughty children if they do not cease crying that the king
will fetch 'em away."[29]

When the news came to America late in 1775 that the British government intended to wage full-scale war rather than

merely to negotiate, Lee came out decisively and even publicly
for separation, as he had told Burgoyne he would, vigorously
urging that step on John Dickinson and Robert Morris, who
were much opposed to it. He informed Dickinson that his last
letter to Burgoyne had given a rather accurate description of
his sentiments. But the news of the British government's formal
announcement that force was to be used, especially since the
British people seemed to be determined to give their support,
left no practical alternative. That people, "once certainly brave
honest and sensible," had endorsed the "accursed bloody measures" of "an obstinate tyrant" in a number of addresses, a
"damning proof that the English nation is lost, and that a separation must (and immediately) take place." Reunion with Britain had become impossible, and delay in declaring independence
would be "dangerous and criminal." French aid should immediately be sought. The help of France would save America many
agonies in her struggle with Britain.[30] Writing to Morris on
January 3, 1776, Lee declared: "The king's speech absolutely
destroys all hope of reunion—I formerly and indeed not long
ago look'd with some degree of horror on the scheme of separation but at present there appears no alternative—we must be independent or slaves."[31]

Later in January, Lee explained his views more fully to the
two members of Congress. He told Dickinson,

I can see no possibility of preserving the connection, the
People of G Britain are so totally lost every thing is so
swallow'd up in the corrupting vortex of the court, such a
general stupidity darkness and depravity have overspread the
land, that they are no longer capable or worthy of being the
presiding part of the empire—tho' I am fond of the thought
of the two countrys returning to their former state of relation I cannot help shuddering at some consequences shou'd
America be restor'd to her ancient priveledges and the war
immediately cease—every engine of corruption will be set
at work, your morals will be in a short time contaminated,
your leading men will be seduced by titles ribbons and pensions, the army left amongst you will be held out as the
means of providing for your children, idle relations and re-
tainers—other notions and principles will take place in the

minds of your youth—attachment to the person of and trappings of a diabolical tyrant will be substituted in the room of honest industry and a reverence for equal laws—such I am convinc'd will be the consequences of returning to your former dependance even with the restoration of your priveledges—yet I own my weakness, I wou'd accept the proposal shou'd it be offer'd—but we may assure ourselves it never will be offer'd. The tyrant is too confirm'd in his resolution to enslave you—He never will relax a jot—the hellish maxims he has imbib'd from his infancy rivett him in the persuasion that to leave you the shadow of freedom wou'd be a treason to his royal dignity. . . .[32]

In the same vein Lee wrote to Morris, demanding that Congress immediately declare independence. Such a step would help to secure aid from Britain's traditional enemies, France and Spain, and it was necessary for the Americans to decide what they were fighting for. "You must no longer hobble on one high shoe and one low." If Congress did "not act more decisively we shall be ruined, decision decision ought to be our word. Are we at war or are we not? . . . do not the people of England . . . support the tyrant? Why are we to eternity whining about a connexion with these depraved people?" And then Lee added significantly, "When you have conquer'd I think you may then with more safety glory and advantage return to your former state of relation."[33] In other words, a declaration of independence need not necessarily be final. It would be an effective weapon as well as an expression of an ideal. Should George III and the British government abandon their efforts to coerce the Americans and offer to them a favorable and guaranteed position in the empire, it would be advisable for the Americans to accept the olive branch. This line of argument was probably used to sway Dickinson and Morris toward independence, but it suggests that Lee himself at that time did not consider a declaration of independence, if one were issued, to be irrevocable.[34]

Morris protested in friendly fashion against Lee's participation in "the hue and cry for independence." Lee responded that he had long hesitated because the jealousies and dissensions between the several colonies were so great that the task of forming an American republic would be a very difficult one. But the conduct of the British government and people had rendered the step indispensable. If that government should be reorganized on true Whig principles, "the man who will vote for independence I shall think a very bad American." In any case, asserted Lee, "I neither think it decent nor proper in my circumstances to be very liberal of my sentiments. I have upon the whole a very great opinion of the Congress whatever they resolve I shall with readiness and zeal assent to."[35]

In February, Lee continued in the same strain. He indicated to Morris, Rush, Dickinson, and Joseph Reed, a prominent Philadelphia lawyer, that he believed a reconciliation with Britain at that time "on secure and absolute terms" to be as possible "as a scheme of incorporation with the Afghan Tartars or any of the interior tribes of Asia." All schemes of reconciliation, he declared, were "idle and dangerous dreams." England herself had deprived the colonists of their rights and was determined to conquer them. True, Britain had recently authorized General Howe and Admiral Viscount Howe to offer amnesty to Americans who would abandon rebellion, but it was doubtful that they had power to negotiate, and even more doubtful that any agreement into which they might enter could be depended upon, because of the treachery of the king and his minions. By all means, asserted Lee, declare independence now and secure an alliance with France. If you can obtain such an alliance, Britain may be forced immediately to cease her military efforts against the Americans. At least the Anglo-American war would be shortened and suffering resulting from it would be greatly diminished.[36] To Dickinson, Lee expressed his views as if he had become a thoroughgoing American. Before the preceding December he had been opposed to separation.

> I weakly flatter'd myself that the [British] nation wou'd be roused—but now when I see that they can tamely suffer the whole youth of England to be exported for the destruction of their relations—when they can be so passive as to behold their garrisons occupy'd by foreign mercenaries with the sole view of enabling a most accursed tyrant to butcher their fellow subjects—my patience and forbearance are exhausted

—I disclaim all connexion with my dastardly native country —I consider myself solely as a citizen of the only free country on the face of the globe—in this character I demand and expect that the legislature of my country shou'd lay aside all childish attachments and prejudices, and make it the sole aim of their politicks—to insure the welfare and safety of this community of which I am an adopted member—you will excuse the heat with which I express myself, but they are the real sentiments of my heart. . . .[37]

Although Lee told Morris he did not think it proper to voice his sentiments too freely, he actually drew up early in 1776 a rough sketch of an essay demanding independence. He obviously entertained the thought of publishing the essay, but he did not do so. Lamenting the slowness of Congress to act, he employed a descriptive metaphor which could hardly have failed to shock. If the members discovered their wives with the Howe brothers *in flagrante delicto*, they would be too indifferent to interfere.[38]

Although Lee was one of the first to demand a declaration of independence and in spite of the fact that he was most vociferous, he was not at bottom devoted to the idea of a permanent independent American republic. Even in his most passionate outpourings on the subject the possibility that such a declaration might sooner or later be rescinded is either expressed or implied; and he suggests more than once that political change in Britain would destroy all thought of an enduring separation. In short, he was embarked upon a troubled sea and headed for a destination to which he did not wish to go. But the troubles which came upon him as a result lay in the future.

For the present there was work to do, and he did it to the admiration of those Americans who desired decisive action. In December, 1775, the American leaders in Rhode Island were much alarmed for the safety of their colony, partly because there were many and dangerous Tories within its narrow boundaries and partly because of rumors of a projected attack by British forces from Boston. They begged Washington for help, and the commander in chief sent Lee with a guard of thirty men and a few riflemen to their assistance. Setting out from the

American camp on December 20, Lee reached Providence two days later. Joined by Israel Putnam, he proceeded to Newport on Christmas Day and remained there until the twenty-seventh. In five hectic days he inspected the harbors of the colony, made recommendations for fortifications, and frightened the Tories. From the known Loyalists he exacted an oath not to give supplies or information to the British and to give their support to the Continental Congress. Three Tories of Newport who refused to take the oath Lee has arrested and sent to Providence. The results of his whirlwind visit were most pleasing to the local patriots, who also rejoiced because the rumored British assault failed to materialize. They presented to Lee a gift in acknowledgment of his services,[39] and Washington heartily praised his efforts in a letter to Congress.[40]

Back at Cambridge, Lee wasted hardly a moment before embarking upon a similar and far more important expedition to New York City. He had long been worried about the situation in that town, for it was obvious to him, as it was to all those possessing any military knowledge, that New York was the strategic center of the colonies, insofar as they had one. He guessed, as did Washington, that the British would soon transfer the bulk of their army from Boston to Manhattan. Under the circumstances, the continued presence of British warships in the New York harbor, the failure of the local patriots to deal with the numerous Tories in and about the town, and the lack of fortifications there called for strenuous action. To Robert Morris on January 3, 1776, Lee asserted that the New York situation made him "uneasy almost to distraction . . . for Heaven's sake why [has Congress] not fortify'd and garrison'd that city. . . . No time, not a single instant is to be lost."[41] If Congress failed to move, "We shall weep repentance with tears of blood," he wrote to Dickinson the same day.[42] Two days later Lee had a plan to deal with the situation which he proposed to Washington. Since for political reasons Congress had not done and probably would not do anything about it, Washington should send him to New York, empowering him to raise a body of volunteers in Connecticut and to call upon the New Jersey militia, to expel or suppress the Tories, and to fortify the town. After all, argued Lee, Washington was entrusted with the defense of the colonies generally, even though his authority did not specifically cover New York; and if he did exceed his powers by sending Lee, Congress would certainly forgive him, since he would be carrying out the secret wishes of that body. Indeed, Lee contended, as soon as he had cleansed the vicinity of the town of Tories and fully committed the local patriots to deeds as well as words, Congress itself would order American troops into the place. Lee's plan was obviously a good one, and it would not require the services of any of the troops besieging Boston, as he did not fail to point out.[43]

Washington promptly saw the merits of his subordinate's proposal but hesitated to act upon it. Fortunately John Adams, temporarily absent from the Congress, was available for advice, and Washington asked his opinion. Adams immediately and courageously gave his approval, knowing that he would be censured more severely than the military men if anything went wrong.[44] The commander in chief accordingly instructed Lee on January 8 to execute his plan, "keeping always in view the declared intentions of Congress." This phrase, which restrained Lee in some degree, would also serve to protect Washington against the wrath of his superiors. How much the commander in chief then valued Lee's services is shown in other phrases calling upon him to keep himself in readiness, insofar as possible, for a speedy return to Boston, should he be needed with the main army.[45]

Lee set out quickly for New York, but he encountered bad weather and did not reach New Haven until January 15. Either on the road to New Haven or at that place he learned that General Richard Montgomery and Benedict Arnold had suffered a disastrous defeat in a desperate assault upon the British garrison at Quebec; indeed, that the intrepid Montgomery had been slain and the bold Arnold seriously wounded. These bad tidings made his errand all the more urgent, since it was now likely that the British would attack the colony of New York from both the south and the north. Fortunately, he also heard good news at New Haven. In response to urging by Washington, Governor Jonathan Trumbull of Connecticut had raised and equipped two regiments of militia to accompany Lee.[46] From these he took twelve hundred men, with whom he expeditiously marched on to Stamford. There he wrote to Congress to explain his mission. He planned to disarm the Tories, giving their weapons to American militia, and to force the Loyalists to deposit half or more of their property with the Congress as a pledge of good behavior. He also intended to demand an ironclad oath from them, with the idea that the most determined Tories, the "desperate fanaticks," would reveal themselves by refusing to swear it. These he would take into custody and send to Connecticut, where they would be harmless. He intended to occupy the town, but not to attack the king's ships. He begged Congress to approve his project.[47]

Simultaneously Lee received at Stamford a communication from the Committee of Public Safety of New York, the acting executive body of the patriots of that province. The committee was almost horrified by the news of his approach. Everything that could be done to deal with the British was being done but it would be impossible to move decisively against them until March. If Lee entered Manhattan with his troops, the British would bombard the town and create havoc. Would not Lee abandon his design? At least he should stop his men at the New York–Connecticut boundary until he had explained his intentions to the committee.[48] His answer must have shocked the committee, although there were ardent patriots both in the town and in the colony who would have given their approval to it. He had no intention of attacking the British; because of the concern of the committee members, he would not bring all his men into the town; but he would come into it with a force sufficient to control it. He predicted that the British would not bombard the town. If they did, "the first house set in flames by their guns shall be the funeral pile of some of their best friends."[49]

As it happened, the Continental Congress had an opportunity to act on Lee's letter before he could execute his design, for he was so severely stricken with "gout or rheumatism, or a mixture of both" at Stamford that he was for some days completely *hors de combat*. He was unable to walk, suffered great pain, ran a fever, and could neither sleep nor eat for eight days.[50]

Meanwhile, a congressional committee consisting of Benjamin Harrison, Thomas Lynch, and Andrew Allen made its way to New York under orders to co-operate with Lee and the local patriots in dealing with the New York situation.[51] That Congress sent the men was fortunate, for that body had previously laid down a ruling which would otherwise have placed Lee and his troops under the command of the New York executive, thus rendering Lee helpless. Lee was exasperated by his physical ills and almost prayed for snow so that he could go forward in a sleigh. Finally he recovered sufficiently to make the journey, partly by litter and partly on horseback.[52] Before he set out he received disconcerting news from Washington, who told him that Henry Clinton had sailed southward from Boston with several hundred soldiers, probably for New York.[53] But the commander in chief also soon sent him another letter encouraging him to go forward with the task which he had assumed.[54]

With his regiment of Connecticut volunteers Lee reached New York on Sunday afternoon, February 4, within a few hours of the arrival of Clinton in the harbor. Many citizens immediately sent their wives and children to the country. Many others accompanied their families from the town. Clinton's appearance, of course, caused fears of a large-scale British attack. When he assured the public he had only a few troops with him, that he had come merely to visit his friend Tryon, who was executing his duties on board a ship in the bay, and that he was on his way to the Carolinas to take part in military operations there, the patriots, including Lee, refused to believe him.[55] Strangely enough, Clinton was telling the truth, insofar, at least, as military affairs were concerned. He *was* headed for the Carolinas. He was making the same extraordinary blunder that Burgoyne made before the battle of Bunker Hill—carelessly giving out valuable information.

Whatever was Clinton's purpose, his appearance jarred the New York patriots; and when Lee and the committee of Congress met their leaders, it was promptly agreed that Lee should take possession of the town and the heights opposite it on Long Island. It was also decided to fortify the town and its vicinity against the day when the British came in force.[56] The Commit-

tee of Safety even ordered three regiments of New York minutemen into the town to assist Lee.[57] Lee secured a second regiment from Connecticut and another from New Jersey, and soon
had twenty-five hundred armed men at his command, although
he was not able to procure reinforcements who would serve for
any great length of time. The members of Congress after a short
stay returned to Philadelphia; but Lee continued to display both
energy and resolution in meeting the various problems arising
from the divided sentiments of the townspeople, many of whom
were devoted Loyalists, and the presence of four or five British
war vessels offshore. One problem to which he found a quick
solution had developed from the presence of a number of cannon on the southern end of Manhattan. The patriots had
planned to carry them off and to make use of them, but had
been deterred by the threats of Hyde Parker, the senior British
naval officer, who had declared that any attempt to remove them
would be a signal for the ships to cannonade the town. Lee
scoffed at Parker's menaces and persuaded the local patriots he
would not dare to fire. Notifying the British officer that the
first house set afire by British bombardment would be the funeral place of several Tories,[58] he had the artillery removed, and
Parker failed to shoot. Instead he let it be known that he refrained because of tenderness toward the citizens, who were
loyal to the king, the removal of the cannon being the work of
New Englanders who were trying to involve the New Yorkers
in their quarrel with Britain. This statement gave both Lee and
Washington a hearty laugh at the expense of Parker.[59] Lee also
cut off the supplies which the British had been receiving from
the town ever since the beginning of hostilities. The American
leaders in New York had not attempted to deprive the ships of
provisions, on the excuse that the British could sever communications between Manhattan and neighboring areas from which
the townspeople themselves derived foodstuffs. Lee scoffed at
the timidity of the local American officials and ignored their
protests against his action. However, he could not prevent the
British from procuring supplies from New Jersey. Lee even laid
plans to cannonade H.M.S. *Asia* when she ran aground in the
harbor, but the ship floated away before he could act.[60]

The local American leaders also resented Lee's strenuous methods of handling the Tories almost as bitterly as did the Tories themselves. The New York Provincial Congress, which had convened not long after Lee's arrival, protested in strong language against his imprisonment of a certain Samuel Gale, in Fairfield, Connecticut, and insisted that as "faithful guardians of the people," they must "protect the liberty and property of our constituents as much as possible in our present unhappy situation." The Provincial Congress denounced arrests made without its consent and demanded to know what charges were made against Gale, so that he could be either punished or released.[61] Admitting that the seizure and incarceration of Gale had been irregular, Lee justified his action on the basis of necessity, and he declared his intention to take the sternest measures concerning the Long Island Tories, since the Continental Congress had instructed him to put New York in a state of defense. If he exceeded his powers, he must undergo "the shame of being reputed foolish, rash, and precipitate" and must accept public censure, but he believed he was doing his duty to the New York patriots, to all America, and to his own conscience.[62] In essence he rejected the authority of the local Congress and continued with his own vigorous program.

To deal with the Long Island Tories, who were particularly obnoxious to many patriots, Lee sent out some militia under Isaac Sears, who had been aggressive in New York in opposing British authority before 1775 and who had helped to initiate Lee's expedition to that place.[63] To increase Sears's influence Lee had given him the rank of adjutant general on the expedition, an appointment which Lee laughingly explained to Washington as made "most impudently by the virtue of the power deputed by you to me (which power you never deputed) . . . ."[64] Sears was soon administering an ironclad oath to various Tories on Long Island, informing those who were inclined to refuse to take the oath that they must comply or be imprisoned in Connecticut. The Loyalists were furious. In retrospect, Thomas Jones, the Tory historian of New York, could use no term milder than "blackguard" to describe Sears,[65] who was probably not at all gentle in carrying out his task. He reported on March 7 from Jamaica that he had tendered the oath to "four of the grate Torries, which they swallowed as hard as if it was a four pound shot, that they were trying to get down." "I can assure your honor," he wrote to Lee, "they are a set of villins in this country, and beleve the better half of them are wateing for soport and intend to take up arms against us."[66]

It is doubtful that much was directly accomplished by forcing on the Tories oaths of allegiance to the American cause; indeed, Lee himself realized that they would refuse to be bound by their oaths as soon as the British should appear in force at Manhattan. He had hoped merely to discover the most dangerous ones—those who refused to pledge themselves—and to put them out of the way.[67] Even that objective was not reached, partly because of the opposition of the Provincial Congress. However, Lee's vigorous campaign against the king's men had served to help achieve another of his objectives, that of leading the New York patriots to take a stronger stand for America. That campaign, however, had another result which was not so happy for Lee. The New York Congress instructed its delegates to protest in Philadelphia against his behavior, and the Continental Congress felt forced to pass a resolution to the effect that no military officer in its employ should force test oaths upon civilians.[68] When he heard about it, Lee wrote to Congress to protest against public censure of his conduct, admitting that he deserved a private reprimand and promising that he would try to avoid taking similar precipitate action in the future. However, Richard Henry Lee pocketed the letter, assuring his friend that he was not named in the resolution, that it applied to the future rather than to the past, and that the Continental Congress as a whole approved of his activities in New York.[69]

Perhaps the most important of those activities in February and March, 1776, in view of later events, was Lee's attempt to meet the purely military problem of New York. Conceivably, because of the fact that the town could not be defended against superior land and naval forces, he should have made no attempt to fortify it. However, both the New York patriots and the Continental Congress desired that it be defended against British attack. Moreover, it was not known at the time that the British would be able to bring a large army to Manhattan, as they did a few months afterward. Lee then thought it possible to hold off the British fleet, or at least to make New York a battle-ground, even though British land forces could probably carry the town in the end. Accordingly he had pulled down the walls of Fort George on the lower end of Manhattan, except for the one facing the bay, so that the old fort could not be used by the British as a defensive position, if they should succeed in making a landing. He laid plans to set up on the island various batteries and protecting walls which might serve to hold off the British fleet and to prevent such a landing. He also made arrangements to place artillery on both sides of Hell Gate with the idea of try-ing to close the passage against flanking movements by the fleet. To cover the artillery on Long Island he proposed to establish there a fortified camp with a garrison of four or five thousand men. Further, he planned to place a garrison at Kingsbridge to guard the only good bridge and the only feasible communica-tion between Manhattan and the mainland, over which a re-treating American army would necessarily pass.

Lee worked assiduously upon his plan; but lack of artillery, a shortage of manpower, and a dearth of engineers held up prog-ress. The works were hardly begun when he was called away from New York early in March; and only a few hundred troops were available for the defense of the town after the middle of that month. As a result Lee was much discouraged and con-cerned for the safety of the place. Eventually the works were completed, and Washington brought to New York the main American army. But the problem of defense was still unsolved, and there really was no adequate answer if the British sent both a fleet and an army more powerful than any which the Ameri-cans could raise. When Lee was asked by the Continental Con-gress in March to give his opinion upon the New York military problem, he argued that the town could not be held indefinitely against superior land and sea forces. He claimed, however, that the British could be made to pay a heavy cost for possession of the town and implied that the American forces could retreat safely in case of necessity to New England. He failed to point out that the British might crush the American garrison on Long

Island, open Long Island Sound to their ships, and then push around the left flank of the Americans, pinning them against the Hudson River and destroying them.[70] New York could be a trap, as events were to prove several months later. Lee himself would eventually discover this fact. Meanwhile, he had much work to do far from the banks of the lower Hudson.

CHAPTER SEVEN

THE SOUTHERN COMMAND

*We want you at N. York—We want you at Cam-
bridge—We want you in Virginia—*
JOHN ADAMS TO MAJOR GENERAL CHARLES LEE
Philadelphia, Feb. 19, 1776

As LADY SARAH LENNOX BUNBURY remarked in 1775,
there was an element in Lee's character which led him
to use dictatorial methods. He liked his own way "as
well as anybody," and would be as tyrannical, given excuse and
opportunity, as George III himself, she wrote. She also predicted
that he would eventually regret the shedding of British and
American blood and his own part in helping to bring on the
War of Independence.[1] Lady Sarah knew men and her man,
and both prophecies proved to be accurate. At New York,
whatever excuses may be offered for his highhanded behavior,
Lee paid little heed to the representatives of the people of the
colony and was apparently arbitrary beyond the necessities of
the situation. Like many persons who flatteringly describe themselves as democrats, he was quite willing to deal with opposition
on the principle that the end justifies the means. That the Tories
of New York came to hate him and some moderate patriots to
dislike him is not surprising. Nor was Lee's behavior in financial
matters at New York beyond reproach, for he failed to pay bills
incurred for personal expenses. The Tory Thomas Jones declares that when a Mrs. De La Montaine, who owned the tavern
where Lee resided, presented her final account, "He damned
her for a tory, cursed her for a ———, and left the house without paying her a sixpence."[2] While Jones is notoriously untrust-
worthy, especially when he discusses patriots, there was probably at least a measure of truth in his statement, for Lee certainly
omitted paying his wine bill—more than six years later the wine
seller was still trying to collect his account. Since Lee's ex-

penses were paid by the Continental Congress and since he received a salary of £75 per month, there was no sound reason for his failure at this time to meet his obligations. It may be that he was exhibiting the avarice which was one of the darker facets of his personality. On the other hand, he was notoriously unbusinesslike in all his transactions, even concerning sums owed to him.

In any case, as far as the Continental Congress was concerned, Lee continued in the winter of 1775-76 in the high favor which he had enjoyed since the beginning of hostilities. The energy which he displayed at the camp outside Boston, in Rhode Island, and in New York added to his prestige; and he was looked upon by the Congress as a pillar of strength. "That God may restore you to health, and crown your endeavors in defence of liberty with success, is the sincere and ardent prayer, of . . . John Hancock," wrote the president of that body to Lee on February 12.[3] The men at Philadelphia, greatly impressed by his abilities and zeal, decided to detach him from Washington's army and to give him a separate and very important command. Indeed, they were so desirous of obtaining his services for their respective colonies that he was ordered within a space of two weeks first to assume leadership of the American army in Canada and then to direct the defense of the southern colonies. There were too few Charles Lees in the winter of 1775-76 to please the talented group of men who sat in Independence Hall. That there was only one General Lee was also bewailed by Abigail Adams, who seems not to have had absolute faith in Washington and who wished Lee to return to Boston in March, 1776. "But how can you spare him from here?" she asked her husband. "Can you make his place good? Can you supply it with a man equally qualified to save us?"[4]

Almost from the beginning in 1775 of the American attempt to conquer Canada, Lee's name was mentioned in connection with the command of the American troops who were sent to the St. Lawrence. Partly because of his fluency in French, the language of the bulk of the inhabitants of that colony, he seemed to many the proper person to execute that most important enterprise, by means of which Congress hoped to add a fourteenth colony and also to transfer the scene of major warfare far to the north. Probably he would have been appointed to the post at the very inception of the attempt, had it not been that his presence seemed necessary at Boston. As it happened, Richard Montgomery, a former British army officer who had married into the Livingston family of New York, and a friend of Lee's[5]—Lee seems to have known almost every officer who served with the redcoats in his time—led the American troops on the St. Lawrence, with the energetic assistance of Benedict Arnold, not yet a traitor.[6] Even as the brave Montgomery was trying to capture Montreal, in November, he modestly urged that Lee be placed above him in the supreme command.[7] In the following month he repeated his recommendation, indicating that he desired Lee's appointment even if he himself should succeed in capturing Quebec. The British, he thought, would certainly try desperately to regain control of Canada, and he wanted Lee to be there to meet their counterattack.[8]

Lee wagered ten guineas that Montgomery and Arnold would complete the conquest of Canada by capturing Quebec, but he did not take sufficiently into account either the difficulties faced by the American troops or the courage of Guy Carleton, British governor of Canada and possibly the ablest military man the royal army possessed in the New World. Montgomery and Arnold did all that human flesh could achieve but failed to carry the walls of Quebec. After Montgomery's death in a final and unsuccessful assault, Arnold, though seriously wounded, assumed control and desperately tried to maintain a blockade of the city for some time. In January, 1776, and again in February, he asked that some experienced officer, preferably Lee, should be sent to supersede him.[9]

When the news of the disastrous defeat of the army at Quebec reached the Thirteen Colonies, Horatio Gates predicted to Lee that Congress would order him to Canada to retrieve the American fortunes there.[10] Washington made a similar prophecy, as he believed Congress would assume that General Philip Schuyler was not available. The commander in chief told Lee that he would regret the loss of his services at Boston, but that Canada would provide an excellent field for the exercise of "your admirable talents."[11] Gates and Washington proved to be accurate prophets. Early in February, Robert Morris wrote to Lee from Philadelphia on behalf of Congress to ask whether he would be willing to assume the responsibility for the approaching campaign in the northern wilderness. Lee was still very weak from "rheumatism" and gout, and he replied that the rigors of the Canadian weather might be fatal to him. On the other hand, he entertained the pleasant thought that he might conquer Canada for the Thirteen Colonies as Wolfe and Amherst had captured it for Britain. In any case, he generously told Morris, he would gladly obey the orders of Congress, whatever they might be.[12] Morris relayed Lee's message to his colleagues at Philadelphia, and Lee was unanimously chosen on February 17.[13]

The news came to Lee in most flattering guise. There was an official notification of February 19 from John Hancock expressing the hope that "the Disposer of events may grant you success equal to your merits and zeal,"[14] and there were private congratulatory letters dated the same day from John Adams, Benjamin Franklin, and Benjamin Rush, carried by no less a personage than the celebrated Tom Paine, who came to New York, at least in part, to make Lee's acquaintance.[15] John Dickinson also sent his felicitations.[16] Franklin, who had accepted an appointment as one of three commissioners from Congress to the Canadian people and who expected to be intimately associated with Lee in his new command, rejoiced that "you are going to Canada. I hope the gout will not have the courage to follow you into that severe climate. . . . God prosper all your undertakings, and return you with health, honour, and happiness. Yours most affectionately."[17] Rush wrote, as might be expected, rather fulsomely. " . . . I tremble only at the price of victory on the Plains of Abraham. I presage your surviving your conquests from one part of your character, and that is you have a wonderful talent of infusing your spirit into the minds of your troops. Should your blood mingle with the blood of Wolfe, Montcalm, and Montgomery, posterity will execrate the plains of Abraham to the end of time. . . . Mr. Pitt conquered America in Germany. Who knows but Gen. Lee may conquer

Britain in Canada?"[18] But it was Adams who heaped the greatest compliments upon Lee, and praise from John Adams was praise indeed.

> The Congress have seen such a necessity of an able commander in Canada, as to destine you for that most arduous service. I tremble for your health, yet I hope the campaign will rather promote it than otherwise.
>
> We want you at N. York—we want you at Cambridge—we want you in Virginia—but Canada seems of more importance. . . . I wish you as many laurells as Wolf and Montgomery reaped there, with an happier fate. Health and long life, after a glorious return. . . .
>
> A luckier, a happier expedition than yours to N. York was never projected. The whole whig world is blessing you for it, and none of them more than Your Friend & Servt.[19]

Even before he received the official notice of his appointment to the command in Canada, Lee began to prepare for the campaign. His first step was to seek Washington's permission to ask Congress for the services of either General Nathanael Greene or General John Sullivan, as his assistant. Both had served under him at Boston, and he had confidence in them.[20] Greene, sanguine, quick-witted, and courageous, and perhaps the ablest of the generals of the War of Independence, was one of Lee's admirers.[21] He also began to collect heavy cannon, men, food, and military stores. He was moving vigorously when he received a letter of February 28 from Hancock ordering him not to set out for Canada without further orders;[22] a day later there arrived another which informed him that he had been placed in charge of a newly created southern military department covering the colonies of Virginia, North Carolina, South Carolina, and Georgia.

The reason for the sudden change was very flattering to Lee. The southern members of Congress, fearing a British attack upon their colonies, were eager to have him command in their area, and they begged insistently for his services. Congress decided on February 27 to establish the southern military district and to place in command of it a general who would be responsible for the defense of the whole region. The same day Edward

Rutledge moved that Lee be given the new post. Northerners opposed the motion because they wanted Lee on the Canadian front. However, Rutledge pushed the matter, and Congress finally approved his motion on March 1.[23]

"After a warm contest . . . , every one wishing to have you where he had most at stake," reported Hancock to Lee, the southerners had their way.[24] Lee received the news with mixed feelings. He wrote to Washington, "As I am the only general officer on the Continent who can speak and think in French, I confess it would have been more prudent to have sent me to Canada, but I shall obey with alacrity, and hope with success."[25] There was an appealing glamor about the Canadian command which must have attracted him. On the other hand, his gout and "rheumatism" would be less exasperating and less dangerous in a southern climate. Moreover, it would appear that he had been interested in a southern post as early as the preceding December, when he suggested to Franklin that a "regular" officer ought to be put in charge of the defense of Virginia because of the danger of a major British assault there.[26] He had told Franklin that "regular" officers were not necessarily superior, but it was an important fact that the public believed them to be so. Such an officer could therefore accomplish more in Virginia than an un-trained civilian, more than, for example, Patrick Henry. In ef-fect, he had implied that he himself could be very useful in Virginia.[27]

Washington, who had not been consulted by Congress re-garding the employment of Lee's services, also looked upon his selection for the new southern department with mixed emotions. He would have preferred that Lee continue at New York, to which the main British army would sooner or later repair.[28] For the sake of the common cause he would rather have sent him to Canada than to the South. As a Virginian he rejoiced that Lee was going to the Old Dominion.[29] To his brother John Augus-tine he expressed his opinion about Lee's appointment, presuma-bly without inner reservations: "He is the first officer in mili-tary knowledge and experience we have in the whole army. He is zealously attach'd to the cause, honest and well meaning, but rather fickle and violent I fear in his temper. However as he possesses an uncommon share of good sense and spirit I congratulate my countrymen upon his appointment to that department. . . ."[30] Eventually Washington would have a very different opinion of Lee.

With much concern for the fate of New York, Lee turned over the command there to William Alexander, Earl of Stirling, who was not an earl and who was an American general.[31] An American by birth and a heavy drinker, Stirling, to give him the name by which he is generally known, was, at least when sober, a good officer. Lee did not worry about New York because of any special defects he saw in Stirling, whom he described as "most zealous, active and accurate,"[32] but rather because of the fact that the town would be left virtually defenseless when the Connecticut volunteers returned home, as they did a few days after his own departure. Reaching Philadelphia on the eleventh, Lee was immediately closeted with a committee of Congress to prepare his report on the New York situation, which was substantially adopted. Four days later he requested Congress to give him instructions for his new post. A committee, including Richard Henry Lee and Franklin, promptly waited upon him and directed him to go immediately to his duties in the south.[33] Proceeding to Baltimore, Lee reached that place on March 20 and advised the Committee of Safety there on fortifications for the port, soon to be of great usefulness to the American cause. Nine days later, with his personal staff, he arrived at Williamsburg in a heavy rainstorm and began his labors in the southern department.

In his new post Lee was actually subordinate only to Congress itself, for he was virtually independent of Washington. As it turned out, he also had the most important American command next to that of the commander in chief, inasmuch as the British army moved aggressively against Charleston, South Carolina, in Lee's district, and New York, where Washington himself assumed charge. In addition he soon became the first in rank after the commander in chief, for Artemas Ward, whose talents, according to Lee, fitted him to be a "church-warden,"[34] resigned from the service in the spring of that year. Nevertheless, he was not all-powerful in his domain, because he needed the full support of local dignitaries in order to carry on his work. Fortunately he received that support in ample measure, though not without some bickering, caused in part by his own aggressive tactics and behavior.

In Virginia, Lee was as energetic in his measures as he had been in Rhode Island and New York; and he did not confine his activities to his district. He was concerned by the continued presence of royal governor Robert Eden in Maryland, who, like Tryon in New York, had not been molested by the patriots. Eden was extremely popular in Maryland, and his very presence at Annapolis tended to place a brake on the patriots— Maryland had only recently instructed her delegates to Congress to vote against independence. Suspecting from captured dispatches containing military information and sent to Eden by the British cabinet that the governor would help British armies which were to be sent to the South, Lee took it upon himself to demand his arrest. Without any authority over Maryland and in spite of the promise he had recently made to be more circumspect in his conduct, he begged Samuel Purviance, chairman of the Baltimore Committee of Safety, to order Eden's seizure. "I shall therefore irregularly address you in the language & with the spirit of one bold determined free citizen to another, and conjure you as you value the liberties & rights of the community of which you are a member, not to loose a moment & in my name (if my name is of consequence enough) to direct the commanding officer of your troops at Annapolis immediately to seize the person of Govr Eden—the sin and blame be on my head. I will answer for all to ye Congress. . . ."[35]

This extraordinary step had the approval of the Virginia Council of Safety at Williamsburg,[36] but it caused commotion in Maryland. Purviance and his Baltimore colleagues took Lee at his word and sent a small armed force to Annapolis to arrest Eden. However, the Council of Safety at Annapolis, which was the executive body for the whole colony, disapproved both of the measure and of the contemptuous manner in which its own authority was slighted. That body prevented the Baltimore men from executing their mission and passed resolutions condemning the Baltimore committee and, in effect, Lee as well. Its members merely placed Eden on parole. Moreover, there was widespread criticism of Lee for highhanded interference in affairs which were none of his business. Somewhat surprised by the violence of this reaction, Lee defended himself on the score of urgency, claiming that he had hoped that additional military information would be found in Eden's papers and that he had urged Purviance to send troops in the mistaken belief that the committee at Annapolis had none at its disposal. He assured the Maryland council that its members did him "the most cruel injustice" if they suspected him of harboring "a wish to extend the military authority or of trespassing upon the civil. . . . I solemnly declare that if I thought it possible that I should ever be intoxicated with military command, I wou'd now whilst I retain my senses, beg leave to divest myself of my present office and serve as a volunteer in the glorious cause, in which I have embarked my person, fortune, & reputation."[37] Whatever merit may be found in these assertions, Lee's conduct with respect to Eden was partly justified by events. Receiving from Virginia the documents upon which he had based his action, the Continental Congress itself ordered Eden's arrest. Instead, the Maryland legislature finally sent Eden off to England unsearched and unscathed.

In Williamsburg, Lee was joyfully received. The Virginia Council of Safety invited him to dinner almost immediately after his arrival there, and the military officers present in the town united to offer him a flowery tribute which now strikes the ear a trifle strangely:

> Your much wished for arrival in Williamsburg affords a pleasing opportunity to the officers of the Virginia forces in this city, to express the high satisfaction they have on your appointment. . . . Perfectly convinced of your great abilities as a commander, and of your firm attachment to the cause of America, we entertain the most sanguine hopes, that the American sword has not been drawn in vain to vindicate violated rights, and in opposition to a blood thirsty king and ministry. We shall rejoice to unite with you in this great design, and endeavour by a strict attention to the duties of our several stations, to establish American freedom on a lasting and permanent basis.[38]

Nevertheless, as the days went on, some Virginians found fault with Lee. There were not wanting persons to express dissatisfaction when he established his headquarters in the governor's "palace." When he tried to turn the College of William and Mary into a military hospital, even the Virginia council protested. On the whole, however, he remained a popular figure. What was more important, his measures were vigorous, not unsuccessful, and generally taken in full co-operation with Virginia officials.[39]

When Lee rode southward in the latter part of March, it was almost certain in his mind and in the opinion of Congress that the British would strike at one or more of the southern colonies, even though their main effort would be directed at New York. At Williamsburg, through the interception of a letter to Eden from the British colonial secretary, Lord George Germain, he learned that the cabinet was sending a fleet and about three thousand men to the coast of North Carolina. At an earlier time Lee would have had some reason to believe it was the British intention to strike at North Carolina, because the Tories in the colony had raised the king's standard. However, this rising had recently been crushed in battle. Since North Carolina contained no strategic center of importance, he concluded that the British would land in force either in Virginia or in South Carolina. For some time he fretted in uncertainty. "I am in a damned whimsical situation . . . ," he wrote to Robert Morris; "I know not where to turn, where to fix myself. I am like a dog in a dancing school. . . . I may be in the north, when as Richard the Third says, I should serve my sovereign in the west. God extricate me out of the scrape with honour to myself and health to the community."[40]

At first, Virginia seemed to Lee the most likely object of attack,[41] especially since Lord Dunmore was already operating off the coast with a fleet and a small army composed of regulars, Tories, and freed Negroes. He decided that Yorktown and Williamsburg were probably the British objectives. Even though this conjecture should prove to be incorrect, it seemed urgent, while he waited for the British to disclose their intentions, to place Virginia in a state of defense, at least against Dunmore.

Fortunately Virginia had raised nine regiments and had placed them upon the Continental establishment. These had been scattered up and down the coast and even in the interior of the colony. Lee immediately ordered concentrations to cover Williamsburg and Yorktown. This measure brought cries of anguish from areas abandoned by the troops, but the Council of Safety firmly supported the change.[42] He also received the hearty assistance of its members in another project which inevitably caused discontent. Lord Dunmore was constantly obtaining supplies and information from the neighborhood of Norfolk. Lee suggested that it was indispensable to remove all the civilians and their stock from that vicinity, with due care for property, and the council gave its approval.[43] Many persons were removed, and a number of houses at Portsmouth were burned so that Dunmore's men could not use them for shelter. Although it proved to be impossible to isolate Dunmore by creating a no man's land around Norfolk, the step was not taken without profit. In addition Lee arranged for the detention of several well-known Tories, including the prominent planter Ralph Wormeley, Jr., and he prudently turned these over to the council for examination and disposal. A few years and Wormeley would be his close friend, so strange are the ways of humankind.

Nor were these measures all that Lee undertook, for he was tireless. He tried to organize a fleet of bateaux to protect the many rivers of Virginia; following an idea which he and Franklin had jointly held for many months, he began to train some of the Virginia troops to use pikes instead of muskets or rifles;[44] he did his best to raise a body of cavalry, for none had been provided; and he enrolled engineers to build fortifications. He secretly and almost frantically pushed the preparation of artillery which might serve to keep Dunmore's fleet away from the coast.

Lee remained in Virginia for about six weeks. Meanwhile the patriots of North Carolina enlisted many troops, raised large sums of money, and did everything in their power to prepare for a British invasion. They feared the British would strike at their colony and earnestly begged Lee to come to North Caro-

lina and to direct their defense. He promised that he would do
so as soon as the British landed in force, and earlier if it were
possible. He suggested that the wives and children of the Tories
in the colony be held as hostages for their good conduct; he
praised the North Carolinians for their energy; and he pledged
military assistance from Virginia when it should be needed.
With South Carolina during this period Lee had very little
contact, for that colony retained control of its own troops, who
were therefore not directly under his command. The South
Carolinians, too, were preparing for invasion and asked for aid
from Lee, which was readily promised. Lee sent Brigadier General
John Armstrong to investigate the situation in South Carolina
and Georgia and to do what he could toward improving
their defenses. Both Armstrong and Brigadier General Robert
Howe, who supervised preparations in North Carolina, gave
Lee enthusiastic assistance. The devotion to duty of Lee and
his aides and of the civil officials in the South, coupled with
the gallantry of the southern troops, made the British task a
difficult one when the day of invasion finally came. It is an
amusing fact, however, that Lee considered the forces available
in the South to be insufficient, and that he begged Congress on
three separate occasions to send help from Pennsylvania into
Virginia. He even contended that it would be wise to weaken
Washington's army in order to strengthen his own department.[45] Congress, with the advantage of a better perspective,
wisely refused to weaken its northern armies unnecessarily.

Congress may have been more influenced by Lee with respect to other public questions in the spring and summer of
1776, particularly whether or not to declare independence, for
he continued to inject himself into public affairs outside the
scope of his military duties. In May, for example, he lamented
that Congress had "thrown away . . . money and attention on
our damn'd fleet," and wisely urged the necessity of conquer-
ing Niagara and Detroit.[46]

Lee remained an ardent champion of a declaration of independence, constantly pushing his friends and acquaintances in
public life to cut the ties between America and Britain. On
April 3 he asserted in a letter to Edward Rutledge that the

American cause needed badly both independence and the establishment of a permanent national legislature. Without taking these steps military supplies and other assistance could not be obtained from France and Holland. Without such help, he insisted, "we cannot, we have not the means of carrying on the war."[47] Two days later he demanded of Richard Henry Lee, "For God's sake, why do you dawdle in the Congress so strangely? Why do you not at once declare yourself a separate independent state?"[48] On April 16 he put further pressure on Robert Morris and offered new and rather remarkable reasons why a declaration must not be delayed. "For God's sake why does your Congress continue in this horrible nonsensical manner? Why not at once take the step you must take soon? I consider every day's delay as the loss of at least 100,000 pds. in money, and the blood of an hundred men—what can you mean by it? You will force at last the people to attempt it without you—which must produce a noble anarchy."[49] Early in May he once more pressed Morris. Congress must declare "at once what you really are and must be—an independent state."[50] A few days later, playing the character of Brutus, he wrote again on the subject to Richard Henry Lee, dramatically and almost beseechingly:

If you do not declare immediately for positive independence, we are all ruined. There is a poorness of spirit and languor in the late proceedings that I confess frightens me so much that at times I regret having embarked my all, my fortune, life, and reputation in their bottom. I sometimes wish I had settled in some country of slaves where the most lenient master governs. However, let the fact of my property be what it will, I hope I shall preserve my reputation, and resign my breath with a tolerable degree of grace. God bless you. I cannot write more at present. "Ah, Cassius, I am sick of many griefs."[51]

He urged action upon John Dickinson in the spring of 1776 and again on July 3, his last letter to the Pennsylvania Farmer arriving too late, of course, to have any possible influence.[52] On the nineteenth of the month, before he learned that the declaration had been voted, he vehemently asked Richard Henry Lee why it was delayed.[53]

How much influence was exerted by Lee's letters to Edward Rutledge, Morris, and Richard Henry Lee cannot be measured, but he contributed, no doubt in a decidedly minor degree, to the steadily rising tide at Philadelphia in favor of independence. Moreover, he labored, perhaps more effectively, toward the same end at Williamsburg, where he tried to convince such powerful persons as Edmund Pendleton, Richard Bland, and Patrick Henry, who were among those who hesitated or pretended to hesitate. As early as April it became evident that an official demand from Virginia for separation would probably lead Congress to act, as Richard Henry Lee informed his friend.[54] It was therefore essential to the cause of independence to persuade that colony's temporary legislature, called the Convention, to issue instructions to the Virginia delegates at Philadelphia demanding that they vote for separation. The Convention, meeting at Williamsburg, did finally issue such instructions on May 15, and Lee may have had some part in bringing about that result. It seems likely, in view of Lee's aggressive composition and his enthusiasm, that he used all the arguments at his command upon every Virginian who would listen to him. Certainly, he was debating the question rather heatedly early in April with Pendleton and Bland. He described the able leader Pendleton as a man of sense who nevertheless put up arguments against immediate separation which would have disgraced "an old midwife drunk with bohea tea and gin."[55] Early in May he was engaged in a discussion of the subject with Patrick Henry, whose attitude might be decisive in the Convention. This discussion led Lee to write a long letter to Henry on May 7, which may have had some little share in the final decision of the Convention. Henry was saying that the colonies should be federated and that American emissaries should be sent to sound the French government before taking the plunge. According to Lee, Henry was expressing a fear that an alliance with France might lead to the resurrection of the French Empire on the North American continent. Indeed, according to statements made by Lee, Henry was concerned lest European intervention in the conflict lead to the partition of the colonies between two or three of the great powers. Lee contended that there was good reason to believe that Congress had already consulted the Bourbon governments of France and Spain and had received assurances that they favored an American declaration. "Disgrace and defeat will infallibly ensue," he insisted, unless arms, ammunition, and military supplies in general were obtained in large quantities from Europe, and these could not be obtained until the Bourbon kings were convinced of the determination of the Americans to fight for nothing less than independence. Shrewdly pointing out that French policy then aimed at developing commerce rather than at acquiring territory, he claimed that there was little ground to fear French efforts to regain territory in North America. In any case, risks—and this one was minor—must be run. Moreover, the people of the colony in general, "except for a very few in these lower parts of Virginia whose little blood has been suck'd out by musketoes," and the soldiers in particular were crying out for separation. Would not "despair, anarchy, and finally submission be the bitter fruits" of further delay? By all means, the Virginia Convention should order its representatives at Philadelphia to vote for independence.[56]

Something has already been said about Lee's motivation and desires in connection with his championship of a declaration of independence. It should be stressed that his argument was largely based on a romantic republican ideal and on military and immediate political advantages to be gained. Even greater emphasis ought to be placed on the fact that it was not founded on American nationalism. One of the most striking features of his correspondence of 1775-76 is that he customarily refers in letters to American leaders to "your" cause rather than to "our" cause, and to "your" army rather than to "our" army. Thus, even in the letter to Patrick Henry discussed above, he expresses a wish that Henry's counsels may be beneficial to "your country." He had not become an American, though he had claimed to be such, and he was therefore not committed heart and soul to independence.

CHAPTER EIGHT

GLORY AT CHARLESTON

Then bugle's note and cannon's roar
The death-like silence broke,
And, with one start and with one cry,
The royal city woke.

MACAULAY, *The Armada*

THERE WAS rejoicing in London early in June, 1776, among the supporters of the king and the cabinet over the news of the capture of General Lee, the "wicked madman" and the "arch-rebel," and there was sorrow among those who sympathized with the American cause. Dispatches to Lord George Germain from Governor Tryon had brought the news that Lee had been seized in Virginia by Henry Clinton, and that the Americans were trying to cover up their dismay by pretending that he had deliberately and traitorously surrendered himself.[1] The report was all moonshine, however, for Tryon had been misled by a false rumor, and Lee was then en route to Charleston, where he met Clinton, but with artillery and rifle fire.

On May 8, Lee received at Williamsburg a dispatch from North Carolina informing him that the British fleet and army long expected from England had arrived on the coast of that colony and had been joined there by Clinton. He put the defense of Virginia under Brigadier General Adam Stephen and set out southward almost immediately, accompanied by thirteen hundred troops the Old Dominion offered for the defense of its neighbors. After some delay at Halifax, caused by a minor mutiny in the Eighth Virginia regiment, he moved on slowly toward New Bern and Wilmington, fearing to advance too rapidly, lest the British use their "canvass wings" simultaneously to attack Virginia. Near New Bern on May 25 he was met by couriers from Charleston who brought news which made it seem likely that the South Carolina capital would be the main object of British attack. At Wilmington on June 1 he learned that the enemy fleet and army had sailed the day before, probably for Charleston. Taking the risk of making a premature and faulty decision, he hurriedly sent off to assist in the defense of that town the Eighth Virginia regiment and seven hundred North Carolinians, and with the troops sixteen hundred pounds of badly needed powder. He arranged for bringing on an additional detachment of Virginians, and he rode on rapidly to Charleston, which place he reached none too soon. On the road he received from General Armstrong and John Rutledge, the chief executive of South Carolina, letters of June 4 which announced the presence of the fleet off Charleston Bar. "For God's sake," wrote Rutledge, "lose not a moment."[2] Quickly committing the defense of North Carolina and Virginia entirely to subordinates, Lee rode on hastily into Charleston. He arrived in the nick of time and was busy preparing for a British onslaught by June 8.

John Rutledge had cause for fear. The British fleet, containing over fifty sail, included two ships of the line, the *Bristol* and the *Experiment*, with fifty guns; six frigates, the *Solebay*, *D'Active*, *Actaeon*, and *Syren*, each carrying twenty-eight guns, the *Friendship* with twenty-six, and the *Sphynx* with twenty; and the *Thunderbomb*, a bomb-ship, which specialized in throwing shells. The fleet was commanded by Commodore Sir Peter Parker, a doughty officer. The army which accompanied it consisted of more than three thousand regulars led by Henry Clinton, who was assisted by Lord Cornwallis. While these forces were obviously insufficient to conquer the southern colonies, they were perhaps powerful enough to capture Charleston and to turn it into a British base. A British conquest of the largest town and most valuable port in the South would be a staggering blow, especially if British attacks made simultaneously upon the middle colonies from the sea and from Canada were successful.

Rutledge's concern was all the more justified because the defenses planned for the town were by no means complete, although he had done his best to prepare for an assault. He had collected 1,950 line troops and about 2,700 militia, a sizable force in view of the relatively small white population of his colony. He had also pushed the erection of fortifications and batteries at and near old Fort Johnson on James Island, on Sullivan's Island, and on the mainland, in the hope of preventing the British fleet from seizing control of the harbor. He had gathered over a hundred cannon and a large quantity of powder. However, he had been unable to obtain a sufficient supply of ammunition for the artillery, and the fortifications and batteries were only partly finished when the British and Lee appeared upon the scene. The South Carolinians had not recognized the peril to which they would be exposed and had not supported Rutledge to their full power. The physical work essential to the building of satisfactory defenses was distasteful to them and had been carried on without much enthusiasm largely by Negro slaves.

Charleston was so inadequately protected when the British fleet appeared off the bar at the mouth of the harbor that it would doubtless have fallen quickly before a swift attack. Luckily for the Americans, the *Experiment* was delayed in passage and did not join the British fleet until the twenty-fifth. Moreover, storm and unfavorable winds deprived the fleet of free use of the harbor for many days. When the weather changed to the liking of the British, they lost still more time in bringing their heavier ships across the shallow water at the bar into the harbor. They were able to land five hundred men under Clinton on Long Island as early as June 8 and to continue to send him reinforcements until the fifteenth, when almost the whole of the army was gathered there. Clinton was also supplied with a few pieces of artillery and some small craft. But the fleet was not ready to act until the twenty-eighth. Lee and the Americans therefore had three weeks in which to make plans, build works, set up batteries, bring up the troops from Virginia and North Carolina, and generally brace themselves for the coming struggle.

After rapid consultations with Rutledge and the South Carolina executive council and after a speedy inspection of the defenses of the town, Lee concluded that the situation was desperate. On James Island the Carolinians were strengthening

Fort Johnson, guarding the harbor on the southern side, and they had erected a battery near the fort. Christopher Gadsden, in command of these defenses, was doing everything possible. On the whole, there seemed to be no great cause for alarm so far as his side of the harbor was concerned, since the British were landing their army on the northern side and apparently intended to make their attack there. But Lee was almost horrified when he learned that the Carolinians, expecting the British assault upon the northern side, were relying almost entirely for their safety upon Fort Sullivan on the southern tip of Sullivan's Island. Their plan was to build the fort strongly on the south and east, from which directions the British fleet was expected to attack, and to neglect the west and north. They had twenty-six guns more or less ready for service. The Carolinians were so sure of their ability to beat off the British from the fort that they were neglecting even to provide adequate means of retreat. The twelve hundred men who had been detailed to garrison it were camping beside it while workmen labored to finish the south and east walls. Lee immediately saw that the British could sail past the fort and bombard it into ruin from the west side. He was therefore greatly concerned about the fate of the garrison. He was even more worried because no real preparations had been made to meet the British on the mainland. They could land their army on the mainland by way of Long Island, lying just north of Sullivan's, without molestation; and they could send their fleet up the narrow channel past Sullivan's to support the army by bombarding Charleston itself. Fort Sullivan could not prevent such a maneuver, although its garrison would be able to send a few shot into the squadron as it sailed past their guns. Nor could Fort Johnson bar the British ships from approaching the town.

Lee went to work with his customary energy and brusqueness. Immediately after the landing of Clinton on Long Island he ordered Colonel William Moultrie, who commanded on Sullivan's, to send several hundred riflemen to attack him before he could receive reinforcements. But this measure seemed of dubious value, and the order was rescinded when additional redcoats joined Clinton. Lee ordered buildings razed and batteries erected in the town; he pressed for the completion of Fort Sullivan; and he placed a body of riflemen on the mainland northeast of Haddrell's Point, where he expected Clinton to make his major effort. His commands, issued rapidly and peremptorily, aroused resentment among the high-spirited Carolinians, particularly because he did not hide his belief that Moultrie's fort, in which they placed so much faith, was nothing but a trap. As early as June 9 some South Carolina officers displayed a disposition to refuse to obey him. Since the soldiers of South Carolina were not upon the Continental establishment and since they were by law under Rutledge's direction, the officers technically were outside Lee's jurisdiction. Rutledge wisely put an end to this difficulty by delegating his authority over the local troops to Lee.

With Rutledge's support Lee personally proceeded to put the town itself in a state of defense against both naval bombardment and an attack by Clinton. He gathered 1,500 men near Haddrell's Point, placing them under the command of General Armstrong; he stationed Colonel William Thompson, an able South Carolina officer, with 780 riflemen on the end of Sullivan's Island nearest Long Island to ward off an attack there by Clinton; and he arranged the main body of his men in and about the town. Moultrie was given about 300 men to defend his fort and to work his guns. One way and another Lee had more than 5,000 men, partly militia, at battle stations when the British finally moved in force.

Lee remained unhappy about Moultrie's fort. He could not even provide a safe retreat from it. There were not enough small boats available to carry the garrison, in case of need, across the mile of shallow water which separated Sullivan's Island from the mainland. He ordered Moultrie to build a bridge, which Moultrie did. But the bridge, made of planks resting upon barrels, proved to be too slight to support more than a few men at a time. Lee was also dissatisfied with the slow progress of the works on the island. In addition, Moultrie himself did not entirely please him, for the general fancied that Moultrie was lax in regard to discipline and lacking in energy.

More and more convinced that Fort Sullivan should be

abandoned, Lee begged for a conference with Rutledge and his council on June 22. He wrote to Rutledge: "As I confess I never cou'd from the conversation I have had with the different gentlemen here, well understand on what principle Sullivans Island was first taken possession of and fortify'd, or on what principle it is to be maintain'd I shou'd be extremely oblig'd to you if you will sometime this day convene the gentlemen of the council, that I may be able to form an opinion whether or no, it will be prudent to risk so many men, and encounter so many difficulties in attempting to support it."[3] The meeting was held, and Lee urged a withdrawal from the fort; but Rutledge and his colleagues insisted that it be maintained and defended. They apparently had little doubt but that it could hold off the British squadron, and they were not much impressed with Lee's view that it was useless and merely a "slaughter pen" for the garrison. Probably they were encouraged to take the stand they did by Moultrie's reports, for Moultrie seems to have contended that he could hold the fort and the island against both the fleet and Clinton's men. The general argued the question vainly.[4] Since Rutledge had the final authority over the South Carolina troops, Lee could do no more than protest. He might have refused to co-operate with the Carolinians, at the cost of an almost certain victory for the British, since co-operation was essential to any sort of successful defense of Charleston. For the common cause, it was essential that he accept their decision, and he did.

Committed unwillingly to the defense of Moultrie's fort, Lee worked heroically in a last-minute endeavor to strengthen it as far as possible. He sent to the island an engineer and a vast crowd of workmen, who managed to throw up light defenses for the northern side of the fort, although they were unable to accomplish much on the western side. He also issued orders for the building of a second bridge between the mainland and the island, so that the troops on the island could be withdrawn or supported as exigencies might dictate. He personally spent many hours on Sullivan's directing the labors of his men.[5]

As the hour of battle approached Lee continued to worry about the fate of Moultrie's fort, its garrison, and Thompson's riflemen upon the island, and also about a shortage of artillery shot. There were only twenty-eight rounds available for the twenty-six guns at Moultrie's fort. Nevertheless, he seems to have awaited the British onslaught with some confidence, evi-

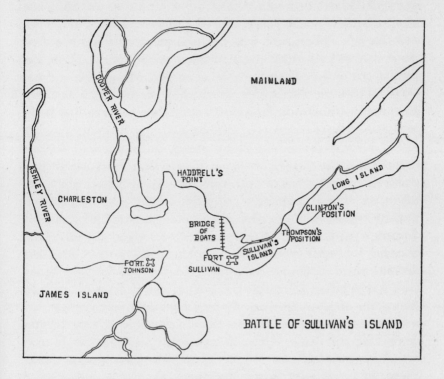

BATTLE OF SULLIVAN'S ISLAND

dently in the belief that he could defend the town, even if Moultrie's and Thompson's forces should be crushed.[6] In any case, he exhibited to his officers and men a cool assurance which heartened them for the fray.[7]

About eleven o'clock in the morning on June 28 the British squadron moved up the channel before a favorable breeze from the south and began a furious cannonade against Moultrie's fort from a distance of not more than four hundred yards. Observing its approach, Lee set out from the mainland for the island in a small boat, with the intention of assuming command there in person. However, the wind and the tide swept his craft back toward Haddrell's Point, and Moultrie had the honor of directing the efforts of the garrison. He responded to the heavy Brit-

ish fire with the twenty-one guns which could be brought to
bear upon the ships, but slowly, in order to save ammunition.
Almost immediately the British began substantially the maneuver Lee had anticipated. While the heavier ships continued to
bombard the fort, the *Syren*, *Sphynx*, and *Actaeon* moved on up
the channel. Their task was to assail the fort from the west.
After it had been silenced, the whole squadron was to bombard
the American defenses upon the mainland. Meanwhile, Clinton
was to attack, or threaten to attack, Thompson's force and help
to conquer the island. Later he was to cross over to the mainland under the protection of the navy.[8]

The British plan was perhaps as well laid as it could be. Fortunately for the Americans, it was dependent for success upon
skillful piloting, since the channel was neither broad nor easily
followed. The frigates were piloted by Negroes who had been
pressed into service, and they failed to do their job. Two of the
frigates fouled each other, and all three ran upon a shoal, where
they lay for hours exposed to American artillery fire. The British also met disappointment with respect to the flanking operation entrusted to Clinton. Ordinarily it was possible to walk
across the channel between Long Island and Sullivan's at low
tide; and they had scheduled their operations so that Clinton
could take advantage of this circumstance and make his advance
simultaneously with the beginning of the naval bombardment.
Again the gods were against them, for the winds had piled up
the waters in the bay to such an extent that the channel remained impassable, except to small boats. Since Clinton did not
have sufficient small craft to move against Thompson in force,
he could only throw a few artillery shot into Thompson's position and make a threatening gesture with his infantry. He put
some of his men into small boats and stationed an armed schooner
and sloop as if he were about to make a descent upon the
Americans, but with no result except to draw fire from a battery which Thompson had erected.

The British chances for victory were thus materially re-
duced at the very beginning of the fray, and Sir Peter Parker
was faced with a rather awkward situation. The grounding of
the three frigates was peculiarly unfortunate for him because

they were essential to the conquest of Charleston and because they were under fire from the fort. There seemed to be only one course open to him: to put his faith entirely in his naval artillery and to batter the fort into silence. Since the British navy in the eighteenth century was accustomed to success in dealing with fortifications on land, he could hardly have entertained seriously the thought that he might be repulsed. His twelve- and twenty-pounders would change the tide of battle. The British ships accordingly maintained their heavy fire upon Moultrie's fort for many hours. Watching from the mainland, Lee feared the fort could not endure their cannonade, the heaviest he had ever seen. He was particularly concerned because of the shortage of ammunition in the fort. He considered sending an order to Moultrie to spike his guns and to attempt a retreat to the mainland when his shot should be exhausted, but he decided to withhold the order. Instead he sent one of his aides, Otway Byrd, in a small boat to the fort to find out the situation there. Meanwhile, he hastily gave instructions for bringing up more ammunition from the mainland. Byrd returned with astonishing news. The garrison, composed largely of raw recruits, was in high spirits and was suffering little from the heavy guns of the British. The palmetto logs with which the fort was built were soft, and they were receiving enemy shot without giving way or splintering. Moreover, the British were being seriously hurt by the slow but accurate fire from the fort.

In midafternoon Moultrie ceased shooting, and Parker assumed that his guns were doing their work. Instead, Moultrie was merely conserving his ammunition. Concerned but hopeful, Lee himself went under fire across to the island about five o'clock to enspirit the garrison, if it should be necessary. His visit was not needed. He was assured the fort would be defended to the last extremity. Congratulating the men upon their valiant behavior, he aimed a cannon or two at the British ships and then returned to the mainland. Before making this visit, Lee sent five hundred North Carolinians to support Thompson, for it had become clear that the mainland defenses were temporarily safe from attack. When Clinton made another small-scale diversionary assault, he was again easily repulsed.

The British kept up their bombardment until nine o'clock in the evening. By six o'clock Moultrie had enough ammunition to resume shooting, but with only two or three cannon. However, his fire was far more effective than that of Parker's ships, and the commodore was finally forced to abandon the struggle. When Parker eventually gave the signal for retreat, his squadron was fairly well battered. He was able to bring off upon a rising tide two of the frigates which had gone aground, but the *Actaeon* had to be abandoned. It was blown up by its own crew. Both ships of the line, the *Bristol* and the *Experiment*, were badly damaged, and the remainder had suffered in lesser degree. The British had scores of casualties, including Parker himself, who had been wounded and who had lost the seat of his pants to an American cannon ball. Moultrie's losses consisted of ten dead and twenty-two wounded; only one of his guns was dismantled by the British bombardment. And Thompson's casualties were negligible.

While the enemy floated at anchor and nursed his injuries just inside Charleston Bar during the days following the battle, Lee joyfully sent the good news to Congress, to the officials of North Carolina and Virginia, and to Washington, Rush, and Horatio Gates. With good judgment and modesty he claimed that the Americans had very effectively checked the British—possibly they had gained a decisive victory. He was reticent also about his own share in driving off the enemy. He praised to the skies Moultrie, Thompson, and their men. Moultrie had gained "eternal credit," Thompson had behaved "most nobly," and the garrison on Sullivan's Island had acquitted itself like Julius Caesar's heroes, the redoubtable Tenth Legion. His own aides had stood fire equally well, "strutting like crows in a gutter." One of them, Jacob Morris, was "a full inch taller in the midst of a hot cannonade than at other times, tho' he is pretty generally upright." He even had praise for those Virginians who had badly conducted themselves so recently at Halifax. He said nothing about his own ceaseless toil, courage, and military knowledge, which had contributed so much to the happy result. But it was a glorious day for him, and he was able to excuse himself gleefully to Gates for not sending a return of his forces because "the adjudant general who is in love has forgot a whole regt."[9] Happily, he was unaware that another June 28 not far in the future would bring him disaster.

Strange to say, Lee is not given much credit by many historians for his part in the success of June 28, 1776. South Carolina historians have understandably tended to exalt at his expense the merits of their own people;[10] and others, finding faults in Lee's conduct at other times and places, have assumed that he had little to do with the results of the fighting.[11] Yet Rutledge, who had had his quarrels with Lee, declared on July 4: "I really think the continent so much obliged to this gentleman, that they should gratify him in every reasonable requisition. This colony, I am sure, is particularly indebted to him, for he has been indefatigable, ever since his arrival here. . . ." At the same time Rutledge took it upon himself to urge that the Continental Congress act, so that Lee would not suffer financial loss because of his adherence to the American cause.[12] William Moultrie gave similar testimony. Lee had been "hasty and rough" in manner, but "he taught us to think lightly of the enemy, and gave a spur to all our actions." Moultrie asserted that Lee's presence at Charleston had been worth a thousand men.[13] The relations between Moultrie and Lee taken into account, this was very high praise. Henry Laurens went further, declaring that "if we do not altogether owe the honor of the 28 June [to Lee], we are certainly greatly indebted."[14] It should be observed that none of the South Carolinians praised Lee with regard to the tactics pursued by the American forces at Charleston. Nevertheless, Lee's judgment that Moultrie's fort was untenable was correct; and it can hardly be doubted that the garrison would have been destroyed, had Parker's three frigates managed to avoid the shoal. It is not too much to say that Lee contributed in very large measure to the successful defense of Sullivan's Island; nor is it too much to say that he had done all anyone could to assure the safety of Charleston. It is a fair guess that his preparations would have assured the security of the town, even in the event that Moultrie's garrison had been crushed.

After the battle Lee was as courteous to the British as he had been generous in his praise of his subordinates. Knowing that the enemy lacked fresh vegetables and fruit, he sent a packet of them to Clinton and to Primrose Kennedy, who served under Clinton. The British general responded with equal courtesy, as befitted an eighteenth-century officer and gentleman. He sent in return a cask of porter and some English cheese to "Charles Lee, Esq. Major General in the service of his Polish Majesty."[15] But if Lee was gracious to Clinton, he did not assume that the danger was over for Charleston. The echoes of the cannonading were hardly ended when he began to push for the completion of Moultrie's fort, even though he continued to believe the fort was very badly located,[16] and to meditate building additional works near Haddrell's Point, for it seemed likely that the British commanders would make a second attack, if only to try to improve their professional reputations. Again the South Carolinians displayed an aversion to labor, and he was able to accomplish little. The British failed to move, however, although the ships remained near Charleston Bar for more than three weeks. Meanwhile the redcoats were shifted about from island to island.

Parker and Clinton could not agree on a scheme to break down the defenses of the town, and it proved impossible to put the ships in good fighting trim. In addition, their forces were suffering from a lack of fresh food. About the middle of July, Lee finally laid plans to take the offensive and to strike a blow at Clinton's army. He hoped to make a real impression on the British, and he felt that he could take risks, in the belief that a check by Clinton would not seriously endanger Charleston. Before he could act, it became evident that the British were about to leave.[17] By July 20 they were on their way to join the main British army at New York. Departing, they left behind a present of fifty-two Highlanders, whose transport wandered into American hands.

The disappearance of the British fleet and Clinton's army did not relieve the southern states entirely from immediate danger, for the Cherokee Indians were on the warpath against the southern frontier and the British still held St. Augustine and Pensacola. Besides, it was likely that another enemy expedition would sooner or later appear off the coast. Lee therefore continued to be occupied for some weeks in attempts to assure the safety of his district. He pressed Virginia and North Carolina to assist South Carolina in an attack upon the Cherokees which rather effectively broke their military power; and he did what he could to strengthen the defenses of the southern ports. He urged again and again upon Congress and upon all who would listen the raising of cavalry as indispensable to the protection of his district,[18] but to no avail. Indeed, he was apparently at that time the only officer of importance in the American army who realized the advantages to be gained from the use of horsemen. Too many Americans believed that cavalry could not be valuable in the rough and wooded country which America then was.

Lee was specially concerned in the latter part of the summer of 1776 with plans to deal with the British in the Floridas. From St. Augustine and an advanced post on the St. Marys River the enemy was constantly sending out parties of regulars, Tories, and Seminole Indians to assail the Georgia frontier. They were carrying off cattle, seizing Negroes, and killing the frontier people. Moreover, British officials were laboring to persuade the powerful Creek nation to send its savage warriors against the Georgia backsettlers. Georgia was sparsely settled and weak, and the situation seemed grave to her leaders. Immediately after the repulse of Parker and Clinton they began insistently to beg Lee for aid and to plead for an attack upon St. Augustine. The town could easily be taken, they contended, if a sufficient force were sent against it.

Lee listened sympathetically to the appeals of the Georgians, as did also the officials of South Carolina. He tentatively decided to make an attempt on St. Augustine. Difficulties developed, however, for the South Carolinians feared for their own safety. They were reluctant to send their men to Florida, especially since they knew the North Carolina and Virginia Continentals might be needed to the north at any moment. On the other hand, the North Carolinians and Virginians were not at all eager to take part in the expedition. They argued that South Carolina should help Georgia as they had helped her. Other troubles regarding command complicated the situation. Most of the South Carolina troops were placed upon the Continental establishment after June 28. However, Lee wanted the services of a regiment which had been kept under state control. The result was a friendly debate between Lee and Rutledge over their respective powers. The debate delayed action, but finally it was agreed that Colonel Peter Muhlenberg's regiment of Virginians, supported by South Carolina troops, should go to Georgia.

Lee made his way southward in August through Port Royal and Purrysburg to Savannah, where he consulted with the Georgia patriots. These made it clear that Georgia could do little to help in the proposed expedition, but, they insisted, it should be sent out. In Lee's opinion they seemed utterly impractical. "I shou'd not be surpris'd if they were to propose mounting a body of mermaids on alligators," he wrote.[19] He came to realize it was almost impossible to supply and transport sufficient men for an assault upon St. Augustine. When news came that the British outpost on St. Marys River had been evacuated, he decided merely to send a raiding party toward the British stronghold.[20] To protect Georgia for the time being, he proposed to raise cavalry, erect small frontier forts, and patrol her broad rivers with armed boats.[21] In the end he did nothing, for he received urgent orders from Congress at the end of August to hurry to the northern states to help defend them against the main British army.

While Lee busied himself in the affairs of his department, the Continental Congress learned of the repulse of Parker and Clinton. Rejoicing over the good news, its members handsomely passed a formal vote of thanks on July 20 to Lee, Moultrie, Thompson, and all those who had fought against the British on June 28.[22] Forwarding the resolution to Lee, John Hancock added his own praises:

> It affords me the greatest pleasure to convey to you . . . the most valuable tribute which a free people can ever bestow, or a generous mind wish to receive—the just tribute of gratitude for rendering important services to an oppressed country.
> The same enlarged mind and distinguished ardor in the cause of freedom, that taught you to despise the prejudices which have enslaved the bulk of mankind, when you nobly

undertook the defence of American liberty, will entitle you to receive from posterity the fame due to such exalted and disinterested conduct. . . .[23]

Receiving this message and the vote of thanks at Purrysburg, Lee responded in heroic style:

. . . The approbation of the freely chosen delegates of a free and uncorrupt people is certainly the highest honor that can be conferr'd on mortal man.

I shall consider it as a fresh stimulus to excite my zeal and ardor in the glorious cause in which I am engaged—may the God of righteousness prosper your arms in every part of the empire in proportion to the justice with which they were taken up—once more let me express the highest satisfaction and happiness I feel in this honorable testimony, and once more let me assure the United States of America, that they cannot meet with a servant (whatever may be my abilities) animated with a greater degree of ardor and enthusiasm for their safety, prosperity and glory. . . .[24]

There is no reason to question the sincerity with which these sentiments were uttered nor to doubt that Lee was pleased by the Declaration of Independence. He rhapsodized about the declaration as a dream coming true. He wrote to Patrick Henry on July 29:

I us'd to regret not being thrown into the world in the glorious third or fourth century of the Romans; but now I am thoroughly reconcil'd to my lot: the reveries which have frequently for a while serv'd to tickle my imagination (but which when awaked from my trance as constantly I consider'd as mere golden castles built in the air) at length bid fair for being realiz'd. We shall now, most probably, see a mighty empire establish'd of freemen whose honour, property and military glories are not to be at the disposal of a scepter'd knave, thief, fool, or coward; nor their consciences to be fetter'd by a proud domineering hierarchy. . . .

Merit, civil and military, would be honored. Learning, eloquence, and poetry would be carried "to the highest degree of perfection," but in simpler and nobler forms than in the Old

World. He saw a "young people" with a great future. Describing himself as "extremely democratical," he also urged that the governor of Virginia should not be immediately eligible for re-election, so that he could not make himself a tyrant and so that he would tend to act not to secure re-election but for the public good. In virtuous republican style he also inveighed against the use of titles in America; "His Excellency and His Honour, the Honourable President of the Honourable Congress, or the Honourable Convention—this fulsome nauseating cant . . . in a great free manly equal commonwealth . . . is quite abominable. . . ." He had heard too much of "His Excellency Major General Noodle" and "the Honourable John Doodle." [25]

But if Lee's sincerity be admitted, it would nevertheless be unwise to take these words as the expressions of settled opinion. He was still playing with dreams, as he virtually admitted in the same letter, when he indicated that his remarks were possibly "cant" and "trivial and whimsical." His use of the phrase "most probably" points to the same conclusion. He was not prepared to sacrifice utterly for his ideal republic, and he had no real faith that such a republic could endure. Indeed, his ideal state was not and has not been of this earth. It was as much a figment of fancy as the noble primitive man associated with the name of Jean Jacques Rousseau.

Although the affair of June 28 increased Lee's continually mounting prestige in the Continental Congress and with the public generally, there were not lacking persons in South Carolina who saw him with critical eyes. True, Thomas Pinckney reported that Lee had "a great deal of the gentleman in his appearance, though homely and in a split shirt." [26] Charles C. Pinckney, however, described him less favorably as "very clever, but . . . a strange animal . . . we must put up with ten thousand oddities in him on account of his abilities and his attachment to the rights of humanity." [27] William Henry Drayton, a proud, opinionated, and obstinate young man, found great fault with Lee. Admitting that he was "very clever," Drayton contended that the general was too positive in his opinions and arrogant in his behavior. Like many South Carolinians, Drayton gloried in the fact that Moultrie's fort had been successfully defended in spite of Lee's opinion that it would fall an easy prey to the British.[28] It is evident that there was a clash of personalities between the two men. Eventually Drayton was in a position to help ruin Lee, and he did not fail to take advantage of his opportunity.

CHAPTER NINE

THE PALLADIUM OF AMERICAN LIBERTY

It was roses, roses, all the way,
With myrtle mixed in my path like mad:
The house-roofs seemed to heave and sway,
The church-spires flamed, such flags they had. . . .
BROWNING, *The Patriot*

THE SUMMER of 1776, a triumphant time for Lee, brought little but disappointment and discouragement to the American armies in the North. Decimated by smallpox, the army in Canada was steadily pushed back until it had lost all its glorious conquests. Before the end of the campaign, in spite of the valorous exploits of Benedict Arnold, it was holding out in northern New York only because the enemy failed to push forward in force. The story, except for smallpox, was much the same with Washington's command. On March 17 the British evacuated Boston, much to the joy of all Americans, and gave the Boston Irish of a later time two reasons to celebrate the day. But evacuation was a minor victory, for the British had never intended to use the town as a base for military operations. They had planned even before the Battle of Bunker Hill to try to smash the American rebellion from New York, and Howe had received instructions to take his army to that place, where he was to be joined by large reinforcements from Europe. Because of pressure exerted by Washington's heavy artillery from Dorchester Heights, Howe was compelled to leave Boston earlier than he desired and to sail to Halifax rather than to Manhattan. His itinerary and his timetable were upset, and British vanity suffered. However, his army was almost intact. In midsummer a vast force of thirty-four thousand redcoats and German mercenaries moved toward Manhattan. It was accompanied by a fleet commanded by Admiral Lord Howe, older brother of the general. Washington was there to meet the British with the main American army, but his forces were inferior in numbers, training, and equipment.

So doubtful did American prospects appear at that time that many Americans, including members of Congress, were eager to negotiate with the Howe brothers, who had been given power not only to attack but also to offer amnesty to those who laid down their arms. They had been authorized to put an end to the conflict and also to issue pardons. Americans desired to deal with the brothers, even though they did not know what terms they could offer, nor what assurances there were that the British cabinet would execute an agreement made by the Howes. Had it not been that the brothers arrived at New York after the Declaration of Independence was voted, they might possibly have been able to secure a peace preserving the integrity of the empire, although they could offer no guarantees that American views of a satisfactory relationship between America and Britain would be definitely and finally accepted by George III and the British cabinet. As it was, when Congress sent a committee to confer with them, they refused officially to receive its members, since they feared that to receive them would in effect recognize the validity of the Declaration of Independence.

Alarmed by the military crisis, the men at Philadelphia frantically tried to strengthen Washington's army. They hurried up men, they gathered supplies, and they sent for Charles Lee, whose victory at Charleston was the only bright gleam of light in the lengthening shadows. They wanted Lee with the main army not only to improve the quality of leadership in it, but also in order to have available a competent commander in the event anything happened to Washington.[1] On August 8, Congress sent off a courier with instructions to Lee to return to Philadelphia with all possible speed.[2] Leaving Savannah at the beginning of September, he reached Charleston on the sixth and rode on northward three days later. He was reported to be at New Castle, Delaware, early in October by Purdie's *Virginia Gazette* of the seventh of that month, which assured its readers that he and Washington would dispose of the British and Hessians. He arrived at Philadelphia on the seventh and was joyfully received. One James Smith was so glad Lee had come that he insisted on writing to his wife about it, although she disliked receiving military news. He would be worth ten thousand men to the American army, exuberantly declared Smith, and the army was eager for his presence.[3]

Lee remained in Philadelphia only a few hours, reported to Congress on military affairs in the South, and then received orders to join Washington, inspecting the defenses of New Jersey en route. Before he left, however, he acquired full ownership of the estate in Virginia which he had purchased from Jacob Hite in 1775. This estate, consisting of about twenty-eight hundred acres and located near Gates's "Traveller's Rest," was a fine property, except that it lacked a good house. To pay for it Lee had borrowed £3,000 from Robert Morris, giving his friend a mortgage as security. He then tried to obtain money from England to repay Morris, but without success, probably because of the refusal of his banking agents to turn over part of his funds in their care. Conceivably the British government had spoken a quiet word to embarrass him, although the cabinet, to its credit, made no attempt to confiscate his property. Deeply concerned by the jeopardous situation in which his fortune was thus placed, Lee had sent a memorial to Congress in the preceding January asking that body to advance him the £3,000 needed to recompense Morris and to give him full title to the Virginia plantation. But Edward Rutledge, to whom the memorial was entrusted, and Robert Morris, whom Rutledge consulted, had thought it unwise at that time to bring the proposal before their colleagues.[4]

Immediately after the battle of Sullivan's Island Lee had again brought his financial status before Congress. He had expressed his concern to John Rutledge, and he had found a sympathetic listener. The South Carolina executive was convinced that Lee deserved to be relieved of the fear of losing everything he owned, and he wrote to seven members of Congress in the general's behalf. He pointed out that Congress could pay off Morris, take a lien on Lee's property in English hands, and be reimbursed in the event it was not confiscated by the British government. If the British seized it, Congress was obligated to the extent of £11,000, the estimate of Lee's fortune in 1775. Lee himself supported Rutledge's proposal in letters to Morris and John Dickinson, begging them to use their influence to secure the approval of Congress. He told them he desired, in addition, £500, and preferably £1,000, to develop the Berkeley estate. He modestly declared to Dickinson that Congress had made "a foolish bargain" with him in 1775, but the bargain was irrevocable. "I have thrown my fortune and risk'd my life and reputation on the fate of America . . . but I cannot at certain times help reflecting that the Congress are compos'd of mortal and changeable men. I cannot help reflecting that I am in a most whimsical state of dependence not only on the word and faith of men but on the chapter of accidents—in short I have nothing that I can call my own—I have nothing realized— had I only a competence secur'd, my mind wou'd be more at ease. . . ." He therefore begged Dickinson "to forward a business which (perhaps weakly) I have so much at heart. . . ."[5] Rutledge's proposal was no more than just, and it seems to have met no opposition in Congress.[6] A committee reported favorably, and Lee was informed before he left Philadelphia that Congress had voted to advance him thirty thousand Spanish dollars[7] on the security of his English property.[8]

The new Virginia gentleman and American hero, "the Palladium of American Liberty," as he was soon to be called, strangely enough was thinking about peace negotiations as well as waging war soon after he crossed the Schuylkill River. From Trenton on October 10 he sent back to Congress some extraordinary political advice. Many American patriots were murmuring because they believed Viscount Howe was prepared to offer peace and generous treatment for America within the empire and because they felt Congress had refused him an opportunity to announce his terms publicly. The Tories were active in encouraging these sentiments. Would it not be advisable, suggested Lee, for Congress to "suffer some gentlemen in the simple character of individuals who are supposed to have influence" to go to Howe and ask what his proposals were? Of course, none of the delegates at Philadelphia should go, for they could not divest themselves of their official character. However, "one or two persons" who had the confidence of Congress could converse with the admiral in a private capacity and would be able to report the substance of his terms to the American public. Thus, argued Lee, it would be shown that Howe had nothing to offer but a demand for unconditional surrender.[9] Lee's suggestion is remarkable because he had hitherto denounced all peace negotiations—and the conversation he urged might well initiate such negotiations. It is possible, moreover, that he himself wanted to be the man or one of the men to talk to Howe.[10] It is not impossible that Lee hoped to work out a plan with Howe which would end the war. Probably he hoped to secure advantage for America. However, Congress gave no sign of interest in his proposal.

On October 12 Lee reached Perth Amboy, from which town he forwarded to Philadelphia a gloomy report on the military situation in the middle states and an exhortation to action. The situation was indeed dark. Before Lee left Savannah the Howes had begun their assault upon the American defenses of New York. These, based on Lee's plan made early in the year, had been made as strong as possible, except for the entrenchments covering the American batteries on Long Island. For some unknown reason the eastern end of their outer lines was left unanchored in open country and exposed to a flank attack. Washington could not have held Manhattan in any case, but the defensive arrangements on Long Island invited disaster. On August 27 General Howe struck with large forces on Long Island, sending detachments against both flanks of the American position. The exposed eastern wing promptly collapsed, and Howe could have overrun all the American defenses on the island, had he seen and taken advantage of his opportunity. The British captured hundreds of prisoners, including Generals Stirling and Sullivan, but Howe failed to move against the final American entrenchments until it was too late. Both Providence and Howe assisted the Americans. Washington managed to ferry the remains of the Long Island garrison across the East River to New York at night under cover of a dense fog, almost under Admiral Howe's guns. New York itself then became untenable, and Washington retreated with the main body of his army to the heights of Harlem. The British occupied the town on September 15. On October 9 British warships made their way up the Hudson, making it clear that American fortifications erected to bar their passage could not do so. The American cause was in great peril, and the American army was in low spirits.

The hasty analysis sent by Lee to Congress from Perth Amboy properly stressed the gravity of the hour. Lee, however, did not yet realize the full danger of the situation. He assumed Howe would not attack Washington; and he predicted that the British would fortify New York and then throw a large force toward Philadelphia. Since Washington could carry his army over the Hudson toward Philadelphia only slowly and with the greatest difficulty, Congress should immediately collect ten thousand men and station them at Trenton. "For Heaven's sake, rouse yourselves," Lee exhorted the delegates.[11]

By October 14, however, after obtaining further information about the state of affairs in the vicinity of New York, Lee realized that Washington's army itself was in the greatest danger. Washington could not hope then to defeat the British in the open field, and it was vital that his army be not destroyed, for it virtually carried the American republic upon its guns. Manhattan had only one usable means of exit, by a bridge at Kingsbridge, and Lee came to see clearly that Howe could land part of his army eastward of Manhattan on the northern shore of Long Island Sound and sweep around Washington's left flank, surrounding him with the British army and fleet and forcing his surrender. The only safe course for Washington to pursue was to retreat to the hills of Connecticut or up the Hudson, where Howe could hardly hope to strike effectively at him before winter set in. Unfortunately, on October 11, Congress had urged very strongly upon the commander in chief the necessity of preventing the British fleet from going up the Hudson. The fleet could not be stopped from sailing up the river in any case, and the only hope of cramping the activities of the navy lay in the artillery of the two American posts of Fort Constitution and Fort Washington, located on opposite sides of the Hudson. To try to carry out the mandate of Congress meant to try to hold the two forts. But Fort Washington was on Manhattan and would be isolated and exposed to British attack if Washington's army retreated beyond Kingsbridge.

When Lee plumbed the state of affairs he became furious. He wrote bitterly, recklessly, and despairingly from Fort Constitution to Gates, saying farewell in the last words of Brutus to Cassius in Shakespeare's *Julius Caesar:* " . . . *inter nos* the Congress seem to stumble every step—I do not mean one or two of the cattle, but the whole stable . . . in my opinion General Washington is much to blame in not menacing 'em with resignation unless they refrain from unhinging the army by their absurd interference. . . . Adieu, my dr. friend; if we do meet again, why we shall smile." [12]

When Lee reported for duty with the army he was joyfully received. As early as September 6, on the retreat from Long Island, General John Morin Scott had heard his men saying they were betrayed and expressing a heartfelt wish that Lee were with them.[13] When he appeared at Perth Amboy and a body of Hessians on Staten Island just opposite promptly moved elsewhere, it was superstitiously assumed that his very presence might have caused their departure.[14] On October 2 William Duer, prominent New York politician, had voiced a fervent hope that Lee would reach the army before Howe again took the offensive.[15] Indeed, there is no doubt the army, including at least one of Washington's aides-de-camp, looked upon Lee as a potential savior.[16] The spirit of the army immediately improved. Possibly Washington's feelings were not those of unmitigated joy. He had carried on a friendly correspondence with Lee while the latter was in the South, and he was unquestionably glad to have his assistance. Yet Washington may have been annoyed that his men placed such great reliance in his subordinate; and the commander in chief was familiar with Lee's whims and tempers.

Lee arrived in the very nick of time, as he had at Charleston, for Howe had finally begun the flanking movement which Lee, Washington, and others had anticipated. On October 12 Howe had landed a force at Throgs Neck, on the northern shore of Long Island Sound, a few miles east of Manhattan. Fortunately for the Americans he had made a mistake in not sending his flanking troops farther up the Sound. The American army was not immediately menaced, because Throgs Point was actually an island connected with the mainland only at low tide. Since there was much rough ground and many stone fences between the point and Kingsbridge, Washington had determined on the thirteenth (for the moment, at least) to try to fend off the flanking movement rather than to retreat.[17]

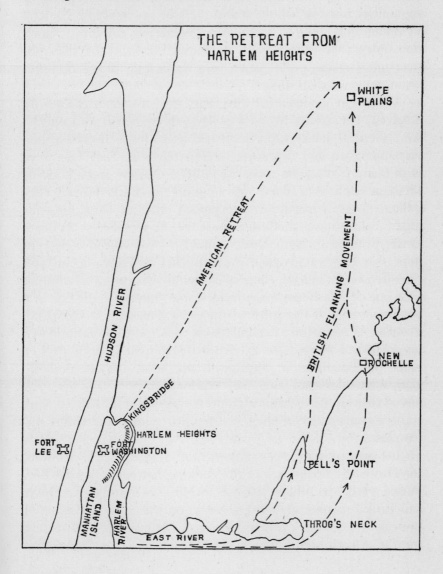

THE RETREAT FROM HARLEM HEIGHTS

The American left wing, placed under Lee's command, by doughty fighting temporarily prevented the British flanking force from advancing, and most of Washington's generals remained or became convinced that the army was reasonably safe on Harlem Heights. Lee vigorously denounced this opinion. He "strongly urged the absolute necessity" of retreat from the island so as to ward off Howe's flanking movement and to occupy higher and more defensible ground.[18] Washington himself seems not to have recognized sufficiently the peril of his army. However, he saw that Lee's opinion was not without reason, and he called a council of war on the sixteenth to consider the situation. According to the historian William Gordon, Lee insisted at this council that the army was in grave danger of being surrounded by the British fleet and army and that retreat was vital. According to Gordon, he convinced the council of the wisdom of this view. The generals, agreeing on retreat, concluded, however, that Fort Washington should be garrisoned and if possible held, "in order to preserve the communication with the Jerseys," as one of Washington's aides reported to Congress.[19] Whether Lee subscribed to the opinion that it was advisable to hold Fort Washington, at least temporarily, is not clear. Certainly, if the main body of the American army withdrew from Manhattan, the fort, located on its northwestern edge, would be substantially isolated and exposed to attack. Its garrison would be in serious danger. In any case, Washington accepted the opinions of the generals. The army moved almost immediately, just in time to evade Howe, who finally sent a large flanking force far enough up the Sound for an effective encircling movement. Lee's advice and aggressiveness may well have saved the American army and the American republic.[20]

As the army retreated to White Plains, Lee commanded the rear guard and acted with his accustomed energy. He apparently did his duty when Howe attacked at White Plains and was beaten off. There is no evidence that he was specially responsible for the check administered to Howe there, and Washington personally is given credit for the achievement.[21] The army was now safe from direct attack by the British, and Lee relaxed a little. Early in November he wrote to Rush that Howe could make only one of two moves before winter and these could probably be checkmated. He informed Franklin on November 6 that the army had done its duty; if America should be conquered it would be the fault of Congress rather than of the soldiers, who had proved their courage.[22] What moves on Howe's part Lee had in mind he did not explain. Whether he anticipated the British general's future motions cannot be learned. In any case, Howe, certain he could accomplish nothing against Washington's army, suddenly reversed his steps and threw the bulk of his troops against Fort Washington and New Jersey.

Observing the southward movement of the British army, Washington guessed its purpose and realized that the fort named after him was imperiled. Lee seems to have urged upon the commander in chief the necessity of withdrawing the garrison.[23] Instead Washington sent to Nathanael Greene on November 8 a discretionary order to remove the men. Further to counter Howe's efforts the commander in chief decided to lead personally the major part of the Continentals across the Hudson to New Jersey. On November 10 he put Lee in command of the remainder of the Continentals and of several thousand militiamen at White Plains. Lee was to defend against a British thrust up the Hudson or into Connecticut. General William Heath was placed in charge of the important American post at Peekskill. If most or all of the British moved into New Jersey, Lee was to join Washington, leaving his sick and the militia to protect Connecticut.[24]

On November 11 in his orders of the day Lee congratulated his men on the news, lately received, that an American force had defeated the Cherokee Indians and that Sir Guy Carleton, after leading a British army from Canada to Ticonderoga, had retreated; and he assured them there was not the "least prospect of success to the enemies of liberty, and mankind," if the American soldiers did their duty.[25] The same day he wrote jokingly to Greene at Fort Lee—recently Fort Constitution and renamed in his honor: "If you should be taken by the enemy it would be really a very serious affair, for I should have a chance of losing my horse and sulky. . . . I begin to think my friend Howe has lost the campaign and that his most Gracious Majesty must request a body of Russians to reestablish order tranquillity happiness and good government among his deluded subjects of America. God bless you, my dr. general. May you live long and reap twice a year an abundant crop of laurels."[26] Five days later, however, he was not so cheerful. Three thousand Massachusetts militiamen prepared to go home, although he begged them to remain in service only a few days longer. What was far worse, he had learned that Greene had not evacuated Fort Washington but had actually reinforced its garrison. He became more concerned than ever about the safety of the garrison, since he was sure the British would attack the fort.[27]

Almost simultaneously the British fulfilled his prophecy. Washington, reaching Fort Lee on the thirteenth, was also alarmed, but failed to act, for he was assured by Israel Putnam and especially by Greene that the fort was not in grave danger. On the sixteenth the British quickly swept the outer defenses of the fort, secured its surrender, and captured over twenty-nine hundred men and a quantity of matériel while Washington looked on helplessly from the western side of the river. The commander in chief sadly reported to Congress that his forces had suffered a "catastrophe." When Lee heard the grim news he flew into a flaming passion and bitterly condemned those who were responsible for the disaster. He exclaimed that "it was a splendid affair for Mr. Howe, who was returning chagrined and disgraced at being able to make no further progress this campaign, thus to have his sores licked by us."[28] He is said to have wept plentifully from "resentment and vexation."[29] He is also reported to have declared afterward that he "was so excited, that he tore the hair out of his head."[30] To Washington he wrote reproachfully, "Oh, general, why would you be overpersuaded by men of inferiour judgment of your own? It was a cursed affair."[31] To Dr. Rush he wrote almost wildly. Asking Rush to let it be known that he was in no way responsible for the capture of the fort, he violently condemned Congress: "I confess your apathy amazes me. You make me mad—you have numbers—your soldiers do not want courage—but such a total want of sense pervades all your counsels that Heaven alone can save you . . . I could say many things—let me talk vainly—had I the power I could do you much good—might I but dictate one week—but I am sure you will never give any man the necessary power. . . ." He added some hints Congress should follow, one of them that "some military man" be put at the head of the Board of War, a recently established office charged with the general oversight of the American military establishment.[32]

It may reasonably be concluded not only that Lee was much disappointed by the turn of events and deeply worried for the American cause, but also that he was ready to assume personally the task of reviving the American fortunes. Probably he did not expect to be made a dictator, to supersede Washington, or even to be placed at the head of the Board of War.[33] Certainly no evidence appears that he carried on a campaign to secure for himself a dominant military position. Nevertheless, rumors that he was about to succeed Washington spread through the American army and Tory circles in New York in December. According to a later story which probably developed from these rumors, a member of Congress from Virginia, presumably Richard Henry Lee, actually offered a resolution to put Lee in Washington's post. There was no truth in the gossip,[34] although many persons both in the army and in Congress must have thought the change might be desirable. Faith in Washington had greatly diminished, and Lee's prestige was greater than ever. It cannot seriously be doubted that Lee was willing to accept the supreme command of the army after the fall of Fort Washington, that he was convinced Washington could not manage it successfully without his advice and assistance, and that he displayed a disposition to act independently of his chief.

A few days after the surrender of Fort Washington the British crossed the Hudson and forced Greene and the garrison to abandon Fort Lee, leaving behind large quantities of stores. Soon Washington was retreating with no more than three thousand men across New Jersey, not stopping until he had crossed the Delaware River. The British followed, establishing a chain of posts from New York to Trenton. For more than a month after the disaster at Fort Washington the American cause was again in dire jeopardy. Washington's men were ill-clothed, ill-shod, poorly equipped, and discouraged. It seemed to many that the new American republic was about to collapse. Washington himself came to feel in December that the game was about ended, unless the tide of battle soon began to turn. From Hackensack on November 21 he ordered Lee to bring his Continentals to New Jersey, unless he and his troops were badly needed where they were.[35]

From Hackensack, Washington's adjutant general, Joseph Reed, who had the panacea for the American difficulties, also undertook to save the cause. In a mood of desperation he wrote to Lee, begging him to join the retreating army and to give it energetic leadership. According to Reed, Washington lacked the ability to act quickly and decisively; such ability was indispensable to military success; Lee had it, and he could supply it to the commander in chief.

> I do not mean to flatter, nor praise you at the expence of any other, but I confess I do think that is entirely owing to you that this army & the liberties of America so far as they are dependant upon it are not totally cut off. You have decision, a quality often wanting in minds otherwise valuable & I ascribe to this our escape from York Island . . . & I have no doubt had you been here the garrison at Fort Washington would have composed a part of this army. Under all these circumstances I confess I ardently wish to see you removed from a place where I think there will be little call for your judgment & experience to the place where they are like to be so necessary. Nor am I singular in my opinion—every gentleman of the family[36] the officers & soldiers generally have a confidence in you—the enemy constantly inquire where you are, & seem to me to be less confident when you are present.
>
> . . . General Washington's own judgment seconded by representations from us, would I believe have saved the men & their arms [at Fort Washington] but unluckily, General Greene's judgt was contrary this kept the generals mind in a state of suspence till the stroke was struck—Oh! General— an indecisive mind is one of the greatest misfortunes that can befall an army—how often have I lamented it in this campaign.
>
> All circumstances considered we are in a very awful &

alarming state one that requires the utmost wisdom & firmness of mind. . . .

. . . I must conclude with my clear & explicit opinion that your presence is of the last importance. . . .[37]

Reed's letter was sufficiently flattering to inflate the ego of any man, and it obviously represented the opinion of several persons close to Washington. Replying, Lee indicated his own judgment of the commander in chief was the same: "I receiv'd your most obliging flattering letter—lament with you that fatal indecision of mind which in war is a much greater disqualification than stupidity or even want of personal courage—accident may put a decisive blunderer in the right—but eternal defeat and miscarriage must attend the man of the best parts if curs'd with indecision. . . . I only wait myself for this busyness of [Robert] Rogers & Co being over—shall then fly to you—for to confess a truth I really think our chief will do better with me than without me."[38]

Unfortunately for Reed's peace of mind Lee's letter was read by none other than Washington himself, who correctly guessed from its contents that his own adjutant general had found fault with his conduct. On November 30 the commander in chief wrote to Reed, saying he had opened it upon the assumption that like other letters from Lee's headquarters it dealt with official business. Washington said that he had had "neither inclination or intention" to examine Reed's private correspondence, but that he had read it.[39] Reed made no response for many months, and Washington seems to have treated him rather coolly. Finally, in March, 1777, when Lee could not display Reed's letter and when it seemed fairly probable Lee never would be able to produce it, Reed tried to get back into the good graces of Washington, after the latter had acquired the laurels of Trenton and Princeton. Reed then declared in a letter of explanation to the commander in chief that he had written nothing to Lee "inconsistent with that respect & affection" he bore to Washington. He had not expected Lee to reply as he did, and he regretted he could not secure his letter from Lee so that Washington could inspect it.[40] This remarkable performance seems to have placated Washington, who responded after a lapse of over two months.

He *had* thought Reed guilty of "disingenuity," and was now inclined to believe "matters were not as they appeared. . . ."[41] Reed then wrote again to Washington, repeating his explanation, and asserted a second time his sorrow that he could not show his letter to the commander in chief.[42] It is not surprising, when Washington and Lee later quarreled bitterly, that Reed defended his chief.

Washington seems never to have mentioned the matter to Lee. Although he could not have been pleased with Lee's opinion of his military abilities, there was nothing to be gained and much to be hazarded by making an issue of an opinion expressed in a private letter. Moreover, Washington himself was probably not at all confident in November, 1776, if ever, that he possessed military genius. He was painfully learning the business of warfare. Soon it would appear that he was a faithful student and one not without major abilities.

CHAPTER TEN

THE KING'S CAPTIVE

O mighty Caesar! dost thou lie so low?
Are all thy conquests, glories, triumphs, spoils,
Shrunk to this little measure?
SHAKESPEARE, *Julius Caesar*

FROM THE moment he crossed the Hudson, Washington expected Lee to come to his aid in the event that the bulk of the British army moved into New Jersey. As early as November 20 he suggested to Lee that he take his troops over the river and wait for orders on the west bank.[1] Accordingly, Lee sent instructions to General Heath at Peekskill to put two thousand men from his garrison across the river, promising to replace them quickly from his own force at Phillipsburg. He argued that this was a wise course, because his army was far from a ferry and time would be saved. Besides, he hoped at the moment to strike a blow at a British corps headed by the noted partisan leader Major Robert Rogers; and he thought it dangerous to leave immediately the approaches to New England undefended, since the British might still advance in force in that direction. Another reason for not moving the main body of his army promptly was a great dearth of blankets and shoes. He began to collect supplies for the march, meanwhile begging the executive officials of Massachusetts and Connecticut to hurry forward blankets and shoes and to send militia to fill the gap which would be created by his departure. Declaring the military situation was desperate—he did not hesitate to tell James Bowdoin of Massachusetts it was so because of indecision on the part of Congress and Washington—he asserted that the British must be driven out of New Jersey or all was lost. He was determined "by the help of God to unnest 'em even in the dead of winter. . . . If Massachusetts and Connecticut do not now exert themselves, they must, and indeed ought to be enslaved; but if they act with the necessary vigour and virtue, I will answer for their success."[2] Looking beyond the existing emergency, Lee also urged upon Bowdoin the necessity of drafting men for service in the campaign of 1777. Congress had called for volunteers to serve for three years or the duration of the conflict. Lee argued that it would be difficult to secure recruits. Instead, every seventh man in Massachusetts—and presumably in all the states—should be called up for service in the Continental forces. It would be wiser to use draftees, he contended, because they would be less likely than volunteers to give their affections to some general who might try to establish himself as a dictator. If the draft were not adopted, the Americans would be forced to call in the troops of the Bourbon princes or submit to Britain.[3] Lee's suggestion was eminently sensible, but it won no favor. It suggests that he himself had no longing, at least at the moment, to be a dictator.

Lee's plans for meeting the immediate crisis were well made. Governor Trumbull of Connecticut and Bowdoin did their duty, and militia from their states were soon trudging along the roads of New England toward the Hudson. However, Lee was unable to secure enough blankets and shoes and was finally forced to set out for Peekskill on November 27 with his Continentals sadly exposed to the elements. Robert Rogers escaped him and Heath twice refused to send part of his force across the Hudson. Washington had ordered him to maintain his post, and he contended that he could not disobey the instructions of the commander in chief.[4]

Arriving at Peekskill on November 30, Lee quarreled hotly with Heath and even personally ordered two of Heath's regiments to march with him. However, Lee received a letter from Washington declaring that he wished the garrison at Peekskill to remain intact, and the order was finally rescinded.[5] Between the second and the fourth of December he crossed the Hudson with about four thousand men.

While Lee made his way to the river, Washington sent letter after letter to him urging him to hasten, before it was too late.[6] On December 2 a frightened Congress ordered Washington to send an express rider to find Lee and to discover the strength of his forces.[7] The next day the commander in chief accordingly hurried off Major Walter Stewart to search for Lee[8] and to take to him another message telling him to waste no time in joining the main army.[9] Nevertheless, immediately after crossing the Hudson, Lee informed the commander in chief that he was meditating an attack or a series of attacks upon the British detachments in New Jersey rather than forced marches to his chief's assistance. He expressed concern lest the British prevent his passage; at the same time he saw an excellent opportunity for destroying redcoat detachments and cutting the long line of British communications between Hackensack and the Delaware River. Thus he might well force Howe's men to abandon their pursuit of Washington and fall back toward New York.[10] Such a method of operation had still another advantage: Lee's force could easily and safely retreat into the hills in the vicinity of Morristown. By December 8 he had reached Morristown. There he had only twenty-seven hundred Continentals, having lost thirteen hundred men from his army during the preceding four days. However, an equal number of New Jersey militia had joined him. At Morristown he met Colonel Richard Humpton, who had been sent on the fifth by Washington to find him and who informed him that about two thousand Philadelphia militia collected through the efforts of Thomas Mifflin were coming up to the aid of the commander in chief. Humpton seems to have carried a letter from Washington, now not to be found, in which the commander in chief said he was thinking of trying to surprise a British detachment at Brunswick. Lee then wrote to Washington to say that Washington with his added strength ought to be safe from attack, especially since, as Lee realized, Howe had no intention of marching in force against Philadelphia. Consequently he himself would take post at Chatham and attack the British advanced base at Brunswick or at some other exposed spot.[11] Before December 8 was ended, however, Major Robert Hoops, who had been ordered by Washington on the seventh to find Lee, appeared at Morristown with the news that the commander in chief had been forced to fall back across the Delaware River. Even then Lee fancied he could do more good to the cause, he told Washington, by hitting at the British rear than by trying to join him. "I shall look about me tomorrow, and inform you further," he wrote to his chief.[12]

Whatever may be the merits of Lee's reasoning—it is apparent his plan was not without military logic—he was ready to disobey Washington's orders on December 8, if not before. It is clear that he valued his own opinion above that of his chief and that he was thinking of acting independently. The odds were, although Washington apparently thought otherwise, that Howe did not intend, and would not be able, to mount a full-scale attack upon Philadelphia. If Lee succeeded in breaking up the British communications and in maintaining a position at Chatham or Morristown, he would gain great credit while Washington acquired none. Certainly such successes would render it impossible for the commander in chief to call him to account for disobedience of orders, difficult to prove in the circumstances. Indeed, Lee might well vault into the supreme command.

It is an interesting fact that the Council of Safety of the state of New York, one of the members of which was Lee's friend William Duer,[13] was trying on that same December 8 to persuade Horatio Gates, who was leading a column from the northern army on the upper Hudson to Washington's camp, to disobey his orders and instead to join Lee. Gates, however, refused to co-operate with the council, and he continued his march toward the Delaware.[14]

As early as December 7, Nathanael Greene warned Washington that Lee would act independently, unless he were strictly confined by orders.[15] Washington was of the same opinion, but he knew of no quick way to compel Lee to obey his instructions. On December 10 he sent off a letter to Lee, saying Howe was unquestionably preparing an advance against Philadelphia: "I cannot but request and entreat you, and this too by the advice of all the general officers with me, to march and join me with all your whole force with all possible expedition. The utmost exertions that can be made will not be more than sufficient to save Philadelphia. Without the aid of your force, I think there is but little, if any, prospect of doing it. . . . Do come on. Your arrival may be happy; and if it can be effected without delay, may be the means of preserving a city whose loss must prove of the most fatal consequences to the cause of America."[16] On the following day the commander in chief wrote again to Lee in the same vein, pleading that his subordinate hasten to support him,[17] and he wrote still again on the fourteenth.[18] Shortly afterward he received astonishing news—that Lee would not join him, but that Lee's army was rapidly advancing toward the Delaware under the leadership of Brigadier General John Sullivan.

From December 8 to December 11 Lee remained at Morristown, uncertain whether to march to Washington's assistance or to attack a British detachment at Brunswick or Princeton. Temporarily he felt unable to move his men at all, because they lacked shoes. On the eleventh he finally set his men in motion toward the Delaware, but with the thought he might strike at the enemy en route. Washington had urged upon him the necessity of avoiding the enemy, keeping to his right, and passing the river far above Trenton. Lee was meditating instead a rapid march across the line of British posts to Burlington, south of Trenton.[19] By the night of the twelfth he had apparently reluctantly made up his mind to follow Washington's plan. He and his army were then a few miles southwest of Morristown. He ordered his second in command, John Sullivan, who had recently been released by the British, to proceed the next day to Germantown on the road to Easton, Pennsylvania.[20] He made a disastrous mistake that night. He decided to spend it at a tavern kept by a widow at Basking Ridge, three miles from camp. With him stayed his personal guard of about fifteen men, his aide-de-camp Major William Bradford, Major James Wilkinson, who had come to Lee with dispatches from Gates, and two French officers who had offered their services to the United States, Captain Jean Louis de Virnejoux and the Sieur Gaiault de Boisbertrand, a lieutenant colonel of cavalry just arrived in America from France. The next morning Lee became a British prisoner of war.

While Washington fled across New Jersey and Lee moved slowly to his assistance, Howe decided to go into winter quarters rather than to try to drive on to Philadelphia. By stringing out his advance forces from Brunswick to Trenton and even to Burlington he exposed himself to attacks such as those meditated by Lee—and, for that matter, by Washington. Lord Cornwallis, who commanded the van at Pennington on December 12, realized the danger he was in, especially from Lee's army, but he did not know where that army was. Consequently, he decided to send out a scouting party to search for it. Lieutenant Colonel William Harcourt, a younger son of Earl Harcourt and an officer in Burgoyne's Sixteenth Light Horse, which had served under Lee in Portugal, asked to be given the privilege of leading the party and was granted his wish.

Harcourt set out on the twelfth with twenty-five privates from his regiment and four officers, including Cornet Banastre Tarleton, afterward famous as a ruthless cavalry leader in the southern states, and a Captain Eustace, one of Cornwallis' aides, who went along for pleasure's sake. That night the party stayed in a house at Hillsborough, which burned down after midnight. All escaped, however, and galloped away early in the following morning on side roads toward Morristown. Four or five miles from Lee's quarters Harcourt and his men met a British sympathizer, who told them they could not safely return by the route they had followed and informed them of the location of Lee's army. Harcourt sent back a captain with four dragoons to reconnoiter, and then pushed ahead once more, taking the Tory with him. At a distance of a mile from Lee's lodgings the British horsemen overpowered two American sentries and questioned them under threats of instant death. The sentinels informed them of the location of the army and also of Lee and asserted that Lee's guard was a small one. Uncertain whether to rely upon these men and not sure what course to pursue, Harcourt sent Tarleton and two men to a near-by hill to examine the countryside. Observing an American horseman approaching, they waited for him, forced him to surrender, and carried him off to their commander. He too was told he would be sabered unless he gave information, and he talked. He was carrying a dispatch from Lee to Sullivan, admitted he had just left Lee, and pointed out the tavern where the general had his quarters. After consulting Captain Eustace and others Harcourt decided

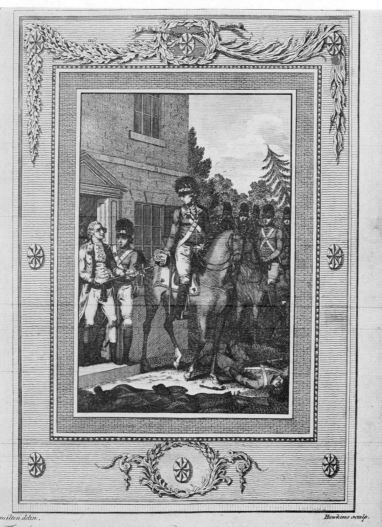

Hamilton delin.

Hawkins sculp.

The American General Lee taken Prisoner by Lieutenant Colonel Harcourt of the ENGLISH ARMY, in Morris Country, New Jersey, 1776.

to try to capture Lee and hastened forward to surround the house.[21]

On the morning of Friday, December 13—an unlucky day for Lee, at least—Lee put his army in motion about eight o'clock, but remained in the tavern for two hours longer, engaged in military business of one sort and another. During that time, while Major Wilkinson waited, he also prepared a letter to Gates, a remarkable document.

"The ingenious manoeuvre of Fort Washington has unhing'd the goodly fabrick we had been building—there never was so damn'd a stroke—*entre nous*, a certain great man is damnably deficient . . . unless something which I do not expect turns up we are lost—our counsels have been weak to the last degree . . . it is said that the Whigs are determin'd to set fire to Philadelphia if they strike this decisive stroke the day will be our own—but unless it is done all chance of liberty in any part of the globe is forever vanish'd—Adieu—my dr friend—God bless you."[22] He had scarcely finished this letter, at about ten o'clock, and was preparing to leave the house when the British horsemen appeared from woods on one side of the house and from a garden on the other. They immediately rode down two sentries and dispersed Lee's guard, which had been quartered in an outbuilding and which was completely surprised. From an upstairs window Lee saw his escort quickly routed. Two of his guards were slain and others were wounded. Then the British began to pour bullets through doors and windows. Captain Virnejoux defended the front door, and other officers with Lee fired in return, but without much effect, merely wounding a horse and cutting the tassel from Harcourt's helmet. Lee himself apparently took no part in the shooting.

Soon it became apparent to the Americans that resistance was useless, for no sign of help from the army was seen and the British threatened to set fire to the house. Boisbertrand tried to escape through a rear door, but was felled by a sword blow upon the head and made prisoner. Mrs. White, the owner of the tavern, begged that her property be spared. About fifteen minutes after the appearance of the British, Lee, after walking to and fro in great agitation in an upper chamber, sent Major

Bradford to tell the British he would surrender. Bradford was greeted by a hail of bullets as he opened the front door, but managed to deliver his message. Harcourt's men immediately ceased firing. A moment or two later Lee appeared at the door, without cloak or hat, and expressed a wish that he would be well treated. Harcourt promised he would be dealt with as a gentleman. When Lee asked for permission for Bradford to bring a cloak and hat, the British officer consented. Bradford obtained the articles but hastily put on clothing belonging to a servant before returning. His ruse succeeded; he was assumed to be a servant and was permitted to re-enter the house. Lee was promptly placed on horseback behind a trooper and carried off with Boisbertrand. The British made no attempt to search the tavern. Virnejoux, Bradford, and Wilkinson, who is reported to have hidden himself in a chimney, therefore escaped.[23]

In spite of efforts by Sullivan, who soon heard the news and sent out a rescue party, Harcourt succeeded in carrying off his captives to the British lines. The evening of the thirteenth the Harcourt party stopped at the home of a "Dutch" physician near the Raritan, where two British officers, Lieutenant Colonel Charles Mawhood and a Major Moyney, were staying. Seeing Lee, Moyney, an old comrade of Lee's, ran out and kissed him. The British officers and their prisoners had dinner with the physician. During the meal the general asked to see the Tory who had helped in capturing him. When the man was brought in, Lee called him a villain and a traitor.[24] A few hours later Lee was a strongly guarded prisoner at the British base at Brunswick, where he was kept for a month. According to one report, the redcoats put on a wild celebration when Lee was brought in, even getting Lee's horse drunk.[25]

Had Lee fought to the death at Basking Ridge, had he committed suicide rather than surrender, he would unquestionably have taken his place in history among the hallowed heroes of the American republic. It is probable that he considered seriously these alternatives to capture. Perhaps he loved life more than principle; conceivably he could discern no practical benefits to be derived from his death; possibly he was not greatly concerned by the place he would occupy in history. It is not likely that he surrendered merely to save Mrs. White's house, as one of his admirers declares.[26]

In any event, Lee's capture was looked upon by almost all Americans as another disaster. A wild story that he deliberately allowed himself to be taken never received credence—except from incautious chroniclers of a later time. Washington, exasperated as he was with Lee because of his conduct immediately before his capture, spoke of the news as "melancholy intelligence." "I sincerely regret Genl. Lee's unhappy fate, and feel much for the loss of my country in his captivity," he wrote to Congress.[27] To Lund Washington he declared, "Our cause has also received a severe blow in the captivity of Genl. Lee.[28] To his brother John Augustine he described the taking of his subordinate as "an additional misfortune, and the more vexatious" because Lee had failed to exercise ordinary prudence in locating his headquarters.[29] "Our country has lost a warm friend and an able officer," he told the legislature of Massachusetts.[30] Nathanael Greene, still smarting from his own failure in the matter of Fort Washington and from the criticism laid against him by Lee, considered his seizure "a great loss to the American states, as he is a most consummate general"—high praise, that, from Greene.[31] Other American military officers shared Greene's sentiment. Young John Trumbull wrote to his father, the governor of Connecticut, "This is a misfortune that cannot be remedied, as we have no officer in the army of equal experience and merit."[32] Lee's "capture had damped the spirit of the army very much, and everything looked very gloomy," General John Cadwalader told Thomas Rodney on December 22 as young Rodney marched forward with some Delaware militia to Washington's aid. Rodney, however, saw a ray of light in the darkness. Hitherto so much confidence had been placed in Lee that Washington had feared to use his own talents without consulting him. Now the commander in chief could use his own abilities freely.[33] At the moment this thought hardly comforted Cadwalader.

Among American civilians also the blow seemed severe. There were lamentations in Boston, especially among the ladies;[34] and Bishop Henry Melchior Muhlenberg expressed consternation. "Saul hath slain his thousands and David his ten thousands," he commented. But David was in the hands of the redcoats.[35] Lee's civilian friends, Robert Morris, Benjamin Rush, Richard Henry Lee, Samuel Adams, and John Adams, were specially downcast. William Shippen, Jr., expressed their thoughts concisely. "Oh! what a damned sneaking way of being kidnapped. I can't bear to think of it." John Hancock expressed the attitude of the Congress in general when he described the news of Lee's capture as "alarming." Hancock was "afraid his loss will be severely felt, as he was in a great measure the idol of the officers, and possessed still more the confidence of the soldiery. . . ."[36]

While the American patriots gave vent to their rage and disappointment the British rejoiced both in America and at home. Informing his older brother that he had taken the "most active and enterprizing of the enemy's generals," Harcourt declared his exploit gave the British so marked a superiority that "it seems to be the universal opinion the rebels will no longer refuse treating upon the terms which have been offered them."[37] A British officer reports that Sir William Howe entertained the same opinion.[38] A Scottish captain vigorously expressed sentiments widespread in the army: "I am happy to hear that Mr. Lee is in custody & I will be still happier to hear in the next acco[un]ts from New York that he has been tried as a deserter condemned & hang'd." [39] Almost inevitably the jubilation of the British and their Tory supporters brought on fits of poetry-writing. An unknown author celebrated in dubious verse:

> When Gates and when Lee turned on Britain their brands,
> Which the favour of Britain had placed in their hands;
> The Congress was glad; but its gladness is o'er,
> Its safety is shipwrecked upon a *Lee shore.*
> The rebels may tremble; they quickly shall see
> That we'll shut up their *Gates* as we've shut up their *Lee!*[40]

In England when the story of Lee's kidnapping appeared, it was not at first believed, for it seemed fantastic. The London *Public Advertiser* of February 14, 1777, and other newspapers pooh-poohed it and reminded their readers of the false report of Lee's capture which had circulated in England in 1776. When the truth of the story became known, there was rather general happiness. In England, too, many felt that Lee's capture heralded the end of the war. No more significant tidings could come from America, asserted one observer.[41] There were celebrations in honor of the event, and a Mr. Hinde of Liverpool at one o'clock in the morning, no doubt after some potations, bet one shilling that Lee would be executed without trial immediately after being brought to England.[42] The king sent his thanks to Harcourt for his brilliant exploit.[43]

Nevertheless, Harcourt's feat was not greeted with universal joy among the British, and he himself was bitterly disappointed to receive merely the thanks of the king. His own brother and sister, who sympathized with the Americans, regretted Lee's capture. Harcourt hoped to be given a colonelcy, but failed to receive it, and considered himself ill-used by the cabinet.[44] On February 18, 1777, the *Public Advertiser* informed its readers that Harcourt was bringing Lee to England, but the announcement proved to be premature.

Disappointment was in store for the British. Their joy over the approaching end of the war turned out to be without foundation. It soon became apparent that Lee was not indispensable to the American cause and that the Continental army was still able to fight. Indeed, the British almost lost their prize captive as the result of amazing counterblows struck by Washington late in 1776 and early in 1777.

Washington was thinking of rapid marches and surprise attacks upon the redcoats before December 8.[45] Reinforced by Lee's army, brought safely into camp by Sullivan, by Gates's column of four regiments, and by Philadelphia militia, he acquired such strength toward Christmas time that he ordered back to Peekskill another detachment which was on the march to join him. He laid plans to attack several British detachments posted on the east bank of the Delaware, and if possible, others in the interior of New Jersey. On Christmas night he personally led a force across the ice-filled Delaware against a garrison of Hessians at Trenton and succeeded in capturing a thousand of the mercenaries there. When Lord Cornwallis hurriedly brought up reinforcements from Brunswick to deal with Washington, he left the British base guarded lightly, by only 250 men, according to a report received on December 30 by General John Cadwalader, who then commanded a detachment of the American army at Allentown, southeast of Trenton. The redcoats had their military chest and large quantities of supplies at Brunswick. Cadwalader saw an opportunity to rescue Lee and to strike a telling blow. He sent off a body of light horsemen at dawn on the thirty-first with instructions to release Lee, if possible. The cavalry rode by way of Cranbury to within five miles of Brunswick, but finally were forced to turn back when scouts learned that twelve hundred British troops were moving into the town from Perth Amboy.[46] Unluckily for Lee, Cornwallis had prudently arranged to cover the weak spot in his communications.

Early in January, 1777, Washington struck again. By January 2, Cornwallis had gathered eight thousand men and was trying to drive Washington back against the Delaware and to destroy the American army. Adopting a plan which may have been proposed by Arthur St. Clair, the American commander decided to try to sweep around behind Cornwallis and capture Princeton and Brunswick. Cornwallis was completely taken in by this maneuver, and the American army captured Princeton. However, Washington's troops met stern opposition there from a British regiment led by Lieutenant Colonel Mawhood, which retreated only after Washington personally led an attack upon it. Besides, his men were tired from their forced march and were suffering from lack of food. Consequently, he had to abandon his hope of assailing Brunswick. Lee's friend Stephen Moylan, who served under Washington, later lamented that the Americans did not have five hundred fresh men. With this added strength, he believed, Washington would have captured the British baggage and probably would have freed "poor Naso."[47] Again Washington had hit effectively, and he was able to establish his army safely in winter quarters at Morristown. All hope of recapturing Lee was, however, now abandoned. On January 13 he was escorted to Perth Amboy. Closely guarded, he was there placed on board an armed schooner and carried across to Manhattan.[48] He was a prisoner in New York for many months.

Had Lee used ordinary caution and avoided capture, had he successfully attacked the British line of communications across New Jersey, he would have been the savior of America, as many expected him to be. As the most successful general in the American army, it is possible that he might have been exalted above Washington. Had he been commander in chief in 1777, it is fairly likely, as the Marquis de Lafayette afterward declared,[49] that he would successfully have used his power to arrange an Anglo-American peace with the Old Thirteen remaining within the British Empire. He was an Englishman, and he was not at heart a republican, as he was soon to indicate. It is more likely, of course, that Washington would have remained nominally in the high command, with the direction of his army entrusted in great part to Lee. How such an arrangement would have worked out in the critical campaign of 1777 one can only guess. Conceivably the American army with Lee supplying the brains would have done better than it did under Washington's command. It is not improbable that a divided leadership would have brought disaster. Perhaps the independence of the United States was hastened by Lee's capture.

CHAPTER ELEVEN

PRISONER AND POLITICIAN

Virtuous and vicious ev'ry man must be,
Few in th' extreme, but all in the degree;
The rogue and fool by fits is fair and wise;
And ev'n the best, by fits, what they despise.

Pope, *Essay on Man*

WHEN LEE was brought to Brunswick, British officers hurried to see him. One young man noted in his journal that he had never seen a general "so dirty and so ungentleman-like." He wore an old blue coat trimmed with red, a battered cock hat, and greasy leather breeches, observed the redcoat.[1] Another junior officer reported Lee was "dejected," that he did not recover from the shock of his capture for several days, and that he praised his own achievements at Charleston and lauded the American soldiers as "the best troops in the world." He ascribed American defeats to "bad luck." He constantly asked what Sir William Howe would do with him and declared that he expected eventually to be exchanged for some British prisoner or prisoners in American hands, in accordance with the custom of the eighteenth century.[2] A third officer, although he did not admire Lee, declared, "I could hardly refrain from tears when I first saw him, and thought of the miserable fate in which his obstinacy had involved him."[3]

Lee was obviously concerned lest he be treated as a traitor or a deserter, in spite of his assertions that he expected to be considered as merely a prisoner to be politely exchanged when circumstances permitted. Harcourt, not unbiased, claimed he was "at least as anxious as one could imagine him" for the preservation of his life.[4] Certainly he had reason for anxiety.[5] Two letters which he wrote to Sir William Howe soon after his arrival at Brunswick were returned without reply to "Lieutenant Colonel" Lee,[6] a direct hint that the British commander believed he was still an officer in the British army and therefore subject to its discipline.

The prevailing sentiment among British officers at Brunswick and New York was that Lee was a deserter and a traitor and merited death,[7] and Howe took the same view. Immediately after receiving the news of Lee's capture he ordered his judge advocate general to Brunswick to prosecute his prisoner on a charge of desertion.[8] But it was soon brought to the general's attention that a military court might not be able to bring in a verdict of guilty against Lee, since he had prudently and publicly resigned his half-pay when he accepted his American commission in 1775. Moreover, there was even real doubt that a half-pay officer was subject to a call to service or to military trial, since half-pay status meant either temporary or permanent retirement from active service. There were no legal precedents which clearly settled these two points. Quite possibly a court-martial would acquit Lee of the charge, on the ground that he was not a member of the British army. In that event he might sue Howe for damages and secure a heavy penalty against him. Should a court find Lee guilty and sentence him to death, the only conceivable penalty, Howe would still be in trouble, for he would surely be attacked both in America and in England as a murderer. On second thought, eager as he was to deal summarily with Lee, he decided to withhold his hand until he had safeguarded himself, at least in some degree. On December 20 he wrote to Lord George Germain to ask for an opinion from English judges on Lee's legal status. If his prisoner were held to be a British officer and if he were sent a written opinion to that effect, Howe would bring Lee to trial, submitting the opinion to the court for his own protection.[9] Sir Henry Strachey, who served as secretary to Viscount Howe and who was also eager to have Lee shot, supported the general's request, urging that he be promptly informed on Lee's legal position.[10]

Long before Germain could respond to Howe's request the Continental Congress gave Howe further reason not to move too swiftly against Lee. The very day the British general wrote to Germain the Congress acted on rumors that Lee's life was in danger. A resolution was passed directing Washington to inquire of Howe what treatment was being given to Lee. If he was not accorded his due as a major general in the army of the United States of America, Washington was to remonstrate. Congress also arranged to forward a sum of money for his use.[11] Its members were grimly determined to protect Lee to the best of their ability, as they would soon prove. From Baltimore, to which place they had fled when Philadelphia seemed in great peril, John Hancock wrote to Robert Morris on December 23 that "the United States are bound, by every tie of justice and generosity, to afford him all the relief in their power."[12] After the battle of Trenton the Americans held as prisoners several Hessian officers and a British lieutenant colonel of engineers, Archibald Campbell. In lieu of a British major general, not available for a trade, Congress directed Washington on January 2 to offer six Hessian officers to Howe in exchange for Lee.[13]

On January 6, learning that Lee had been placed in custody although British officers in American hands were put on parole and given freedom of movement locally, Congress denounced Howe's treatment of Lee as "totally unworthy of that gentleman's eminent qualifications, and his rank in the service of these United States, and strongly indicative of further injuries to his person." If he were not exchanged and if Howe refused to place him on parole, Washington was to inform the British general that Lieutenant Colonel Campbell and five Hessian officers would receive "exactly" the same treatment accorded to Lee. To punctuate this stern threat of retaliation Congress made preliminary arrangements to imprison the Germans and requested the authorities of Massachusetts, where Campbell was held, to co-operate.[14] These actions brought an immediate protest from Colonel William Irvine of Pennsylvania, who pointed out that retaliation, if carried through, would prevent the exchange of Pennsylvania officers captured before Lee. Irvine wrote arrogantly to the executive officials of his state, " . . . let me ask what great services has he yet done."[15] Samuel Adams asserted, however, that Congress would "certainly" execute its threat.[16] On January 13 Washington communicated the demands of his superiors to Howe. If Howe refused the offer of exchange, Lee must be placed on parole, like any other American officer held by the British. Any violence on his life or liberty would be precisely retaliated on Campbell and the Hessians.[17] Howe made no answer for several weeks.

The same day Lee was removed to New York, where quarters had been prepared for him in the council chamber of the city hall in accordance with orders issued soon after his capture.[18] There he was kept until the following June. He had a large and comfortable living room, and two smaller chambers. He was furnished firewood, candles, excellent food, and wine, at British expense. Thomas Jones, the Tory historian, ironically reports that he was permitted to have as many as six friends to dinner and that he had a comfortable bed, "into which he tumbled jovially mellow every night (for to do him justice he loved good fellowship, a long set, a good dinner, and a convivial glass, when he could enjoy them at any other expense than his own)."[19] No doubt, Lee was well housed and fed, both at Brunswick and in his new quarters, for he himself acknowledged in the summer of 1777 that he was treated with kindness and respect from the moment of his capture.[20] Jones did not exaggerate the comforts, luxuries, and freedom extended to Lee. The captive general may not have been "mellow" every night, but he certainly was some nights.[21] Although his personal wants were well cared for and although he was later permitted to have one of his dogs and his servant, Guiseppe Minghini, an Italian whom he had picked up in his European travels, Lee was carefully guarded by an officer and fifty men.[22]

In New York as at Brunswick the famous prisoner was promptly visited by many persons, for there was great eagerness to see the archrebel in his cage. To friends in the British army, especially after he had had a few glasses of wine, he talked about the military events of the war. To others he spoke freely of his travels in Europe. He gave an appearance of cheerfulness, which was possibly assumed rather than genuine. Immediately before January 20 he refused to discuss political questions with General James Robertson, military governor of the town, and with "some more principal people."[23] Nevertheless, Lee was hardly settled in his new quarters before he was engaged in an effort to bring the war to an end. Strangely enough, he was soon dealing with the Howe brothers and Sir Henry Strachey, this in spite of the fact that Sir William and Strachey, if not the viscount, were eager to have him executed. Strachey made two calls on Lee by February 9. The British official Ambrose Serle noted in his journal that day that Strachey "pd. a 2d. visit to L. of which I am not glad; for an honest man has no chance with a rogue; nor can an unprincipled man be depended on." [24] Serle, who later described Lee as a "blasted scoundrel," feared he would hoodwink Strachey. Perhaps Lee did eventually do that very thing.

How it happened that Strachey, acting for the Howes, began conversations with Lee, is not known. Since the British habitually tried throughout the War of Independence to win over American leaders who fell into their hands and to use them for their own purposes, it is possible they took the initiative. Lee could conceivably be very useful to them, and they could suggest that services rendered by him might save him from a military trial and death. It is probable, however, that he himself made the first serious overture to his jailers. His capture must have given a rude shock to his romantic republicanism; American resistance, in spite of Washington's brilliant successes at Trenton and Princeton, was seemingly still weak; and he may have felt the Americans were certain to be defeated without his assistance. Doubtless he was reminded directly and indirectly again and again of a fact he had not forgotten, that he was himself an Englishman. It is not unlikely that he was convinced— or that he convinced himself—that the Howes could and would give generous terms which would make America happy within the empire. There were good—and honorable—reasons why he should try to help make peace. Perhaps there was another reason, a hope that useful service in bringing the conflict to a close would save his own life, but thoughts of his personal welfare probably did not influence him in a major degree. He knew long before February 9 that the Continental Congress was trying to save him, and he was aware of the legal obstacles in the path of those who desired his punishment by court-martial. That he was not motivated by fear for his own life is indicated by the fact that he continued to labor toward a negotiated peace between Britain and America after his personal safety was definitely assured.

The Howe brothers and Strachey did not believe at the time that Lee honestly and altruistically desired to help bring about peace.[25] They were willing to make use of him, but they did not promise any personal reward. Indeed, Sir William was to display for many months his eagerness to encompass Lee's destruction.

What Strachey and Lee talked about on February 9, and perhaps earlier, is at least partly clear. They discussed a scheme to persuade Congress to send representatives to New York for a discussion of peace terms. Whose plan it was cannot certainly be learned, but it probably emanated from Lee. It was put into effect immediately. In a message to his commander in chief dated the same day Lee sent a letter to the Congress, requesting Washington to forward it promptly. "As Lord & General Howe have given me permission to send the inclosed to Congress, and the contents are of the last importance to me, and perhaps not less to the community, I most earnestly entreat my dear general that you will dispatch it immediately & order the express to be as expeditious as possible. . . ." Requesting Washington to send him one of his aides-de-camp so that he could give some directions on private business, Lee went on in an utterly different strain: "I am likewise extreamly desirous that my dogs should be brought as I never stood in greater need of their company than at present. God bless you, my dear sir, and send you long life and unhappiness."[26]

It is not surprising that Lee wanted the solace he derived from the companionship of his dogs, but very few men would have coupled a wish for the presence of canine friends with a possibly momentous affair of state. His lack of a sense of proportion once more appears.

Lee's letter to Congress, dated February 10, ran:

> As it is of the greatest consequence to me, & I think of no less to the public, I am persuaded that the Congress . . . will permit two or three gentlemen to repair to New York to whom I may communicate what so deeply interests myself & in my opinion the community—the most salutary ef-

fects may & I am convinced will result from it. . . . If my own interests were alone at stake I flatter myself that the Congress would not hesitate a single moment in acquiescing with my request; but this is far from the case, the interests of the public are equally concerned; at least in the opinion of one, who is, and ever shall be most sincerely attached to their welfare.

Indicating that the Howes had granted safe conduct to the American representatives, Lee urged haste.[27] Obviously he hoped Congress would comply with his request, either from concern for his welfare, for public purposes, or for both reasons. It is evident that he expected to open up a discussion of peace terms.[28]

Forwarding Lee's letter to Congress, Washington told him he would send to him as soon as possible his aide-de-camp, Jacob Morris. He could not immediately send the dogs, which were in Virginia, and he regretted that Lee must be deprived "of the satisfaction and amusements you hoped to derive from their friendly and companionable dispositions."[29] Lee was also disappointed by the response of Congress.

While Lee meditated a scheme to end the war, Washington was vainly trying to get a clear statement from Howe regarding his view on Lee's status. The British general refused to exchange Lee for the Hessian officers and indicated he believed his prisoner to be amenable to the laws of Britain. He would say no more, and both Washington and Congress correctly concluded that he intended to have Lee brought to trial for desertion. It was then believed in Congress that Howe would send Lee to England for trial.[30] When Lee's request that two or three gentlemen be sent to talk to him was brought before Congress for consideration, that body was also facing the fact that Howe had given no assurance of sparing Lee's life because of the American threat of retaliation. Both problems seemed extremely serious, and the members debated upon a course of action for many hours. Most of the delegates were eager to do everything in their power to save Lee, although at least one seems to have thought him an Englishman and therefore subject to British law.[31] But this attitude was contrary to common sense and public faith, and Congress determined to put its threat of reprisal into execution. On February 20, Congress declared its "unalterable resolution" to retaliate precisely whatever ill treatment the British meted out to Lee and ordered Lieutenant Colonel Campbell and five Hessian officers "into safe and close custody." They were to be permitted to write to their friends in the British army, so that their plight would create dissatisfaction in it, especially among the Hessians.[32]

With respect to sending persons to confer with Lee, opinion in Congress was unanimously opposed, although the delegates were well aware that Lee's proposal meant the opening of peace negotiations. They believed the Howes were using Lee as "a decoy duck," and that the brothers really had no terms to offer which could be seriously considered. They saw behind Lee's request an attempt to delude the Americans with hopes of peace, to divide them, to lessen their war efforts, and to hinder their attempts to obtain French aid, hardly to be secured when peace discussions were in the air. Yet they did not wish to go on record as refusing to listen to peace terms. They were in something of a dilemma, and some were critical of Lee for placing them in it. It was seriously suggested that Congress pretend Lee asked a conference only for private matters,[33] but the members finally faced the issue squarely on February 21. It was ordered that Lee be told no effort would be spared to save his life and to procure his liberty, but Congress would not send any of its members to see him, since it could not perceive that to do so would "tend to his advantage or the interest of the public." [34]

Strange to say, the two decisions which Congress made almost unanimously on the twentieth and twenty-first of February displeased not only the Howes but also Washington, Nathanael Greene, and other officers in the Continental army. On March 1 the commander in chief formally and vigorously protested against the Congressional threat of retaliation. He condemned it on several grounds. Since he had been exchanging prisoners with Howe for some time, in accordance with an agreement previously established, the British could well argue the agreement was violated by the American refusal to exchange Campbell and the Hessians. Moreover, American prisoners in British hands (and their relatives) protested because they could not be traded for the British officers. Washington also argued that retaliation was an unwise policy, in general because of the bloodshed which might result, and in particular because the enemy held ten times as many American officers as the Americans held British officers. Reprisal carried out might punish the United States much more severely than Britain. Congress should not insist upon executing an unwise policy because of "the distresses of one brave unfortunate man."[35] On March 2, Washington made the same points in a letter to Robert Morris, adding in this "private" communication an urgent request that Congress send two or three private persons to New York to hear what Lee had to say. No possible harm could be derived from such a conference, the commander in chief contended.[36] Tench Tilghman, Washington's aide-de-camp, wrote lengthily to Morris the same day, explaining in detail his superior's attitude. While urging the abandonment of the policy of retaliation, Tilghman strongly advised compliance with Lee's request, so that Lee's many friends could not say Congress had failed to do everything possible to protect him![37] On March 3, Greene supported the arguments of Washington and Tilghman in a message to John Adams.[38] Three days later the commander in chief again formally protested against the policy of retaliation.[39]

The pleas of Washington to Morris had the desired effect upon him, and Morris tried to persuade several delegates that Congress should revoke its decisions, but in vain.[40] John Adams, who was temporarily absent when the decisions were made, was quite unimpressed by Greene's arguments and informed Greene he would give his firm support to both of them. Adams was rightly convinced that the only reason Lee asked for a conference was to open peace negotiations, and he could see no possible benefit and much harm arising from a conference. He was also rightly of the opinion that Congress' threat of retaliation would force the British to treat Lee as an ordinary prisoner and that it would bring no bloodshed.[41] On March 14 the Congress reconsidered its decisions in the light of the protests of Washington, Greene, and Morris. There was much talk about technical points, but Congress reaffirmed its judgments. Several members laid much stress upon a fact Washington and Greene had ignored, that Lee, a major general of the United States, was not receiving the treatment due to his status. They argued cogently that the British, not the Americans, were responsible for the discontinuance of the exchange of prisoners.[42] A few days later Washington made another attempt to persuade Congress to drop its policy of reprisal, sending Greene personally to advise the delegates upon this and other matters.[43] However, it was to no avail. Indeed, after conferring with a committee, Greene reported to Washington on March 21 that he now believed Howe would agree to consider Lee as an ordinary prisoner, a fact indicating that Greene had been convinced of the wisdom of the threat of reprisal.[44] On March 24, Congress acted even more vigorously than before, specifically ordering the commander in chief to exchange no more prisoners until Howe had acknowledged Lee to be exchangeable.[45]

Much criticism of the conduct of the Continental Congress in the War of Independence has been offered, but the delegates can hardly be censured for refusing to send emissaries to Lee, and they deserve only the highest praise for their loyal insistence that their servant, even though a former British officer, should not suffer because of his adherence to their cause. Congress took the only honorable course, in spite of the difficulties and dangers certain to result. Indeed, if persons involved in the discussion of American policy at this juncture must be blamed for their behavior, Washington and Greene should properly be the targets of attack. It may well be asked why their views differed so sharply from those of Congress, why they brought such heavy pressure upon that body, and why they were unwilling to meet inconveniences and to run risks to save their fellow officer. Their seeming unconcern about Lee's fate may be explained on personal grounds. Neither man had any special reason to love him, and both had recently had cause to dislike him.

While Washington and Greene debated with Congress on Lee's request and on retaliation, Lee waited in New York for many weeks without authentic news, since Washington, hoping to persuade Congress to reverse itself, did not undertake to notify him of its decisions until April 1.[46] Washington's delay may have constituted tragedy for Lee. Soon after the middle of March he was visited by his aide, Jacob Morris,[47] who may have informed him of the discussions revolving about him among the American leaders, but who could not have assured him Congress would spare no effort to protect him. Lee, uncertain until after April 1 that Congress was determined to save him, fearing perhaps that he would be abandoned to the mercies of the British, may have decided to try to preserve his life by turning traitor. On March 19 he again asked Congress to send men to talk to him, a request probably innocent of malicious intent.[48] Ten days later, on March 29, before he could receive an answer, he submitted to Strachey an amazing document, ostensibly drawn up for the purpose of forcing the Americans quickly to lay down their arms and to bring America once more within the British Empire.

In this remarkable paper Lee began by declaring that Britain would conquer the Americans, but only after an exhausting struggle, unless the British adopted a certain special military measure. Both Britain and America would suffer very heavily if the war continued for a long period. He asserted that America would be particularly the gainer if the war were ended while the Howes held office, for they might be succeeded by others without power or desire to offer terms as generous. He expressed confidence that the brothers would be indulgent to "individuals who have acted from principle" and that they would surely be equally indulgent in regard to general conditions of peace, since otherwise the Americans would again revolt whenever England should be involved in a European war. On these several grounds, said Lee, "I shall most sincerely and zealously contribute all in my power to so desirable an end, and if no untoward accidents fall out which no human foresight can guard against I will answer with my life for the success." Accordingly, to bring the war quickly to an end, Lee proposed an addition to British plans for the campaign of 1777. He had learned or guessed that Howe intended to advance upon Philadelphia with about twenty thousand men while John Burgoyne, supported by a small force under Barry St. Leger coming down the Mohawk Valley, struck southward toward Albany from Canada with a second army. Lee characterized these arrangements as insufficient to break down American resistance, and he urged that Howe send four thousand men to occupy Annapolis and Alexandria, and either Baltimore or the west bank of the lower Susquehanna River. This relatively small army could cut communications between the middle and the southern states while Washington was busy trying to check Howe's main body. Lee predicted that the Germans of Pennsylvania and Maryland, loyal to the American cause but concerned for their property, would quickly abandon resistance. The Loyalists of Maryland would rise. Since the New Englanders would be walled off by Burgoyne and the Hudson, American opposition generally would soon collapse, indeed within two months after the redcoats appeared on the shores of Chesapeake Bay, unless war broke out in Europe. He claimed that the conflict would be ended with very little further bloodshed.[49]

Although there is no evidence to prove it, Lee's plan was probably brought to the attention of General Howe, and possibly Admiral Lord Howe, by Strachey. That the general was much impressed does not appear. It is unlikely that he altered his projects for the coming campaign in the slightest because of it. Conceivably it influenced him to move against Philadelphia by way of the Chesapeake rather than directly by land across New Jersey,[50] as he had earlier intended. If he took Lee's suggestion seriously, he certainly gave Lee no credit for his assistance, for he was determined even as late as June to do what he could toward punishing him for serving in the American army.

Did Lee sincerely wish to help the Howes so as to end the war quickly—or was he trying to aid the Americans? After the British drive of 1777 failed to achieve its object and after he had lost his prestige among the Americans, he claimed that he had not committed an act of treachery, indeed, that he had saved America when he was a prisoner; that is, he had deliberately persuaded Howe to waste much time by taking a southern sea route to Philadelphia while Burgoyne marched to his doom at Saratoga.[51] Since there is no evidence that Lee was a habitual liar—indeed, much praise was given him by contemporaries because he seemed to have an exceedingly high respect for truth—

Lee may well have been trying to mislead the Howes. It was certainly legitimate for him to attempt to do so. If he tried, he was probably not very successful, since it is clear that the Howes believed they owed him nothing for his ideas.[52] Lee himself wrote to Washington on April 2, commenting on the refusal of Congress to send persons to see him, "I am unfortunate in all things, and this stroke is the severest I have yet experienced."[53] It is quite plausible that the phrase "all things" included failure to deceive the Howes.[54] In any case, the defective planning which permitted Burgoyne to advance unsupported to the destruction of his army was probably the work of Lord George Germain, General Howe, and Burgoyne himself, without benefit of Lee's advice. In 1779 and 1780 Lee may honestly have believed he had succeeded in deceiving the general and his brother. It must be recalled, however, that Lee's claim was made partly in order to regain standing among the Americans. It can be argued that it has validity simply because he dared at that time to assert it.

That Lee's proposal was deliberately conceived to fool the Howes is also suggested by the very nature of his plan and by the fact that it gave no information about the American army. Cutting communications between the middle and southern states, even coupled with the two major British offensives, could not possibly have forced the Americans to submit with little fighting in two months time. The British could not win the war by occupying strategic positions except for a long period, and such a policy would have required more troops than the British had in America. Moreover, Lee's proposal, if adopted, would have weakened the army Howe intended to lead against Washington. The only real chance for quick British success with the forces they had available lay in a sustained offensive with all the troops Howe could muster against the main American army under Washington. The destruction of that army might well have led the Americans to sue for peace. But was Lee aware of the realities of the military situation? Probably so, for he had argued insistently after October, 1776, that the Americans should avoid full-scale battle and wage a war of "scorched earth" and attrition. However, he was by no means infallible in military matters, and it is quite possible that he underestimated the strength of the new Continental army enlisted in the latter part of 1776 and the early months of 1777. He did not have the advantage of hindsight.

It is not improbable that Lee's plan was intended to accomplish what he claimed it would when he presented it to Strachey. Conversing constantly only with the British, and hearing them voice optimistic views, he may well have concluded that an eventual British victory was certain and that an early end of the war was best for all concerned. Conceivably he was prepared to claim credit from both sides, no matter what the event.[55]

If Lee was trying to help the British win an early victory, was he a traitor to the United States? The ugly name has often been applied to him, and he has been described as a Mephistopheles, a monster more horrible than Benedict Arnold himself. Even Arnold has not wanted defenders, but nothing has hitherto been said, except for some comments by Charles Carter Lee, in behalf of Lee, if indeed he did attempt to aid the British. Yet it can be argued on technical grounds that he could not have been guilty of treason because he had not taken an oath of allegiance to the United States, since such oaths were not taken by the Continental army until after his capture. Professional soldiers in the eighteenth century attached great importance to their oaths. That Lee was not bound by a formal pledge, especially since he was born an Englishman, may have led him to think himself free to work toward a conclusion of the war with the Americans receiving less than independence. Although one may well believe that an American military court would have considered him to be bound in honor to the United States, oath or no oath, it is worth recalling that Arnold was American born and that he had taken the oath long before he went over to the British in 1780.

If Lee was doing his best to aid the British, are there any excuses for his behavior on moral grounds? If he sold his ideas for money, there could be none, but there is no evidence of weight indicating that money was an object with him in this affair. Arnold, it will be remembered, dickered with the British over his price for sixteen months before he took the plunge. If Lee in fear and desperation tried to secure his own personal safety by giving his ideas to the Howes, a plausible excuse for his conduct may be found. Not until after he had drawn up his plan did he know of Congress' unyielding determination to protect him,[56] in spite of the efforts of Washington and Greene to deprive him of the effective support of Congress.[57] He probably knew of the activities of his fellow generals. It will readily be admitted that had Congress refused to do everything in its power to save him Lee would have owed nothing whatever to the United States. Other excuses of some moral validity might be offered. The idea of ending the war on the basis of a quick and almost bloodless British victory with generous terms for the Americans was certainly not intrinsically immoral; nor was it impractical. The Howes, not unfriendly to the Americans, hoped for just such an end to the war. Moreover, in March, 1777, when the Declaration of Independence was less than nine months old, no one could say that the breach between Britain and America was final. Many Americans had approved of the declaration with great reluctance and at least some had approved it as a means of taking an extreme bargaining position, so that when the conflict should be settled, the Americans could obtain more favorable arrangements—as part of the empire. Unquestionably, although they could not commit themselves openly, there were many patriots in March, 1777, who would not have objected too strenuously to a return to their old allegiance on satisfactory terms. Lee's English background and his championship of universal liberty, rather than of American nationalism, may have led him to that conclusion. It is significant that he was trying to promote a reconciliation immediately before he drew up his plan.

Admitted that Lee's proposal of March 29 was intended to effect a quick British victory, it would be highly improper to describe him as a mere criminal traitor, for it is apparent that his motives were not completely selfish if indeed they were selfish at all. Had his plan fallen into American hands when he could be brought before a military court, it is not unlikely that he would have been found guilty of treachery and sentenced to death. But even if he did do his best to help the British, a tribunal of coolheaded philosophers would probably bring in the verdict of "guilty, with extenuating circumstances"—the verdict so famous in the Dreyfus case. As it happened, Lee's plan remained unknown to the American public and to all the world, except for a very few persons, until more than seventy years after his death.

CHAPTER TWELVE

TOWARD FREEDOM

"England! with all thy faults I love thee still. . . ."
BYRON, *Beppo*

WHEN THE British cabinet received Sir William Howe's letter of December 20, 1776, asking that he be relieved of any legal responsibility which might arise from bringing Lee before a court-martial, Lord North and his colleagues must have been puzzled as to what course to follow. What they decided to do in the way of punishing Lee is not known, but after a formal cabinet meeting on February 25, 1777,[1] Germain sent an order to Howe telling him to put the prisoner on board the first warship leaving New York for England.[2] It may be assumed that the ministry did not plan to give Lee a hero's welcome in London or Bristol.

Whatever the purpose of the cabinet in ordering Lee sent to England—and it is not at all certain that the cabinet sought his life—the ministry was relieved of the necessity or pleasure of dealing with him through the action of the Continental Congress. While Germain's letter made its way across the Atlantic, Washington, carrying out the mandates of Congress, conducted a lengthy discussion with Howe regarding Lee's status, the related question of exchange of officer prisoners, and the treatment meted out to Lieutenant Colonel Campbell and the Hessians by the Americans. Howe wished to divorce the Lee question from the matter of exchange, and to try to put the American commander in the position of absolutely refusing to trade officer prisoners. Thus he hoped to make Washington appear cruel and vindictive in the eyes of his British and Hessian officers. He feared to deal drastically with Lee until he had some assurance that American reprisals visited upon Campbell and the Hessian prisoners would be blamed on Washington rather than on himself. As Congress had foreseen, he was especially anxious lest such reprisals cause great dissatisfaction among the German mercenaries. If he could convince them that their brethren suffered only because of American brutality, he might be able to deal summarily with Lee without too serious repercussions in his own army. Accordingly, Howe condemned Washington for ceasing to trade officer prisoners, demanded that exchanges be resumed, and insisted that the American commander had no right to ask for the return of Lee to the American army until he had in his hands a British major general.

Howe met disappointment in his scheme, for Washington carefully executed his instructions and avoided extreme statements. He made it clear that the Americans asked not for Lee's freedom but that he be recognized as an ordinary prisoner eligible for exchange if and when a British major general fell into American hands. He admitted that Howe had the right to refuse to trade Lee for a batch of officers of lesser rank, as he had done. Washington would make no further exchanges until the American view of Lee's status was accepted. Howe was still hoping to put his opponent in the wrong when he received Germain's order to send Lee to Britain. He did not dare, however, to execute the order, because of the effect reprisals might have upon his German troops. Early in June he informed Germain that he was taking the liberty of postponing Lee's departure until he was assured it would have no serious effect upon his own army.[3]

Meanwhile, five Hessian lieutenant colonels and majors captured at Trenton were closely confined in their quarters at Dumfries in Virginia, receiving treatment which American officers in command there considered equivalent to that meted out in New York to Lee. They were apparently not abused in any way. It was another story with poor Archibald Campbell, by all accounts an amiable gentleman. On February 1, even before Congress requested that Campbell be confined in the same fashion as Lee, the executive authorities of Massachusetts deprived him of local freedom on parole and ordered him thrown into a dungeon in the jail at Concord. Apparently, they did so in the belief that Lee had been given similar accommodations. But they kept the unfortunate Campbell in a filthy hole for four months, long after it became apparent that Lee was well housed, even though carefully guarded. He was even put on a diet of bread and water, it is said.[4] The British officer rained protests upon Howe, upon General Heath, who commanded in Massachusetts at the time, and upon Washington, but to no avail. Howe continually demanded of Washington—and with justice—that Campbell be released from the dungeon.[5] Washington was sympathetic, and assured the British commander as early as March 3 that steps would be taken to make Campbell as comfortable as possible.[6] He had asked the Massachusetts people on February 28 to give the British engineer decent quarters, indicating that Lee was well housed.[7] The executive council of the state paid no heed, and Congress failed even to consider seriously Campbell's plight until the end of May. On May 17 Lee himself wrote to Boston begging gracious handling of the British officer. He was sure the Massachusetts leaders were acting upon misinformation, since "severity and harshness is not the characteristic of New England." Lee's letter apparently convinced the authorities at Boston, for Campbell was finally removed to a house in Concord.[8] Congress did not take any action to relieve him until June 2, when evidence that Lee was handsomely housed and fed was overwhelming.[9]

The tragicomedy of retaliation and threats of retaliation was not yet played out. Just as Campbell was led off to better quarters, Lee was taken from the New York city hall and put on board the British warship *Centurion*, anchored in New York Bay. On June 4, the birthday of George III, there was much celebrating by the British. On land and sea, cannon roared; Governor Tryon gave a handsome dinner; the Howes did likewise; and the general added a fillip to the occasion by sending Lee off to the *Centurion*.[10] Possibly General Howe took this step because he was about to put to sea with the major part of the British army, leaving Clinton with a relatively small force in command at New York. He may have feared that an American attack on New York during his absence might result in Lee's enlargement. Lee could scarcely be rescued from the warship.[11] Probably Howe was also finally preparing to send him to England. If so, the British general soon found reason not to issue the decisive order.

When the news came to Philadelphia of the placing of Lee on board ship, Congress immediately concluded that Howe was about to hurry him off to Britain and once more acted energetically. On June 10 the delegates again put pressure upon Howe in an ominous resolution. If persons employed in the service of the United States were carried off to Britain and lodged in prison, Congress would order the equivalent for British prisoners under American control.[12] This resolution had exactly the effect intended. Howe did not dare to send off Lee, for fear Congress would deal drastically with the Hessian prisoners at Dumfries. On July 8 he passed on his problem to Lord George Germain, asking for instructions.[13] Germain also bent before the inflexible will of the stubborn men at Philadelphia. On August 6 he approved Howe's decision not to forward Lee immediately to Britain.[14] On September 3 he informed the British general that the cabinet had surrendered to the demands of Congress. He likewise believed it was dangerous to risk dissension among the German mercenaries. Lee deserved the "most exemplary punishment," but there must be "an end to fruitless negotiation." He ordered Howe to handle him as an ordinary prisoner of war, eligible for exchange.[15]

Meanwhile, in July, a Connecticut officer, Lieutenant Colonel William Barton, hit upon a scheme to obtain Lee's freedom. He decided to try to capture Major General Richard Prescott, the commanding British officer in Rhode Island, so as to enable Congress to offer him to the British in a trade for Lee. With thirty-eight men he made his way through Prescott's lines, pulled Prescott out of bed, and carried him off, almost without interference. Poor Prescott, who had been an American prisoner earlier in the war, thus was captured a second time.[16] Congress gave Barton a vote of thanks, presented a sword to him, and promoted him to colonel. On July 16 Washington happily suggested to Howe a Lee-Prescott trade.[17] The following day he ordered Prescott to be closely guarded in Connecticut without the privilege of local parole, giving him the same treatment accorded to Lee.[18] Congress gave its hearty approval to these measures. On August 7 Campbell and the Hessians were ordered on parole, Prescott being substituted for them, Congress resolving that the British general was to be held "as a pledge for the good treatment and release of Major General Lee, and that he be treated as nearly as circumstances will admit, in the same manner as the enemy shall treat the officer last mentioned."[19] Henry Laurens, delegate from South Carolina, declared that he was quite willing, if Lee were executed, to have Prescott hanged.[20]

By the fall of 1777, Lee's personal safety was assured, and Howe was authorized to exchange him. Howe could have accepted Washington's offer of a Lee-Prescott trade, but he refused it for many months. He seemed to be in no hurry to regain the services of a general so susceptible to capture as Prescott; he was not at all eager to release Lee; and he was angry because of the defeat inflicted upon him by Congress. He was determined that the Americans should not have their own way entirely or quickly. He did not even reply to Washington's offer.[21] When Washington repeated it in September, Howe responded that exchanges in general must be resumed before he would consider a Lee-Prescott bargain.[22] He kept Lee under lock and key until December 27, when he relented sufficiently to permit Lee local freedom on parole in New York, and Prescott received the same privilege in Connecticut.

Lee spent more than six months on board the *Centurion*. He was permitted to have the companionship of Guiseppe Minghini and one of his dogs, and he was also allowed to have visitors. On July 5 he entertained Nicholas Cresswell, a young Englishman who had been caught in America by the outbreak of the war and who had spent three years in Virginia. Cresswell was familiar with Lee's plantation, and Lee gave him tea and chatted with him at length about his own estate and other matters.[23] But Lee could not have the company of all his friends, and he found his captivity aboard the *Centurion* very trying. It is possible that he was abused. On August 22 he wrote to Clinton, begging that something be done to improve his situation. He then told Clinton he was worse off than he would be in a common jail.[24] It is conceivable that Richard Brathwaite, commander of the ship, dealt too harshly with his prisoner. Clinton promised to do all he could for Lee—consistent with Howe's orders.[25] Presumably Clinton, not an inhumane man, saw to it that the prisoner's lot was improved.

Given the freedom of the city on December 27, Lee found quarters in a house with his old friends Major William Butler and Major Daniel Disney, the latter an officer in the Forty-fourth regiment when Lee first entered the British army. Clinton and Major General James Robertson supplied him with horses. On December 30 he informed Washington that his situation was as "easy, comfortable and pleasant as possible for a man who is in any sort a prisoner." "I have nothing left to sigh for," he told his chief, except complete freedom.[26] He had failed again in an attempt to secure money from his English agents,[27] but Congress and his friends saw to it that all his financial needs were met. Accordingly, he was able to entertain freely, and there is no doubt that he was very active socially until the following March, when he was sent to Philadelphia. Many British officers, even of the highest rank, now sought his company, including, of course, Clinton and Robertson. He chatted with Clinton about the battle of Sullivan's Island, but he was probably more intimate with Robertson than he was with his former antagonist.[28] It is reported that insulting remarks made about the American army by a young British officer at one dinner attended by Lee during his captivity aroused his wrath, to the discomfiture of the redcoat, who was forced to apologize.[29] It is clear, however, that Lee was generally offered respect and even affection by several British officers after his release on local parole. Probably he was given a farewell dinner when he finally left New York.[30]

While Lee enjoyed himself at Manhattan, Washington and Howe, unable to reach an agreement for a complete exchange of prisoners, did make an arrangement to trade officer prisoners on general parole. By this arrangement prisoners could be returned to their own lines, promising in return for the privilege not to take an active part in the war. By January 17, 1778, Howe was prepared to barter Lee's general parole for Prescott's.[31] Accordingly Washington sent Prescott into New York toward the end of January.[32] Washington expected, of course, that the

British would promptly accept Lee's formal pledge not to take part in the fighting and that he would promptly be released. However, as in all the negotiations between the two commanders regarding Lee, difficulties developed. Before Prescott arrived at New York, Howe had arranged to have Lee sent to his headquarters at Philadelphia, so that he could personally take Lee's parole, as he claimed. There was no point in compelling Lee to go to Philadelphia to give his pledge. Actually, Howe wanted to talk to him, and about means to end the war. Washington protested against the delay in releasing his subordinate which would result from Howe's plan and also against sending him by sea, because Lee had expressed fear of an attack of gout while on board ship. The British general permitted him to travel by land, but insisted on taking his parole at Philadelphia.[33]

Lee himself was eager to go to Philadelphia. He informed Clinton on March 16 that he had business of the greatest importance to transact there.[34] And so he did, for he had again offered his services to the Howes as a mediator between Britain and America, and his desire to see Sir William was possibly as great as that of the British general to see him.

Early in 1778 Lee once more approached the British authorities on the subject of Anglo-American relations. In a lengthy letter to James Robertson he expressed his obviously sincere opinions on those relations and suggested that Robertson relay its contents to the Howe brothers. He contended that continuation of the war would ruin Britain, even if she should triumph in a military way, because of her vast debt and the heavy expenses of the war. On the other hand, argued Lee, America would likewise suffer even in the event of an American victory, for "confusion anarchy and civil wars" would follow independence; " . . . is there no means to prevent these calamities to both parties? perhaps there is not—but it is the business of a good man to devise and attempt some means." Lee then had little hope that the war could brought promptly to an end but suggested terms which he thought might possibly satisfy both moderate Britons and moderate Americans. Parliament should pardon all the Americans and solemnly renounce all power to tax them for revenue; and the British army should be withdrawn from America, at least until the Americans should consent to its return. For their part, the Americans should renounce independence and give "every possible security" for observing the British acts of trade governing American commerce, modified in particulars which were especially burdensome to them. Lee feared that these proposals would shock "many a partial overbearing Englishman" and "Americans sore from the calamities and desolation . . . spread over their country, and from their own individual sufferings and losses. . . ." Nevertheless, if Lord Howe and General Howe would empower him to propose them to the Americans he would do so, even at the risk of his own popularity.[35] Since Viscount Howe was in England at the time, Robertson had forwarded Lee's offer to General Howe at Philadelphia. Lee's offer interested Sir William, especially since the British government was about to embark upon a campaign to secure a negotiated peace which would leave America in the empire.

Crossing New Jersey in the care of a British artillery captain and Joshua Loring, British commissary of prisoners, Lee reached Philadelphia on March 25, remaining there until April 5. On April 3 he had a conference with Howe, who, although Lee was quite unaware of the fact,[36] was soon to be relieved of his command. As a result of this interview and perhaps of earlier ones, Lee's respect for Howe warmed into affection, an affection which he boldly declared after his release, in a letter to Rush. He then described the British general as candid, goodnatured, brave, and sensible, but indolent, and corrupted by the fashion of the times to worship "every scepter'd calf, hog, or ass. . . ." He correctly assessed Howe as a great soldier on the field of battle and as an otherwise lazy and incompetent commander, a judgment which has been often quoted and which has been rather generally accepted. As Lee put it, Howe "shut his eyes, fought his battles, had his little whore . . . ," and then repeated the process. In this last interview, according to Lee, the British commander virtually admitted that he had made a mistake in taking the American command under George III and Lord North and awkwardly apologized for the stern treatment he had meted out to Lee. The two men conversed about the political situation. According to Elias Boudinot, Howe declared the Americans could not possibly win their independence and said, " . . . and as for you Lee what in the devil could get into you to be so crazy" as to believe it possible? Lee again asserted that he did not desire independence for America, but rather a prompt cessation of hostilities and freedom for America within the British Empire. He seems to have told Howe that the Declaration of Independence was not intended as a final statement of American purpose, but as a means of taking a strong bargaining position from which the Americans could recede at the proper time. Since Howe himself desired as much freedom as possible for America under the British flag, Lee's statements pleased him. Lee promised the British general he would use what influence he had among the American leaders toward bringing about peace negotiations. Possibly, neither man had been completely frank. They parted on good terms, probably because each had tried to state his views in such a way as to please the other. The British general even sent wine and spirits to Lee's house to comfort him upon his journey to the American camp at Valley Forge. However, some British soldiers broke into his cellar and carried off the stimulants.[37]

On the morning of April 5, Lee signed his parole, pledging his "faith & sacred honor" that he would neither "directly, nor indirectly give any intelligence to the king's enemies, nor say nor do anything contrary to the interest of his majesty or his government. . . ."[38] Actually, in spite of its phrasing, the parole merely prevented Lee from taking the field, for it was understood in the eighteenth century that the pledge was not to be taken literally. Lee then promptly departed for Valley Forge.

Meanwhile, during the last few months of Lee's captivity there had again arisen in the American army, in Congress, and elsewhere a belief that Washington was unfitted for the supreme American command. This belief was not widely held among American patriots in private life. Indeed, patriots who were not immediately concerned with public affairs hardly knew that serious dissatisfaction with Washington existed. Moreover, both in the army and in Congress there were many who had faith in the Virginian, in some cases almost an idolatrous faith. Those who thought Washington was not sufficiently talented for his great responsibilities began to consider measures toward his removal, not only on the ground of insufficient ability, but also on the principle that the continuance of one man in control of the army over a lengthy period was a menace to republican institutions. There was no planned, secret, and concerted drive to replace Washington and therefore no vicious "Conway Cabal" against him; nor is it true that the motives of those who wished his removal were utterly base. Their motives were undoubtedly mixed, but it cannot be contended that their objections to continuing Washington in the supreme command were without foundation. It is true that they underestimated his abilities and that they did not properly assess his devotion to republican principles. Their chief candidate for his post was, of course, Horatio Gates, who had won magnificent laurels by forcing Burgoyne's surrender at Saratoga; the glorious victory of Gates over Burgoyne was inevitably contrasted with Washington's defeats at Brandywine and Germantown. Some of the disgruntled ones also surely believed Lee to be the proper person to succeed the commander in chief.[39] It is even sometimes said that Gates was merely the ostensible candidate for the post and that Lee was the real candidate, but there is no contemporary evidence of any weight to substantiate this view,[40] and Lee, a prisoner, could hardly be pushed for the supreme command.

No public action had been taken against Washington. Indeed, Gates's conduct in the winter of 1777-78 was so inept that he injured his own chances. When the contents of a letter from the French General Conway to Gates containing criticism of Washington were bruited about, Gates acted in such a way that he could be made to appear ridiculous.

Nevertheless, Washington had been made most uncomfortable by the attack upon him, and it was more important to him than ever that his army should be successful in the campaign of 1778. Lee might be a great help in the campaign.[41] Washington seems therefore to have set aside any grievance which he may have entertained against Lee because of the latter's disobedience of his orders in December, 1776. When he learned that Lee was to leave the British lines on Sunday morning, April 5, he sent

Lieutenant Colonel Richard Kidder Meade, one of his aides, with a small body of horse to escort Lee to his own headquarters. Lee was received with suitable dignity and apparently genuine cordiality. In the evening Washington and Mrs. Washington gave a dinner at which Lee, Greene, and several other high officers were guests.[42] Lee spent the night in a chamber back of Mrs. Washington's sitting room. The next morning he rose tardily, and breakfast was delayed for him. "When he came out he looked as dirty as if he had been in the street all night," Elias Boudinot, who was present, later recalled. According to Boudinot, he soon afterward discovered a reason for Lee's belated appearance. Lee had brought "a miserable dirty hussy with him from Philadelphia (a British sergeants wife) and had actually taken her into his room by a back door and she had slept with him that night."[43] However, Boudinot hated Lee.

Lee remained only a short time at Valley Forge. On parole he could not, of course, assume active military duty. He soon set out on a sorry-looking nag to visit York, Pennsylvania, where the Congress was in session. Before he left, as Elias Boudinot tells us, Lee insisted to him that Britain would win the war and that the Americans should move themselves en masse to the Mississippi and freedom by way of Pittsburgh. Moreover, Boudinot relates that Lee expressed the opinion Washington was "not fit to command a sergeant's guard."[44] But again it must be remembered that Boudinot's reminiscences, when they reflect upon Lee, should be heavily discounted because of Boudinot's violent antipathy toward the Englishman.[45]

Lee reached York on April 9,[46] and remained there for a few days. He conferred tête à tête with Henry Laurens, then president, and also with other members of Congress. He presented to them a "Plan for the Formation of the American Army," which called for an almost complete reorganization of the army along new lines and which emphasized the importance of cavalry. Lee claimed that the reorganization could quickly be accomplished. But his plan also included advice on the conduct of the campaign of 1778. Lee argued that the American army was inferior to the British in discipline, in officers, and even in ardor and numbers. It would therefore be "insanity" to attack the British in the open field. It was well, of course, to tell the American soldier that he was the equal of the British soldier! The Americans should maintain the defensive, harassing and impeding the enemy whenever possible. The British would certainly take the offensive in one form or another, Lee claimed. They might try to attack Washington, in which case Washington could decide how to act. They might carry on a war of devastation, against which bodies of cavalry and light infantry would be the most effective defense. They might try to occupy large regions such as the valley of the lower Susquehanna and the region about Baltimore, living off the country and wearing down American resistance. To meet this danger Lee urged that Lancaster and Baltimore be placed in a state of defense.[47] According to the information then available, Lee's advice to act on the defensive was sound, whatever may be said regarding the respective merits of British and American troops. Nor was he foolish in believing the British would take the offensive, for neither he nor Congress knew at the time that France was entering the war and that orders from London would consequently soon put the main British army on the defensive. However, Lee's ideas were very coolly received.[48] Laurens predicted that a British force marching to Lancaster would be cut off.[49] Indeed, Lee himself was apparently viewed with jealous eyes. Laurens later declared Lee had made dark hints in private conversation regarding the shortcomings of Washington and also concerning the wisdom of a negotiated peace between America and Britain, hints which greatly displeased Laurens.[50]

Other business which Lee did with Congress concerned his own exchange. It will be recalled that Congress had insisted that Washington should demand the final exchange of Lee for Major General Prescott before entering into any general agreement. It was, of course, the intention of Congress that Lee should be exchanged before any other American officer in British hands. However, when Washington arranged for Lee's release on parole from Philadelphia, he also secured the final exchange of Ethan Allen for Archibald Campbell. Washington had therefore violated the spirit, and indeed the letter, of his instructions from Congress. Sentiment in that body against Washington was running high when Lee reached York. Indeed, on April 10, Congress approved a draft of a letter to the commander in chief which contained a stern reproof and a declaration that justice to Lee and the honor of Congress itself demanded that Lee be freed before any American officer. Indeed, it was generally believed in Congress that various officers about Washington were jealous of Lee and were influencing their chief toward postponement of Lee's exchange. However, Lee urged Congress to waive his exchange as a preliminary to a general exchange, and that body therefore adopted on April 13 a second draft in which Washington was ordered merely not to conclude a general cartel unless its terms included the final exchange of Lee for Prescott.[51] Lee had helped Washington out of a nasty situation. It is not likely that he did so from love of Washington, but rather that he believed his release was certain and that it might well be earlier if it were not stipulated as a preliminary to a general cartel. On April 17 while on the road to Virginia, Lee sent to Henry Laurens a proposal that he and one or more other American officers be bartered for Burgoyne. Lee declared that Howe set no value on Burgoyne and that the latter would be of no value to the British. On the other hand, argued Lee, "I am well and hope always shall be with General Washington—and to speak again vainly I am perswaded (considering how he is surrounded) that he cannot do without me." It was Lee's opinion that Washington needed powerful assistance and that he was not receiving it from his subordinates.[52] However, bargaining on the basis of Burgoyne for Lee plus was not undertaken, for Lee's final release in exchange for Prescott was arranged by Washington only a few days later.

Before Lee left York, shortly after the middle of April, he sent Washington a copy of his plan for reorganizing the American army, along with his ideas regarding the approaching campaign. Washington responded on April 22, remarking that he hoped Lee would have an easier time riding his hobby of army reorganization than he did riding his old nag from Valley Forge to York. The commander in chief said he would talk to Lee about his plans and ideas when he saw him again. More important, he informed Lee that his exchange had been definitely arranged on April 21. After Lee's parole was obtained from the British, "I shall most cordially, and sincerely, congratulate you on your restoration to your country . . . ," wrote the great Virginian. Washington spoke also of the "rejoicing" which he felt because of imminent return of Lee to the army, and urged Lee to rejoin him as soon as possible.[53]

CHAPTER THIRTEEN

APPROACH TO MONMOUTH

Onward he flies, nor fix'd as yet the goal
Where he shall rest him on his pilgrimage....
BYRON, *Childe Harold's Pilgrimage*

Washington's handsome and generous welcome of his return to the American army reached Lee at his Virginia estate, to which he had given the name "Prato Verde." From Prato Verde on April 28, Lee responded that the news made him happy and that he would set out for Valley Forge as soon as a fit of the gout permitted, and he made bitter reference to "the impudence of North and his colleagues" and "the patience or rather stupid forbearance of the [British] people in not tearing them to pieces."[1] But Lee's condemnation of North and the cabinet did not mean that he had entirely given up his hopes for a negotiated peace, America to remain in the empire. Rather it indicates a thought on Lee's part that if George III and North and their friends had not been in power, he himself would not be torn between his feelings as an Englishman, his views of a satisfactory Anglo-American relationship, and his duty as an officer in the American army. He was not happy. Lee's talk at York to Laurens and other members of the Congress of the power of the British army and of the advisability of continuing on the defensive, and also his hints that a peace bringing America less than independence might be desirable, were intended to furnish an impulse toward negotiations with General Howe. He had kept his promise to Howe before his release that he would try to exert his influence with Congress for that purpose, but to no avail, except to arouse suspicions in Congress regarding his own abilities and his own loyalty.

Leaving Prato Verde when he was able to travel, Lee went to York, where he spent some days. Little can be learned of his activities there except that he petitioned Congress for a promotion. He pointed out that several persons had been elevated to the rank of major general since his appointment in June, 1775, but that his status had remained unaltered. He claimed that Washington had long before expressed an opinion that Congress must have overlooked him when promoting others and that he could certainly have attained the rank of lieutenant general in the Polish, Portuguese, or Russian army, had he been in service in Europe rather than in America during the period 1775-78.[2] However, no action was taken on his petition, possibly in part because Lee as the only lieutenant general in the army would have been in a position to push hard for the supreme command in the event that Washington's post became vacant. Moreover, a raise in rank for him would probably have brought forth applications for similar promotions on the part of other major generals, and Congress had suffered grievously from the jealousies and conflicting claims of the army officers.

Before Lee left York for the army, if not before he reached that town, he learned that Britain was embarking upon a great peace offensive, that Parliament had repealed all the laws passed since 1763 which had proved to be obnoxious to the Americans, and that Britain was sending a commission headed by the Earl of Carlisle to deal with Congress in the hope of obtaining a peace leaving America within the empire. Exactly what terms the cabinet and Parliament were prepared to approve is not clear, but they would have given America as much freedom within the empire as most Americans had asked before 1774. The commission was willing to abandon all claim to the power to tax in America except for the purpose of trade regulation, the proceeds of any taxes for such regulation to be used exclusively for the benefit of the Americans. In other words, Britain was now seemingly ready to make substantial concessions to America, although Britain apparently would not go so far as to accept an arrangement such as Lee had proposed to James Robertson and the Howes. Before Lee left York he also learned that France had signed a treaty of amity and commerce with the United States on February 6, and that France was entering the war as an American ally. This news was known to Congress on May 2. The participation of France in the war virtually assured

American independence, as many Americans realized. The news caused great rejoicing in Congress and in the army at Valley Forge, the army celebrating with a military pageant on May 5.

Nevertheless, there were not lacking persons, even in Congress, who were reluctant to receive the ancient French enemy as an ally, who feared America might fall under French domination, and who were disposed to make peace with Britain, if satisfactory terms could be secured, rather than to continue the war in the expectation that the French alliance would bring independence instead of other untoward results. Since America had been committed to the goal of independence for almost two years and since the war had brought desolation and sorrow to so many Americans, these people could hardly speak freely, but it is likely that they were fairly numerous, although probably in a minority in Congress. Lee's sympathies undoubtedly lay with these people, and must have been all the stronger because he wished Britain to continue prosperous and powerful. He therefore continued to be receptive to ideas of an Anglo-American agreement.

Nor was Lee ignored by British officials in America carrying on the drive for peace. James Robertson, after learning that Clinton was about to succeed Howe, sent to him on May 3 a copy of the letter which Lee had written to him while Lee was still within the British lines. Clinton read the letter.[3] He reached Philadelphia on May 8 and assumed command on May 11. Before or immediately after landing he ordered Robertson to write to Lee, and Robertson did so. His letter to Lee has not been found, but it is clear that Robertson asked Lee to meet him and to confer with him and that Lee received the letter. How the message passed through the American lines is also unknown. During the latter part of May or early in June, Lee replied in a letter which reached Robertson. It, too, is missing, but it is clear that Lee said he could not or would not meet Robertson and that he doubted anything could be done toward ending the war. Perhaps he insisted upon the withdrawal of the British forces as a preliminary to negotiation, as he had in his first letter to the British general. He remarked that the devastations of a British force in New Jersey between May 7 and May 10 had greatly strengthened American hostility to Britain. On June 4, Lee is reported to have told a British officer "that he was very unhappy in and very averse to the present course of affairs," and that he "wished for nothing so much as to promote every idea of peace." At the same time Lee sent to Clinton his best wishes, whatever the result of "the present unfortunate contest" might be.[4] On June 17, Robertson wrote a second time to Lee, expressing a personal liking for him and regret that he could not joyfully embrace him in the knowledge that they had succeeded in making peace between the two countries they both loved.[5] With this letter, which may not have reached Lee, the correspondence ended. So far as can be told, Lee's efforts toward reconciliation had also ended. One can guess they were abandoned in part because of a belief that they were hopeless, in part because they were dangerous to Lee himself.[6] It should be stressed, in view of later events, that nowhere in this correspondence is there any suggestion that Lee might be paid for his services, nor is there any suggestion that he might conduct himself in such a fashion as to betray the American army to the British.

It was then a Lee desiring, but despairing of, an Anglo-American peace who traveled to Valley Forge in May, 1778. He arrived on the twenty-first, together with Benedict Arnold, "to the great joy of the army."[7] He took his old place beside Washington as the senior major general and second in command. Reporting his coming, Nathanael Greene noted that Lee had "his usual train of dogs" and that there had been many and happy changes in the army and its fortunes during Lee's long absence as a prisoner.[8] Greene himself as quartermaster general had contributed not a little to the improved prospects of the army by reorganizing the supply system, even though he employed his own relatives as subordinates in not unprofitable positions. Baron von Steuben, who had sold his services as a professional soldier to Congress, had arrived at Valley Forge and was increasing its efficiency by his labors as a drillmaster. The young Marquis de Lafayette had also entered American service. Not yet twenty-one, he was a major general and was valuable because of his connections with the French court, if not for his military abilities. The long, hardship-filled winter of 1777-78 had passed, large reinforcements were coming in, and French aid was soon to appear.

Lee was immediately given a command commensurate with his rank and was asked to offer an opinion regarding strategy for the coming campaign. After a council of war completed on May 8 the consensus among Washington's generals had been that the army was not sufficiently strong to attack the British either at Philadelphia or at New York and that it should remain on the defensive for the time being. Lee subscribed to this decision on May 22.[9] Indeed, he was very strongly against taking the offensive. In an undated memorandum, probably prepared somewhat earlier in the month, he indicated an opinion that Howe would try to strengthen his position in the middle states and declared he had "the strongest reasons" to believe Howe would send a force by way of Chesapeake Bay to move against and occupy the region between Annapolis, Alexandria, and the lower reaches of the Susquehanna River. Lee pressed Washington to take steps to meet such an attack.[10] It is clear that Lee's advice here was good advice if the British were able to take the offensive. Baltimore had become extremely important as a port and particularly as the receiving point of military supplies from Europe; and a British occupation of Baltimore and the area indicated would partly sever the American states and embarrass the American war effort. But Lee continued to express concern about such an attack even after June 4, when Clinton announced that the British would soon evacuate Philadelphia.[11] As late as June 15, partly on the basis of information secured from Dr. Robert Wellford, a physician who had just deserted the British army because his sympathies lay with America, partly because of data supplied by a Mr. Willing, Lee urged Washington to be prepared for a possible British thrust directed against Lancaster either from Philadelphia or from the Chesapeake. It was then commonly believed that Clinton would retreat to New York; but Lee contended that if the British evacuated Philadelphia and went on the defensive they would establish themselves in southern Delaware and eastern Maryland, where they could be supported indefinitely by the British fleet. Until June 15—perhaps until June 18—Lee thought largely in terms of defense and not at all in terms of offense.

It is an interesting fact that Lee also suggested changes in the organization of the army on the ground that under existing arrangements a major general would command men in the field whom he did not control in camp. Lee believed it to be important that a major general should be steadily in command of the same men so that there would be no lack of co-operation because officers and men were unknown to each other.[12] Washington's reply to Lee's suggestions upon strategy and army organization is also interesting. He indicated that steps had been taken to guard the lower Susquehanna, although he did not expect a British attack there. He said a change in the organization of the army was desirable but could not be made because Congress had not approved a plan which he had proposed; and he claimed a change was not vitally necessary, since a major general's command in the field would include his command in camp and since the major generals were well known throughout the whole army. He ended by thanking Lee for his suggestions, declaring he would always be "happy in a free communication of your sentiments upon any important subject relative to the service, and only beg that they may come directly to myself. The custom, which many officers have, of speaking freely of things and reprobating measures, which upon investigation may be found to be unavoidable, is never productive of good, but often of mischievous consequences."[13] It seems likely that Lee was among the "many officers" whom Washington criticized and that the commander in chief was well aware of the fact. Certainly Lee made comments about Washington's "blunders" in the campaign of 1777 and Gates's achievements in the Saratoga campaign in a letter to his friend Rush on June 4.[14] It is therefore probable that the commander in chief and his principal subordinate were once again not on the best of terms.

It is also possible that Lee at the time did not enjoy friendly relations with Greene. Lee was told after his release that the Quaker general had urged Washington to let Lee remain a prisoner as long as possible. Greene was advised to see Lee and deny the story.[15] If Lee believed the tale, he could hardly have failed to resent it. It is likely, however, that it arose from Greene's attitude toward the extreme measures taken by Congress to protect Lee during his captivity, and that Lee realized such was the case, even if Greene never discussed the matter with him. In any event, Greene later expressed friendship for Lee when the latter had become Washington's open enemy.

There were, of course, personal likes and dislikes in the army. There was much secret backbiting and perhaps as much open quarreling. Before the campaign of 1778 was finished, the European concept of personal honor had developed so fully among the officers that the duel became a common mode of settling such quarrels. As yet, however, duels were infrequent. There were also national jealousies in the Continental army which were most vexing to both Washington and Congress and which at times threatened seriously to disrupt the army. The French, German, and Polish officers—all of whom did not have the merits of Steuben and Kosciuszko—always demanded for themselves lofty rank from Congress, and not infrequently succeeded in obtaining it. Lafayette's receipt of a commission as major general before he was twenty-one was not the only case in which an officer from the European continent was given high rank before he had proved himself of value to the American cause. Very humanly, officers of American, British, and Irish extraction who had fought since the beginning of the war and who saw European soldiers suddenly placed above them upon the military ladder were bitterly resentful. As a result the Americans, British, and Irish tended to line up against the French, Germans, and Poles. The situation seemed dangerous in May, 1778. Washington therefore sought assistance in dealing with it from Lee, senior officer in the first group, and from Lafayette, ranking officer in the second group. He suggested that Lee and Lafayette discuss the problem and try to find a remedy. They talked about it as some length, and Lafayette finally proposed a solution which was heartily endorsed by Lee. This was to enlist all European troops, together with deserters from the British army, in a special foreign corps, thus preventing in some degree disputes over rank. Both men also recommended this solution on the ground that discipline would be improved, since European soldiers had little respect for American officers and communicated their contempt for those officers to the American soldiers. Strangely enough, both men also urged the change because it would lessen the amount of contact between the European and American soldiers and would therefore tend to prevent the moral corruption of the American soldiers. It is also an interesting fact that in his own report Lee asserted that care should be taken to avoid offending the French officers and soldiers because America should be grateful to the French "court and nation for the generous part they have acted."[16] Some will find new evidence of duplicity on Lee's part in this statement, but it could be argued that it does him honor. The proposals made by Lafayette and Lee were so sensible that they were eventually carried out in part, to the benefit of the army.

Before the campaign of 1778 opened, the British veteran and the volatile young Frenchman were associated in another curious episode. On February 3, 1778, Congress had passed a resolution demanding that every officer in the American army take an ironclad oath of allegiance. The oath ran:

> I, _____ _____, do acknowledge the United States of America to be free, independent and sovereign states, and declare that the people thereof owe no allegience or obedience to George the third, King of Great Britain; and I do renounce, refuse and abjure any allegience or obedience to him; and I do swear (or affirm) that I will to the utmost of my power support, maintain and defend the said United States against the said King George the third, and his heirs, and successors, and his and their abettors, assistants and adherents, and will serve the United States in the office of _____ which I now hold, with fidelity, according to the best of my skill and understanding. So help me God.

Most of the officers at Valley Forge had taken this oath in May, but Lee and Lafayette were absent at the time, and arrangements were made to swear them on June 9. Washington himself presided at the ceremony. Lafayette's oath was taken without event. However, as the Frenchman afterward recalled, while Washington was reading the oath, Lee twice removed his hand

from a Bible used in the ceremony. Washington stopped reading and asked Lee why he had taken away his hand. Lee replied, "As to King George, I am ready to absolve myself from
all allegiance to him, but I have some scruples about the Prince
of Wales," and then proceeded to complete his oath. Lee's remark aroused laughter among the spectators;[17] perhaps they
believed it was one of his jokes. But it is certain that the oath
was obnoxious to him, and that he felt Congress had no absolute
right to deprive him of his freedom of opinion and of action on
pain of abandoning his commission. He bitterly condemned a
similar oath required by Virginia in 1779 from persons suspected
of Toryism on penalty of sequestration or confiscation of their
property. Lee then argued that a situation might arise in which
the Americans might wish to rejoin the empire under "a just
and amicable prince." The Virginia oath was therefore "horrid
and insane," and " no conscientious man of any reflection ought
to take it." Lee argued that Virginia should require an oath of
loyalty merely to the "government de facto established by the
consent of the people."[18] No doubt, Lee still believed on June 9
that an Anglo-American reconciliation under certain conditions
was desirable. The vigor of his denunciation of the Virginia
oath probably reflects his anger because of the oath which he
himself took in 1778. It has been and will be contended that Lee
was "wicked" in taking an oath to which he did not commit
himself heart and soul. Yet it is true that oaths can and may be
variously construed, as any casual visitor to a courtroom will
readily testify. A reasonable judgment of Lee's behavior on
June 9 is that he internally pledged himself, to use his own
phrase, to be loyal to a "government de facto established by the
consent of the people."[19] It is to be suspected that no man who
took the oath seriously and thoughtfully intended to pledge himself to more than that. Certainly, Lee's behavior in taking the
oath and his later condemnation of the Virginia oath indicate
that he did not pledge himself coldly and deliberately to con-
cepts in which he did not fully believe.

While the American army waited at Valley Forge for the
opening of the campaign, the peace commissioners sent out from
England—the Earl of Carlisle, George Johnstone, Sir William

Eden, and Viscount Howe—reached Philadelphia on June 6. There they met Clinton, who was also a member. They promptly sent into the American lines a copy of their instructions together with a peace offer in a letter sealed with an image of a fond mother caressing her children. Congress received these documents on June 13. The peace terms which the commissioners suggested cast oblivion upon the past and substantially promised autonomy for America within the empire. They would surely have been acceptable to most Americans in 1775, even in the early part of 1776, but they were not sufficient in 1778, even though they were apparently somewhat more generous than George III and the cabinet intended to offer. Congress promptly responded by resolving that it would not deal with the commission until the British should withdraw their armies and navy from the American states or acknowledge American independence.[20] The commission could not meet either of these stipulations, and some of its members despairingly tried to win over influential Americans by cajolery and bribery. But these efforts failed ingloriously. Indeed, the labors of the commission were virtually doomed before it reached Philadelphia, for orders from Germain to Clinton to evacuate Philadelphia had preceded them to America. The evacuation of the city was a powerful support to those Americans who desired nothing less than independence. They could well argue that independence would soon be a reality. On August 11, Congress definitely ended all hope of a negotiated peace by formally declaring that it would have no further dealings whatever with the commission.

The entrance of France into the war not only gave impetus to British efforts to make peace but also greatly altered the military situation. The Earl of Sandwich had been responsible for the British navy for several years before the War of Independence, and he had allowed the navy to dwindle both in size and in efficiency. Meanwhile, France had been rebuilding its navy. The result was that Britain lacked sufficient sea power to deal effectively with the French navy and that France was able to send to America in the spring of 1778 a squadron from Toulon under the command of the Count d'Estaing. This squadron was ordered to the Delaware Capes, and preparations for its departure aroused great concern in London. Partly because of this squadron, partly because of the fact that Britain was forced, at least for the moment, to go on the defensive generally, instructions were sent to Clinton to concentrate his forces at New York and to carry on limited offensives against the New England seaports and in the West Indies. When Clinton learned early in June that D'Estaing would soon appear at the Delaware Capes, he hurried his plans for evacuation. He might have gone by sea, but he did not have enough transports to carry his whole force, its baggage, and fleeing Loyalists. Moreover, he feared that New York might be attacked and captured while he was at sea. He therefore sent his heavy baggage, the Loyalists, and a body of German mercenaries, in whom he did not have full reliance, by water and prepared to march with the bulk of his army and a large part of baggage by land across New Jersey. He calculated that his army could reach New York in ten days and that he would meet difficulties on the march, but not major ones.[21] D'Estaing was too late to attack the transports, and they reached New York without incident. Clinton himself encountered greater difficulties than he anticipated.

On the night of June 8 the British army began to cross the Delaware, and Clinton's whole force was on the New Jersey side on the morning of June 18. Altogether he had about ten thousand men, most of whom were reliable British veterans, but including also a body of Hessians under Baron von Knyphausen. His troops were well supplied with food. His chief cause for concern was his long baggage train, which would offer a target for attack. But troubles soon came upon him. Rain, heat, and his baggage slowed his march; and New Jersey militia under Major General Philemon Dickinson rendered his progress still slower by destroying bridges and wells and by cutting down trees in his path. Moreover, a force of twelve hundred New Jersey Continentals under General Maxwell began to press upon his left flank. Clinton therefore did not reach the Monmouth Courthouse at Freehold until June 28. It would seem that he made no great effort to hurry and that he remained confident of his ability to reach New York, even though Hessians deserted him by scores. His men were short of water, but he had brushed aside with ease the harassing attacks made upon him by Dickinson and Maxwell, although Dickinson reported to Washington in the evening of June 27 that the militia were increasing in numbers and that he believed Clinton might suffer the fate of Burgoyne.[22] The British army was partly in camp near the courthouse and partly on the road toward Sandy Hook on the morning of June 28, when it was attacked by Washington. The fighting which followed has ever since been called the "Battle of Monmouth," although "Engagement at Monmouth" would be a more accurate term.

Before the last of Clinton's army had left Philadelphia, Washington was certain of the fact of the evacuation, and he called a council of war to consider the situation on June 17. At this gathering Lee again expressed his opinion that the British on the defensive would establish themselves on Chesapeake Bay.[23] Washington, however, had information which made it clear that the redcoats were moving toward New York by way of South Amboy or some other port to the south of that place. On the assumption that Clinton would move toward South Amboy the commander in chief asked the assembled generals to give their opinions upon four possible courses of action: to attack the British in force immediately; to march to the lower Hudson on a line parallel to Clinton's march without striking at the British; to try to harass and strike at them without engaging in a general action; or to attack them somewhere in New Jersey with all available forces. There were divergent opinions in the council, and Washington therefore asked the participants and also General Cadwalader to give their opinions in writing, which were handed in on the eighteenth. No one favored an immediate attack. Anthony Wayne, always bold, urged an attack in force upon Clinton as he marched, on two grounds: Clinton because of his baggage could not pursue if he gained an advantage, and such an attack would at least make it appear that he was fleeing before the Americans. John Cadwalader agreed with Wayne, emphasizing that it would be difficult to assail the enemy after the British reached New York. Greene was against a general action, unless the Americans had a decided advantage in position or some similar factor in their favor,[24] and the other officers were emphatically against one. Lord Stirling put the case against full-scale battle very clearly: ". . . in any case it will

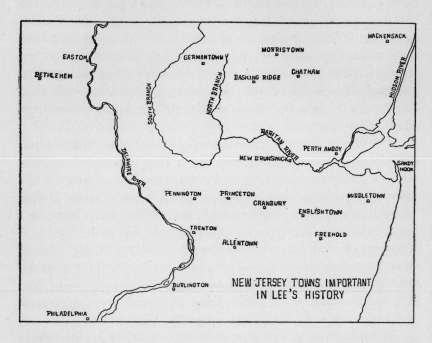

NEW JERSEY TOWNS IMPORTANT IN LEE'S HISTORY

be imprudent to risque a general battle; if the affairs of the United States can be maintained in their present situation, the enemy loose their point; if we loose a general battle or suffer our army to be much impaired, the United States are ruined." Lee took the same view as Stirling and in even stronger terms, arguing that it would be "criminal" to attempt a full-scale attack. Baron von Steuben advised Washington to follow the British, keeping on their left flank, but "carefully avoiding a general action." John Paterson explicitly supported Stirling and Lee, pointing out that Washington had previously gained great advantages over the British by not fighting and urging that he continue the same policy. Opinions varied, however, upon the advisability of making a partial stroke against the British. Lee suggested that one might be attempted, provided that the New

Jersey militia were able to embarrass the British march. Greene, Henry Knox, and William Woodford believed circumstances might permit one. Jedediah Huntington declared there would be very little chance to hurt the British, and Charles Scott went so far as to say that the British could not possibly be injured. Benedict Arnold, as yet a loyal American, and never backward with respect to fighting, was also strongly against a partial stroke, because he believed it would inevitably bring on a general action, to be avoided because the British army was stronger than the American. The consensus was, therefore, to harass the British; if feasible, to strike a partial blow; but to avoid a total clash.[25]

The line of thought taken by most of the generals was obviously largely based on the fact that a British removal to New York was in itself equivalent to a great American victory. They believed it to be unwise to jeopardize the happy results of that removal, the main American army, and the American cause in a battle which was likely to end in defeat. It will be recalled that Washington had never risked his army in a full-scale assault against the British army, and that he certainly had not defeated that army. No doubt the opinion of the generals was that American chances in a pitched battle, if one were necessary, would be as good or better at a future time.

Washington was not bound to act according to the advice of his generals, but he commonly used the collective thought of his subordinates. In this case he accepted the cautious counsel given by the majority of the generals. On June 18 he ordered the army to march eastward across the Delaware on a line parallel to Clinton's march, and he instructed Lee, who commanded the first division, to halt after crossing the river "till further orders, unless you should receive authentic intelligence, that the enemy have proceeded by a direct route to South Amboy, or still lower.[26] In that case you will continue your march to the North [Hudson] River."[27] In other words, if Clinton marched by a northerly route across the Raritan River, Washington hoped to attack him, perhaps with assistance from a force commanded by Gates on the Hudson. If Clinton took a southerly route, Washington then had no real hope of hurting the British army. And Clinton did take a southerly route to Sandy Hook.

As the American army advanced, however, Washington quite properly reconsidered the whole situation. It is altogether likely that he deeply desired to win at least a minor success over the British. Those who had pushed to replace him with Gates had censured him because of the many defeats he had suffered since the spring of 1776. Giving little weight to difficulties beyond his control and to his successes at White Plains, Trenton, and Princeton, they had contrasted the American rout on Long Island, the loss of Fort Washington, Brandywine, and Germantown with the victorious campaign of the northern army under Gates against Burgoyne. Even a minor success against Clinton might serve to still or soften the voices of his critics. Personal considerations made some sort of attack desirable. And besides, a successful assault upon Clinton, even a major one, was obviously not impossible. On June 24, Washington therefore called another council of war in Hopewell township in New Jersey. Addressing the generals, he informed them that Clinton had between 9,000 and 10,000 troops and that the American force numbered 11,884, plus about 1,200 New Jersey militia. He noted that the militia and Maxwell's Continentals had had little success; and that Clinton had traveled only forty miles in seven days. Should a general attack be made upon Clinton? The council replied in the negative. Should an attempt be made to "annoy" the British army? The collective advice of the generals, recorded and signed by all except Wayne, was that a force of 1,500 Continentals should be sent to harass Clinton's left flank and rear while Maxwell's Continentals and the New Jersey militia continued their efforts.

But again there were divergent opinions. Lee spoke very vigorously against a general action, saying that he would like to build a golden bridge over which the British could retreat to New York; that the armies were about equal in size; that it would be extremely unwise to assail them in full force; and that the French alliance was far more effective toward securing independence than any military victory could be. He urged that the force sent against Clinton should engage merely in harassing operations and that it should therefore consist of fifteen hundred men or fewer. He opposed sending a larger detachment to attempt a partial stroke against the British, on the ground that a general action would result. Five officers, including Stirling and Knox, agreed with him. Six generals, however, including Greene, Lafayette, Wayne, and Steuben, believed that the detachment should be larger and that it should join the Jerseymen in making a partial attack. They did not make their view wholly clear at the council. After the meeting broke up, Greene, Wayne, and Lafayette wrote letters to the commander in chief to clarify and urge their opinions. Greene declared that the army, since it had pursued the British, must disappoint American public opinion or do more than merely harass Clinton. An attack sufficient to make a real "impression" should therefore be made, with the main body of the army close at hand to give support in case of need. Greene said that he did not desire a general action, but that the army could if necessary fight efficiently. Wayne offered the same advice. Lafayette, without too great modesty, denounced councils of war as gatherings addicted to hairsplitting logic, strongly urged a partial stroke, and asserted that he was sure Washington himself was not content with mere harassing operations. It should be stressed, because there has been so much misunderstanding regarding the councils of war of June 18 and June 24 and of the events which followed, that *not a single American officer urged a general attack upon Clinton.* The only difference of opinion arose over the advisability of striking a partial blow or of merely continuing harassing operations. It is clear that the generals believed the British would have the better chance for success in a full-scale battle.[28]

Lafayette seems to have read Washington's mind correctly. Before the day was over the commander in chief ordered Daniel Morgan forward with 600 riflemen to join the New Jersey Continentals, the combined force of 1,800 men to operate on the British right flank, and he sent Brigadier General Charles Scott with 1,440 picked men against the British left flank. On the following morning he ordered still a third detachment, of 1,000 picked men under Wayne, to push forward against Clinton; and simultaneously with this move he put the rest of the army in motion. In all, 4,240 Continentals and 1,200 militia were thus committed against the British. At the same time Washington ordered Lafayette forward to assume command of all the advanced Continental forces, with instructions to concentrate upon Clinton's left flank, to harass, attack by detachment, or attack with his whole command, in case an opportunity offered.[29] Meanwhile, Dickinson was to continue to impede the enemy's march as much as possible. Lafayette immediately began to increase pressure on Clinton.

At this point difficulties over command developed. When asked by Washington, Lee had given his approval to sending Lafayette forward as the commander of one of the Continental detachments, although he seems to have considered seriously asking for the command for himself.[30] But Washington had not obtained Lee's consent to his decision to place all the advance forces under one commander, Lafayette. Ordinarily, by military custom, Lee, as senior major general, would have been asked to assume such an important post. Perhaps because he thought it unwise to have Lee undertake responsibilities which might include the partial stroke that Lee had deprecated, the commander in chief had passed over him. But he had likewise passed over Lord Stirling and Greene, who were also senior to the young Frenchman. Both Lee and Stirling were wounded in their military pride, and Lee's friends expressed concern for his honor. Lee perhaps felt more deeply offended than Stirling. In any case, in the evening of the twenty-fifth, after some vacillation on the part of Lee and Stirling,[31] Lee asked for the command of the advance forces. His request was a reasonable one, and it could hardly be denied. On the other hand, to replace Lafayette was likely to injure the young man's vanity, a quality which Lafayette did not lack. However, he had indicated a willingness to serve under Lee, because of the respect which he had for the veteran. Washington therefore tactfully arranged on the twenty-sixth to send Lee forward with reinforcements. As senior officer he would, of course, assume command of all the advance forces. Thus it was unnecessary to supersede Lafayette directly. Moreover, it was agreed between Washington and Lee that Lafayette should be allowed to complete any operation he had begun before Lee's arrival.[32]

Lafayette strove mightily to catch up with the British and to begin an attack before Lee should arrive, but was unable to do so. Heat and lack of food and water finally forced him to call a halt at the very moment when it became possible to establish contact in force with the British, who camped at Freehold (Monmouth Courthouse) on the night of the twenty-seventh. Lee therefore had the privilege and the responsibility of leading the advance corps when the hour of crisis came.

CHAPTER FOURTEEN

MONMOUTH FIGHT

I found no truth in one report at least—
That if you tracked him to his home, down lanes
Beyond the Jewry, and as clean to pace,
You found he ate his supper in a room
Blazing with lights, four Titians on the wall,
And twenty naked girls to change his plate!
BROWNING, *How It Strikes a Contemporary*

ON THE MORNING of June 27, Lee and the American advance forces, except for Dickinson's and Morgan's men, were in and near Englishtown, where they had been ordered to halt by Washington. Dickinson was trying to embarrass the British left and Morgan the British right. Soon after noon Washington sent for Lee to come to his own headquarters at Manalapan, where he conversed with Lee and gave him instructions, in the presence of Lee's subordinates, Lafayette, Wayne, Scott, and Maxwell. It was clear then that Clinton was headed for the neighborhood of Sandy Hook and that a long day's march would put him beyond attack. If anything substantial were to be ventured against him, it could not be postponed. Washington ordered Lee to attack the British rear on the following morning with the troops under his immediate command, about forty-two hundred men, and he requested Lee to confer with his subordinates that afternoon regarding a plan. Lee accordingly met with them later in the day, but offered no proposals, saying the situation and numbers of enemy detachments were unknown and that the ground was also unfamiliar. He indicated a scheme of attack would necessarily be postponed until the following morning. Lee has been severely criticized for not making a plan at that time,[1] but he was no doubt correct in concluding that a workable one could not then be formed. Late at night he received further orders from Washington, to send out a force of from six to eight hundred men to watch

Clinton, to skirmish and delay the British if they began to move, and to keep Lee informed of their actions. Washington also desired that Morgan be instructed to push against the British in the event they began to march. These orders were promptly executed.

In the morning of June 28, hearing that the British were marching eastward from the courthouse, Washington sent additional orders to Lee by his aide, Richard Kidder Meade, and by John Clark, a war-office employee. According to Meade's later testimony, he informed Lee that Washington wished him to "bring on an engagement, or attack the enemy as soon as possible, unless some powerful circumstance forbid it, and that he [Washington] would soon be up to his aid." These orders were delivered after desultory fighting had already begun. Meade also testified later that in his opinion Washington then intended to instigate a general action.[2] However, Clark afterward said that the instructions he carried to Lee were to "annoy the enemy" as much as possible, but to "proceed with caution" and to prevent the British from drawing him "into a scrape."[3] Did Washington really desire a full-scale conflict with Clinton, either on June 27 or in the morning of June 28? If so, he gave little weight to the almost unanimous opinion of his generals. It is certainly difficult to believe he was insistent upon a general action regardless of the nature of the terrain. Clinton believed at the time and later that Washington never intended to challenge the whole British army. The British general pointed out that under Washington's orders the main American force under Washington was at Englishtown at ten o'clock on the morning of the twenty-eighth, seven miles behind Lee and separated from him by ravines crossable only through three narrow defiles, surely a poor position from which to support the advanced force.[4] But perhaps the best testimony on the point comes from Washington himself. Writing to Horatio Gates at six o'clock in the morning of the twenty-eighth, he said, "This morning . . . the enemy began to move; we are following fast, and mean to harrass them as much as possible."[5] At the same time he reported to Congress that Lee had been ordered to attack the British rear, "if possible." It is apparent Washington wished to make an "impression," and if an opportunity presented itself, to deliver a damaging stroke, rather than to engage Clinton's men *in toto*. Washington hoped that Lee would be able to deliver a smart blow against the British rear guard and that Clinton, because of position and the necessity of protecting his baggage, would be unable to attack Lee in great force. If Clinton did stage a major counterattack, Lee presumably had enough strength to hold him off until Washington could come to his assistance. To be sure, the terrain between the commander in chief and Lee would give Clinton a great advantage, in the event he drove Lee back. Washington probably knew something about that terrain and decided to take the risk. Apparently, he was so anxious to strike that he did not give sufficient weight to the tactical situation.

Washington, in accordance with his plan, moved forward toward Englishtown early in the morning of the twenty-eighth, and Lee simultaneously advanced from Englishtown toward the British near the courthouse. At four thirty Dickinson had discovered that the British were beginning to march from their encampment and had sent a messenger to inform Lee and Washington. Lee issued orders for the advance at five o'clock, but his troops did not actually move until seven o'clock. He ordered left behind four or five hundred men, including the sick, the lame, and a guard for his baggage. His force passed through a defile over a bridge across the first of three ravines—the west ravine—between Englishtown and Monmouth, entering relatively open country extending to the courthouse and surrounded by swampy woods.[6] Then Lee received information from Dickinson, which later proved to be inaccurate, that Clinton had not moved. Concerned lest Clinton attack in major force, Lee halted his men. Meeting Dickinson, he was given further cause for alarm. Dickinson told him the British had not moved and that the bridge over the west ravine was the only means by which artillery could be moved across it. He warned Lee that an advance would place him in a perilous situation, because a successful retrograde movement would be almost impossible.[7] In other words, he feared Clinton would attack, pin Lee's force against the ravine, and destroy it. Lee saw the force of Dickinson's remarks, but he was also receiving intelligence that the British *had* moved forward to the east of the courthouse. Exasperated by these contradictory reports, he hesitated for some time. Finally, after examining the situation further, he decided to ignore his various informants, to assume that the British army was moving away, and to push forward. Accordingly, the main body of his troops moved ahead through two more defiles across two more ravines—the middle and east ravines—the latter stretching from the courthouse roughly at a right angle across his line of advance. Lee was warned that the east ravine was a menace to him, and was concerned about it, but decided nevertheless to attack.[8] At the time he seems not to have realized fully that the three ravines would place him in a very poor position should Clinton attack in strength, since Lee could be pinned against them and since it would be difficult to bring up the main army across them.

Reaching fairly open country beyond the courthouse, the Americans saw before them a British force of from fifteen hundred to two thousand men, Clinton's rear guard, mostly infantry, together with two batteries. This rear guard was well arranged and protected on its left by a wood. Clinton's baggage train, with his Hessians and part of the British troops, had actually begun to march early in the morning. Strung out in a long line, they were headed for some heights near Middletown, where a successful American attack would be impossible. However, Clinton and over four thousand men, including a few Hessians and comprising some of the best soldiers in the world at that time, were still near at hand and ready to support the rear guard, although Lee was quite unaware of the fact. Clinton had not expected an American attack in force, but he was prepared for one, even for a full-scale battle. Clinton knew that the main American force could not have passed the defiles, that in case of need he could bring up the British troops accompanying the baggage train as quickly as Washington could traverse the defiles to support Lee, and that he would have all the geographical advantages.[9] Clinton, indeed, had been annoyed by the harassing maneuvers of Dickinson on his front and left and of Morgan on his right, although the latter had achieved nothing whatever. Morgan, operating independently of Lee, found the

British in such close order on June 27 and June 28 that he could not attack.[10] His six hundred riflemen were therefore of no help whatever to Lee, even less valuable to him than Dickinson's militia, who did fire a few shots at the British on the morning of the twenty-eighth. In any case, Sir Henry desired to free himself of the threats of Dickinson and Morgan; and he hoped to accomplish this end by striking at the American center—that is, as fortune would have it, at Lee.[11] Clinton, though small of stature and unimpressive in appearance, was an experienced commander who knew something about his business. As he is supposed to have said later, on June 28 he "fought on velvet."[12]

In happy ignorance of Clinton's arrangements and plans Lee saw a chance to strike an effective blow by isolating and destroying the British rear guard. He therefore ordered Wayne to press against the British front. He stationed troops led by General Maxwell and Colonel Jackson on Wayne's left. To the extreme left he sent a detachment led by General Scott. Lee went to lead personally Scott's men through some woods to strike at the British right flank[13] and rear and to cut off the British rear guard from their supports. In the meantime Lee hoped that Morgan would move against the left flank of the British rear guard. But Morgan, for some unknown reason or reasons, did not appear.

While Lee was maneuvering his men into position for his intended attack, the British light cavalry in the rear guard advanced against Wayne's men. Hitherto there had been little actual fighting, but there was a smart skirmish before the light horse retreated. Lee still felt sure he had the situation well in hand and sent a message to Washington to say he was almost certain of cutting off the British rear guard. This report was made, of course, on the assumption that Clinton would not promptly support his rear guard, in which assumption Lee quite understandably erred. Before he could complete his arrangements, Wayne, always eager for the fray, insistently begged for reinforcements so that he could assail the British front. Wayne was not content to obey his orders and had not been informed of Lee's plan. Lee, of course, did not comply with the request. In the meantime, the British rear guard was reinforced by Clinton, who brought up his supporting troops, and a British column began to move toward the courthouse and the American right wing. Lee left his strong right wing and went to examine the situation. Warned by Lieutenant Colonel Alexander Hamilton and others that the British advance was a real threat, he ordered Lafayette to lead three regiments to the endangered flank to meet the expected assault. Lafayette personally led one regiment to the exposed spot, leaving the colonels of the other two to bring them up. The regiment under Lafayette immediately came under British artillery fire. At the same time he sent out Lafayette, Lee ordered Major John Francis Mercer, one of his aides, to tell General Scott, who was stationed in a wood on the extreme left with the troops who had been entrusted with the flanking movement, that it was most important that he hold firm on that side.[14]

At this point the trend of the engagement changed. Lieutenant Colonel Eleazer Oswald, who commanded a battery on the right flank just beyond the east ravine, ran out of shot. His ammunition wagon lay west of the ravine, and he began to retreat toward it. Lee personally rode up to him and imperiously demanded the reason for his action. Oswald explained his situation, and Lee therefore permitted him to take the new position. This was the first retrograde American movement. Still worried for fear Scott would not hold firm on the extreme left, Lee then hurried off a second aide, Captain Evan Edwards, to Scott to repeat the instruction carried by Mercer. Mercer and Edwards did not find Scott and did not deliver Lee's orders. Instead they soon returned with a report that Scott was retreating, and that a British detachment was moving toward Scott's former position. Mercer had seen a body of Americans moving to the rear on the left flank and had assumed, perhaps correctly, that it was Scott's force. It would seem that both Mercer and Edwards erred seriously in not finding Scott and delivering their message. Mercer had convinced Edwards it was not worthwhile to follow up Scott, and that it was wiser to inform Lee quickly of the situation. Lee received the news, erroneous so far as the British detachment was concerned, with anger and disappointment, and was all the more worried when he observed that Lafayette and the regiment under him were at some distance from Wayne's right and seriously exposed. It had been intended that the two regiments advancing toward Lafayette's position should take post on his right, but Lee hurried off orders to them to take a position on a knoll behind Lafayette and to his left. Lee's intention was to strengthen and to reorganize the right wing.[15]

As the fates would have it, Lafayette misunderstood Lee's purpose. He observed the two regiments taking position to his rear and he noted that the regiment with him and Oswald's battery were both without solid support. According to Lafayette, someone—he was never able to state whom—but someone not sent by Lee, told him Lee desired him to fall back across the ravine and to join his regiment with the two behind him in a new position based on the courthouse. This maneuver seemed to be a wise one to Lafayette, and he therefore undertook it. He thought of it as merely a temporary withdrawal. But Scott, if he had not previously withdrawn in the mistaken belief that the right wing was retreating, learned of Lafayette's movement and withdrew his own men from the wood on the right to a position west of the ravine.[16] Wayne was also informed of the maneuver on the right. He galloped over to Lafayette who explained what he was doing. Wayne was not convinced Lafayette's withdrawal was necessary. Indeed, he sent an aide to Lee urging an advance upon the enemy. Wayne believed the British column advancing toward the courthouse contained no more than eighteen hundred men.[17] Lafayette, however, continued to fall back, and sent an order to Oswald to do likewise. Oswald refused because Lee had shortly before commanded him to hold his position. Lafayette then went to him and told him it was Lee's instructions that he do so. Oswald accordingly withdrew to an eminence indicated by the young Frenchman. Again Lafayette had ordered a withdrawal without instructions from Lee.[18] Since the remainder of Lee's troops were falling back, Wayne did not wait for orders, but also withdrew to the west of the morass, where he and Scott reorganized their men. Wayne was still not convinced any withdrawal was necessary, and he urged Lee instead to order an advance.[19]

Although Lee had ordered neither Lafayette nor Oswald to

retire, he believed Lafayette's maneuvers were proper. Indeed, he later expressed the opinion that he was at fault in not instructing the young Frenchman to do as he did. He ignored Wayne's advice and went personally to the right wing, sending Lafayette into the village surrounding the courthouse[20] to find out whether it would serve as an anchor for that wing. Lee's thought then was to take position behind the east ravine with the village of Freehold as a base for his right. Lafayette discovered that the wooden houses in the village and scanty woods in the neighborhood offered no real protection. Lee also examined the village and came to the same conclusion. Receiving a new report from Lafayette that the British column was still moving slowly toward the village, and learning that Clinton had brought up large reinforcements, Lee decided the right wing must fall back further, especially since he remained ignorant of the position of the left wing. He feared that the British cavalry would sweep around his right flank. According to Clinton, Lee withdrew just in time to avert such a sweep.[21] After the right wing had fallen back, he hoped to reorganize his whole force. At the moment he was not greatly worried about the left wing, since it was far stronger and seemingly in much less danger than the right.[22]

As yet, Lee had not informed Washington of the difficulties he had encountered. Earlier in the morning two messengers had come to him from Washington, by one of whom he was told that the commander in chief was at Englishtown. He had sent back messages by them to the effect that he hoped to isolate and capture the British rear guard.[23] Just as he was arranging to withdraw, Lieutenant Colonel John Laurens, one of Washington's aides, came to him with a letter from the commander in chief. According to a later and probably prejudiced statement by Laurens, this letter declared that Washington was at Englishtown, was moving up with his men, and was prepared to support Lee. In it Washington certainly asked for information about Lee's fortunes. Laurens asked Lee to read the letter and give him a report for the commander in chief. Lee hesitated, then indicated he did not know what to say. According to Lee, he sent no message because he did not know to what position he would withdraw and because he did not wish to send useless information. Lee later denied that the letter said Washington was coming up to his aid. He continued to act on his own responsibility, he stated, on the assumption that the commander in chief was at Englishtown, at too great a distance to advise or to assist him. It is conceivable that Washington's message did not unmistakably portray his intentions.[24]

In any case, Lee ordered his right wing to fall back, while he sought a stronger position in the rear. Noticing some hills just west of the middle ravine, he ordered General du Portail, a French engineer in American service, to examine them and to report. Du Portail soon returned, saying that these hills were defensible. Lee therefore had the right wing move toward this spot. Meanwhile the long-threatened British attack came in the form of a brisk advance against Lee's right, which retreated as American officers realized that Clinton's men were coming up in major force. There was some confusion in the minds of the American officers, and their men did not move in perfect parade order. But Lee's command was by no means disorganized, although many of the officers and men were exhausted from their exertions and suffering from lack of water in the heat of a torrid June day. It is perhaps worth mentioning that Lee tried to march the right wing back through woods so as to protect his men both from the heat and the British.

Arriving at the position behind the middle ravine recommended by Du Portail, Lee was disconcerted to find that an eminence upon his front was higher than a hill which was the base of his own force. From it he believed the approaching British could command his position. Moreover, his right wing was still exposed to a flank attack. A successful British attack would pin his force against the west ravine. He was therefore in a dangerous spot. When the British began to advance in force from the courthouse, Lee accordingly decided to withdraw once more.[25] Still believing, as he said, that Washington and his men were at Englishtown, he sent off John Clark, a war-office clerk who had volunteered his services, to that place to inform the commander in chief of his intention. He requested Clark to tell Washington that by *"too much precipitancy in one of his brigadiers & false*

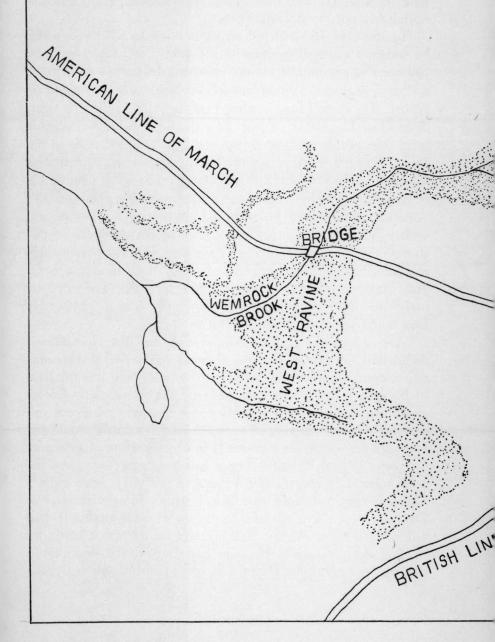

BATTLE OF MONMOUT

AMERICAN LINE OF MARCH

BRIDGE

WEMROCK BROOK

WEST RAVINE

BRITISH LIN

intelligence his troops were thrown into confusion & that he was retiring." Clark delivered the message to Washington.[26]

While attempting to discover a defensible position to his rear, Lee made arrangements to check Clinton's advance so as to make possible an orderly and safe withdrawal. He placed some artillery in a good position and lined up four regiments behind the middle ravine. The artillery was effectively served, and it checked Clinton's advance for a time. Fortunately for Lee and his men, he was now informed of a defensible position. Peter Wikoff, a captain in the New Jersey militia who lived near by and who was well acquainted with the neighborhood, approached him at this juncture and offered his services. The general received him joyfully and begged him to indicate a spot where the British advance could be stopped. Wikoff suggested two locations, both of which seemed unsatisfactory to Lee. Wikoff then mentioned a hill west of the third ravine. There were woods on both sides of the hill. With the ravine in front, it was obviously an excellent choice. Lee therefore instructed Wikoff to lead his men to this spot, giving him authority for the purpose.[27]

Wikoff did his best to perform the task which he had assumed, and soon Lee's force was moving back and across the ravine. Until this third retrograde movement Lee's command had kept good order. But many of his men were in very poor shape because of their exertions, the heat, and lack of water. There was therefore some slight disorganization in the third withdrawal. Moreover, all of Lee's officers did not know they were expected to post themselves upon the hill west of the ravine. In the confusion attendant upon the march, some of Lee's men, without orders, continued as if in full retreat.

Throughout the morning Lee had shown courage, coolness, and perfect self-control. He had perhaps taken too many duties upon himself and had perhaps devoted too much personal attention to his endangered right wing without giving sufficient care to his left. But it is truly difficult to find valid and weighty grounds upon which to criticize his conduct or his tactics. Certainly he himself was satisfied that he had done his best—indeed, that he had performed rather brilliantly. But shortly after noon, while he was making arrangements further to safeguard the retirement of his men across the west ravine, he met Washington and received what was no doubt one of the greatest shocks of his life.

Washington and his troops had reached Englishtown in mid-morning. While the commander in chief had a late breakfast in the village, his troops pushed toward Monmouth. He found time to write a brief message to Congress at eleven thirty, and then moved forward himself. He had not gone far when he received news through a straggler that Lee was retreating. It is not certain who first brought him reliable information of the withdrawal, but Lee's messenger Clark was one of several persons who reported the situation to him.[28] Alarmed, Washington sent forward two aides, Richard H. Harrison and John Fitzgerald, to secure further information, and he rapidly followed in person. Harrison and Fitzgerald met some of Lee's troops crossing the west ravine. When questioned, officers declared disgustedly they were retreating and they knew not why. Harrison and Fitzgerald went on and found Lee, who asked Washington's location. Lee promptly rode back and met Washington east of the bridge over the west ravine. The conversation that followed in the presence of a considerable group of officers was an amazing one.

Washington was bitterly angry and had lost control of his temper. "I desire to know, sir, what is the reason, whence arises all this confusion?"

Lee was so stunned by Washington's severe manner and intonation that he seemed not fully to comprehend his meaning, and stammered, "Sir, sir—."

Washington repeated his question. Lee then declared there was no confusion except that caused by contradictory intelligence and disobedience of his orders by Scott and others. The commander in chief asserted that Lee's retiring maneuvers were unnecessary because he had reliable information to the effect that Lee was fleeing before a mere "strong covering party" of the enemy. Lee retorted that Washington's information might be correct, but that the British were stronger than his force, and that it would have been unwise to act in any other way than he did. Washington then asserted that Lee should not have accepted his assignment if he had not intended to attack the British. Upon the assumption that Washington was demanding to know why he had not initiated a general action, Lee retorted that he had been opposed to one, but had been willing, and had done his best to execute his orders.[29]

Washington then rode off, giving commands toward making a stand against the British. Lee also began to issue instructions, but his aide Mercer informed him that the commander in chief had apparently taken over and suggested that it would be unwise for him to give contradictory orders. Lee then rescinded his orders, upon the assumption that he no longer had authority, and rode away after Washington.[30] Washington personally checked Lee's retreating men, trying to use some and sending back others who were exhausted. He particularly called upon Wayne to stem the British advance. Meanwhile, he was making arrangements to place his own men on the position behind the west ravine pointed out to Lee by Peter Wikoff. The British were pushing forward and their artillery was supporting them. At this time Washington no doubt began to suspect that Clinton had more than a "strong covering party" on the field. Clinton had come to the conclusion that his baggage was safe after Lee fell back across the middle ravine, but he had decided to push on toward the west ravine in the hope of driving the Americans against it. He calculated that it was a venture which would cost little and which might bring him a handsome victory.[31] But the tactics followed by Lee and independently continued by Washington destroyed the British general's opportunity.

Lee, following Washington, found him busily engaged upon a hill. Washington saw him. Knowing that the major British threat which Lee had guarded against and which he himself had discounted was a reality, the commander in chief possibly felt some uneasiness regarding his recent behavior toward the Englishman. Deciding that his presence was needed in the rear, he asked Lee to assume command of the troops covering the retirement. Lee responded, evidently with some tartness, that Washington had already entrusted that command to him. The Vir-

ginian answered merely by saying that he expected Lee to take
proper measures to check the enemy at that spot. Lee asserted
that Washington's order would be obeyed and that he would
not be the first to leave the field, whereupon Washington rode
away.[32] Alexander Hamilton, who was present, enthusiastically
exclaimed that he would fight with Lee upon that spot until
death. Lee, once more cool and collected, dryly observed to
Hamilton that he still had command of his senses, that the hill
upon which they stood was worth no great sacrifice, that he
must first of all care for his command, and that he would then
willingly join Hamilton in a defense of the hill until death.[33]
Later Hamilton did not remember this scene with any great
pleasure and asserted that *Lee* was not in full control of himself
at this juncture.

Meanwhile, Wayne under Washington's direction had taken
position to Lee's left in a wood. Lee sent orders to him to stand
until the last man (which Wayne considered superfluous) and
arranged for the defense of the hill upon which he was and the
grounds immediately to his left. Posting artillery there, he himself took a position in the center. The British attacked promptly.
They were resisted, but Lee eventually found it necessary to
send his center and left successively back across the bridge over
the west ravine, while Wayne continued to hold in the wood.
Lee himself brought up the rear of his retreating columns.[34]
While these events were in progress, Washington's men had
come forward and had taken up a strong position upon and near
the hill west of the ravine. Lee again met Washington upon the
hill, commented to him that the difficulties which had developed
arose from British superiority in open country because of their
cavalry, and again declared that he was opposed to a general
action.[35] He asked Washington what he should do with his
spent forces. Washington ordered him to lead them to Englishtown and to re-form them there, in a defensible position, where
they might be useful in the event that Washington was unable
to hold the hill. However, the commander in chief later stopped
some of Lee's detachments and called upon them to support his
own men. Lee moved on toward Englishtown, leaving the scene
of the fighting. There he began to reorganize his men. But

Steuben soon appeared with orders from Washington to undertake that task. Lee abandoned the job to Steuben, indicating that he was very tired.

While Lee, joined by one of his dogs, unhappily made his way from the field, the fighting increased in intensity. Clinton realized that Washington's position behind the west ravine, with Wayne in the woods on Washington's left, was a very strong one and that a direct frontal attack would be expensive and hazardous. However, some of his troops charged without orders; Clinton was therefore forced to cover their advance and was accordingly committed to an attack upon Wayne and Washington's left, and also upon Washington's right flank. Neither of these movements was very successful, and Washington counterattacked in some strength. Clinton's men, like the Americans, were suffering from exhaustion and the heat. Later, Clinton asserted that he would have continued his assaults, had he had one additional brigade of fresh troops. As it was, he decided to fall back to a position east of the middle ravine. There he placed his men upon a spot where his flanks were more or less protected by woods on both sides, with the ravine in front. Washington ordered his men forward to renew the struggle, but night fell before he could accomplish anything more.

In the afternoon of the twenty-eighth Clinton sent orders to General James Grant to bring back toward Monmouth a large part of the force which had covered the baggage train. Clinton then planned to assail Washington with the bulk of his army on the twenty-ninth, should Washington give him an opportunity. However, for some unknown reason, Grant failed to obey his orders. Consequently, about midnight, after his troops had recovered somewhat from their weariness, Clinton quietly left the field and marched rapidly off toward Middletown.[36] The American army seems not to have noticed his retirement, although it is difficult to believe the movements of the British were noiseless. In any case, Washington saw no hope of achieving anything by following Clinton because, if for no other reason, he could not catch the British before they reached Middletown, where they would have great geographical advantages in their favor. Clinton reached Sandy Hook without further molestation. Lord Howe, who had in the meantime sailed from Philadelphia and who had managed to escape D'Estaing's fleet, met him there. Early in July Clinton's army was safe in New York.

Who was the victor at Monmouth? In reporting the engagement to Congress on July 1, Washington did not claim a victory. His report was cautiously worded, although he claimed that British losses were larger than his own.[37] Three days later he wrote to John Augustine Washington, his brother, saying that the "battle . . . from an unfortunate and bad beginning, turned out a glorious and happy day," and that the American army had "recovered the field of battle."[38] On July 6 Henry Laurens spoke of the engagement as "a partial victory" for the Americans.[39] On July 2, however, Congress unanimously passed a resolution of thanks to Washington for his "important victory." It was, of course, sound psychologically for the Americans to claim a "victory," and the word has frequently appeared in descriptions of the engagement by American writers. Indeed, American historians who have made no study of the Monmouth fight sometimes go so far as to declare that Washington might have or would have won an overwhelming victory, had it not been for Lee's bad behavior. Lee's view in retrospect was that the Americans had effectively checked Clinton's counterattack, but that they could not have driven Clinton from the field. He remained convinced that a general action between the two armies could not have ended in a major American success.[40] Clinton's later analyses agree substantially with Lee's judgment. The British general emphasized the fact that his forces as well as those of Washington remained upon the field at the close of the day. He insisted that his assault upon the American position behind the west ravine was actually only a protective operation, and that his withdrawal beyond the middle ravine at the end of the day was dictated not by American pressure but by tactical considerations. He continued to argue that a general action would have ended in an American defeat. Moreover, Clinton contended that he checked the American attack at Monmouth, protected his baggage, and secured a safe retreat to New York—in effect, that he obtained important advantages and that the American secured none.[41] There is much sound logic in the

British commander's analysis. It is true, however, that the main American army, which had not won any major victories and which had suffered a number of serious reverses in earlier campaigns, had given a good account of itself and had held its own in the fighting. Certainly, Washington's management of his troops on the field deserved praise. It would seem that his plan for assaulting Clinton, if it contemplated a partial stroke, exhibited no great genius; if—what seems to be very unlikely—he intended to make a general attack, his arrangements were not without serious faults.[42]

CHAPTER FIFTEEN

COURT-MARTIAL

They out-talk'd thee, hiss'd thee, tore thee!
Better men fared thus before thee....
ARNOLD, *The Last Word*

W HAT WASHINGTON thought about Lee immediately
after the engagement at Monmouth cannot now be
ascertained. Washington, in relative tranquillity at
least, possessed that great quality called good judgment; and it
is therefore to be suspected that he was not at all sure Lee's behavior had been reprehensible. He may even have regretted his
stern reprimand on the field. On the other hand, he could hardly
have failed to resent the open and implied criticism which Lee
had thrown out against him, both at their first memorable meeting and at their third meeting on the field. Moreover, officers
attached to Washington, on the basis of their observations of the
fighting and their loyalty to him, probably spoke to him against
Lee. Even as Washington had assumed command on the field
his aide John Fitzgerald had told the commander in chief that
he "expected" Lee's behavior "would be subject of enquiry for
a future day."[1] Lee declares that even Washington's reprimand
was "instigated by some of those dirty earwigs who will forever
insinuate themselves near persons in high office."[2] Recalling that
before Lee rejoined the army he had spoken slightingly of the
abilities of the officers surrounding Washington, that Lee was
something of a rival of Washington for military glory, and that
relations between the two generals were not cordial before the
engagement, one is therefore inclined to believe that members
of Washington's staff, especially his young and hotheaded aides-
de-camp, were hostile to Lee before the Monmouth fight and
that they censured his conduct both during and immediately
after it.[3]

There can be no question but that Lee deeply resented Washington's reprimand both at the time and later. His vanity was grievously wounded, especially since he believed he had prevented Clinton from achieving a major success. His vanity was hurt all the more because of the implication in the remarks made to him by Washington and Hamilton that he was not in full possession of himself upon the field. Those remarks seemed to reflect unfavorably not only upon his abilities but also upon his courage. As Lee rode toward Englishtown after leaving the scene, he met Dr. David Griffith, physician and chaplain in a Virginia regiment. In a conversation with Griffith, heard by other officers, he defended his own actions and angrily inveighed against Washington's tactics. At Englishtown he carried on publicly in similar vein.[4] That evening he drafted a letter to Richard Henry Lee, bitterly protesting against the treatment he had received, and asserting that his maneuvers had saved the army, and perhaps America.[5]

That Washington did not intend, at least immediately after Monmouth, to accuse Lee formally of misconduct is indicated by the fact that on June 30 he selected Lee to serve as executive major general for July 1. But reports of Lee's angry talk after he left the field, and possibly of other statements by Lee, undoubtedly reached his ears and further annoyed him. He was certainly in no mood to admit he himself had erred, either in his military actions or in his treatment of Lee. And Lee demanded of him an opportunity to clear himself of imputations placed on his conduct by the commander in chief in their remarkable conversation on the battlefield!

A prudent man in Lee's position after Monmouth would have guarded his tongue and would at least have waited until Washington had had time to consider calmly the situation and events of June 28. It was hardly likely that the commander in chief would ever admit—because of his pride if for no other reason—that his subordinate had acted in admirable fashion. It was possible, however, that Washington, after learning for certain that Clinton had had sufficient men upon the field to crush Lee's advanced force and even to strike effectively at the bulk of the American army, would have made it clear to the army and the public that Lee had not been seriously at fault. A coolheaded man in Lee's predicament might have accepted a temporary and not too unfavorable verdict on himself with the thought that time and more careful consideration would give him his due. Lee might conceivably have attempted to discuss the whole affair privately with the commander in chief and to persuade him that an injustice had been done. Certainly to demand an immediate public inquiry was a most imprudent step, for a verdict favorable to him would inevitably inflict some damage upon Washington himself. But Lee was not prudent, not modest, and not timid. He obviously did not realize he could hardly win a public contest between Washington and himself, even though the facts were heavily in his favor. On June 29 or June 30 he wrote angrily to Washington. By mistake he dated his letter July 1:

> From the knowledge I have of your Excellency's character, I must conclude that nothing but the misinformation of some very stupid, or misrepresentation of some very wicked person, could have occasioned your making use of so very singular expressions as you did on my coming up to the ground where you had taken post; they imply'd that I was guilty either of disobedience of orders, of want of conduct, or want of courage; your Excellency will, therefore, infinitely oblige me by letting me know on which of these three articles you ground your charge, that I may prepare for my justification, which, I have the happiness to be confident, I can do to the army, to the Congress, to America, and to the world in general. Your Excellency must give me leave to observe that neither yourself nor those about your person cou'd, from your situation, be in the least judges of the merits or demerits of our manoeuvres; and, to speak with a becoming pride, I can assert, that to these manoeuvres, the success of the day was entirely owing. I can boldly say, that had we remained on the first ground, or had we advanc'd, or had the retreat been conducted in a manner different from what it was, this whole army, and the interests of America, would have risk'd being sacrificed. I ever had, (and hope ever shall have) the greatest respect and veneration for General Washington; I think him endow'd with many great and good qualities; but in this instance, I must pronounce that

he has been guilty of an act of cruel injustice towards a man who certainly has some pretensions to the regard of ev'ry servant of this country; and, I think, sir, I have a right to demand some reparation for the injury committed, and unless I can obtain it, I must, in justice to myself, when this campaign is closed (which I believe will close the war), retire from a service at the head of which is placed a man capable of offering such injuries; but, at the same time, in justice to you, I must repeat, that I from my soul believe, that it was not a motion of your own breast, but instigated by some of those dirty earwigs who will forever insinuate themselves near persons in high office; for I am really convinced, that when General Washington acts for himself no man in his army will have reason to complain of injustice or indecorum.[6]

Lee's demand that Washington make a specific charge or charges against him so that he could defend himself "to the army, to the Congress, and to the world in general" was in effect a request for a court of inquiry or a court-martial. Conceivably, Lee would have been satisfied with a written statement from Washington which he himself could refute in print, Washington having the privilege of rebuttal. But the commander in chief, not a man of the pen, would never have accepted Lee's challenge to such a contest. And of course, such a debate would have been seriously hurtful to the American cause. Washington could have treated Lee's letter as the product of an embittered man and could have attempted privately to reach an amicable understanding with him. However, the letter came to Washington on June 30, almost simultaneously with a formal condemnation of Lee's behavior at the beginning of the engagement sent to him by Anthony Wayne and Charles Scott. Scott's actions upon the field had been assailed by Lee, and statements by him should have been received with reserve. However, this document no doubt led Washington toward a decision to deal sternly with Lee.[7] The same day he informed Lee that he would have an opportunity to justify himself in a military investigation.

I received your letter (dated through mistake the 1st of July), expressed, as I conceive, in terms highly improper.

I am not conscious of having made use of any very singular expressions at the time of my meeting you, as you intimate. What I recollect to have said was dictated by duty and warranted by the occasion. As soon as circumstances will permit you shall have an opportunity either of justifying yourself to the army, to Congress, to America, and to the world in general, or of convincing them that you were guilty of a breach of orders, and of misbehaviour before the enemy on the 28th inst. in not attacking them as you had been directed, and in making an unnecessary, disorderly, and shameful retreat. [8]

Although its purpose was not of a nature to please the commander in chief and in spite of the fact it contained much self-praise, Lee's letter to Washington was couched in respectful terms and expressed the belief that Washington would not knowingly commit an injustice. The commander in chief's reply was contemptuous in tone and vindictive in content. His notice that Lee would be accused of having made a *"shameful"* retreat indicates animus against his subordinate and a disposition to hurt him as much as possible.

When John Fitzgerald brought Washington's reply to Lee, the latter's rage may be imagined. He hurried off a rejoinder, misdating it June 28: "I beg your Excellency's pardon for the inaccuracy of misdating my letter. You cannot afford me greater pleasure than in giving me the opportunity of shewing to America the sufficiency of her respective servants. I trust that the temporary power of office, and the tinsel dignity attending it, will not be able, by all the mists they can raise, to offiscate the bright rays of truth; in the meantime, your Excellency can have no objection to my retiring from the army." [9] But Lee was not satisfied even with this tart and unsubmissive statement. He soon addressed a third letter to his superior, asking for a court-martial rather than a court of inquiry, because a court of inquiry would probably be too slow and too inefficient. In making this request Lee dared Washington to do his worst, for a court of inquiry could merely give an opinion, while a court-martial could impose sentence. Lee obviously believed he would not be found guilty of the charges Washington proposed to bring against him.

> Since I had the honour of addressing my letter by Colonel Fitzgerald to your Excellency, I have reflected on both your situation and mine, and beg leave to observe, that it will be for our mutual convenience that a court of enquiry should be immediately ordered: but I could wish it might be a court-martial, for if the affair is drawn into length, it may be difficult to collect the necessary evidences, and perhaps might bring on a paper war betwixt the adherents to both parties, which may occasion some disagreeable feuds on the continent, for all are not my friends, nor all your admirers. I must intreat, therefore, from your love of justice, that you will immediately exhibit your charge, and that on the first halt, I may be brought to a tryal. . . .[10]

It can hardly be denied that this letter and its predecessor were a trifle less than completely respectful to Washington.

Washington wasted no time in proceeding against Lee. After reading these letters and before June 30 had ended he ordered Colonel Alexander Scammell, deputy adjutant general, to place Lee under arrest and to read to him the charges upon which he would be tried by court-martial.[11] He did not coolly consider the situation, and he hastily added a new charge against Lee: that the first two letters he had received from Lee that day had exhibited disrespect for the commander in chief. The indictment which Scammell read to Lee accused him of "disobedience of orders, in not attacking the enemy on the 28th of June, agreeable to repeated instructions"; "misbehaviour before the enemy on the same day, by making an unnecessary, disorderly, and shameful retreat"; and "disrespect to the commander in chief in two letters dated the 1st of July and the 28th of June."[12] The added charge must have astonished Lee; and apparently it arose from personal animus rather than from public duty. It is difficult to discern any public loss which would arise from the omission of the charge; and it is not easy to find any considerable public good which might have been derived from publishing the letters and securing Lee's conviction.[13] It would seem, to describe Washington's action in military parlance, that the commander in chief threw the book at Lee. If he were found guilty of all the charges, or of the first two, death was not an illogical penalty.

Possibly Washington's determination to bring his subordinate before a military court is explained in part by a belief that Lee was guilty of treachery on the battlefield, that he acted as he did to assist the British. Almost immediately after the battle John Laurens and Alexander Hamilton, Washington's aides, expressed such a suspicion.[14] His friend Lafayette may have shared the sentiment with Laurens and Hamilton.[15] It is fairly likely that the commander in chief entertained the same suspicion. Sometime in July he wrote to his stepson, John Parke Custis, that there was at Monmouth "a capital blunder or something else somewhere."[16] Indeed, questioning of Lee's loyalty was probably widespread in the army within a few days after the battle. On July 6, Colonel John Bannister, a Virginia officer, noted that Lee was "under great suspicions of misconduct and bad intentions."[17] If Washington thought Lee was guilty of treachery on the battlefield, there was no direct evidence—and no indirect evidence worthy of the name—to support his view. To bring a charge against Lee on that score would of course have been absurd.

Washington wasted no time in setting the judicial machinery in motion. On July 1 he appointed the court-martial to hear his charges against Lee. The Earl of Stirling was chosen president. With him were selected Brigadier Generals Smallwood, Poor, Woodford, and Huntington, and Colonels Johnston, Wigglesworth, Febiger, Swift, Angell, Clark, and Grayson. John Laurance, judge advocate general, personally acted for the United States. Stirling was ready to proceed to business on July 2, but the trial was held up by Lee, who objected to the earl as a member of the court, because he had been told that Stirling had already expressed an opinion on the case unfavorable to himself. "I think it more eligible for many reasons that Monsr de Calb [Kalb] shou'd be president instead of yourself," Lee wrote to Stirling. Stirling replied that he had neither expressed nor formed an opinion, and he offered to resign a "most disagreeable" office if Lee continued to object to his presence on the court. Lee probably wanted Baron von Kalb to serve because of the baron's extensive experience in European warfare, possibly also because he was on friendly terms with the baron. He may have thought Stirling too friendly to Washington to be impartial.[18] On the other hand, if Stirling stepped aside, Washington might appoint in his stead some officer more attached to himself than was the American lord. In any case, Lee did not repeat his objection. The trial was delayed again while Colonel William Grayson was replaced by Colonel William Irvine, so that Grayson, who had participated actively in the battle, could testify for the prosecution. This change was no doubt an unfortunate one for Lee, since Irvine was probably hostile to him[19] and Grayson was no doubt his friend.[20] The court heard evidence from July 4 to August 9, and finally gave its verdict on August 12. Lee conducted his own defense. Since the army was on the move toward the lower Hudson during this period, and since the services of the officers hearing the case might be needed at any time, it met at various places in New Jersey and New York.

While the public eagerly and vainly tried to penetrate the veil of secrecy surrounding the proceedings of the court-martial, Lee fought effectively for his life, his reputation, and his military career. The most important witnesses for the prosecution were Wayne, Scott, and some of Washington's aides-de-camp. As was to be expected, Wayne and Scott did their best to damage Lee, especially since they could most effectively avert criticism of their own conduct by attacking his. With less excuse for doing so John Fitzgerald, Alexander Hamilton, John Laurens, Richard Kidder Meade, and Richard H. Harrison also said everything they could against Lee. All young, they were no doubt eager to display their loyalty to their chief.[21] Conceivably, they also realized that it was to their interest to support Washington against Lee. It cannot be said they were not honestly convinced that the prisoner deserved severe punishment. In any case, they consistently represented Lee's actions and conversation in the most unfavorable manner, and they made much of what they did not see him do and of what they did not hear him say. Indeed, they were so eager to secure Lee's condemnation that they overreached themselves. Thus they tried to make it appear that Lee was confused, flustered, and embarrassed on the battlefield, only to be completely refuted by half a dozen other witnesses who asserted that he was cool, collected, and in complete control of himself. Hamilton, cross-questioned by Lee on this contention, was made to seem foolish. The animus which dominated their testimony and which they did not hide discredits it now and must have cast doubt upon it in the minds of the members of the court.

The testimony of other prosecution witnesses is open to even more serious criticism. Thus Pierre l'Enfant[22] was called upon by the prosecution to relate a conversation he had with Lee upon the field—and needed an interpreter, because of his unfamiliarity with English! Lee could hardly have conversed with him in French, because Lee's French had become rusty. Indeed, Lee declared he could not even remember talking to him. The unfavorable testimony of L'Enfant was almost ludicrous, and Lee treated it and L'Enfant with contempt. The remarks of Dr. David Griffith, another prosecution witness, were worth even less than those of the Frenchman. He was not on the battlefield, and his evidence was concerned only with statements made by Lee after he had left the field—statements, moreover, without much reference to the issues before the court.

As might be expected, Lee's principal witnesses were his aides, including Evan Edwards, John Francis Mercer, and John Brooks, the latter, Lee's adjutant. These young men defended him as ardently as Washington's aides attacked him; and their motivation was no doubt partly similar. They were not inferior in character and ability to their counterparts serving Washington. Edwards was a lean and lanky Pennsylvanian who was studying at the college in Rhode Island (later Brown University) in preparation for the Baptist ministry when the war broke out. He promptly enlisted and served throughout the war. Although he had acquired polish under Lee's tutelage, he never took a great part in public life; but he was highly respected and liked for his modesty, good humor, honesty, and abilities. Both Mercer and Brooks in maturity were prominent in public affairs, Mercer serving as governor of Maryland and

Brooks holding the same office in Massachusetts. Edwards, Mercer, and Brooks strove mightily to exculpate their chief, and not without effect. They were given strong support, especially by several artillery officers, including Eleazer Oswald, Major Samuel Shaw, and Henry Knox,[23] the commander of the artillery branch. Peter Wikoff contributed a sworn statement which went far toward justifying Lee's behavior.

The witnesses for the defense, Lee's cross-questioning, and Lee's long address to the court after the taking of evidence had been concluded, made it clear that the case against him was extremely weak, except with reference to the charge of disrespect to the commander in chief. Lee could and did defend himself against that accusation on the ground that his resentment against the treatment given him by Washington had provoked him. He also cogently argued that his letters to the commander in chief were private rather than public. But his defense against this charge, though reasonable, tended to excuse his behavior rather than technically to acquit him of it.[24]

Strangely enough, Lee, confident of the outcome, failed to obtain the services of a witness who could offer most valuable testimony in his behalf. Indeed, he afterward declared that he refused to use several persons who desired to speak for him, in the belief that their statements would not be needed to obtain an acquittal.[25] Certainly he omitted calling upon Major John Clark, who could have described the contents of the message he carried from Washington to Lee and of that he carried from Lee to Washington. It would seem Lee had even forgotten Clark's name.[26] Clark's evidence would have tended to prove that Washington expected Lee only to harass Clinton. What was equally important, it would have countered the evidence of others to the effect that Lee did not keep his superior informed of his situation and plans. While the prisoner was not charged with neglecting to inform Washington, his cause was weakened by the omission of Clark's evidence.

The man who might have cleared Lee beyond all reasonable doubt was never in the courtroom, for Clinton's evidence and opinions could not be received. Clinton's report on Monmouth to Lord Germain, written on July 5, was not seen by Americans until long after Lee's trial was ended; and the many notes he made concerning the battle remained unknown for decades. It is likely, however, that even the Gospel according to St. Mark would not have sufficed to save Lee. On August 12, three days after he made his final appeal to the military tribunal, the verdict and a sentence was announced by the court. He was found guilty of the first charge. With respect to the second, he was convicted of "making an unnecessary, and in some few instances, a disorderly retreat." The court failed to accept Washington's adjective "shameful," and inserted the strange phrase "in some few instances." Lee was also declared guilty of the third charge. He was sentenced to be suspended from any command in the army of the United States for a period of one year.[27]

Although those little familiar with the details of Monmouth and the trial, including historians, entertain a belief that there was something sinister in Lee's conduct on the field, the verdict was utterly inconsistent with the facts now known regarding the Monmouth engagement and it was almost equally inconsistent with the testimony given at the trial. Many persons at the time were well aware of the startling discrepancy between the testimony and the verdict; and almost every scholar who has examined the trial record with some care without—and even with—a desire to find Washington perfection itself has noted the amazing contrast between the known facts and the official opinion of the court.[28] Forty-five years afterward, when Jacob Morris wished to defend the memory of his mentor and friend, he merely republished the official record.[29] Many persons at the time and careful, informed scholars since have also observed the gap between the enormous crimes of which Lee was convicted and the relatively light punishment imposed upon him. If he was actually guilty as found on the first and second charges, the death penalty could have been imposed. It has been concluded accordingly that the court, even after watering down Washington's charges, was not convinced of the justice of its verdict, and that it therefore chose the lightest penalty possible. It seems fair to say, as these persons have said, that Lee was guilty only of disrespect to the commander in chief, neither a great crime nor under the circumstances an inexcusable one.[30]

Reaching the conclusion that Lee was innocent with respect to the major charges laid against him, one must admit that the anger he exhibited because of the treatment given him by Washington was not unjustified. He certainly displayed moral courage, if not prudence, in challenging the commander in chief. Other American officers who were made to feel their chief's displeasure on other occasions in less public fashion apparently failed energetically to protest, except Hamilton, who also possessed moral courage in high degree.

The conclusion that Lee was not guilty in regard to the two important charges leads almost inevitably to another judgment, that he was innocent of treachery on the day of Monmouth. Upon superficial consideration one may be tempted to transfer the suspicion of Lee's motives arising from his plan of March 29, 1777, to the battlefield. One may similarly be inclined to interpret the events of the day in terms of Lee's desire for a peace giving America less than independence. But there was in Lee's plan, even according to the most unfavorable view of his intentions, nothing in the nature of betrayal of his comrades in battle; and there is certainly no substantial reason to believe that his opinion regarding the Anglo-American relationship points toward betrayal at Monmouth. On the other hand, his military reputation and his personal pride were at stake at Monmouth. He insisted on having the command of the advanced force because he believed his military honor required that he have the command; and it is difficult to believe he did not do his best to preserve that honor on the field. That he did his best for the American army is rather clearly indicated by the evidence brought before the court.

It is not at all improbable that Lee, guilty neither with regard to the official charges made against him nor of treachery, actually rendered most valuable service to the United States on June 28, 1778—service far more important than that which he gave on and immediately before the June 28 when he led the Americans to victory over Clinton and Parker at Charleston. It is quite likely that his retrograde movements at Monmouth prevented Clinton from delivering a smashing counterattack, as both Lee and Clinton contended. A thesis put forth by the

British soldier and contemporary historian Charles Stedman[31] that Lee far outshone both Clinton and Washington in generalship on that torrid June day is by no means untenable.

If it be admitted, as it must, that the judgment of the military court was inconsistent with the facts, we must ask why the court deliberately committed an act of grave injustice. Perhaps many of its members were honestly convinced that Lee deserved punishment, in spite of the evidence, but it is not likely. A partial explanation is surely to be found in the fact that the judges as army officers were largely dependent upon Washington for future promotion. The determining factor in the minds of the judges, however, was that they saw the trial, whether or not they confessed it to themselves, as a contest for prestige and power between the commander in chief and his aggressive subordinate. The charges against Lee were obviously made by Washington personally; and it was equally apparent that Lee had challenged the wisdom and behavior of his superior. If Lee were acquitted, Washington would surely be greatly disappointed. Indeed, he would suffer a serious blow. On the other hand, if Lee were convicted, the commander in chief would be exalted. A further reason for finding against the defendant arose from Lee's well-known friendship with Gates and the fact that Lee was believed to be in sympathy with those who had attempted to secure the replacement of Washington by the hero of Saratoga during the previous winter.[32] Almost certainly the judges viewed the trial not only as a contest between Lee and Washington but also as one between the members of the "Conway Cabal" and Washington. They must have feared confusion at headquarters, indeed that the services of Washington might be lost, should they find Lee innocent. The commander in chief then had a far more numerous following than Lee in the army and no doubt commanded the loyalty of several members of the court. Perhaps others, not specially admirers of Washington, wanted no part in a verdict which might lead to his resignation or removal, to dissension in the army, and possibly even to disaster for the American cause.[33]

That such were the sentiments and considerations which swayed the court cannot be proved by statements from its members, who apparently preserved a prudent silence. These sentiments and considerations were, however, expressed by others at the time of the trial. Statements made by Benedict Arnold to Clinton after Arnold went over to the British have some value— truth may come from the mouth of a traitor. Sir Henry recorded Arnold's remarks: "Arnold told me speaking of Monmouth & W that at all the councils of W. where he assisted A was determined not to risk general action that A has often heard the officers express their disapprobation of W. conduct private as well as publick on that day. That Lee's was generally approved. That W. had condemned it in a hurry & his pride would not let him acknowledge the truth & that all the officers in general have said since, that W. popularity & Lee unpopularity determined them to back him."[34] A statement made by Gershom Mott, an army officer who was a Washington partisan, undoubtedly throws some light on contemporary opinion of the issues in the trial. He wrote to Colonel John Lamb on July 25: "The devils are now cock a hoop, flattering themselves, that they now shall have it in their power to ruin G. Washington on acct of his arresting Lee. . . . Now Gates & tools will work like the children of Hell."[35] Whether Gates and his satanic followers actually hoped to use the trial to discredit Washington is not known, but Dr. William Shippen, Jr., assured Richard Henry Lee after the verdict was given that Gates, Henry Knox, Samuel Holden Parsons, Alexander McDougall, Benjamin Lincoln, and other officers were convinced that an injustice had been done.[36] The attitude of Washington's supporters appears even more explicitly in a statement by John Penn, a member of Congress from North Carolina, whose opinions and actions were to be of the utmost importance to Lee. On July 15 he declared that Lee "has made it a quarrel with Genl Washington, and of course you know he must fail."[37] An entry made in his journal on July 16 by Major Samuel Shaw, who testified in Lee's behalf and who was firmly convinced that he deserved praise rather than punishment, is equally revealing. Predicting his conviction and punishment, Shaw commented: "However, people may, on the one hand, pity that unfortunate officer, and lament the severity of his fate,—or, on the other, lend their assistance to asperse a reputation in military matters, till that unhappy affair, unsullied,—yet it seems the general and prevailing sentiment, that it will not be for the good of America, should he be again admitted to command. It may be so,—perhaps it is expedient that it should be so."[38] Still further light upon the situation is derived from statements by Samuel Holden Parsons, who urged disposition of Lee at the time of the trial purely on ground of public welfare. Hearing a false report that Lee had been convicted and dismissed from the army early in July, he insisted the verdict and sentence should be revoked. He feared that a disgraced Lee would do serious hurt to the American cause by going over to the British. He therefore argued that Lee should merely be transferred to some post where he could do no harm, or that he should be executed, again so that he could do no injury to the United States.[39] Parsons thought then wholly in terms of the necessities of the state and not at all of justice, whatever may have been his attitude later.

It cannot be seriously doubted but that the court-martial sacrificed Lee because of partisan passions in the army and a belief that the public welfare should override all other considerations. It remained to be seen whether its work would stand, for American military law then required the confirmation of the verdict and sentence by Congress itself. Conceivably, Congress, directing a struggle in behalf of human freedom, would reverse the judgment of the court in the interest of justice.

CHAPTER SIXTEEN

THE JUDGMENT OF CONGRESS

Pshaw! we all must bear
The arrogance of something higher than
Ourselves—the highest cannot temper Satan,
Nor the lowest his vicegerents upon earth.
I've seen you brave the elements, and bear
Things which had made this silkworm cast his skin—
And shrink you from a few sharp sneers and words?
BYRON, *Werner; or, the Inheritance*

THE WASHINGTON-LEE quarrel reached the newspapers and the public almost as soon as the report of the Monmouth engagement itself, and it promptly became the center of heated discussion. Washington's version of the events of June 28, contained in his official report to Congress of July 1, was the first to reach the public, for Congress promptly ordered his letter published. Washington referred only briefly to Lee in this document. The commander in chief reported that he felt "great surprise and mortification" when he met "the whole advanced corps retreating, and as I was told, by General Lee's orders, without having made any opposition except one fire given by the party under the command of Col. Butler." Remarking that Lee was to be tried by court-martial, he said that the "peculiar situation of Gen. Lee at this time requires that I should say nothing of his conduct." He had said enough, of course, to suggest his complete disapproval of Lee's behavior. He described in some detail the occurrences on the field after his own arrival, quite properly giving himself much credit for checking the British counterthrust.[1]

It quickly became known that Lee had a different version. Governor William Livingston of New Jersey prepared an account of Monmouth which was amended by Joseph Reed and printed in the *New Jersey Gazette* at Trenton on July 1. This description contained nothing positively unfavorable to Lee. It did declare, however, "Our success, under heaven, is to be wholly ascribed to the good disposition made by his Excellency, supported by the firmness and bravery of both officers and men. . . ."[2] Good judgment would have led Lee to ignore this account, but he protested bitterly in a letter of July 3 to Isaac Collins, the publisher, denouncing it as "a most invidious, dishonest, and false relation." "Before long" he would supply "a minute, just, and faithful" description. In a postscript larger than the letter, he indicated briefly but not specifically that part of the credit for checking the British counterthrust belonged to him and that he wanted recognition of his services. He asked Collins to see to it that his protest was published in Philadelphia. Collins printed it in his newspaper on July 8.[3]

July 3—the day before his trial began—must have been a busy day for Lee. He was preparing for his trial, and he dashed off letters to Robert Morris and Joseph Reed in addition to that to Isaac Collins. His letter to Morris was another effort to tell confidentially his side of his quarrel with Washington to those he considered his best friends in Philadelphia, Morris, Richard Henry Lee, William Duer, and others. He feared that Washington's official report and private letters of those supporting Washington might permanently sway both public and Congressional opinion against him unless he offered a prompt rebuttal. He bitterly poured out his heart to Morris.

> . . . have we not a gracious prince on the throne? is he not still the same? I trust he is; but there is something rotten betwixt him and his people—not content with robbing me and the brave men under my command of the honor due to us—a most hellish plan has been formed (and I may say at least not discourag'd by head quarters) to destroy for ever my honour and reputation—I have demanded a court martial which has fortunately been granted—if I had been let alone, I should with patience have suffered 'em to pick up the laurels which I had shaken down and lay'd at their feet; but the outrageous attacks made are enough to drive patience itself to madness . . . .

Washington, "by all that's sacred," had hardly more to do at Monmouth than "to strip the dead." He himself, threatened by the flower of the British army and especially by a cavalry flanking attack, had withdrawn his men safely, in spite of the "temerity, folly, and contempt of orders" of Wayne and the refusal of other officers to heed his commands. He had maneuvered the British into a position where they could not hope to gain any advantage. After Washington took over, there was a cannonading on both sides, but the British could not and did not attempt an attack in force.

> The general has the madness to charge me with making a shameful retreat—I never retreated in fact . . . but a necessary and I may say in my own defence masterly manoeuvre. . . . Such is my recompense for having sacrificed my friends, my connexions, and perhaps my fortune for having twice extricated this man and his whole army out of perdition, and now having given him the only victory he ever tasted. Do not my dr friend imagine I talk in this heated manner to every man—to you I venture to pour out my indignation—but I give you my word I am so sensible of my ticklish situation that I am with others perfectly moderate and guarded.

He requested Morris to show "the cool parts" of his letter to Richard Henry Lee, Duer, and to "what others you think prudent."[4]

To Reed, Lee protested against the account of Monmouth which appeared in Collins' newspaper, and more particularly against Reed's behavior in helping to prepare it. Reed, who had been present as a civilian observer at Monmouth and who had merely made some corrections in, and additions to, the description written by Livingston, insisted that he had done no ill to Lee. The two men met shortly afterward near Morristown, and Reed gave an explanation which apparently soothed Lee. Later, however, Reed reopened the subject. He seems to have feared that Lee was still dissatisfied with him and that Lee might publish that letter of November 21, 1776, in which the Pennsylvania politician had commented so severely upon Washington's military abilities. He did not want that letter seen either by the commander in chief or by the public! On the other hand, he was determined to give his support to Washington. He wrote to Lee, defending in some detail his conduct in helping to prepare the Collins publication, and he tried to secure Lee's silence with respect to that most embarrassing letter by means of a thinly veiled threat. He was then a member of Congress and he could not "discover the prudence or wisdom of diminishing the number of your friends at such a time,—& especially those who have seats in Congress where alone you can expect to have those 'enormous injuries' redress'd of which you complain. . . ." In reply, on June 22, Lee assured Reed of his friendship, and he vigorously asserted that he had no intention of publishing Reed's letter to "embroil" him with Washington. Nor was he interested in playing politics in order to gain backers. ". . . I despise the thought—I ask only for common justice—I know, I am conscious that nothing but cabal artifice, power, and iniquity can tarnish my name for a moment. . . . I never entertained the most distant wish or intention of attacking Gen. Washington . . . but if the circle which surrounds him chuse to erect him into an infallible divinity, I shall certainly prove a heretick, and if great as he is, he can be perswaded to attempt wounding evry thing I ought to hold dear, he must thank his priests, if his deityship gets scratch'd in the scuffle. . . ." Even if his friends were carried away "in the general torrent of delusion, raised by all the wicked arts that hell can prompt . . . the dread of no power on earth shall prevent me from exposing the wickedness of my persecutors." If he were not permitted to defend himself, then the sacrifices made in the war were in vain. Lord North himself would not have established in America "a more odious despotism."[5] The result of this exchange of opinion was the complete collapse of friendly relations between the two men.[6]

If Lee sent his story to Richard Henry Lee and Robert Morris before the dust of battle had descended, at least one of his enemies also sent *his* story to Philadelphia before the air had cleared. Washington's aide John Laurens wrote to Henry Laurens, President of the Congress, on June 30 and again on July 2. To be sure, it was highly proper that the son should correspond with the parent. Through these family letters, however, the President of Congress received a narrative highly unfavorable to Lee, for the younger Laurens did not hesitate to accuse Lee of misconduct and to suggest that he was disloyal. Simultaneously he gave the highest praise to Washington. Had it not been for Lee, he mistakenly argued, Clinton's "whole flying army" would have fallen into American hands.[7] Since the father was already hostile to Lee, particularly because of Lee's effort to open a discussion of peace terms with the British before the battle, he promptly accepted the son's version. He made it clear that he would heartily support Washington—"I love and reverence him"—and that he, too, believed Lee guilty of treachery. The President of Congress, thus condemning Lee on July 6, did so before he could have known much, if anything, about Lee's defense.[8] John Laurens had struck Lee a very heavy blow.

Alexander Hamilton, by his own statement anything but an admirer of Washington at the time, wrote lengthily on July 5 to Elias Boudinot at Philadelphia in a similar vein. Lauding the commander in chief in lofty terms, he savagely assailed Lee as "either a driveler in the business of soldiership or something much worse." Yet he feared the court-martial would not condemn him, because of a "preconceived & preposterous opinion of his being a very great man." "Some people" were "very industrious in making interest for him." Whatever the court-martial might decide, Hamilton would "continue to believe and say—his conduct was monstrous and unpardonable."[9] (Hamilton was old enough to vote.) In reply Boudinot expressed hearty approval of Washington and Hamilton and exclaimed against those who "could be capable of betraying" America. He was thankful that the "Supreme Disposer of human events" baffled "not only the formidable & open force of our enemies, but also the more dangerous & secret efforts of false or lukewarm friends."[10] To lend a helping hand to the "Supreme Disposer" he asked or permitted the printer of the *Pennsylvania Packet* of Philadelphia to publish a part of Hamilton's description on July 16. The result, although Hamilton's savage comments on Lee were excised, was a public and anonymous attack on Lee.

Although sentiment in the army was by no means uniform regarding the Washington-Lee quarrel, opinion in Philadelphia was heavily against Lee during and immediately after his trial, in part no doubt because the published versions of the events of June 28 favored the commander in chief. After Evan Edwards had given his testimony Lee sent him to the American capital to get in touch with Richard Henry Lee, Thomas Mifflin, and probably others, in order to defend himself more effectively before Congress, if and when the military court held against him. Edwards found Lee's conduct "so cursedly represented in this place that I have been almost mob'd in defending you—ten thousand infamous lyes have been spread that I never heard before to byass the minds of the people against you. In the name of God, what are we come to?—So much for our republicanism."[11] Even Benjamin Rush, giving no credit to the accusation of treachery, concluded that Lee had probably blundered. Expressing his friendship and asking Lee for an explanation, he wrote an unsigned letter to him, in order to avert criticism.[12] In general the news of Lee's conviction and sentence must have been greeted with pleasure rather than anger in Philadelphia.

If Lee was confident of honorable acquittal at the beginning of his trial, he knew the tide was running against him long before its close. Nevertheless, the pronouncement of the court, even though the sentence was relatively light, was a staggering blow. To Richard Henry Lee he described himself at the end of September as a "blasted mortal."[13] But he was determined never to give up the struggle. Immediately after the court made known its decision he scolded Rush in friendly fashion for not daring to sign a letter indicating a measure of sympathy for Charles Lee.

> Your letter . . . ought . . . either to make me laugh or make me cry. If it is from excess of personal prudence, it ought to make me laugh—and if really the state of affairs are such that the force of party cabal and official power can be already grown to so dangerous a heighth that not less circumspection is necessary now in the infancy of your states than it was under the tyrannical administration of Cardinal Richelieu and Mazarine it is really a very melancholy situation . . . what the devil is it you are so all damnably afraid of?

He assured Rush that the publication of the proceedings of the court-martial would exonerate him beyond doubt, and that "G. Washington saw, knew, and was almost as little concern'd in the affair of the 28th as he was in the battle of Philippi." Daniel Jenifer, Lee's former aide, who carried the message to Rush, would give the physician the truth.[14] Lee could have resigned from the army, thus exhibiting his contempt for the decision of the military court. His resignation from the army, however, would have given his enemies almost precisely what they desired, and it would have been seen by some as an admission of guilt and by others as an act of cowardice. Instead he was resolved to fight to the last for his reputation and career. There was reason to believe that an examination of the proceedings of the court-martial by Congress might possibly lead its members to exonerate him, especially since he still had some friends in that body.

In order to put his case more effectively before Congress, Lee tardily asked Major John Clark on September 3 to give on his honor a statement regarding his actions at and his knowledge of the engagement at Monmouth. Clark did so, and Lee sent his statement to Congress, asking that it be considered as evidence together with the record of the court-martial.[15] On September 15, toward the same end, he asked Washington for permission to leave the army and to go to Philadelphia,[16] which was promptly granted.[17] Departing from the Hudson, he lingered for some days in New Jersey and finally arrived at Philadelphia early in October. He had little hope of success there, and expected to be "shunned and treated as a scoundrel," although he had friends in the army who were trying to win support for him in Congress. On September 12 Dr. William Shippen, Jr., a good friend to Lee, wrote to Richard Henry Lee, his brother-in-law, urging the Virginia delegate to fight against ratification of the verdict. He seems to have written in behalf of a large group, Gates, Henry Knox, Benjamin Lincoln, Samuel Holden Parsons, Alexander McDougall, and other officers who believed in Lee's innocence.[18]

The Congress which received the proceedings of the Lee trial on August 21 was not the Congress of 1775 and 1776, for most of the great leaders of the Revolutionary generation and several of Lee's friends were no longer members. Franklin and John Adams were in Europe on diplomatic business; Jefferson was in Virginia; and Washington, of course, was with the army. John Dickinson, John Hancock, Edward Rutledge, and Benjamin Rush were also absent from the national councils. Congress had deteriorated as to ability and character, and even in numbers. In the latter part of 1778 it contained little genius and was riddled with personal and factional strife. Statesmanship from this body in dealing with the Washington-Lee quarrel was hardly to be expected, and it did not appear. The delegates, discussing the problem in secrecy, delayed their decision for more than three months and finally acted largely on the basis of personal and partisan consideration. Lee found champions in Congress—Samuel Adams, William Paca of Maryland, and especially Richard Henry Lee. But Washington also had his ardent friends, including Henry Laurens, William Henry Drayton, and John Penn of North Carolina.

If the issue had depended merely upon Laurens, Drayton, and Penn, Congress would promptly have confirmed the action of the military court. Laurens had made up his mind long before he knew anything very much of Lee's side of the controversy. An honest man, he might conceivably have changed his opinion upon more careful consideration, but it was almost impossible for him to reverse his stand. Penn and Drayton, recently elected to Congress, acted from less laudable motives and also committed themselves against Lee before they examined the facts and arguments in his defense. Drayton, an enemy of Lee since the summer of 1776, had gone out of his way in 1777 in an address to a grand jury in South Carolina to accuse Lee of disobeying Washington's orders in December, 1776. What this performance had to do with the business of the grand jury it is difficult to discover; and it is equally difficult to find out why Lee's behavior in 1776 was properly a subject for pronouncements by Drayton, who was not familiar with all the facts and who had no authority in the matter. On July 5, Drayton, unknown personally to Washington, wrote to the commander in chief, congratulating him upon the Monmouth fight. He assured Washington that he was "tenderly and anxiously interested in every thing respecting your safety and glory."[19] In other words, Lee could expect short shrift from Drayton. Penn's attitude was equally remarkable. On July 15, he reported to Governor Caswell of North Carolina that the outcome of Lee's trial was not yet known. "However, he has made it a quarrel with Genl Washington, and of course you know he must fail."[20] Prejudging the controversy, both Drayton and Penn energetically pushed for the ratification of the judgment of the court-martial. Nothing specific about Penn's activities against Lee can be learned;[21] and Drayton did Lee much greater harm.

Although the proceedings of the military court were received in Philadelphia on August 21, the Lee case was not discussed in Congress until October 23. The delay was partly caused by the need of printing the court record, so that it could be examined by all the delegates; partly it developed from the reluctance of some members, perhaps many, to face the issue. Delegates seem to have hoped Lee would resign, saving them the necessity of making a difficult decision.[22] On September 7 the Congress quite properly refused to consider the evidence of Major Clark, which was not officially a part of the record, no matter the importance of his statements.[23]

Shortly after the Washington-Lee quarrel came before Congress, a substantial majority was in favor of confirming the action of the military court. As the weeks went on, however, the tide of opinion began to turn, partly because of the efforts of Lee and Richard Henry Lee, partly because members had had an opportunity to read the court proceedings. Those who had earlier favored the replacement of Washington by Gates tended to support Lee and to demand that the verdict of the court be set aside.[24] In debate on the floor on October 23 the opposing sides were almost evenly divided. "General Lee's affair hangs by the eyelids," wrote Gouverneur Morris to Washington on the twenty-sixth. The merits of the issue were not discussed, but merely important questions of procedure. In general, members who were hostile to Lee asked for a vote approving or disapproving the verdict and sentence. Those favoring his cause demanded consideration and votes on the charges individually, a procedure which would have been much to his advantage.[25] By following such an arrangement, members who were convinced of his guilt on the third charge but not on the more serious ones would be encouraged to express their opinion. Moreover, members who feared the influence of Washington and his friends and their supporters could soften their criticism by finding Lee guilty of disrespect and at the same time cleanse Lee's reputation. William Paca was one of those who pushed hard for separate decisions on the charges. William Henry Drayton fought vigorously for a verdict upon the accusations as a whole.[26] In the end Lee's friends lost their fight for separate votes.

If the opposing sides were about equally divided in terms of potential votes on October 23, it is a fair conclusion that a majority of the delegates did not believe Lee had been given justice by the military court. Anxiety not to offend the commander in chief, his supporters, and the members of the court, and fear that the American cause would suffer by a reversal in Lee's favor undoubtedly led some to set aside private justice for their own comfort and what seemed to be the public interest. Others, it is fairly certain, avoided the contest by remaining away from meetings. Rush, not an unprejudiced observer, for he feared Washington-worship and had become convinced that Lee had received grossly unfair treatment, reported the situation on the twenty-seventh to John Adams: "The Congress I believe disapprove of the sentence, but are so much afraid of the workmanship of their own hands, that they are afraid to reverse it. I blush for my country when I tell you that several members of Congress leave the house when the affair is bro't on the carpet."[27]

To many the fate of Lee must have seemed unsettled until Congress finally voted, early in December. He himself, however, realized that his cause was doomed before the end of October. His support in Congress suddenly weakened in the latter part of the month, probably because Richard Henry Lee gave up the struggle and prepared to return to Virginia. On the thirtieth, obviously in order to expose the nature of the arguments made against him, he requested Congress to open its doors to the public when the issue was debated. He told Laurens he wished "the whole world, at least the whole military world were to form the audience." He had been found guilty by the military court "to the astonishment not only of myself but of every man in the army who was present at this court, and every man out of the army who has read the proceedings." He urged an early decision, since the number of delegates present in Congress was steadily decreasing. Congress, however, continued to debate his destiny in secret and to delay its decision.[28] Lee could hardly have expected that his requests would be approved. They arose from desperation, caused at least partly by the impending departure of Richard Henry Lee for Virginia. Without the support of his most vigorous champion Lee knew he was almost certain to lose the contest in Congress. And Richard Henry left for home on November 3, supposedly because of family affairs.[29] The significance of this event was not lost on General Arthur St. Clair, who wrote meaningfully from Philadelphia to Washington some days later, "I suppose Your Excellency has heard that Mr. R. H. Lee is returned to Virginia."[30]

Lee was so certain that his cause was lost that he prepared a paper in order to vindicate himself to the public before Congress acted decisively. Meanwhile, the delegates hesitated. Finally, on December 2, his fate was again formally debated. It was then moved that the judgment of the court-martial be confirmed. Knowing that the resolution would be passed, Lee's friends countered with a motion to postpone. William Henry Drayton demanded the yeas and nays in order to put the delegates on record. The vote was thirteen to ten in favor of postponing. However, Congress balloted by states rather than by head, and it was determined to proceed with the original motion by a vote of five states to four.[31] Discussion was resumed until adjournment. On December 4 the matter was again taken up. A vote was averted by Edward Langworthy, delegate from Georgia and a supporter of Lee, who requested delay until the following session.[32] On the fifth, with Drayton again forcing a vote by yeas and nays, the delegates approved the judgment of the military court.

In the end, six states voted against Lee; two were for him, and three were divided. Two states, New Jersey and Delaware, were not sufficiently represented to cast a ballot. Fifteen individual votes, including those of Laurens, Drayton, John Penn,

Francis Lightfoot Lee, Roger Sherman, Oliver Ellsworth, James Duane, and Gouverneur Morris, were counted against him. Seven individual votes, by William Whipple, Samuel Adams, James Lovell, William Carmichael, Meriwether Smith, Cornelius Harnett, and Edward Langworthy, were cast in his favor. Although Lee's appeal from the judgment of the court was decisively turned down, it is obvious that opinion among those voting was far from unanimous against him.[33] It is equally clear that several members absented themselves in order to avoid committing themselves. In view of what has been said, few will doubt that among the absentee members those who were inclined to support Lee were more numerous than were those who were against him.[34]

Was it necessary for Congress to choose absolutely between Washington and Lee, and to strike such a heavy blow at Lee? There were alternatives. Had there been greater wisdom and less partisanship in that body, a reasonably satisfactory compromise could have been reached. Thus, Congress could have annulled the judgment of the court-martial, at the same time honorably discharging Lee from command under Washington with generous thanks and treatment for his services to the cause. Both the commander in chief and his antagonist would have been at least partly satisfied with such a solution. Moreover, it would have ended rivalry between them in the army.

Not surprised by the result,[35] Lee was of course deeply chagrined. When he heard the news he is reported to have pointed to one of his dogs and to have exclaimed, "Oh, that I was that animal! that I might not call man my brother."[36] In October he had wittily informed Aaron Burr, who had fought at Monmouth and who had defended his conduct, that whatever action Congress might take, he would resign his commission, "retire to Virginia, and learn to hoe tobacco, which I find is the best school to form a consummate general."[37] But he did not resign—he did not do so, as he later declared, because of advice from the "devil's eldest brother";[38] nor did he go off immediately to Virginia to labor in a tobacco field. Instead, he was resolved to continue his fight for vindication, and he remained in and near Philadelphia until the following spring. Even before

Congress voted, he began an appeal to the public, reprinting and distributing the court-martial proceedings[39] and publishing a lengthy and well-reasoned explanation of his conduct at Monmouth in the *Pennsylvania Packet* on December 3. In this essay he pointed out that the military court had made no real effort to find out the nature of the orders given him by Washington before Monmouth; and he argued most effectively that he could not possibly have disobeyed his instructions, unless they had called for an attack without respect to situation or consequences. Such instructions, as he indicated, Washington could not possibly have given, unless the commander in chief was hopelessly incompetent. He also offered an effective defense of his tactical maneuvers, making clear the reasons for his retrograde movements. He refrained from discussing the charge of disrespect and his relations with Washington; and his language was cool and restrained. Referring to efforts made in the trial to prove that he held a low opinion of the American soldier, he made an excellent case to the contrary and subtly turned the charge against Washington. Praising the troops to the skies and lauding them as the best in the world, he mentioned American victories won by them under commanders other than Washington; and he asserted that American defeats and disasters, mentioning specifically the fall of Fort Washington, could not be explained by faults either in the ranks or among the junior officers. He left the reader to draw his own conclusion, that the commander in chief lacked military ability and was responsible for several major defeats in the field.[40]

Simultaneously, but anonymously, Lee struck hard in another essay at the charge of disrespect, using the misfortunes of General Thomas Conway as his vehicle. Conway, the Irish-born French officer who had joined the American army and whose name has been immortalized and besmirched in the phrase "Conway Cabal," had a low opinion of Washington, and he said so in a letter to Gates. Its contents being revealed, he was attacked at the time and since as a sinister conspirator attempting by dishonorable means with other shady characters to force the removal of Washington as commander in chief. An unpopular though capable officer, he had been refused a certificate of honorable service when he resigned from the American army. Lee asked the reason and gave the answer. Conway had committed no crime, but had commented adversely upon the commander in chief. Lee then pointed out that General James Wolfe, the Duke of Marlborough, and even Frederick the Great had responded to the censure of subordinates by brilliant exploits in the field rather than by bringing them before military courts on the charge of disrespect. That Wolfe had behaved in this fashion was well known in America. Lee thus scored a point against Washington. Lee also argued that the clause in the American military code concerning disrespect, copied from the British, was intended partly as a gesture of courtesy to the commander in chief and partly to prevent officers from offering public and licentious criticism tending to create confusion among the rank and file. It was not intended to impose "a dead, torpid, idolatrous silence." His interpretation was sensible. He thus made out a strong case to the effect that Conway had been mistreated. Further, in doing so, he also defended himself rather effectively against the third charge brought against him.[41]

On December 10 the *Pennsylvania Packet* published still another item from Lee, the statement of Major Clark regarding Monmouth. These three pieces, together with the circulation of the proceedings of the court-martial, could hardly fail to have an effect. That they caused an immediate and important change in opinion in Philadelphia or elsewhere does not appear. As time went on, however, the conviction spread, even among army officers friendly to Washington, that Lee had been the victim of a great injustice.[42]

Lee's vindicatory essay of December 3, whatever its other immediate results, aroused the wrath of Washington, the two Laurenses, and Alexander Hamilton. The commander in chief poured out his injured feelings and his anger privately to Joseph Reed. Lee had "most bare-facedly misrepresented facts in some places, and thrown out insinuations in others" that had not "the smallest foundation" in truth. Lee had planned from "the moment of his arrest (though it was an event solicited by himself)" to pose as a persecuted man and a victim of "party." Washington denied he had acted because of rivalry with Lee, "unless bringing him to tryal at his own request is considered in this light." He had avoided even mentioning Lee's name so far as possible after the beginning of the trial.

If he conceives I was opposed to him because he found himself disposed to enter into a party against me—if he thought I stood in his road to preferment, and therefore that it was convenient to lessen me in the esteem of my countrymen, in order to pave the way for his own advancement—I have only to observe, that as I never entertained any jealousy of, or apprehension from him, so neither did I ever do more, than common civility and proper respect to his rank required, to conciliate his good opinion. His temper and plans were too versatile and violent to attract my admiration; and that I have escaped the venom of his tongue, and pen, so long, is more to be wondered at than applauded; as it is a favour, that no other officer under whose immediate commands he ever served has the happiness, if happiness can thus be denominated) of boasting.[43]

"First in war, first in peace, first in the hearts of his countrymen," the Virginian was mortal. Here is not a description of a conflict penned by an unbiased observer, nor even one drawn up by a participant in relative tranquillity long after the event. It will be recalled that not until he published his vindication did Lee charge Washington with making a deliberate effort to ruin him; and that even then he condemned Washington personally only because the commander in chief charged him with disrespect. All along Lee had argued that his antagonist had unfairly censured him on Monmouth field; that Washington's "earwigs," including no doubt Hamilton and John Laurens, had misled him; and that the commander in chief, having mistakenly taken a stand against him, had erred in refusing him redress. Lee *had* asserted—and with ample reason—that Washington partisans strove to destroy his reputation. It should also be observed that Washington implied his opponent had sought a court-martial in order to strike at him. This charge, made earlier by his defenders, is quite surely unfounded, for it is clear that Lee wanted his hurt pride soothed and his military credit maintained. If it be admitted—and it is generally admitted by qualified scholars—that the rebuke he received on the battlefield was without just cause, then it may be argued that it was Washington's duty as a gentleman, as soon as he learned his error, to make amends. But the commander in chief never admitted making a mistake. The real aggressor was, then, Washington, although Lee reacted with violence. It is perhaps worth adding that Washington *had* offered Lee more than ordinary courtesy in the early part of the war.

Washington had too fine a sense of dignity and too good judgment to enter into a literary quarrel with Lee. Yet he feared that Lee would sway public opinion against him, unless he were answered.[44] John Laurens resolved to reply to Lee's "infamous" vindication but came to the conclusion that Hamilton could do a better job. He asked him to undertake the task, and Hamilton seems to have consented.[45] However, nothing from his pen appeared in the press. Possibly Washington put a stop to the project. If he did so, he displayed both prudence and wisdom. After waiting out the year of suspension Lee might return to the army to plague him. But Lee was under a cloud; many things might come about during the year, including the end of the war. If he were unanswered, he might in the end hurt himself more than Washington by continuing his campaign in the newspapers.

Certainly Lee had won little active support from the newspapers. The only printer who dared to say he had been ill-used was his old friend and enemy, James Rivington. Rivington had established a newspaper, the *Royal Gazette,* in New York in 1777. On December 19 he informed his readers that Lee had been found guilty by the court-martial and by Congress when all the "intelligent" world knew he had saved the American army from destruction. Rivington's opinion must have been known to Lee, and he may have derived some slight consolation from it. To be sure, what the Tory printer had to say hardly won friends for Lee among the Americans.

CHAPTER SEVENTEEN

DUELS

And my whole soul revolves, the cup runs over,
The world and life's too big to pass for a dream,
And I do these wild things in sheer despite,
And play the fooleries you catch me at,
In pure rage!

BROWNING, *Fra Lippo Lippi*

SEVERELY battered by the struggle with his enemies and critics, Lee remained in Philadelphia and its neighborhood for
more than four months after publishing his defense. He
stayed on partly in order to obtain funds, for his pay had, of
course, been cut off. He had managed to get £1,500 from his
English properties some time in 1778, but this sum had been invested in South Carolina and brought him no income at the
moment. On February 27, 1779, Congress finally voted to lend
him another £300 so that he might develop his Virginia estate
and meet his current expenses. The sum was voted grudgingly,
on condition that Lee abandon efforts to secure money through
Colonel William Butler and other friends in the British army.[1]
But his money difficulties were not the principal cause for his
continued residence in the Quaker city. He would admit neither
that he had been guilty of misbehavior nor that the judgment of
Congress was final, and he was eager to face, and to do battle
with, his foes. Since some of his enemies were disposed to destroy him utterly, he did not lack for adversaries. Indeed, he
was challenged so directly that he could not depart for some
time because of the code of honor of an eighteenth-century
gentleman.

Trying to make political capital, Lee maintained his friendly
relations with Benjamin Rush, and with Samuel Adams and
James Lovell, who were among the members of Congress who
had supported him. He revived his former intimacy with

Thomas Mifflin, who had recently retired from the commissary department of the army under a cloud of accusations of misconduct; Mifflin was also trying to vindicate himself. Lee established cordial relations with Benedict Arnold, not because he had any affection for or trust in Arnold, but because they had a common enemy in the person of Joseph Reed. He struck up an alliance with James Wilkinson, likewise an unpopular man at the moment. He had no more love for Wilkinson than for Arnold, but he associated with both men because they might be useful, even though they were bitter enemies of his old friend Gates. None of these officers, including Gates, could effectively help him at the time, nor could Rush, who had left the medical department of the army after a squabble. Mifflin and Rush eventually regained public esteem, but not in time to achieve anything for Lee. By April, 1779, Lee knew it was at least temporarily useless for him to continue his efforts to win vindication through politics. Abandoning the fight, he advised Gates to resign before he too was besmirched by Washington's partisans. He congratulated Gates because he was serving in virtuous, republican New England rather than in Pennsylvania or New Jersey, "which are inhabited by the refuse of the Irish, the descendants of the worst part of the Germans and by the first hypocrites of the most hypocritical sects—stiff neck'd Presbyterians, Quakers, New Light men and the whole family of the devil. They have the gasconade thievery and lying of the Irish —the stupidity avarice and sordid disposition of the lower Germans—to sum up the whole, Washington is their God, Joe Reed their dictator, or rather despotic prince, and Roberdeau is a saint amongst them. . . ."[2] Lee had much more success in meeting the personal attacks of his adversaries. Receiving hard blows, he returned them in full measure.

Even before Congress finally ruled against him, Lee was assailed by Baron von Steuben. In the military court Lee had made some comments which the German general found distasteful. Lee had scoffed at testimony offered by the baron: "Of all the very distant spectators of the manoeuvres on this day, and those a very trifling part of them, the Baron Stubens is, I think, the only gentleman who has stepp'd forth to prove their demerits;

he has certainly shewn a very laudable zeal for bringing a criminal officer to condign punishment; but the next time he takes the field of prosecution in the cause of an injured community, I hope his prudence will dictate to him the necessity of being furnished with a better apparatus."[3] In what way these rather tart remarks reflected upon the honor of Steuben, it is now somewhat difficult to see, but the German seems to have claimed they cast doubt upon his courage. The fact that Lee and other American generals had been jealous of Steuben because of the wide powers given him early in 1778—and later diminished—and the fact that Steuben was on good terms with Hamilton and Washington may serve in some degree to explain his injured feelings. In any case, being told that Lee's remarks aspersed him, he came to Philadelphia, inspected the printed record, and demanded satisfaction in a letter of December 2. Steuben wished to see Lee as near and as soon as possible—Lee to choose the place, time, and arms; the baron preferred not to be a spectator, either distant or tardy, on *this* occasion.[4] Lee promptly responded that he had had no intention of questioning the baron's courage, but that he had been vexed by his "forwardness" in serving as a prosecution witness.

He was prepared to make this statement publicly. Nevertheless, declared Lee, "If you found that I have not dealt honestly, I am ready to satisfy you in the manner you desire. . . ." Steuben, left without any measurable ground for complaint, had to accept this straightforward explanation, perhaps against his will, as satisfactory.[5] Alexander Hamilton, who gave his blessing to the baron, offered a startling verdict on this affair. He wrote to Steuben not long afterward: "I have read your letter to Lee, with pleasure—it was conceived in terms, which the offence merited, and if he had any feeling must have been felt by him. Considering the pointedness and severity of your expressions, his answer was certainly a very modest one and proved that he had not a violent appetite, for so close a *tete a tete* as you seemed disposed to insist upon. His evasions, if known to the world, would do him little honor. . . ."[6] Much later this young man who was such an excellent judge in matters of honor and courage freely cast aspersions upon the character of Aaron

Burr, was called to account, tried to avoid a duel without offering an honest apology, and was forced to go to his untimely death upon the duelling field.

Steuben disposed of, Lee was almost immediately confronted with another demand for satisfaction, from John Laurens. Not gifted with the pen and unable to use it effectively against Lee, Laurens, who was a brave man, decided to use other weapons. He accused Lee of casting reflections upon Washington's character, and as Washington's aide-de-camp and friend insisted on an accounting from Lee. He was obviously as little familiar with the eighteenth-century code of honor as was his friend Hamilton.[7] Lee could have replied that Laurens should avoid meddling in affairs which were none of his business. But Lee undoubtedly looked upon Laurens as one of his persecutors, and there was real danger that he would be ridiculed, should he turn aside a second challenge from his enemies. He therefore determined to deal with Laurens. Admitting he had expressed a low opinion of Washington's military abilities, he denied making any attack upon his character. He indicated slyly that it was a little odd for one gentleman to fight the battles of another in the eighteenth century. However, if Laurens wished to revive the medieval custom whereby any knight might be called in to serve as a champion for old women, widows, and priests, and if Laurens refused to accept his denial, he was ready to meet him.[8] The young officer was determined to fight. The duel was postponed for some days because Lee was injured by a fall from a horse and because he was having trouble with his ancient enemy, the gout. On December 22 he wrote to Laurens to say he would meet him at half past three the following afternoon on the edge of a wood near Philadelphia, unless it should rain. He chose pistols as the weapons to be used, indicating that his recent illness and his accident prevented him from using the sword.[9]

On the afternoon of the twenty-third Lee, accompanied by Evan Edwards, who was to serve as his second, reached the appointed spot. Laurens and Hamilton, his second, were very late, and Lee and Edwards passed the time as gentlemen and scholars by discussing predestination versus free will. Finally, Edwards suggested that Laurens and Hamilton would fail to keep the engagement. Lee insisted that they would keep it, and they made their appearance shortly afterward.[10] There was some discussion about the most suitable mode of procedure. Lee suggested one which was apparently then new in America, that he and his opponent face each other from a distance and advance toward each other firing at will. His proposal was approved by the others.

The principals, provided with pistols, took their places and walked toward each other. At a distance of some five or six paces they fired almost simultaneously. Laurens was untouched. Believing his opponent was also unhurt, he was preparing for a second discharge when Lee announced he had been hit. Assuming he had been seriously wounded, the young South Carolinian hurried forward to assist him, as did Edwards and Hamilton. Upon investigation, however, Lee discovered his enemy's bullet had merely grazed him in the side, although the flow of blood was for a short time rather profuse, and he expressed a desire for a second shot. The seconds protested, contending that the requirements of honor had been met, but Lee repeated his request, and Laurens agreed. Hamilton suggested that Lee ought to be satisfied, unless he felt personal animosity toward his opponent, Edwards again insisted the duel be halted, and Lee finally consented to abide by the decision of the seconds reached after consultation between them. While Edwards and Hamilton considered the situation, their principals talked about their quarrel. Lee again asserted that he had not vilified Washington's character, because he had respect for the commander in chief as a man and because the utterance of personal abuse was incompatible with the behavior of a gentleman. He declared that he had expressed an unfavorable opinion of Washington as a military leader, and he said he might do so again. He refused to consider himself accountable to Laurens for such remarks. He said he had no personal feeling against his opponent and had consented to meet him merely to defend his own honor. The affair ended when the seconds returned, announcing there was no good reason for continuing hostilities.

The Lee-Laurens duel was carried out in proper style, and the seconds warded off wild tales about it by publishing an account of it in a Philadelphia newspaper.[11] Lee, in fact, is reported to have said afterward that he had come to respect Laurens[12] and that he admired Laurens' courage. "I could have hugged the noble boy, he pleased me so."[13] If Lee came to entertain a measure of good feeling toward Laurens, he certainly found nothing praiseworthy in the conduct of Elias Boudinot, who anonymously attacked him a few days later.

Elias Boudinot sent no challenge to the Englishman. Somehow or other he secured possession of a savage assault upon Lee written by a Tory and printed early in the war in a newspaper published under the auspices of the Earl of Dunmore. The Tory described Lee as a mercenary soldier, miser, villain, scoundrel, profligate, and traitor. Boudinot supplied this piece of calumny, together with an introductory letter he signed "A. B.," to Isaac Collins, who printed both items in his New Jersey Gazette on December 31. In his introduction he compared Washington and Lee to Virtue and Vice, Good and Evil; accused Lee of trying to seize Washington's post; and asserted that the Tory had told the truth.[14] According to Lee, he even altered the Tory blast, inserting in it some abuse of his own. Stung by these publications, Lee learned that Boudinot was responsible for them. Protesting vigorously to Governor Livingston of New Jersey, he asked the governor to punish him by removing him from a post he held as commissary of prisoners for that state. Livingston, indicating that he believed Boudinot had been guilty of "forgery" and ungentlemanly conduct, responded that he lacked the power to punish him and suggested Lee sue him for libel,[15] small consolation to Lee. Collins, however, made some reparation by inserting in his newspaper on January 27, 1779, a letter from Evan Edwards which must have made Boudinot wince. Edwards explicitly denied that Lee had ever designed to oust Washington, and asserted that "every man who is a friend to this community, a friend to virtue or justice, and every man who would reprobate Genl Lee in any attempts to depreciate so valuable a character as General Washington's, must despise the rancorous villain, who, from the baseness of his soul, could be capable of composing, or instrumental in publishing such false, such dastardly, and such malignant calumny."[16] Perhaps Edwards' letter helps to explain

why Boudinot in his reminiscences failed to accuse Lee of treachery at Monmouth.[17]

With Steuben, Laurens, and Boudinot striking at Lee, it is
not surprising that Mad Anthony Wayne also assailed him. Lee
was at Elizabethtown early in January, 1779, trying to secure
money from his English property through the help of friends
in the British army. There on the seventh, Wayne, who despised
Boudinot's performance, questioned Lee regarding remarks he
had made during his trial. Mad Anthony accused him of trying
"to injure my military character in the eye of the world," asked
him to acknowledge he had done so, and requested that he give
"that satisfaction which one gentleman has a right to claim of
another, feeling himself injured in so tender a point." Wayne's
demand for satisfaction was about as well grounded in the code
of honor as was that of Steuben. He received a straightforward
reply. Lee admitted that he had been critical of Wayne's tactics
on Monmouth field and that in defending his own military opinions and dispositions he had found fault with the latter's. He
had made no personal attack. Did Wayne have any just cause
for taking offense because of testimony he was forced to give
in his own defense? Lee urged Wayne not to permit his name
to be enrolled among those of his own "persecutors." However,
if Mad Anthony was still not satisfied, he would meet him, as
soon as he had fully recovered from his fall and had completed
some pressing business. Wayne responded that he was not
pleased with this answer and that he hoped to meet Lee on the
duelling ground at a suitable time.[18] After further explanation,
however, Wayne apparently withdrew his challenge.[19] Not
long afterward he wrote to Lee in highly complimentary
fashion.

It is somewhat strange that Steuben, Laurens, and Wayne
all came to believe within the space of a few weeks that Lee had
insulted their honor as gentlemen; and it is interesting that Hamilton endorsed Steuben's conduct and seconded Laurens. Had
Lee really injured these men sufficiently to compel them to seek
his life? Or did Steuben and Wayne as well as Laurens challenge Lee, in part at least, as adherents of Washington? Since
Lee spoke to Wayne about the "list" of his "persecutors," it

seems probable that he then believed there was a cabal to destroy him. Certainly he believed so at a later time, when he went so far as to assert that Washington himself was responsible for attempts to assassinate him.[20] There are some curious parallels in the history of General Conway and of Lee, which the latter may have observed. Conway expressed a low opinion of Washington; Washington discussed Conway's conduct with correct reserve in a letter to Congress; Laurens and Hamilton savagely attacked Conway in letters to Henry Laurens and Governor George Clinton respectively; and John Cadwalader challenged him, with almost fatal results for Conway. Lee became an enemy of Washington; Washington discussed his behavior at Monmouth with correct reserve in a letter to Congress; Laurens and Hamilton bitterly assailed Lee in letters to Henry Laurens and Elias Boudinot respectively; and Steuben, Laurens, and Wayne challenged Lee.[21] These circumstances do not, of course, warrant placing any accusation against the commander in chief.

If Wayne's name was not placed by Lee on the list of his "persecutors," that of William Henry Drayton certainly appeared there. Lee, in conversation with Richard Hutson, a member of Congress from South Carolina, bitterly censured Drayton. Hutson informed Drayton of Lee's remarks,[22] and early in February Drayton initiated a correspondence which must be read to be appreciated. On the third he wrote to Lee:

My colleague Mr. [Richard] Hutson, hath this day mentioned to me a conversation you had with him, in which you expressed yourself as injured by a misrepresentation of your conduct immediately preceding your captivity by the enemy, in a charge I had the honour to deliver, as chief justice, to the grand jury of Charlestown, South Carolina.

I must inform you, sir, that, on the one hand, I have been repeatedly assured the representation I then made was a true one; and that, on the other hand, I have also been assured, that it was not founded on fact; and that, immediately upon this latter assurance in South Carolina, I took that step which was most likely to lead me to a certainty on the subject, with the avowed design, that if I had injured your reputation, I might be enabled to make the most ample reparation; but I did not receive the necessary materials. Those sentiments of propriety which dictated the first advance on my part then, to acquire them, now dictate a like conduct when another opportunity seems to open itself for my arriving at the truth, and to do that justice which the case may require. And I do assure you, that if I can be enabled to declare, that you did not violate the orders of the commander in chief, respecting your injunction with him, when he had retreated to the Delaware in 1776, I shall not only do so in the most pointed terms, but beg your pardon for having through error and misrepresentation, published the contrary. . . .

Those principals of honour which must make you feel an injury, make me feel even an idea of having done an injury, and impels me to make a reparation where it is due.[23]

In other words, Drayton, who had prejudged the Washington-Lee controversy, who had taken a leading role in securing the confirmation of Lee's sentence by Congress, who had admittedly and unnecessarily attacked Lee's conduct in December, 1776, without any real knowledge about it, was willing to retract his statement to the grand jury—if the general could convince him it was unwarranted. Under the circumstances his letter would have provoked a man of much milder temper than Lee possessed. Two days later he replied in deliberately offensive language, probably with the intention of goading Drayton to issue a formal challenge.[24]

I should have done myself the honour of answering your letter yesterday, but was prevented by a variety of business. If I have violated any orders of the commander in chief, to him, and the Congress only, am I responsible; but certainly am not amenable to the tribunal of Mr. William Henry Drayton. I shall therefore remain entirely indifferent whether you are pleased to think or dream that I designedly threw myself into the hands of the enemy, or whether I was not taken by a concurrence of unfortunate circumstances such as happen in the course of all wars. The only remark I shall make on your extraordinary requisition, that I should clear myself on this point to you simply, Mr. William Henry Drayton, whom I consider but as a mere common member of Congress, is, that you pay a very ill compliment to the general. You must suppose him either miserably deficient in understanding, or in integrity as a servant of the public, when you suppose that he would suffer a man, for a single day, to act as his second in command, whom he knows to be guilty of such abominable military treason. This ingenious supposition, therefore, is, in my opinion, a greater affront to the general than to myself.

I am sincerely concerned that my friend Eustace should have degraded himself so far as to enter into any discussion of this matter with Mr. William Henry Drayton; and I shall reprimand him for not understanding his dignity better. I shall now only take the trouble of adding, that if you can reconcile your conduct in stepping out of the road, (as I am informed you did in your charge to the grand jury,) to aggravate the calamities of an unhappy man, who had sacrificed every thing to the cause of your country, and as he then conceived, to the rights of mankind; who had sacrificed an ample, at least an easy and independent fortune, the most honorable connections, great military pretensions, his friends and relations: I say, if you can reconcile your stepping out of the road to aggravate the calamities of a man who had notoriously made these sacrifices, and who, at the very time you were displaying your generous eloquence, had no less than five centinels on his person, and was suffering extremely in body and mind—if you can, I repeat, reconcile such a procedure to common humanity, common sense, or common decency, you must still be a more singular personage than the public at present consider you.[25]

Drayton's reaction was vigorous, but he wished to close the discussion rather than to continue it with sword or pistol. Throwing off the mask of politeness which he had assumed in his first message, he replied on the eighth.

At nine o'clock last night, I received yours of the fifth instant in answer to mine of the third. But, as I have neither time nor inclination to enter into a competition, whether Mr. Charles Lee, or Mr. William Henry Drayton, can raise the most ingenious supposition, say the keenest thing, and pen the most finished period with parenthesis; nor ambition to correspond with you in your simple character of Mr. Charles Lee, whom I cannot consider but as legally disgraced for being guilty of abominable military treason against a community of the most liberal, just, and generous, and I must add, merciful people on the face of the globe: I say, perfectly satisfied with my simple character of Mr. William Henry Drayton, "a mere common member of Congress," and "a mere chief justice of South Carolina," I shall do myself the honour, out of breath as I am with parentheses, to make only one observation in reply, absolutely terminating the correspondence on my part, that I verily believe we equally remain entirely indifferent with respect to what either is "pleased to think or dream." And now, finally taking my leave of Mr. Charles Lee, with common decency from respect to my simple character, I subscribe myself . . .[26]

Lee could not permit the pompous[27] Drayton to have the last word. Waiting until March 15 to reply, he used blistering language in an effort to exasperate Drayton into a challenge.

As I have now settled all my affairs, and as I am given to understand that you may probably soon set out for Carolina, I take the liberty of addressing this letter to you, which is to close our correspondence for ever—until very [lately] I was taught to consider you only as a fantastick pompous dramatis personae, a mere Malvolio, never to be spoke or thought of but for the sake of laughter, and when the humour for laughter subsided, never to be spoke or thought of more—but I find I was mistaken. I find that you are as malignant a scoundrel as you are universally allow'd to be a ridiculous and disgusting coxcomb. You are pleas'd to say that I am legally disgrac'd—all I shall say in reply is, that I am able confidently to pronounce that every man of every rank in the whole army who was present at the tryal, every man out of the army, every man on the continent who has read the proceedings of the court martial (perhaps indeed I might except Mr. Penn of North Carolina and Doctor Scudder of the Jerseys with a few others of about their size in understanding) is of opinion that the stigma is not on him on whom was pass'd but on those who pass'd this absurd

iniquitous and preposterous sentence—for to be just, I do
not believe you quite blockhead enough to think the charges
had a shadow of support—and if ever by some wonderful
metamorphosis you shou'd become an honest man [you]
will confess it—as to the confirmation of this curious sentence, I do not conceive myself at liberty to make any comments on it, as it is an affair of Congress for which body I
ever had and ought to have a profound respect, I shall only
lament that they are disgraced by so foul a member as Mr.
William Henry Drayton—you tell me the Americans are the
most merciful people on the face of the earth. I think so too,
and the strongest instance of it is that they did not long ago
hang up you and every advocate for the Stamp act,[28] and do
not flatter yourself that the present violent airs of patriotism
you give yourself, and your hard labour'd letters to the
[British] commissioners and the king will ever wash away
the stain—if you think the terms I make use of harsh or un-
merited my friend Major Edwards is commission'd to point
out your remedy.[29]

Drayton is reported to have replied that his position as chief
justice of the State of South Carolina prevented him from engaging in a duel,[30] but his answer, if he penned one, has unfortunately been lost.

Who won in the exchange of abuse between Drayton and
Lee is not certain. Each man evidently felt the sting of his op-
ponent's pen. There can be no question, however, but that Lee
was the winner in a contest of wit with Miss Rebecca Franks, a
Philadelphia belle of the Jewish faith and of Tory sympathies.
Miss Franks was one of the beauties who had graced the famous
Mischianza, the lavish entertainment given by the British officers
in honor of Sir William Howe immediately before his departure
for England, and she possessed a witty and malicious tongue.
Several of her victims had been sadly embarrassed by her sal-
lies.[31] It was an unlucky day for her, however, when she chose
some breeches worn by Lee, the boon companion of Laurence
Sterne and John Hall-Stevenson, as a subject for her remarks.
The breeches had leather inserted on the inside of the thighs and
were used for riding on horseback. Miss Franks, perhaps not at
her best, asserted that Lee wore green breeches "patched" with

leather. The letter of protest which he wrote to her may have amused her a little; it certainly made her angry. Dated December 20, it has as much sparkle as any of his writings, and though a trifle broad, might be described as almost a minor masterpiece. Cheerfully making fun of his own predicament, he managed not only to discomfit his talented antagonist, but also to strike at his masculine enemies in passing.

Madam,

When an officer of the respectable rank which I bear is grossly traduced and calumniated, it is incumbent on him to clear up the affair to the world, with as little delay as possible. The spirit of defamation and calumny (I am sorry to say it) is grown to a prodigious and intolerable height on this continent. If you had accused me of a design to procrastinate the war, or of holding a treasonable correspondence with the enemy, I could have borne it: this I am used to; and this happened to the great Fabius Maximus. If you had accused me of getting drunk as often as I could get liquor, as *two Alexanders the Great*[32] have been charged with this vice, I should, perhaps, have sat patient under the imputation; or, even if you had given the plainest hints, that I had stolen the soldiers' shirts, this I could have put up with, as the great Duke of Marlborough would have been an example; or if you had contented yourself with asserting, that I was so abominable a sloven as never to part with my shirt, until my shirt parted with me, the anecdotes of my illustrious name-sake of Sweden would have administered some comfort to me. But the calumny you have, in the fertility of your malicious wit, chosen to invent, is of so new, so unprecedented, and so hellish a kind, as would make Job himself swear like a Virginia colonel.

Is it possible that the celebrated Miss Franks, a lady who has had every human and divine advantage, who has read, (or, at least, might have read,) in the *originals*, the New and Old Testaments; (though I am afraid she too seldom looks even into the translations:) I say, is it possible that Miss Franks, with every human and divine advantage, who might, and ought to have read these two good books, which (an old Welsh nurse, whose uncle was reckoned the best preacher in Merionethshire, assured me) enjoin charity, and denounce vengeance against slander and evil speaking; is it possible, I again repeat it, that Miss Franks, should, in the face of the day, carry her malignity so far, in the presence of three most respectable personages; (one of the oldest religion in the world, one of the newest; for he is a new-light man; and the other, most probably, of no religion at all, as he is an English sailor:) but I demand it again and again, is it possible, that Miss Franks should assert it, in the presence of these respectable personages, "That I wore green breeches patched with leather?" To convict you, therefore, of the falsehood of this most diabolical slander; to put you to eternal silence, (if you are not past all grace,) and to cover you with a much larger patch of infamy than you have wantonly endeavoured to fix on my breeches, I have thought proper, by the advice of three very grave friends, (lawyers and members of Congress, of course excellent judges in delicate points of honour,) to send you the said breeches, and, with the consciousness of truth on my side, to submit them to the most severe inspection and scrutiny of you and all those who may have entered into this wicked cabal against my honour and reputation. I say, I dare you, and your whole junto, to your worst; turn them, examine them, inside and outside, and if you find them to be green breeches patched with leather, and not actually legitimate *sherry vallies*, such as his Majesty of Poland wears, (who, let me tell you, is a man that has made more fashions than all your knights of the Meschianza put together, notwithstanding their beauties;) I repeat it, (though I am almost out of breath with repetitions and parentheses,) that if these are proved to be patched green breeches, and not real legitimate *sherry vallies*, (which a man of the first *bon ton* might be proud of,) I will submit in silence to all the scurrility which, I have no doubt, you and your abettors are prepared to pour out against me in the public papers, on this important and interesting occasion. But, Madam! Madam! reputation (as "Common Sense", very sensibly, though not very uncommonly observes,) is a serious thing. You have already injured me in the tenderest part, and I demand satisfaction; and as you cannot be ignorant of the laws of duelling, having conversed with so many Irish officers, whose favourite topic it is, particularly in the company of the ladies, I insist on the privilege of the injured party, which is, to name his hour and weapons; and as I intend it to be a very serious affair, I will not admit of any seconds; and you may depend upon it, Miss Franks, that whatever may be your spirit on the occasion, the world shall never accuse General Lee with having turned his back upon you. . . .

P. S. I have communicated the affair only to my confidential friend _____, who has mentioned it to no more than seven members of Congress and nineteen women, six of whom are old maids; so that there is no danger of its taking wind on my side; and, I hope, you will be equally guarded on your part.[33]

Miss Franks suffered the more because this *jeu d'esprit* was soon widely published, arousing much laughter at her expense. Lee circulated the letter among friends and acquaintances, in Philadelphia, and Dr. James Craik gave a copy of it to Hugh Henry Brackenridge, who was about to publish the first issue of his *United States Magazine.*[34] Brackenridge printed it in January, 1779,[35] and various newspapers promptly reprinted it. Lee, learning that Miss Franks had been sadly vexed, then wrote her a letter of apology, assuring her he had intended only a "harmless joke."[36] He sent this apology to the *Pennsylvania Gazette* of Philadelphia, and also a denunciation of Brackenridge. Lee claimed Brackenridge had altered the piece and had made it more offensive to Miss Franks.[37] In March, James Rivington gleefully entered the affair, giving the readers of his *Royal Gazette* the original letter, two nasty forgeries claimed to be Miss Franks's response, and an obscene message from "Sly-boots" to Lee. One of the forgeries was ascribed to Cyrus Griffin, member of Congress from Virginia.[38] Griffin promptly denied the authorship, and was defended by Lee in the *Pennsylvania Packet* of Philadelphia of April 6.

At this point the Lee-Franks affair developed into a contest between Lee and Brackenridge. The publisher felt he had been unfairly placed in the wrong and was not disposed to accept blows without trying to return them. In a letter printed in the *Packet* of April 13, and also in his magazine,[39] he made a virulent attack upon Lee. He asserted the general's *jeu d'esprit* was beneath Lee's dignity; accused him, apparently unfairly, of sending it to Rivington; claimed the general associated with Tories; insinuated that Lee's behavior at Charleston in 1776 was unworthy because he wished to evacuate Fort Sullivan; declared Lee had recently been repulsed in advances to a lady with Negro ancestors, whose guardian was considering the use of a cudgel upon him;[40] and ended by describing him as "a wild animal." Lee met this assault by demanding from Congress an opportunity to justify his conduct at Charleston—secretly, to avoid disclosures concerning the defenses of Charleston—or that Congress republish the vote of thanks it had given him in 1776.[41] The delegates were forced to accede to his request,[42] and the vote of thanks accordingly reappeared in the *Pennsylvania Packet* on April 15. He also sent a formal challenge to Brackenridge, who had a nice sense of humor as well as a caustic pen and who laughingly refused to meet him. Lee then secured a horsewhip and watched for an opportunity to chastise his enemy. Observing him on Market Street one day, Lee gave chase, horsewhip in hand. Noticing his pursuer, Brackenridge rushed into a tavern and bolted the door in the face of the angry general, who cursed him and begged him to come out and fight like a man. Brackenridge gave answer that he did not like being the target for a pistol and would remain within, if Lee did not mind, which brought further and "dreadful" oaths from Lee and a promise that he would whip him, if only he would venture out. Brackenridge responded that he had not liked whipping as a child and that he had not changed his opinion. He remained safely inside the tavern until Lee departed amid the laughter of a large crowd which had gathered to enjoy the show.[43]

Some time before his departure from Philadelphia Lee seems to have dealt with Joseph Reed. According to General Samuel Smith, Lee made it a point in polite company to assert that Reed's face was stamped "with the devil's favorite brand." Overhearing this remark on one occasion, Reed demanded, "What was that, sir?" Lee bowed and repeated his observation, amid roars of laughter. Reed declared that Lee would hear from him shortly. "I doubt that," responded the general. No challenge was offered.[44]

Almost immediately after his encounter with Brackenridge, Lee must have left for his Virginia estate, since he passed through Lancaster about April 20, accompanied, according to report, by "his dogs and doxey." [45] He could accomplish nothing more, at least for the time being, in Philadelphia. He had made an effective defense of his conduct on Monmouth field, and he had dealt courageously and rather successfully with his personal enemies. Nevertheless, his many quarrels and his willingness to meet all comers either with pen or pistol hardly made him generally popular in polite society, even though many, including young James Monroe, sought his acquaintance and friendship. Some of those who had entertained him and who had championed him were undoubtedly relieved by his departure. The embittered man who puts heart and soul into a losing cause may be admired; but his company is not universally sought; and he may become something of a nuisance. Probably even Benjamin Rush did not regret his going. During his stay at Philadelphia, Lee had been attracted by a sister of Rush's wife and had once more entertained the thought of marriage, even though the young lady, a daughter of Richard Stockton of New Jersey, was a niece of Elias Boudinot. Rush, however, warded off a proposal from Lee by hints upon the disparity of age between the young lady and the general in middle years. [46]

CHAPTER EIGHTEEN

ROAD TO OBLIVION

I will have such revenges on you both,
That all the world shall—I will do such things,—
What they are, yet I know not; but they shall be
The terrors of the Earth. You think I'll weep;
No, I'll not weep:
I have full cause of weeping; but this heart
Shall break into a hundred thousand flaws,
Or e'er I'll weep.—O fool, I shall go mad!
SHAKESPEARE, King Lear

WHILE LEE the fighting man strove manfully against his enemies early in 1779, Lee the romantic dreamer amused himself by writing "sev'ral crude reveries." One of these was an extraordinary plan for setting up an ideal military colony in "some happy climate of America," a scheme he considered "perhaps as wild, 'tho not quite so poetical," as Horace's to transplant the Romans to the Fortunate Islands.[1] Inspired in part no doubt by his readings in Horace and Jean Jacques Rousseau and by his own unhappy situation, he created imaginatively the society in which he believed he could be truly happy. In this curious bit of literature he reveals himself as a true child of the Enlightenment and offers some views and ideas in certain respects much like those held by Franklin, Jefferson, and Tom Paine. Not attempting to devise a Utopia for all men, he wished to establish a military and agrarian community having as little contact as possible with existing society. The colony was to be composed of ten thousand soldiers and their families, soldiers being insisted upon as essential to its defense. Indeed, every male was to be brought up in the practice of arms for the common protection.

There was to be as little industry and commerce as possible in the colony. Every able-bodied man was to be a soldier,

hunter, and an "agricultor," with lands distributed according
to rank, but with the highest officers owning no more than five
thousand acres and the privates not less than four hundred. Such
"effeminate and vile" occupations as tailoring, barbering, shoe-
making, and weaving would be left to women, slaves, and weak
and deformed men. No professional merchant was to be permitted to reside within the community, for commerce did not
bring riches, strength, happiness, or glory. Trade "must emas-
culate the body, narrow the mind, and in fact corrupt every
true republican and manly principle; nay, I think it must destroy all sensibility for real pleasure and happiness." The conversation of commercial men was "dull, languid, and stupid;
their pleasures confined to gross eating and drinking; their only
idea of mirth, to the roaring of some vile, hoarse singer; and of
wit, to the storyteller of the club or some wretched punster,
who lives on catches and crotchets." Since commerce was
nevertheless essential, Lee would have one or more fairs each
year on the frontiers of the colony, where his blessed people
could meet merchants and peddlers of all nations and exchange
produce of their lands for needed articles. Lawyers were likewise to be barred from the holy precincts, for they were as de-
structive as a plague. But little law would be needed in the community. Property would be inherited equally by children of
both sexes, and a simple civil code would suffice. Every gentleman in the colony would know sufficient law to decide all civil
disputes justly. Nor would the punishment of criminals be a
difficult problem. Lesser offenses would be punished by slavery
or labor on public works, and major ones by mutilation and
exile. Following the teachings of the Marquis di Beccaria, Lee
would bar the death penalty, particularly because it did not prevent crime. To prove that a simple legal system could be easily
managed without the aid of professional lawyers Lee pointed to
the example of the early Roman republic.

Nor were sectarian priests or clergymen to be permitted in
the colony. All the inhabitants were to be Christians, and every
person was to attend divine worship, for Lee insisted that religion was vitally important to man. Religious ceremonies were
to be held under the leadership of a *pontifex maximus* or su-

preme servitor, who was to be chosen not for theological learning but for his dignified appearance and pleasing voice. There would be no preaching, short prayers, and much poetry and music. A colonist would be required, beyond attendance at services, only to acknowledge the existence, providence, and goodness of God and a reverence for Christ. Lee was acutely aware that these proposals would "shock quakers, puritans, and rigid sectarists," but he detested and despised them "from the bottom of my heart." " . . . I speak to men and soldiers, who wish and are able to assert and defend the rights of humanity; and, let me add, to vindicate the character of God Almighty, and real christianity, which have been so long dishonoured by sectarists of every kind and complexion; catholics, church of England men, presbyterians, and methodists." Rather amusingly, Lee insisted upon bathing and cleaning of teeth before attendance at religious services. (If slovenly with respect to his clothing, he was less averse to bathing than many eighteenth-century gentlemen—and ladies.)

Poetry and music, so important in the religious establishment, would also, with the study of history and polite literature, form the basis of education and of public life in the community. Private and public virtue and true civilization would be assured through refining and ennobling pursuits and studies. Lee said little specifically about government, although he took for granted the existence of a capital and a legislature. Presumably the officers and gentlemen would lead the privates and humbler folk. In this ideal society, of course, governmental processes would be simple and uncorrupted by personal and partisan interests.[2]

Where Lee's never-never colony was to be located, except that it was to be set up in America, is not known. Certainly the Virginia to which he went in the spring of 1779 and where he resided until 1782 offered no paradise for the unhappy of existing society. Lee made no attempt to forswear the great world, nor did he settle down to a quiet and humdrum existence at Prato Rio. It was not in him to vegetate. Instead he continued his efforts to clear his record, to regain public esteem, and to hurt his enemies; and he remained a center of public controversy for many months.

Before leaving Philadelphia, Lee had prepared some "whacking queries" which he circulated among his friends and which he proposed to publish in the hope they would interfere with Washington's digestion.[3] Just before his departure he thought the time to strike had come, for the *Pennsylvania Packet* had printed an extract of a letter from an unnamed gentleman of South Carolina. The letter, written to Benjamin Rush by his friend Dr. David Ramsay, later a famous historian, ardently defended Lee; and Rush or Lee had arranged for its appearance in print. After reading the proceedings of the court-martial Ramsay was convinced that Lee had been the victim of a great injustice. He declared he was "sorry for the ingratitude of my country," and asserted that Lee had deserved thanks instead of censure for his conduct at Monmouth. Had he been in Congress, he would have voted to reverse the judgment of the military tribunal. He sharply and properly condemned the evidence offered by members of Washington's staff, for they seemed to display a "mean inclination to bring Lee in guilty. They deal much in negatives & have not the appearance of simplicity." Ramsay saw Lee as an "unfortunate hero."[4] Lee fancied that the appearance of Ramsay's remarks would give him a greater number of sympathetic readers,[5] but his "whacking queries" did not reach the public until July, possibly because he could not immediately find a man bold enough to put them in his paper. On June 7 he sent them to the famous printer William Goddard, and Goddard arranged for their publication on July 6 in the *Maryland Journal and Baltimore Advertiser*, a Baltimore newspaper which appeared under the name of Goddard's sister Katherine, but which was actually controlled by Goddard himself. Eleazer Oswald had signed a partnership agreement with Goddard on June 8 but had not yet assumed any authority.

"Some Queries, Political and Military, Humbly Offered to the Consideration of the Public" were printed anonymously under a Philadelphia date line. There were in all twenty-five questions, devoted in the main to self-justification and to an assault upon Washington, but containing also some items well calculated to make Joseph Reed, who had become president of the council of Pennsylvania, most unhappy. The most pointed were:

9th. Whether it is salutary or dangerous, consistent with, or abhorrent from, the principles and spirit of liberty and republicanism, to inculcate and encourage in the people, an idea, that their welfare, safety, and glory, depend on one man? Whether they really do depend on one man?

10th. Whether, amongst the late warm addressers, in this city [Philadelphia], to his Excellency General Washington, there was a single mortal, one gentleman [Reed] excepted, who could possibly be acquainted with his merits?

11th. Whether this gentleman excepted, does really think his Excellency a great man; or whether evidence could not be produced of his sentiments being quite the reverse?

12th. Whether the armies under Gates and Arnold, and the detachment under Stark, to the northward, or that immediately under his Excellency, in Pennsylvania, gave the decisive turn to the fortune of war?

. . . .

14th. On what principle was it that Congress in the year 1776, sent for General Lee quite from Georgia, with injunctions to join the army under General Washington, then in York-Island, without loss of time.

. . . .

18th. Whether, when General Howe . . . fell back towards York-Island, orders should not have been immediately dispatched for the evacuation of Fort Washington, and for the removal of all the stores of value from Fort Lee to some secure spot, more removed from the river? Whether this was not proposed and the proposal slighted?

19th. Whether the loss of the garrison of Fort Washington, and its consequent loss of Fort Lee, with the tents, stores, had not such an effect on the spirits of the people, as to make the difference of twenty thousand men to America?

20th. Whether, in the defeat of Brandewine, General Sullivan was really the person who ought to have been censured?

21st. Whether, if Duke Ferdinand [of Brunswick] had

commanded at Germantown, after having gained, by the valour of his troops, and the negligence of his enemy, a partial victory, he would have contrived, by a single stroke of the bathos, to have corrupted this partial victory into defeat?

.   .   .   .

23d. Whether the trials of General St. Clair, of which court-martial General Lincoln was president, and that on General Lee, were conducted in the same forms, and on the same principles? Whether in the former, all hearsay evidences were not absolutely excluded; and in the latter hearsay evidence did not constitute a very considerable part?

24th. Whether, if the Generals Schuyler and St. Clair, had been tried by the same court-martial as General Lee was, and instead of Congress, General Washington had been the prosecutor, those gentlemen (unexceptionable as their conduct was) would not have stood a very ugly chance of being condemned? And whether, if instead of General Washington, Congress had been the prosecutor, General Lee would not probably have been acquitted with the highest honour?

25th. Whether it must not appear to every man who has read General Washington's letter to Congress, on the affair of Monmouth, and the proceedings of the court-martial, by which General Lee was tried, that if the contents of the former are facts, not only General Lee's defence must be a tissue of the most abominable audacious lies, but that the whole string of evidences, both on the part of the prosecution and prosecuted, must be guilty of rank perjury, as the testimonies of those gentlemen, near forty in number, delivered on oath, scarcely in one article coincide with the detail given in his Excellency's letter? [6]

Goddard must have expected trouble when he published these stinging questions. Well-meaning, contentious, and perhaps unworldly, he had printed in his paper in 1777 an anonymous letter urging acceptance of peace terms erroneously reported to be offered by the Howes, and he had been rudely and rather brutally handled by the local Whig Club, an organization devoting itself to rooting out secret enemies of the American cause. Sturdily defending the freedom of the press and refusing to divulge the name of the contributor, he had finally won out in the resulting struggle.[7] The Whig Club was almost certain to resent the publication of the "Queries." Perhaps Goddard was encouraged by Oswald, who was about to join him in the management of the paper. Both men were convinced that Lee had been abused. In any case, the appearance of the "Queries" created a furor in Baltimore, and the Whig Club promptly undertook to deal with Goddard.

On the night of July 8 a mob of "ruffians, composed of Continental recruits, mulattoes, or negroes, fifers and drummers," numbering about thirty men and led by three Continental officers, invaded Goddard's bedroom. They demanded his surrender and appearance before the Whig Club. Goddard managed to grasp a sword, called Oswald to his side, and refused to be browbeaten. He offered to meet the leaders of the club in an amicable way at a near-by coffeehouse the following morning, and his offer was accepted. Fearing that this agreement would not be kept, in the morning he went to four magistrates demanding protection, but none gave any. His fears were certainly well grounded. A mob led by Colonel Samuel Smith, afterward United States Senator from Maryland, caught him in the street, maltreated two neighbors who tried to defend him, and carried him off. Helpless in the hands of his captors, Goddard felt forced to yield, at least for the moment, revealed that Lee was the author of the objectionable questions (a fact which hardly needed stating), and promised immediately to apologize in his paper for calumniating General Washington. Released, he published his apology in the issue of July 9. The Whig Club had evidently won a complete victory. Goddard, however, had merely been prudent in the face of overwhelming physical force and soon renewed the fray, supported by one of the doughtiest fighters for the freedom of the press America has known, Oswald, who had hitherto remained pretty much in the background.

Eleazer Oswald, who was unquestionably one of the heroes of Monmouth, according to report was born in Falmouth, England, in 1755, and was therefore still a very young man. He was living in New Haven and operating a distillery when the news of Lexington and Concord came. Promptly joining the army, he served as Arnold's private secretary in the Canadian campaign, was captured and released, and rejoined the army. Soon after Monmouth, whether because he was passed over in rank or because he sympathized with Lee, or for both reasons, he resigned his commission. Having married a daughter of the printer John Holt and possessing a good education, he logically turned to the printing business and associated himself with Goddard, who was a fine craftsman. Oswald was equally willing to fight with the pen or with dueling weapons, as those who hectored Goddard, especially Samuel Smith, soon discovered.

On July 11, Oswald put Smith to the ultimate test. Smith had hurt the interests and the reputation of Goddard's new partner, and Oswald demanded satisfaction on the field of honor. Smith, although he saw nothing wrong in leading a mob, indicated in reply that he considered duels immoral, and he claimed he had done Oswald no wrong. On July 15, Oswald responded, bluntly accusing Smith of cowardice. Meanwhile, Goddard and Oswald had petitioned the state authorities, telling the story of the mob attacks, forthrightly defending Lee, and demanding public protection of the freedom of the press. In the July 16 issue of their newspaper they struck fiercely at their enemies. They championed Lee's cause, printed the correspondence between Oswald and Smith, and retracted the apology forced from Goddard. Their enemies were silent and inactive. Goddard continued, with and without a partner, to publish his paper in Baltimore for thirteen years longer, and he was never again molested. Perhaps an opinion expressed by the state authorities in favor of freedom of the press had an effect. Perhaps Oswald's challenge to Smith suggested that a printer who suffered at the hands of a mob was not without means of redressing his injuries.[8] Goddard and Oswald had won a victory for freedom of the press. Yet they paid a price. They were too unpopular in Baltimore to openly operate the newspaper, which was temporarily returned to the management of Goddard's sister.

The "Queries," detested by Washington partisans in Baltimore, hurt both Reed and Washington, although it is not known that the digestion of the commander in chief suffered. Lee's subtle references to that lamentable letter of November 21, 1776, sorely vexed Reed because of the effect the reference might have on his relations with Washington and on his standing with the public, and he was provoked into an open reply, sent to Goddard and promptly printed by him. Asserting that he would not have answered except that Lee was trying to strike through him at the commander in chief, Reed scored a point by accusing Lee of violating "private and confidential correspondence." He then gave his readers a most extraordinary version of the contents of the letter. *Before* the fall of Fort Washington, while Washington hesitated whether to abandon or defend the fort, Reed was so eager that it be abandoned that he wrote to Lee, begging him to support that opinion with the commander in chief. Reed's comment on Washington, as he recollected it, was, "With a thousand good and great qualities, there is a want of decision to complete the perfect military character." Reed had observed this "want of decision" in Washington upon this *one occasion only;* it had arisen from diffidence and modesty; with added experience and confidence Washington had overcome it. Presumably the commander in chief had become that *rara avis,* a military genius without a flaw. Since Reed could not possibly have forgotten so completely the contents of that embarrassing letter, he must be found guilty of disingenuity.[9]

Washington, though much vexed, wisely made no public response. He told Reed that Lee had been his enemy from the beginning of their association and that Lee had pursued him "under the mask of friendship" before they broke openly. Lee had related "self-known" falsehoods about him. Asserting the purity of his own conduct in the service of America, he suggested that in publishing the "Queries" Lee had other "motives, still more hidden and dark" than to hurt the commander in chief and to exalt himself. Perhaps he was accusing Lee of treason. To Reed, Washington also defended his own behavior in the matter of Fort Washington, placing the blame for the disaster chiefly upon Congress, Greene, and his other advisers. He thanked Reed for writing publicly in his defense.[10]

Sharply condemning the "banditti" who had attacked Goddard, Lee eagerly sought to continue the fray. He composed an explanatory supplement to the "Queries" in which he once more defended his conduct at Monmouth and once more denied that he accused Washington either of doing him a deliberate wrong or of deliberate deceit. He sent this piece to Goddard, but for unknown reasons Goddard did not print it. He also wrote a lengthy letter to Joseph Reed in reply to Reed's. Both of these essays, together with a copy of the letter of 1776, he sent to Philadelphia in the summer of 1779 in the care of young John Skey Eustace, formerly his aide-de-camp at Charleston and still his friend. Eustace tried to secure the publication of the essays, but could not find a printer there who was willing to use them. Perhaps the newspaper men in Philadelphia saw Goddard's difficulties in Baltimore as a warning to themselves. Lee then directly asked Reed himself to secure their publication. Surely Reed believed in freedom of the press. If Reed objected to their contents, he could reply through similar means.[11] Reed was not interested in helping his enemy to strike at his own reputation, and the essays failed to reach the public. This blow to Lee's campaign for vindication was heightened by the collapse of the friendship between Lee and young Eustace, whom Lee had declared to be his heir and adopted son. In the summer and fall of 1779, Eustace was declaring in company in Philadelphia that Alexander Hamilton perjured himself in Lee's trial and was vainly trying to provoke him into a duel. Simultaneously, however, he was turning Lee's money to his own use without permission, a thing which he had done on an earlier occasion. Moreover, Eustace became friendly with Joseph Reed, and finally accepted an appointment as his aide-de-camp. Mutual acquaintances warned Lee against Eustace; the general complained; and Eustace disassociated himself from Lee forever.[12]

The appearance of the "Queries" marked the end of Lee's campaign for vindication in the newspapers, although Lee continued to write essays in his own defense. Goddard and Oswald remained his stanch friends, but they could not help him reach the public for several years. Oswald finally began to publish the *Independent Gazetteer* in Philadelphia in 1782, but it was too late. By 1780, Lee had virtually ceased to write for publication; indeed, he had abandoned the struggle against his enemies as useless.[13]

Attempting to revive his prestige and to heal his wounded self-esteem in the latter part of 1779, Lee claimed, probably for the first time, that he had saved the American cause when he was a British prisoner. He privately told two persons whom he trusted that he had succeeded in persuading Sir William Howe to follow defective strategy in 1777. In a letter to Benjamin Rush he made the same claim in vague terms, promising details when they should meet again. "America owes me more than she yet knows," he told Rush.[14] The fact that he dared to seek credit for misleading Howe suggests, as the writer has already remarked, that such was his intention in preparing his "treason" plan of March, 1777. In any case, Lee did not and could not demand public recognition for his dealings with Howe, since his enemies would have had an additional ground for accusations of treachery. Nor could restricted private circulation of the claim give him any real advantage.

It is highly doubtful that the "Queries" gained Lee any friends and they probably caused him to lose in public esteem. As the period for which he was suspended from command drew to a close, public opinion among the Americans was apparently against him rather than for him. As a result there was a drive in Congress to prevent him from resuming army service and in fact to dismiss him absolutely from the Continental forces. On December 4, the day before his sentence expired, James Forbes, delegate from Maryland, offered a resolution, "That Major General Charles Lee be informed that Congress have no further occasion for his services in the army of the United States of America." There was strong support for the resolution, although no reason except Lee's quarrel with Washington and a spurious claim of economy could be offered as causes for his release. However, Henry Laurens had left the Congress, William Henry Drayton had died, and the membership of the house had been considerably altered since the preceding year. Forbes's resolution was voted down. It was approved by only three states, six being opposed, with one divided and three not voting.

Nevertheless, the vote by individuals was close, nine members favoring and twelve opposing the resolution.[15]

In accordance with this decision by Congress, Lee could have re-entered the army. Just as he was leaving Prato Rio for Winchester he received the news, together with advice from a friendly delegate not to accept pay—in order to avert dismissal on the score of economy. He was ill and in a hurry, and he fell into a fury. That so many delegates should so malevolently pursue a much-abused man! That he, almost penniless, should toil without pay in order to hold his commission! Although unable to write in his own hand, he quickly sent off a vicious note to the Congress which ended all possibility of further service. "I understand that it is in contemplation of Congress, on the principles of economy, to strike me out of their service. Congress must know little of me if they suppose that I would accept of their money since the confirmation of the wicked and infamous sentence which was passed upon me." His letter, whatever its justification, was highly insulting to his employers. If sent at all, it should have contained in addition his formal resignation. Half mad with rage, he merely gave vent to his feelings without considering the consequences, which could only be unfavorable to himself. When the note reached Philadelphia, at least one of Lee's friends contended it was a forgery. On January 10, 1780, the motion of dismissal voted down in December was again introduced. A fruitless effort was made to postpone action, and the resolution was carried by a count of five states to four, with three divided and one not voting. Twelve individuals favored the measure, and nine opposed it. If any one of the twelve affirmative ballots had been cast in the negative, the resolution would have been defeated.[16] Close as the result was, the decision of Congress was final. Lee accepted the action of Congress with good grace, apologizing for his ill-tempered letter. He informed the delegates that he had intended to resign formally in any case, because he could not have served "with safety and dignity" under Washington. His resentment of the treatment he had received and the unfortunate circumstances under which he had written to Congress had led him to commit against that body a wrong, for which he sincerely asked pardon. He concluded in manly fashion, wishing that Congress might find "many servants ready to make as great sacrifices as I have made, and possessed with the same degree of zeal for their service as has from the beginning governed all my actions; but with the good fortune never by one act of imprudence to incur their displeasure; and I can, without arrogance, assert, on self-examination, that this is the only step in the whole line of my conduct which could justly furnish matter of offence."[17]

So ended the connection which had begun so auspiciously between Charles Lee and the army of the United States; the "Palladium of American Liberty" was cast aside, without ceremony and without thanks. When Congress published his letter of apology but failed to award him even a word of praise, Lee wrote a third letter to the delegates, asking Congress to offer some recognition for his services and asking also that Congress express its disapproval of its predecessor's decision in confirming the judgment of the military court. Aware that his letter might do more harm to him than good, he sent it to Rush, leaving it to his friend to decide whether or not it should be submitted to the delegates.[18] The physician apparently pocketed it.

As Lee's insulting letter to Congress indicates, he had become half mad on the subject of his wrongs by the winter of 1779. Always temperamental and unstable, he had controlled himself fairly effectively in a most trying situation until the preceding summer. Then, as the publication of the "Queries" suggests, his real and fancied wrongs began very seriously to affect his judgment. In September, 1779, he reported a scheme of Washington partisans in Virginia to assassinate him.[19] In December, warning Gates against the machinations of Washington, he claimed that the commander in chief himself was plotting his utter destruction, and for the first time, in writing at least, he violently assailed Washington's character. " . . . I am confident as I am of my own existence, that it is the determin'd purpose of that dark designing sordid ambitious vain proud arrogant and vindicative knave W: to remove me from the face of the earth by assassination direct or indirect, and to ruin your fame and fortunes forever—for my own part, who have no family, and am tired of this rascally planet, I am indifferent when the stroke is struck. . . ."[20] No doubt Lee had in mind the attacks made on him by Laurens, Hamilton, and Boudinot, and the challenges he had received from Steuben, Laurens, and Wayne. Quite humanly he had come to see them as part of a plan formed by Washington.

Certainly, although Washington had neither desire nor need to murder him, there was one anonymous gentleman who was eager to destroy the public credit Lee still retained after his final dismissal from the army. Shortly after the discovery of Benedict Arnold's treason and his flight to the British, in October, 1780, this unknown enemy republished in the *Pennsylvania Packet* a wild report from an Irish newspaper that Lee had accepted a bribe from Clinton before Monmouth. In an accompanying letter he accused Lee of being Arnold's accomplice. "It cannot now be doubted that LEE and ARNOLD upon their meeting at Valley Forge, upon the former's arrival from the city [Philadelphia], had agreed to do everything they should ever have in their power to ruin the army of the States, and to sacrifice our illustrious chief."[21] When this nasty accusation appeared on October 3, Lee was preparing an appeal to Congress for financial help, for he was in serious straits because of lack of money. He hurriedly added to his letter a request that Congress use its influence "to keep in some decent order this scoundrel calumniator." After some consideration he wrote again to the delegates, contending that this "hellish malignant libel" was intended to point him out "as a proper subject for assassination." To prevent "some wild fanatick or a collection of 'em" from killing him he begged that Congress publicly denounce the canard.[22] His requests were ignored for more than two months. A committee, of which Samuel Adams was a member, finally recommended that both be ignored. The committee expressed the surprising opinion that Lee deserved no financial assistance because he had not given proof of losses incurred because of his service in the American army—a view quite inconsistent with the attitude taken by the delegates in earlier years.

The house accordingly took no action upon the request for money. With respect to his second petition it was resolved, "That Mr Lee be informed that Congress are fully persuaded of his attachment to the interest and well being of the United State of America, therefore are of the opinion the illiberal insinuations complained of by him are unworthy either of his or the attention of Congress."[23]

Strangely, even Horatio Gates and Robert Morris began to doubt Lee's loyalty to the United States in the late spring of 1781. They came to believe it was possible he was going over to the British out of pique and resentment. In June, Gates, then estranged from Lee, noted that he visited Tories such as Daniel Dulany in Maryland and Ralph Wormeley, Jr., in Virginia and that the Wormeley properties were close to that part of the British army operating in the state. He expressed a fear to Morris that their old friend had actually gone over to the British.[24] Although Gates and Morris were not aware of the fact, Lee's opinions continued to be much the same during the period 1779-82 as they were in 1777-78; and he was not disposed to do anything actively to help the British. In September, 1779, he was arguing that American freedom was already won, that the chief danger to the United States lay in a crushing defeat for Britain which would expose America to imperialistic designs of the Bourbons. Another danger to American freedom existed in the lack of devotion to true republicanism among the Americans—too many of them, outside of New England, worshipped one man.[25] In December, 1779, and again after Cornwallis' defeat at Yorktown had assured American independence, he suggested that the United States ought to sign an armistice with Britain for three, four, or six years. During this period of quiet the Americans could consider their situation and decide whether or not they were capable of managing their affairs under a "federate republican government." If their decision was in the negative, they could seek the "protectorship" of either Britain or France.[26] In March, 1780, he was consulting with Ralph Wormeley, Jr., about organizing a coalition of "true" Whigs and moderate Tories in order to restore what he thought of as genuine republican government in Virginia. Then he even con-

ington erred in not completely adopting it. After the British captured Fort Washington and began to push across New Jersey, he again outshone the commander in chief. While Washington prepared to defend against a British attack upon Philadelphia, Lee correctly concluded that Howe did not intend such an attack and correctly urged the wisdom of taking post on the British right flank in the region of Morristown. Then, loitering near Morristown, against Washington's orders, in the hope of striking a blow at the redcoats, he became suddenly a British prisoner.

Lee's capture dealt a stunning blow to his romantic republicanism; the realist and the Englishman in him asserted themselves; and he began to work for peace and an Anglo-American accommodation. There is no special reason to believe he did so for his personal safety. Whether he intended to reach these ends by giving the British useful military advice in his "treason" plan must remain doubtful; it is quite likely he was trying to prevent a complete British victory. If he was really trying to bring the war to an end quickly and with little bloodshed, he was hardly a mere black-hearted traitor, and his name should not be linked with that of the mercenary Benedict Arnold, for there was not in Lee the cold calculator of self-gain.

Having made up his mind as a prisoner that America ought to rejoin the British Empire and to accept substantial freedom within it, Lee seems to have clung steadily to that conviction during the remainder of his life. He did not wish America to be a victim of British tyranny, and there is no reason to suspect him of treachery after his return to the American army. He may not have performed brilliantly at Monmouth, although the evidence suggests that his tactics were fundamentally sound. Certainly the evidence points clearly to a conclusion that the verdict and the sentence given on his conduct by the court-martial were unjustified, and that both the court and Congress found against him because of personal and political considerations. Against Washington and his partisans Lee fought his most courageous fight, and a losing one. Whatever his shortcomings, there was something admirable in the dauntless bravery which he displayed in defying his many enemies.

When the proud, turbulent, whimsical, unhappy, and valiant

spirit that was Charles Lee vanished at Philadelphia in 1782, one of the most remarkable men ever to set foot in America left the human scene. His career was one of almost dazzling contrasts, and he who was a guardian angel of the American cause in the early months of the War of Independence later seemed to many to be the offspring of Satan. Fundamentally there was little of the satanic in him. He saw heavenly vistas on earth for man and tried to reach them. Aware nevertheless in high degree of the need to solve existing problems with the materials at hand, he also tried to find satisfactory solutions others would accept. After laboring mightily and romantically for American freedom, he came to believe an American republic was impractical and strove to close the widening gap between Britain and America. Had he been consistently romantic or consistently realistic, he would have been a happier and perhaps a more successful man. In deed and in word he displayed selfishness. That he was more selfish than the human race generally is, however, highly doubtful, for Lee could not and would not hide his faults behind a mask of prudence and respectability. Certainly, whatever were all of his motives in throwing himself against his own country in 1774-75, one of them was a devotion to a generous ideal. In offering his services to America he risked more than any American. No doubt he took those risks in part to satisfy his detestation of George III and his friends and to fulfill his own ambitions, but he did not make the great gamble merely for himself. Or if he did, he lost almost utterly.

When proper allowance for poetic license is made, a poem written by an unknown person "To the Memory of General Lee" and published soon after his death tells his tale.

> Warrior, farewell! eccentrically brave,
> Above all *kings*, and yet of gold the *slave;*
> In words a very *wit*—in deeds *less wise;*
> For ever *restless*, yet would never rise;
> At least no higher, than to meet the ground;
> If strong the *blow*, the greater the *rebound.*
> Of all men *jealous*, yet *afraid* of none;
> In *crowds* for ever—ever still *alone,*

At once the pride and bubble of a throng,
Pursuing *right*, and yet forever *wrong;*
By nature form'd to play the *monarch's* part
At *best* a sad republican at heart.

　　But to cast up the aggregated sum—
Above all *monarchs*, and below all scum;
Unsettled *virtues*, with great vices mix'd,
Like the wide welkin, where few stars are fix'd,
Rest, *restless* chief! thy sword has taken rust;
Peace to thy *manes*—honour to thy *dust.*[38]

BIBLIOGRAPHICAL NOTE

It was not thought necessary to prepare a formal bibliography for this volume. References to manuscripts and printed materials have been given for newly discovered or rediscovered facts and also for new and disputable interpretations. It is believed that these are sufficiently detailed for those who wish to examine the sources which were the basis for comparatively novel portions of the text. First citations of manuscript collections and of books are quite complete; for convenience, later citations of the same sources are conventionally abbreviated.

It is perhaps worthwhile to remark that this volume is based in large part on eighteenth-century documents, particularly on the writings of Charles Lee. Also, something should be said about the nature and scope of the documents used.

Considerable effort has been made to secure all the documents in print or in manuscript throwing light upon Lee. It is certain that the search, like others of the same type, has not been completely successful. Indeed, the writer found it impossible to obtain permission to examine a very few Lee letters owned by private persons in the United States, but has reason to believe that his ill fortune with respect to these items has led to no serious errors of omission or commission.

Lee's own writings are, of course, of fundamental importance in this study. Fortunately, he was not so careless about his papers as he was in other matters. He often kept letters written to him, and he frequently preserved drafts of letters and essays which he himself composed. At his death a substantial collection of his papers was turned over to his friend William Goddard. A part of these was published in a memoir by Edward Langworthy only ten years later. A much larger part, if not the bulk of the collection, was safeguarded by Goddard and his descendants for a century. Between 1871 and 1874 the New-York Historical Society was apparently permitted to print all the papers that then remained in the possession of the Goddards. The same highly valuable institution added all the obtainable items emanating from Lee or concerning him. The happy result—happy particularly because the documents in the hands of the Goddard family were afterward very largely destroyed or lost—was the publication by the Society of four sturdy volumes of Lee Papers.

The four volumes form the backbone of this study. Many of the documents printed in them cannot be obtained elsewhere. It is pleasant and rather comforting to record that the editing was generally well done. Comparison between these printed documents and Lee manuscripts still preserved proves the fidelity of the editors.

To be sure, the volumes do not contain all the now available documents concerning Lee, nor do they contain even all those written by him. The writer secured access to a number of unprinted Lee letters and essays, in the form of originals or photocopies, in the Amherst Papers, in the British War Office Series; the British Colonial Office papers; the Sir Henry Clinton MSS and the Nathanael Greene MSS in the William L. Clements Library; the Washington MSS in the Library of Congress; the collections of the Lansdowne family at Bowood; and the Robert R. Logan Family Papers. At least one such Lee letter was found in a Revolutionary newspaper. In addition, it was possible to locate and to identify several very important anonymous and pseudonymous essays written by Lee and published by him in newspapers both in England and in America. It is not unlikely that additional Lee publications of this nature will be found and identified in the future.

NOTES

CHAPTER ONE

1. The baptismal record reads: "Charles, son of Coll. John Ley was baptized on ye twenty sixt day of January 1731/2." The date given, is, of course, Old Style. Lee's birthdate is commonly given as 1731. He was born late in 1731, New Style, or, more likely, early in 1732. The writer is much indebted to Mr. P. H. Lawson, of Chester, for a copy of the baptismal record and for other information about the Lee family.

2. Ann Lee, founder of the Shakers, is described as a niece of Charles Lee in James Thacher, *Military Journal of the American Revolution* . . . (Hartford, 1862), 141-42. Thacher erred. Ann Lee was of humble origins.

3. For Lee's ancestry see George Ormerod, *The History of the County Palatine and City of Chester* . . . , 3 vols. (London, 1819), I, 466-67; II, 216-17.

4. *Ibid.*, I, 466-67; letter from Mr. P. H. Lawson to the writer, Nov. 21, 1947. Mr. Lawson's letter gives baptismal records of the twins, not mentioned by Ormerod.

5. *The Lee Papers*, 4 vols. (*Collections of the New-York Historical Society for the Year 1871, . . . 1872, . . . 1873, . . . 1874* [New York, 1872-75]), II, 376. Hereinafter these papers are cited as *LP*.

6. *Ibid.*, I, 149. Possibly Lee's studies at Bury St. Edmunds preceded those which he undertook in Switzerland. However, he states that he was a "boy" when he was at the academy.

7. S. H. A. Hervey, *Biographical List of Boys Educated at King Edward VI Free Grammar School, Bury St. Edmunds* . . . (Vol. XIII of *Suffolk Green Books* [Bury St. Edmunds, 1908]), 466.

8. *LP*, II, 376; III, 311.

9. Hervey, *Boys Educated at King Edward VI Free Grammar School*, 52, 465-67.

10. State Papers Domestic, Entry Books (SP44), Military, Vol. 186, folio 282, in British Public Record Office. It has frequently been said, incorrectly, that Lee was only eleven years of age when he received his first commission.

11. Charles S. Terry (ed.), *The Albemarle Papers* . . . , 2 vols., I, Vol. XXIV of *New Spalding Club Publications* (Aberdeen, 1902), 206, 276.

12. Franklin B. Dexter (ed.), *The Literary Diary of Ezra Stiles* . . . , 3 vols. (New York, 1901), I, 455.

13. A search made for the writer by Mademoiselle Yvonne Fernillot of the municipal library of Reims proved unavailing.

14. London *Chronicle*, Aug. 29-31, 1775. His name does not appear in the published lists of scholars at Westminster and Oxford.

15. R. Lamb, *An Original and Authentic Journal of Occurrences during the Late American War* . . . (Dublin, 1809), 102.

16. *LP*, I, 38, 97, 231.

17. *Ibid.*, IV, 26.

18. *Ibid.*, I, 149; IV, 100.

19. *Ibid.,* I, 230.

20. *Gentleman's Magazine,* XX (1750), 380.

21. Colonel Lee's will, executed September 5, 1749, is now located in the National Library of Wales. Charles was sworn at Chester as sole executor on August 21, 1750.

22. *LP,* I, 1.

23. *Ibid.,* 105, 110; Edith R. Curtis, *Lady Sarah Lennox An Irrepressible Stuart 1745-1826* (New York, 1946), 129.

24. *LP,* I, 105-106; Countess of Ilchester and Lord Stavordale (eds.), *The Life and Letters of Lady Sarah Lennox 1745-1826* . . . , 2 vols. (London, 1902), I, 291-93.

25. *LP,* I, 33, 110.

26. Lamb, *An Original Journal,* 101, states that Lee's height was about five feet, eight inches. The description of Lee offered here is compiled from many sources, in which no serious disagreement appears.

27. *LP,* I, 3.

28. *Ibid.,* 1.

29. In 1779, Lee filed a legal statement to the effect that he had served in Virginia in 1755. Lyman Chalkley (ed.), *Chronicles of the Scotch-Irish in Virginia* . . . , 3 vols. (Rosslyn, Va., 1913), II, 505.

30. Lee's name is not listed among those of the officers wounded. See *LP,* IV, 348-49, for some remarkable comments by the historian George Moore about Braddock's defeat. Moore informs us that Washington covered the retreat of the regulars (which Washington did not do) and "the young subaltern" (Lee), and implies that Lee must have behaved less than bravely in the battle. Moore, the latest historian to write at length about Lee, seems to have believed it his duty to condemn him at all costs and, on the contrary, to exalt Washington at every opportunity.

31. *Ibid.,* I, 3.

32. *Ibid.,* I, 3-5; *The Works of John Hall-Stevenson,* 3 vols. (London, 1795), II, 188-90. The twins are mentioned only in an epitaph written by Lee's friend John Hall-Stevenson, just cited. It is conceivable, but not likely, that Hall-Stevenson did not confine himself to fact.

33. *LP,* IV, 164. The "queen" referred to may be another woman. In taking to himself an Indian wife Lee did nothing extraordinary. Several officers of the Forty-fourth acquired Indian consorts. One of them married a sister of Silver Heels. Another announced that he expected to father a Seneca warrior.

34. *Ibid.,* 70-72.

35. *Ibid.,* I, 15-17.

36. William Smith, *The History of the Late Province of New-York,* 2 vols. (New York, 1829-30), II, 317.

37. Stanley M. Pargellis, *Lord Loudoun in North America* (New Haven, 1933), 349-50. Lee's anti-Scottish prejudices of this period appear in a curious anecdote in *The American Museum,* II (1787), 200. Drinking with an old Scottish officer at Albany, Lee is said to have asked forgiveness in advance, because in his cups he always abused the Scots. The old officer then similarly asked Lee's forgiveness, for he had a habit, whether drunk or sober, of laying a cane across the shoulders of anyone who abused his people. According to the anecdote, Lee was unusually polite that night. Lee had good Scottish friends at this

time, and his anti-Scottish sentiments, like those of Dr. Samuel Johnson, may easily be exaggerated.

38. *LP,* I, 7; Mrs. Anne Grant, *Memoirs of an American Lady* . . . , 2 vols. in one (Boston, 1809), II, 33, 37-38. Mrs. Grant's reminiscences, of course, must be used with caution.

39. *LP,* I, 6-15. Many myths developed about Lee. For a curious one arising from the Ticonderoga campaign see John Armstrong, *Life of Richard Montgomery* (New York, 1860), note, 185-86; *LP,* I, 8.

40. *LP,* I, 5.

41. *Ibid.,* 18, 27-29.

42. *Ibid.,* 27.

43. *Ibid.,* 19-22.

44. A journal kept by Lee on this expedition is printed in Sylvester K. Stevens and Donald H. Kent (eds.), *The Papers of Col. Henry Bouquet,* Series 21644, Part II (mimeograph, Harrisburg, 1941), 137-39.

45. *LP,* I, 26; Thomas Gage to Sir Jeffrey Amherst, Dec. 25, 1759, Sir Jeffrey Amherst Papers, War Office, 34/46, British Public Record Office.

46. The King *v.* Charles Lee, Recognizance, April 28, 1760, Autograph Collection, Historical Society of Pennsylvania; Lee to Amherst, July 9, [1760], Amherst Papers, War Office, 34/21.

47. Thomas Jones, *History of New York during the Revolutionary War,* 2 vols. (New York, 1879), II, 350.

48. Lee to Amherst, July 9, [1760], Amherst Papers, War Office, 34/21.

49. *LP,* I, 24-25.

50. *Ibid.,* 22-23.

51. *Ibid.,* 30.

CHAPTER TWO

1. *LP,* I, 30-31.

2. (London, 1761, printed for R. and J. Dodsley, in Pall Mall.) This pamphlet, and others of the period 1759-61, has been ascribed to Lee. There can be no question but that Lee wrote it, since the writer states that he had been on the river "*au beuf,*" obviously the stream on which Fort Le Bœuf was located. The style is also Lee's. It has likewise been conjectured that Lee wrote *Considerations on the Importance of Canada, and the Bay and River of St. Lawrence,* but the ascription is almost certainly without basis in fact. This pamphlet was published in London in 1759, while Lee was in America, and it is too sober and too heavy to be his product. It has also been suggested that he wrote *A Letter to an Honorable Brigadier-General, Commander-in-Chief of his Majesty's Forces in Canada,* an attack upon General George Townshend for attempting to take credit from Wolfe for the capture of Quebec. This pamphlet, published in 1760, cogently expresses Lee's sentiments on Townshend and Wolfe. See *LP,* I, 27; IV, 95. However, the writer is inclined to believe Lee was not responsible for it. Stylistically, it does not seem to have quite his touch.

3. According to Edward Langworthy, a contemporary of both Franklin and Lee, and a personal acquaintance of Lee, Franklin declared "that it would not fail of making a salutary impression." *LP,* I, 122.

4. Horatio Gates to Lord Thanet, Oct. 26, 1777, Horatio Gates MSS, New-York Historical Society.

5. *LP*, I, 31-33.

6. Lewis P. Curtis (ed.), *Letters of Laurence Sterne* (Oxford, 1935), 140, 141 n.

7. *United States Magazine*, I (1779), 168.

8. R. B. Peake, *Memoirs of the Colman Family* . . . , 2 vols. in one (London, 1842), I, 375-76; Francis Hardy, *Memoirs of the Political and Private Life of James Caulfeild, Earl of Charlemont* . . . , 2 vols. (London, 1812), I, 182-84.

9. *LP*, I, 33.

10. Upton, an Irish gentleman known as "Tatty," became Lord Templetown in 1776. He remained Lee's friend at least until 1772, when he invited Lee to visit him in Switzerland. *Ibid.*, 106-107.

11. Lee to Earl of Shelburne, Jan. 12, 1762, Lansdowne MSS, Bowood.

12. *Id.* to *id.*, July 10, 21, Aug. 24, 1762, *ibid.*

13. More properly, perhaps, Graf von Lippe-Schaumburg.

14. Lee to Shelburne, July 10, 1762, Lansdowne MSS.

15. *Id.* to *id.*, July 21, 1762, *ibid.*

16. *Id.* to *id.*, Aug. 24, 30, 1762, *ibid.*

17. *Id.* to *id.*, Oct. 11, 1762. *ibid.*

18. Colonel Cosnan to Lee, Dec. 6, 1762; Lee to Cosnan, Dec. 6, 1762; Lee to Count William La Lippe, Dec. 7, 1762; La Lippe to Lee, Dec. 8, 1762. *ibid.*

19. *LP*, I, 51-52.

20. James Sullivan *et al.* (eds.), *The Papers of Sir William Johnson*, 9 vols. to date (Albany, 1921———), IV, 320, 341, 362; *LP*, I, 35-36. Lee's writings against Amherst have not been identified. An attack signed "Z. Milis" and printed in the London *Public Advertiser*, January 14, 1764, may be Lee's product. It expresses his sentiments.

21. See Lee's later condemnations of Bute and of the extension of the royal authority, *LP*, I, 38, 40-41, 43.

22. Curtis (ed.), *Letters of Laurence Sterne*, 226-27.

23. John Hill Burton (ed.), *The Autobiography of Dr. Alexander Carlyle of Inveresk 1722-1805* (London and Edinburgh, 1910), 475-78.

24. *LP*, I, 34-35, 48-51, 55, 115-16; James Sullivan *et al.* (eds.), *Johnson Papers*, IV, 609, 767-68, 773, 788; *Calendar of N. Y. Colonial Manuscripts Indorsed Land Papers in the Office of the Secretary of State of New York, 1643-1803* (Albany, 1864), 354-79.

25. Petition of Lee and Patterson, Nov. 29, 1764, Colonial Office, 5/1130, British Public Record Office.

26. *LP*, I, 36.

27. Lee to Charles Yorke, May 27, 1765, British Museum, Additional MSS, 35,637, folios 153-55. These MSS are hereinafter referred to as Add. MSS.

28. *LP*, I, 37.

29. John Moore, *A View of the Society and Manners in France, Switzerland, and Germany* . . . (Boston, 1792), 334.

30. Lee to Yorke, May 27, 1765, Add. MSS, 35,637, folios 153-55.

31. *Ibid.; LP*, I, 38.

32. *LP*, I, 42-43.

33. *Ibid.*, 44-45.

34. *Ibid.*, 38, 40-41, 43. See also Lee to Charles Yorke, April 27, 1766, Add. MSS, 35,656, folios 454-56. In conversations with Stanislaus, Lee defended the justice of the execution of Charles I.

35. *LP*, I, 45.

36. See *ibid.*, 48, where it is indicated that Lee wrote a letter from Lyon in 1766.

37. *Ibid.*

38. *Ibid.*, 51-52, 55-56.

39. Paget Toynbee (ed.), *Satirical Poems Published Anonymously by William Mason with Notes by Horace Walpole* . . . (Oxford, 1926), 99. It was charged in the London *General Evening Post* in October, 1774, that a promise of promotion to Lee had not been kept. The charge was promptly denied. See the New York *Gazetteer*, Dec. 2, 1774. The writer believes, as indicated in the text, that there was some sort of pledge. Certainly Lee's exploit in Portugal deserved recognition.

40. It has been suggested that Lee asked for military preferment beyond his deserts. His services were as valuable as those of others who were given much higher rank. For example, those of Brigadier General John Burgoyne before 1762 were almost nonexistent. Burgoyne had married into the powerful Stanley family.

41. *LP*, I, 56-61, 69, 70.

42. *Ibid.*, 77.

43. W. L. Grant and James Munro (eds.), *Acts of the Privy Council of England, Colonial Series*, 6 vols. (London, 1908-12), IV, 815; V, 63, 69, 590; VI, 369.

44. *LP*, I, 59.

45. Albert H. Smyth (ed.), *The Writings of Benjamin Franklin*, 10 vols. (New York and London, 1905-1907), V, 117-18; Lee to Benjamin Franklin, April 7, 1768, Benjamin Franklin Papers, II, No. 120, American Philosophical Society.

46. *LP*, I, 78.

47. Charles K. Scott Moncrieff (ed.), *Memoirs of the Duc de Lauzun* (London, 1928), 38-39.

48. Hall-Stevenson to Gates, July 17, 1767, Davers to Gates, Jan. 7, [1768], Gates MSS.

49. *LP*, I, 66-70; Davers to Gates, April 18, [1768], Gates MSS. It is possible Lee had another, but not an overwhelming, objection to marriage—venereal disease. In an epitaph upon Lee written long afterward, Hall-Stevenson declared he was not conquered by the sword, fire, pestilence, *"nec tactu Veneris malignae." The Works of John Hall-Stevenson*, II, 192. Perhaps Hall-Stevenson's phrase referred merely to the fact that Lee never married, except by Indian ceremony. However, Lee mentions gonorrhea very casually. *LP*, III, 321. And Lee's "rheumatism," from which he suffered at least as early as 1766, could have been a result of that disease.

CHAPTER THREE

1. *LP*, III, 52-54, 55-66.
2. *Ibid.*, 68, 69, 71.
3. *Ibid.*, 75-66.
4. *Ibid.*, 83.
5. *Ibid.*, 71-75.
6. *Ibid.*, 77-78, 81-83, 85.
7. *Ibid.*, 84-85.
8. *Ibid.*, 77, 81.
9. *Ibid.*, 85, 89.
10. *Ibid.*, 79-80.
11. *Ibid.*, 86-88, 90-91.
12. *Ibid.*, 81, 86, 91.
13. *Ibid.*, 93-94, 97.
14. *Ibid.*, 93, 96.
15. The Earl of Pembroke reported to Hall-Stevenson in the winter of 1770-71 that Lee had been living in the best house in Lucca, but "observ'd it was so unnatural a connection yt [that] it could not subsist any time. . . ." Hall-Stevenson to Gates, Feb. 8, 1771, Gates MSS.
16. Davers to Gates, June 30, [1771], *ibid.*
17. *LP*, I, 94-99; IV, 126. No contemporary evidence regarding the duel has been found, but it is mentioned in Edward Langworthy's brief memoir of Lee, published in 1792. The report is therefore credible. It may have been based upon Lee's papers, to which Langworthy had access.
18. *Ibid.*, I, 99, 100.
19. The last charge against Grafton was certainly justified, for Grafton brassily flaunted his mistress before the public.
20. *LP*, I, 91. Lee does not mention Grafton by name, but he is clearly the person Lee had in mind.
21. *Ibid.*, 93.
22. *Ibid.*, 94-96.
23. *Ibid.*, 97-98.
24. Lee mentions writing this essay, *ibid.*, 101, 106. It was apparently reprinted in several English newspapers.
25. See "An Account of a Conversation, Chiefly Relative to the Army" and "A Political Essay," *ibid.*, IV, 91-108.
26. *Ibid.*, I, 101-104.
27. *Ibid.*, IV, 234-35.
28. W. Robertson Nicoll and Thomas J. Wise (eds.), *Literary Anecdotes of the 19th Century* . . . , 2 vols. (London, 1895-96), II, 208.
29. The Lee-Junius thesis was rather effectively destroyed in a brief article in *British Critic*, XXX (1807), 334-35. The thesis has not been revived by a serious student of Junius.
30. *LP*, I, 104-106.
31. [Davers] to Gates, Sept. 22, [1771], Gates MSS.
32. *LP*, I, 107.
33. Davers to Gates, Aug. (?), 1772, Gates MSS.

34. *LP*, I, 109-10.

35. *Ibid.*, 110-11.

36. Davers to Gates, Aug. (?), 1772, Gates MSS.

37. *LP*, I, 116.

38. Charles R. Leslie and Tom Taylor, *Life and Times of Sir Joshua Reynolds*, 2 vols. (London, 1865), II, 99. Lee probably came into contact with Reynolds and Burke through his cousin, Henry Bunbury, who was intimate with them.

39. Lee's association with Mrs. Macaulay and Dempster is mentioned in *LP*, I, 111. Regarding his acquaintance with Phipps, see his letter to Phipps, *ibid.*, 166-68. Phipps is mentioned as one of Mrs. Macaulay's intimates in Dr. Benjamin Rush's Journal, Part II, 84, American Philosophical Society.

40. *LP*, I, 108-109.

41. *Ibid.*, 97, 101.

42. *Ibid.*, 127-28.

43. Comte de Lauraguais to Comte de Maurepas, Feb. 3, 1778, Benjamin F. Stevens, *Facsimiles of Manuscripts in European Archives Relating to America 1773-1783* . . . , 25 vols. (London, 1889-98), VIII, No. 782.

44. New York *Gazetteer*, Oct. 14, 1773; New York *Journal*, Oct. 14, 1773.

CHAPTER FOUR

1. Frederick Haldimand to Thomas Gage, Nov. 2, 1773, General Thomas Gage MSS, William L. Clements Library, University of Michigan.

2. Gage to Haldimand, Jan. 5, 1774, Frederick Haldimand Transcripts, B, 20, Archives of Canada.

3. Haldimand to Gage, Nov. 2, 1773, Gage MSS.

4. This sketch, if not written by Lee, was based upon information secured from him by the publisher, James Rivington.

5. *LP*, IV, 239.

6. New York *Gazetteer*, Dec. 2, 1773.

7. *Ibid.*

8. *LP*, I, 117-19.

9. Smyth (ed.), *Writings of Benjamin Franklin*, I, 174.

10. John H. Campbell, *History of the Friendly Sons of St. Patrick and of the Hibernian Society* (Philadelphia, 1892), 37.

11. *LP*, I, 121; Williamsburg *Virginia Gazette* (Purdie and Dixon), Feb. 17, 1774.

12. Lee and Mason traveled together to Westover to make a visit. Two letters from Thomas Taylor Byrd to William Byrd, [1774], *Virginia Magazine of History and Biography*, XXXVIII (1930), 358. See also Lee to William Byrd, April 6, [17]76, Henry E. Huntington Library and Art Gallery.

13. The ancestry of *the* Lees of Virginia has been traced to several sources, but not to the Lees of Dernhall.

14. Moncure D. Conway, *Omitted Chapters of History Disclosed in the Life and Papers of Edmund Randolph* (New York and London, 1888), 15-16; Paul Leicester Ford (ed.), *The Works of Thomas Jefferson*, 12 vols. (Federal Ed., New York and London, 1904-1905), I, 9-10.

15. *LP*, I, 121-22.

16. *Ibid.*, 123-26.

17. June 29, 1774. The address was sent to John Holt, publisher of the New York *Journal*, on June 5, and was reprinted by him on July 7.

18. Tom Paine is sometimes given credit for putting forth the idea that America was the "last asylum" of liberty and that the American cause was that of mankind. Lee anticipated Paine both in thought and in expression. As noted above, Lee used the "last asylum" idea as early as 1765.

19. The pseudonym and the style point directly to Lee, and he was in Philadelphia at the time. However, we need not rely upon such evidence. Lee himself states that he wrote the address. *LP*, I, 137. One "Brutus," attacking "Anglus Americanus," in the Philadelphia *Pennsylvania Gazette*, July 20, 1774, suggests that "A Younger Brother," who was also writing for the newspapers, was the same person as "Anglus Americanus." However, Lee makes it clear that he was not "A Younger Brother." See *LP*, I, 137.

20. An extract of a letter by a Tory writer in the New York *Gazetteer*, December 22, 1774, declares the address pleased the populace, but not the thinking people, *i.e.*, the Tories.

21. The address was printed in the Boston *Gazette*, Aug. 1, 1774; the Hartford *Connecticut Courant*, Aug. 2, 1774; the Providence *Gazette*, Aug. 6, 1774; and the Newport *Mercury* (Supplement), Aug. 8, 1774. Lee states that he wrote the address. *LP*, I, 137.

22. Lee to Samuel Adams, July 21, 1774, Samuel Adams MSS, New York Public Library.

23. Haldimand to Gage, July 21, 1774, Haldimand Transcripts, B,5.

24. Gage to Haldimand, July 30, 1774, *ibid.*

25. Providence *Gazette*, July 30, Aug. 6, 1774.

26. Dexter (ed.), *Literary Diary of Ezra Stiles*, I, 453-54.

27. *Ibid.*, 455.

28. *Ibid.*, III, 417-18.

29. Lee to Samuel Adams, July 21, 1774, Samuel Adams MSS.

30. Richard C. Ballagh (ed.), *The Letters of Richard Henry Lee*, 2 vols. (New York, 1912-14), I, 110; Margaret W. Willard (ed.), *Letters on the American Revolution 1774-1776* (Boston and New York, 1925), 35; *LP*, I, 148.

31. *Royal Historical Manuscripts Commission*, Fourteenth Report, Appendix, Part X, Vol. II, 225-26.

32. Astraea, the goddess of justice, the last of the deities to leave the earth at the end of the golden age.

33. *LP*, I, 133-35. The original letter is in the Gage MSS and is dated August 6.

34. *LP*, I, 169-72. The letter is not dated, but internal evidence makes it clear that it was written in August, 1774. Concerning the date of the letter see also Boston *Evening-Post*, February 27, 1775. It was printed in many American newspapers in February and March, 1775.

35. Hugh E. Egerton (ed.), *The Royal Commission on the Losses and Services of American Loyalists 1783 to 1785* ... (Oxford, 1915), 170.

36. Dr. Thomas Young to Samuel Adams, Aug. 21, 1774, Samuel Adams MSS.

37. *Id.* to *id.*, Aug. 19, 1774, *ibid.*

38. *Id.* to *id.*, Aug. 21, 1774, *ibid.*

39. Dr. Benjamin Rush's Journal, Part VI, 243.

40. Charles Francis Adams (ed.), *The Works of John Adams* . . . , 10 vols. (Boston, 1856), II, 386.

41. *Ibid.*, 392.

42. *Ibid.*, 397.

43. Newport *Mercury*, Oct. 3, 1774.

44. See C. F. Adams (ed.), *Works of John Adams*, II, 392.

45. *LP*, I, 119-21, 130-32.

46. *Ibid.*, 135-37.

47. *Ibid.*, 140-43.

48. C. F. Adams (ed.), *Works of John Adams*, II, 401.

49. Stanislaus Hamilton (ed.), *Letters to Washington and Accompanying Papers*, 5 vols. (Boston and New York, 1898-1902), V, 86, 116.

50. The plan is printed in Worthington C. Ford (ed.), *Correspondence and Journals of Samuel Blachley Webb*, 3 vols. (New York, 1893-94), I, 85-87. A manuscript copy in Lee's writing is in the Miscellaneous Collection, New York Public Library.

51. *LP*, I, 137.

52. For examples, Williamsburg *Virginia Gazette* (Pinkney-Rind), Dec. 1, 1774; Boston *Massachusetts Spy*, Dec. 1, 1774; Salem (Mass.) *Essex Gazette*, Dec. 6, 1774.

53. The essay is unsigned, but it can be ascribed to Lee without serious question. A statement accompanying it declares that it was written, as internal evidence proves, by "a person who has long known him [Gage]." The writer gives facts concerning Gage's youth which very few men in America could have known and with which Lee as a fellow officer in the Forty-fourth was no doubt familiar. The opinion the writer expresses of Gage was that held by Lee at the time; the lucid style of the piece suggests Lee's authorship; and the item was first printed in Philadelphia while Lee was in that city. Moreover, the essay contains a quotation in Italian, which few men in Philadelphia, except Lee, could have used. It should be added that Lee gave a fact about Gage—that his formal education was completed at a French academy—which does not appear in the present writer's *General Gage in America* (Baton Rouge, 1948).

54. *LP*, I, 211; III, 366-67, 399; IV, 12.

55. See Hamilton (ed.), *Letters to Washington and Accompanying Papers*, V, 65.

56. For examples, see Salem *Essex Gazette*, Jan. 17, 1775; and Hartford *Connecticut Courant*, Feb. 6 and 13, 1775.

57. *LP*, I, 153-66.

58. Salem *Essex Gazette*, Jan. 17, 1775.

59. Irving Brant, *James Madison, The Virginia Constitutionalist* (Indianapolis and New York, 1941), 164.

60. Winthrop Sargent (ed.), *Letters of John Andrews, Esq., of Boston, 1772-1776* (Cambridge, 1866), 81, 85.

CHAPTER FIVE

1. Clarence E. Carter (ed.), *The Correspondence of General Thomas Gage with the Secretaries of State . . . 1763-1775*, 2 vols. (New Haven, 1931-33), II, 175-76.

2. The note was reprinted in the New York *Gazetteer*, December 22, 1774.

3. *Ibid.*

4. *Ibid.*

5. *Ibid.*, Jan. 26, 1775.

6. *Ibid.*, Feb. 16, 1775.

7. A thorough search has failed to discover it in any newspaper.

8. *LP*, IV, 108-12.

9. *Ibid.*, 239.

10. *Ibid.*, I, 230-32.

11. *Ibid.*, 143.

12. William L. Saunders (ed.), *Colonial Records of North Carolina . . .*, 10 vols. (Raleigh, 1886-90), IX, 156.

13. John C. Fitzpatrick (ed.), *The Diaries of George Washington, 1748-1799*, 4 vols. (Boston and New York, 1925), II, 175-81.

14. That Washington was much interested in Lee's plan is indicated in Hamilton (ed.), *Letters to Washington and Accompanying Papers*, V, 86, 117.

15. *LP*, I, 168.

16. There is no direct evidence of this visit, but it seems very likely it was made at this time. Soon afterward Lee opened negotiations toward purchasing Hopewell—something which he would scarcely have done without seeing it. Moreover, he owed Gates a visit, and was doubtless glad to meet him again and to talk over both public affairs and their private concerns. That they conversed about the estate and about joining the not-yet-formed American army is suggested in *LP*, I, 180.

17. The "Queries" are assigned to Lee partly because of their intimate knowledge of Gage. They refer, for example, to an illness suffered by Gage in England just before the Braddock campaign. The style is that of Lee. There is conclusive proof in the fact that passages in the "Queries" are identical in language with portions of a letter Lee wrote to Edmund Burke from Annapolis on December 16, 1774. Cf. *LP*, I, 145-46, with the "Queries."

18. Williamsburg *Virginia Gazette* (Purdie), Feb. 24, 1775. A draft of this essay was found in Lee's papers. See *LP*, IV, 112-16. The essay was prefaced in the newspaper by a note stating that it was written by an officer of "low rank." It should be added that the king's behavior as to the Fabrigas-Mostyn affair was not so vicious as Lee claimed it to be.

19. *LP*, I, 172-78.

20. *Ibid.*, 149-50.

21. All sorts of wild rumors about Lee flew about in 1774-75. In February, 1775, it was reported in New York that he would soon assume command of an army to be raised by Connecticut. The London *Public Advertiser* of February 16, 1775, even reported a duel between Lieutenant Colonel George Clarke of the Forty-third regiment and "the noted Colonel Lee." The latter was said to be mortally wounded.

22. *LP*, I, 144-49.

23. *Ibid.*, 143-44. This interpretation of Lee's cryptic phrases seems justified, especially since Rush was a devout republican. It is difficult to think of any other step which would cause a "conflagration."

24. *Ibid.*, 168-69.

25. Fitzpatrick (ed.), *Diaries of George Washington, 1748-1799*, II, 191-92.

26. Henry Lee to Lee, July 5, 1775, Gage MSS.

27. It is an interesting fact that Washington's diary records the arrival of Gates at Mount Vernon immediately after Lee's departure. Did Gates too wish to talk to Washington about things military?

28. Almon's *Remembrancer*, I (1775), 9-10.

29. C. F. Adams (ed.), *Works of John Adams*, X, 163-64.

30. *Ibid.*

31. George Cuthbert to John Dalling, [1776], *Pennsylvania Magazine of History and Biography*, LXVI (1942), 209; William Duane (ed.), *Extracts from the Diary of Christopher Marshall* . . . *1774-1781* (Albany, 1877), 29; *LP*, I, 179.

32. James T. Austin, *The Life of Elbridge Gerry*, 2 vols. (Boston, 1828-29), I, 79.

33. C. F. Adams (ed.), *Works of John Adams*, X, 164-65.

34. *Ibid.*, II, 418.

35. Edward S. Delaplaine, *The Life of Thomas Johnson* (New York, 1927), 115-16.

36. C. F. Adams (ed.), *Works of John Adams*, IX, 358; George Cuthbert to John Dalling, [1776], *Pennsylvania Magazine of History and Biography*, LXVI (1942), 209.

37. C. F. Adams (ed.), *Works of John Adams*, IX, 358, 362; *Warren-Adams Letters, Collections of the Massachusetts History Society*, 2 vols. (1917-25), I, 61, 64.

38. John Adams to [James Warren?], June 21, 1775, Miscellaneous Collection, New-York Historical Society.

39. Edmund C. Burnett (ed.), *Letters of Members of the Continental Congress*, 8 vols. (Washington, 1921-36), I, 133.

40. *Warren-Adams Letters*, I, 58.

41. Worthington C. Ford, *et al* (eds.), *Journals of the Continental Congress*, 34 vols. (Washington, 1904-37), II, 97-99.

42. There is fairly reliable evidence of Lee's occasional liking for money. For statements on the point by two persons who knew him and who were not his enemies, see Dr. Benjamin Rush's Journal, Part VII, 379; Mrs. Mercy Warren, *History of the Rise, Progress and Termination of the American Revolution*, 3 vols. (Boston, 1805), I, 292. There is also some evidence of generosity with money on Lee's part. See *LP*, I, 83-84; and John Bernard, *Recollections of America 1797-1811* (New York, 1887), 103. Bernard, it should be noted, relates several anecdotes concerning Lee which must be heavily discounted, although they are very interesting. Bernard is notorious for his ignorance of American history. He reports Lee as saying the Americans admired Washington because he was a patriot, Lee because he was a soldier, and Gates because he was a gentleman.

43. In December, 1774, Lee declared that for him to think himself qualified to be commander in chief—"the most important charge that ever was committed

to mortal man"—would be "the last stage of presumption." He continued, "Nor do I think the Americans would, or ought to confide in a man (let his qualifications be ever so great) who has no property amongst them." *LP*, I, 148.

44. *Warren-Adams Letters*, I, 69-70.

45. *Ibid.*, 89.

46. Dexter (ed.), *Literary Diary of Ezra Stiles*, I, 625. Unfortunately this letter has not been found.

47. *Ibid.*, 207-208.

48. *Ibid.*, 208-209.

49. *Warren-Adams Letters*, I, 137.

50. C. F. Adams (ed.), *Works of John Adams*, II, 419-20.

51. Lee to John Dickinson, Jan. 18, 1776, Robert R. Logan Family Papers.

52. *LP*, I, 185-86.

53. Richard A. Roberts (ed.), *Calendar of Home Office Papers . . . 1773-1775* (London, 1889), 378, 381.

54. *LP*, I, 186-87.

55. *Ibid.*, 187.

56. For an appreciation of his services at this time by Colonel William Thompson see William T. Read, *Life and Correspondence of George Read . . .* (Philadelphia, 1870), 128.

57. *LP*, I, 197-98.

58. *Proceedings of the Massachusetts Historical Society, 1875-1876*, First Series, XIV, 83.

59. John C. Fitzpatrick (ed.), *The Writings of George Washington*, 39 vols. (Washington, 1931-44), III, 416-17.

60. That Lee helped to write it is suggested in *LP*, I, 203, where Lee states, on August 12, "We sent in yesterday a most serious message to Gage but I cannot give you a copy without G. Washington's consent." The fact that he helped to write his chief's second letter upon the subject also points to a conclusion that he assisted in preparing the first.

61. Washington's letter is printed in Fitzpatrick (ed.), *Writings of Washington*, III, 430-31. Compare it with Lee's draft in *LP*, I, 200-202. See also *ibid.*, 211, where Lee indicates that his draft was the foundation of Washington's reply.

62. Fitzpatrick (ed.), *Writings of Washington*, III, 478-80. Lee corrected the proof of the address, and its elevated language suggests his pen.

63. Charles Francis Adams (ed.), *Familiar Letters of John Adams and His Wife Abigail Adams during the Revolution* (Boston, 1875), 79.

64. *Ibid.*, 128.

65. Dr. Jeremy Belknap, "Journal of my Tour to the Camp, and the Observations I made there," *Proceedings of the Massachusetts Historical Society, 1858-1860*, First Series, IV, 82-83.

CHAPTER SIX

1. From the American camp outside Boston, Lee wrote letters to several British officers besides Burgoyne. One letter of November 6 went to his friend Primrose Kennedy. Denouncing as usual George III, North, and Lord Mans-

field, and predicting the British evacuation of Boston, Lee promised comfortable quarters to Kennedy if he was captured. London *Chronicle*, Feb. 22-24, 1776.

2. *LP*, I, 180-85, 193, 196.

3. *Royal Historical Manuscripts Commission*, Fourteenth Report, Appendix, Part X, 337.

4. *The Kemble Papers, Collections of the New-York Historical Society for the Year 1883* (New York, 1884), 46.

5. *LP*, I, 188-93.

6. Edward B. De Fonblanque, *Political and Military Episodes . . . Derived from the Life and Correspondence of . . . John Burgoyne . . .* (London, 1876), 174-79.

7. *LP*, I, 193.

8. *Ibid.*, 193-94.

9. *Ibid.*, 194-95.

10. De Fonblanque, *Political and Military Episodes*, 174-79.

11. Henri Doniol, *Histoire de La Participation à L'Établissement des États-Unis d'Amerique . . .*, 6 vols. (Paris, 1886-99), I, 149-51, 160-61, 168.

12. Lee himself was no doubt responsible for initial publication of the correspondence.

13. The lofty phrase "the wide arch of her empire" exhibits the influence of Shakespeare upon Lee. It is derived from *Antony and Cleopatra*.

14. *LP*, I, 222-25.

15. *Ibid.*, 197, 203-204.

16. *Ibid.*, 199.

17. *Ibid.*, 211-12.

18. *Ibid.*, 214-16.

19. Alexander McDougall to Lee, Dec. 20, 1775, Alexander McDougall MSS, New-York Historical Society.

20. *LP*, I, 228.

21. Lee to William Palfrey, Nov. 5, 1775, Emmet Collection, New York Public Library.

22. *LP*, I, 210.

23. *Ibid.*, 219.

24. Lee to Franklin, n. d., Franklin Papers, XLII, No. 45, American Philosophical Society. The letter is mentioned as of recent date in another to Franklin of Dec. 10, *ibid.*, IV, No. 75. The plan is repeated in part in a letter to Richard Henry Lee of Dec. 12. *LP*, I, 229.

25. Because of the exposed border position of South Carolina, Lee was willing for South Carolina to have her own military establishment.

26. *LP*, I, 285-86.

27. *Ibid.*, 207.

28. *Ibid.*, 212.

29. *Ibid.*, 213-14.

30. Lee to Dickinson, Jan. 1, 1776, Robert R. Logan Family Papers.

31. *LP*, I, 233-34.

32. Lee to Dickinson, Jan. 18, 1776, Robert R. Logan Family Papers.

33. *LP*, I, 255-56.

34. Lee seems to have offered similar arguments in a letter to Edward Rutledge. *Ibid.*, 255.

35. *Ibid.*, 266-67.

36. *Ibid.*, 317-19, 325, 334; Lee to Dickinson, Feb. 22, [1776], Robert R. Logan Family Papers.

37. Lee to Dickinson, Feb. 22, [1776], Robert R. Logan Family Papers.

38. In April, 1776, the unfinished and unsigned draft was picked up by a British sympathizer in quarters formerly occupied by Lee. It was sent to Lord George Germain by Tryon, and may be seen in Colonial Office, 5/1107, pp. 615-18, Library of Congress transcripts.

39. Lee to Governor Cooke, Jan. 9, 1776, *Proceedings of the American Antiquarian Society*, New Series, XXXVI (1926), 300-301.

40. Fitzpatrick (ed.), *Writings of Washington*, IV, 197.

41. *LP*, I, 233.

42. Lee to Dickinson, Jan. 3, 1776, Robert R. Logan Family Papers.

43. *LP*, I, 234-36.

44. C. F. Adams (ed.), *Works of John Adams*, IX, 370-71.

45. Fitzpatrick (ed.), *Writings of Washington*, IV, 221-23.

46. *LP*, I, 240.

47. *Ibid.*, 247-51.

48. *Ibid.*, 242-44.

49. *Ibid.*, 256-58.

50. *Ibid.*, 297.

51. *Ibid.*, 262.

52. *Ibid.*, 259, 269, 271.

53. Fitzpatrick (ed.), *Writings of Washington*, IV, 266.

54. *Ibid.*, 293-94.

55. *LP*, I, 271-72.

56. *Ibid.*, 272.

57. *Ibid.*, 279.

58. *Ibid.*, 341.

59. *Ibid.*, 295-96; Fitzpatrick (ed.), *Writings of Washington*, IV, 351.

60. *LP*, I, 302-303.

61. *Ibid.*, 349-50.

62. *Ibid.*, 350-52.

63. Fitzpatrick (ed.), *Writings of Washington*, IV, 222; *LP*, I, 296.

64. *LP*, I, 296.

65. Jones, *New York during the Revolutionary War*, II, 340-42.

66. *LP*, I, 359. The date of Sears's letter is printed inaccurately.

67. *Ibid.*, 348.

68. Burnett (ed.), *Letters of Members of the Continental Congress*, I, 389-90; Ford *et al.* (eds.), *Journals of the Continental Congress*, IV, 195.

69. *LP*, I, 360-61, 362-63.

70. *Ibid.*, 354-57. Lee also recommended that the children of the leading New York Tories be held as hostages.

CHAPTER SEVEN

1. Ilchester and Stavordale (eds.), *Life and Letters of Lady Sarah Lennox 1745-1826*, I, 245-46.

2. Jones, *New York during the Revolutionary War*, I, 82.

3. *LP*, I, 293.

4. C. F. Adams (ed.), *Familiar Letters of John Adams*, 139. An advertisement in the New York *Gazette and Weekly Mercury*, April 1, 1776, throws some light upon public opinion of Lee at that time. It announced for sale swords ornamented by the head of Washington, William Pitt, John Wilkes, or Lee.

5. Lee sent his "love" to Montgomery in a letter to Philip Schuyler, September 10, 1775, Schuyler MSS, New York Public Library.

6. Philip Schuyler was first given the command, but he abandoned it because he was ill.

7. Jared Sparks (ed.), *Correspondence of the American Revolution; Being Letters of Eminent Men to George Washington* . . . , 4 vols. (Boston, 1853), I, 481, 491.

8. Richard Montgomery to Robert R. Livingston, Dec. 17, 1775, Robert R. Livingston MSS, New York Public Library.

9. Sparks (ed.), *Correspondence of the American Revolution*, I, 118, 156.

10. *LP*, I, 251-52.

11. Fitzpatrick (ed.), *Writings of Washington*, IV, 293-94.

12. *LP*, I, 280-81. See also his statement upon the Canadian command to Washington. *Ibid.*, 297.

13. *Ibid.*, 304.

14. *Ibid.*, 310-11.

15. *Ibid.*, 313. In the spring of 1775, Franklin and Lee had vainly urged that Congress authorize the training of pikemen. On February 11, 1776, Franklin made to Lee his famous suggestion that some Continentals be taught to use the bow and arrow. *Ibid.*, 285.

16. Lee to Dickinson, Feb. 22, 1776, Robert R. Logan Family Papers.

17. Paine was Lee's guest at dinner in New York. Lee reported to Rush that Paine had "genius in his eyes". *LP*, I, 325. This phrase was widely circulated and became famous.

18. *Ibid.*, 313-14.

19. *Ibid.*, 312.

20. *Ibid.*, 308.

21. See *ibid.*, 246; George W. Greene, *Life of Nathanael Greene* . . . , 3 vols. (Boston and New York, 1890), I, 131.

22. *LP*, I, 333.

23. "Diary of Richard Smith in the Continental Congress," *American Historical Review*, I (1896), 506, 507; William A. Duer, *The Life of William Alexander, Earl of Stirling* . . . , *Collections of the New Jersey Historical Society*, II (New York, 1847), 131-32.

24. *LP*, I, 342-43.

25. *Ibid.*, 343.

26. At that time Lee believed the British might make their chief efforts in 1776 in the Chesapeake Bay region, using Norfolk as a base. This opinion was based upon information found in captured documents concerning the activities and plans of Lord Dunmore. Lee to [Richard Henry Lee], Dec. 18, 1775, Henry E. Huntington Library and Art Gallery.

27. Lee to Franklin, Dec. 10, 1775, Franklin Papers, IV, No. 75, American Philosophical Society. Lee reported to Franklin a humorous incident at Boston

illustrating public opinion upon the value of regular army officers. He was accompanied on a tour of the lines by a respectable citizen of New Haven. A cannon shot flew overhead. Lee, busy with his thoughts, neglected to throw himself upon the ground. His companion, copying him, also remained erect!

28. Fitzpatrick (ed.), *Writings of Washington*, IV, 289, 353.

29. *Ibid.*, 397-98.

30. *Ibid.*, 451.

31. Alexander tried to secure recognition in England of his right to bear the Stirling title, but he failed. However, Americans did not deny him the distinction.

32. *Ibid.*, 309.

33. "Diary of Richard Smith in the Continental Congress," *American Historical Review*, I (1896), 512; Ford *et al.* (eds.), *Journals of the Continental Congress*, IV, 206.

34. *LP*, II, 146-47.

35. *Ibid.*, I, 381.

36. *Ibid.*, 473; II, 19.

37. *Ibid.*, I, 472-74.

38. *Ibid.*, 364.

39. In letters to Philadelphia and to General Washington, Lee was severely critical of some members of the Virginia Council of Safety. Robert Morris accordingly warned him to guard his conduct. *Ibid.*, 467.

40. *Ibid.*, 425.

41. *Ibid.*, 433.

42. *Ibid.*, 403-405.

43. *Ibid.*, 387, 406-408.

44. See his brief but curious account of this experiment, *ibid.*, 417.

45. *Ibid.*, 433, 449, 477.

46. Lee to Richard Henry Lee, May 10, 1776, Lee MSS, I, American Philosophical Society; *LP*, II, 17.

47. *Ibid.*, I, 372-73.

48. *Ibid.*, 380.

49. *Ibid.*, 426.

50. *Ibid.*, 467.

51. *Ibid.*, II, 20.

52. Lee to Dickinson, July 3, 1776, Robert R. Logan Family Papers. Lee's passionate and insistent letters to the reluctant Dickinson also contained some judicious flattery. "I think you much my superior in parts, and equal in integrity to any mortal breathing," he wrote to the Pennsylvanian.

53. *LP*, II, 148.

54. *Ibid.*, I, 443.

55. Lee to Richard Henry Lee, April 5, 1776, Lee MSS, I.

56. *LP*, II, 1-3.

CHAPTER EIGHT

1. William Tryon to Germain, April 17, 1776 (Private), Colonial Office, 5/1107, Library of Congress transcripts; E. B. O'Callaghan (ed.), *Documents*

Relative to the Colonial History of the State of New York . . . , 11 vols. (Albany, 1856-61), VIII, 677. When Tryon first received the report, he wrote to Germain, "God grant" that it be true. Thomas Hutchinson heard the news on June 3. It was sent to the French government on June 4. Another false report that Lee had been captured was circulated in the region of Chesapeake Bay in November, 1775. A Tory commented, " 'tis too good news for Tyburn to be true." Hugh Scott to ———, Nov. 6, 1775, Emmet Collection.

2. *LP*, II, 53-54.

3. *Ibid.*, 80-81.

4. The only available account of this meeting by a participant is that in William Moultrie, *Memoirs of the American Revolution* . . . , 2 vols. (New York, 1802), I, 141. Moultrie's relation is probably colored in his own favor. However, Lee expressed contempt for the fort after the battle of Sullivan's Island as well as before it. See p. 130.

5. So averse were many of the South Carolinians to physical labor that Lee was forced on June 19 both to order and to urge all the men under his command to work upon the fortifications. He was compelled to point out that labor upon the works might be more valuable than gallantry under fire. *LP*, II, 73-74.

6. *Ibid.*, 81.

7. Moultrie, *Memoirs of the American Revolution*, I, 141.

8. Clinton later argued that it was not intended that he attack Sullivan's. For an example of his attitude see annotations by Clinton, pp. 17 and 42, and the last page of Edward Langworthy, *Memoirs of the Life of the Late Charles Lee* . . . (London, 1792), copy in the Division of Manuscripts, Library of Congress.

9. *LP*, II, 92-97, 100-103, 107-11. An amusing anecdote of the battle is that one of Lee's aides seemed to shrink from the flying shot. "Death sir," cried Lee, "what do you mean, do you do[d]ge? Do you know that the king of Prussia lost above an hundred aide-de-camps in one campaign?" "So I understand, sir," replied the officer, "but I did not think you could spare so many." Lamb, *An Original Journal*, 99.

10. See, for example, John Drayton, *Memoirs of the American Revolution* . . . , 2 vols. (Charleston, 1821), II, 282-95.

11. Cf. *LP*, IV, 370.

12. *Ibid.*, 369.

13. Moultrie, *Memoirs of the American Revolution*, 141.

14. *LP*, II, 220-21.

15. *Ibid.*, 121, 155.

16. *Ibid.*, 230-31.

17. *Ibid.*, 148-49.

18. *Ibid.*, 97, 100, 102-103, 109-10.

19. *Ibid.*, 246.

20. *Ibid.*, 236.

21. *Ibid.*, 243-44.

22. *Ibid.*, 155. About the same time Lee threatened to resign his commission. Earlier in the year news was sent to Congress from Europe that the services of an unidentified European military genius could be obtained, provided he were made second in command of the American army. Reporting this suggestion to

Lee on May 28, Richard Henry Lee indicated a belief the officer was Lee's old enemy John Beckwith. Lee was furious at the thought that he might possibly be superseded by Beckwith, "so despicable a character . . . a generally reputed coward, (and a b——d sycophant)." He violently asserted his own claims to preferment. "Great God! is it come to this? I am not, it seems, an American; but am I not . . . *Americanior ipsis Americanis?*" Lee announced that if Congress insisted on employing Beckwith he intended to resign the service and ask Congress to reimburse him for his English estate. He said that he would gladly serve under a true genius like La Lippe and that Washington also ought to be willing to do so. *Ibid.*, 146-48. The unidentified European general was apparently the Duc de Broglie.

23. *Ibid.*, 154.

24. *Ibid.*, 239.

25. See *ibid.*, 177-79.

26. Charles C. Pinckney, *Life of General Thomas Pinckney* (Boston and New York, 1895), 31.

27. Robert W. Gibbes (ed.), *Documentary History of the American Revolution . . .*, 3 vols. (New York, 1853-57), II, 4.

28. *Ibid.*, 28-29.

CHAPTER NINE

1. Burnett (ed.), *Letters of Members of the Continental Congress*, II, 56-57. The efficiency of the British intelligence system at this time was hardly remarkable. Ambrose Serle, Lord Howe's secretary, reported home that Lee's stock was very low among the Americans. He also related a curious anecdote regarding Lee's behavior in the South. According to Serle, an American official there suggested it would be wise to proclaim a day of fasting and prayer. Lee is supposed to have responded, "Give me ten thousand more good fighting fellows; and God Almighty may then be on which side he please." Stevens, *Facsimiles*, XXIV, No. 2041.

2. *LP*, II, 205-206.

3. James Smith to Mrs. [James] Smith, Oct. 7, 1776, Emmet Collection.

4. *LP*, I, 233-34, 266; Lee to Dickinson, Jan. 3, 1776, Robert R. Logan Family Papers. Lee also asked Dickinson to support his request.

5. *LP*, II, 118-19; IV, 368-69; Lee to Dickinson, July 3, 1776, Robert R. Logan Family Papers; Peter Force (ed.), *American Archives . . .*, Fifth Series, 3 vols. (Washington, 1848-53), III, 998-99.

6. Dickinson was not a member of Congress at the time, but cordially promised Lee he would exert influence in his behalf. *LP*, I, 167.

7. The equivalent of £3,000.

8. Ford *et al.* (eds.), *Journals of the Continental Congress*, V, 851.

9. *LP*, II, 259-60.

10. Benjamin Rush told Congress early in 1777 that Lee wished to be one of a commission to interview Howe in 1776. "Historical Notes of Dr. Benjamin Rush, 1777," *Pennsylvania Magazine of History and Biography*, XXVII (1903), 141.

11. *LP*, II, 260-61.

12. *Ibid.*, 261-62; Colonel Joseph Wood to Robert Morris, Nov. 19, 1776, Nathanael Greene MSS, I, William L. Clements Library. In the second document cited Colonel Wood explains Lee's views at Fort Constitution on the fourteenth and says he gave Lee information which led the general to adopt them.

13. Henry P. Johnston, *The Campaign of 1776 around New York and Brooklyn . . . , Memoirs of the Long Island Historical Society*, III (Brooklyn, 1878), 227 n.

14. W. T. Read, *Life and Correspondence of George Read*, 202.

15. Johnston, *The Campaign of 1776 around New York*, 267.

16. *Ibid.*, 269 n.; Force (ed.), *American Archives*, Fifth Series, II, 1095. See also William Gordon, *The History of the Rise, Progress, and Establishment of the Independence of the United States of America . . . ,* 3 vols. (3d ed.; New York, 1801), II, 117.

17. Fitzpatrick (ed.), *Writings of Washington*, VI, 197.

18. See a statement by Richard H. Harrison, Washington's aide, *ibid.*, note, 214-15; *LP*, II, 261-62; Gordon, *History of the Independence of the United States*, 117-18; Dexter (ed.), *Literary Diary of Ezra Stiles*, III, 85. Lee is described as urging at this time that Howe be given a "fee-simple" to Manhattan. Alexander Graydon, *Memoirs of His Own Time*, ed. by John S. Littell (Philadelphia, 1846), 175. The unreliable James Wilkinson relates an interesting story he claimed to have received from Lee. According to this very doubtful tale, Lee found Thomas Mifflin exulting over the prospect of fine winter quarters and insisted that the Americans retreat before Howe supplied them with quarters. James Wilkinson, *Memoirs of My Own Times*, 3 vols. (Philadelphia, 1816), I, 103.

19. Fitzpatrick (ed.), *Writings of Washington*, VI, note, 214-15.

20. Washington's biographers have tended to depreciate or to ignore Lee's influence and services at this critical juncture. The writer is nevertheless convinced that Lee's counsel and energetic action were at least partly responsible for extricating the bulk of the army from a *cul de sac*. The official report on the council points toward this conclusion, and such was the contemporary public belief. Joseph Reed, Washington's secretary, who was certainly familiar with the facts, held that Lee saved the army. Similar statements were made by Lee himself and by William Gordon. Lafayette, although he was an intimate of Washington and certainly no friend of Lee, offers the same opinion in his memoirs. *LP*, II, 288, 293-94; Gordon, *History of the Independence of the United States*, II, 117-18; *Memoires, Correspondances et Manuscrits du Général Lafayette . . . ,* 2 vols. (Brussels, 1837-38), I, 31. Tom Paine, long after the event, at a time when he was sharply critical of Washington, made statements leading toward the same conclusion. Philip S. Foner (ed.), *The Complete Writings of Thomas Paine*, 2 vols. (New York, 1945), II, 922.

21. Lee afterward apparently criticized Washington's tactical arrangements at White Plains. Gordon, *History of the Independence of the United States*, II, 120 n.

22. *LP*, II, 262-63, 266-67.

23. *Ibid.*, 283-84, 288-89.

24. Fitzpatrick (ed.), *Writings of Washington*, VI, 263-65.

25. Lee Orderly Book, entry for Nov. 11, 1776, Library of Congress.

26. *LP*, II, 270.

27. *Ibid.*, 283; Gordon, *History of the Independence of the United States*, II, 125. According to Gordon, when Lee heard the fort would be defended he declared, "Then we are undone."

28. Josiah Quincy (ed.), *The Journals of Major Samuel Shaw* . . . (Boston, 1847), 27.

29. Gordon, *History of the Independence of the United States*, II, 125.

30. Lambert Cadwalader to Timothy Pickering, May —, 1822, *Pennsylvania Magazine of History and Biography*, XXV (1901), 261.

31. *LP*, II, 288.

32. *Ibid.*, 288-89.

33. As usual, Lee's language is stronger than would be used by another to express the same sentiments and thoughts. Not long afterward Greene commented that Lee "don't know the power he has over the Americans, and is consequently not cautious enough in his recommendations not to abuse it." G. W. Greene, *Life of Nathanael Greene*, I, 313.

34. The historian William Gordon later wrote Washington to ask if he knew anything about the introduction of a resolution to supersede him with Lee. Washington replied that he had never heard of any design in 1776 to exalt Lee above him. *Proceedings of the Massachusetts Historical Society*, *1929-1930*, LXIII, 369-70; Fitzpatrick (ed.), *Writings of Washington*, X, 337-38.

35. Fitzpatrick (ed.), *Writings of Washington*, VI, 297-300.

36. Washington's staff.

37. *LP*, II, 293-94.

38. *Ibid.*, 305-306.

39. Fitzpatrick (ed.), *Writings of Washington*, VI, 313.

40. Joseph Reed to Washington, March 8, 1777. Washington MSS, Library of Congress.

41. Fitzpatrick (ed.), *Writings of Washington*, VIII, 247.

42. Reed to Washington, June 18, 1777, Washington MSS.

CHAPTER TEN

1. *LP*, II, 289-90.

2. *Ibid.*, 291, 300, 301, 303-304, 325.

3. *Ibid.*, 323-24. Lee also prudently urged the New England governors to lay an embargo upon privateering, so that the Continental forces could be strengthened. Large numbers of men were engaging in that profitable business. *Ibid.*, 318-19.

4. *Ibid.*, 299-300, 304, 305, 313-14.

5. *Ibid.*, 306, 326, 328; Rufus R. Wilson (ed.), *Heath's Memoirs of the American War* (New York, 1904), 104-106.

6. Fitzpatrick (ed.), *Writings of Washington*, VI, 297-300, 305-306, 309, 312, 318.

7. Ford *et al.* (eds.), *Journals of the Continental Congress*, VI, 1000.

8. Fitzpatrick (ed.), *Writings of Washington*, VI, 325.

9. *Ibid.*, 326.

10. *LP*, II, 329-30.

11. Fitzpatrick (ed.), *Writings of Washington*, VI, 329; *LP*, II, 336-37.

12. Fitzpatrick (ed.), *Writings of Washington*, VI, 336; *LP*, II, 337-38. To one of his letters to Washington of this time, probably his first one of December 8, Lee added a characteristic postscript: "Since I seal'd my letter I am told you have the gondolas from Philadelphia with you, for Heaven's sake what use can they be of? I hope if you leave Trent Town you will set it on fire." Stanislaus V. Henkels, *Catalogue*, No. 1021.

13. *LP*, II, 459.

14. Samuel W. Patterson, *Horatio Gates, Defender of American Liberties* (New York, 1941), 105-107.

15. Force (ed.), *American Archives*, Fifth Series, III, 1108.

16. Fitzpatrick (ed.), *Writings of Washington*, VI, 340-41.

17. *Ibid.*, 348.

18. *Ibid.*, 370-71. Lee later denied, at least inferentially, that he disobeyed Washington's orders at this juncture. *LP*, III, 307. His statement is supported by a contemporary letter of the committee of the Continental Congress for foreign correspondence, which asserted that he had orders either to join Washington or to assail the Britsih detachments. Ballagh (ed.), *Letters of Richard Henry Lee*, I, 235. However, Washington's several known orders to Lee to join him hardly gave Lee a chance to exercise discretion. It is difficult to believe that these instructions were mere camouflage, and that Lee had other secret orders of which no direct evidence remains. The committee of Congress may have been misinformed.

19. *LP*, II, 345.

20. Force (ed.), *American Archives*, Fifth Series, III, 1232. It was reported that Lee was determined to put an end to the activities of the "Tories" in Bethlehem, Pennsylvania, on December 13, and "to offer his men amusement in the Sisters' House," a quasi convent of the Moravian Church in the town. Kenneth G. Hamilton, *John Ettwein and the Moravian Church during the Revolutionary Period* (Bethlehem, 1940), 166-67. Wilkinson later asserted that Lee's intention as late as the thirteenth was to assail Princeton. General John Armstrong afterward declared Lee was planning on the thirteenth to attack Brunswick. Wilkinson, *Memoirs of My Own Times*, I, 109-110; Jared Sparks MSS, CXLI, h, p. 183, Houghton Library, Harvard University.

21. These two paragraphs are largely based upon a detailed letter from Cornet Tharleton [Banastre Tarleton] to Lord Vaughan, [Dec., 1776], Hardwicke Papers, Add. MSS, 35,912, folio 239, Library of Congress transcripts. See also statements of Harcourt in Edward W. Harcourt (ed.), *Harcourt Papers*, 14 vols. (Oxford, [1880-1905?]), XI, 182. There is a story, often told in contemporary, but second- or third-hand, accounts, that a Tory who visited Lee on the twelfth hurried off to the British and led Harcourt's party to Lee's quarters. The story probably originated from Major Bradford. See Force (ed.), *American Archives*, Fifth Series, III, 1265. It conflicts seriously with Tarleton's account, no doubt reliable, except possibly with reference to Tarleton's own services. There can be no doubt that a Tory was with Harcourt, for there is ample evidence to that effect. The writer's conclusion is that he was the first informant met by Harcourt's party, that he accompanied Harcourt, and that his information was no more valuable than Tarleton's account indicates. A contemporary document seems to identify the Tory as Major Richard V. Stockton,

a famous guide who assisted the British on several occasions and who was captured on February 18, 1777. Hugh Hughes to Joshua Huntington, March 2, 1777, *Collections of the Connecticut Historical Society*, XX (1923), 53. However, the report was apparently erroneous. If it were true, other references to Stockton's services to Harcourt would doubtless be available. None has been found. As a Loyalist, Stockton might well have asked compensation later from the British government on the score of helping Harcourt, had he done so. It does not appear he made any claim to that effect.

22. *LP*, II, 348.

23. The writer's account of this spectacular incident is largely based upon Tarleton's story, cited in note 21 of this chapter; relations from Bradford in Dexter (ed.), *Literary Diary of Ezra Stiles*, III, 105-106, and Force (ed.), *American Archives*, Fifth Series, III, 1265; and a description by General Howe in a letter to Clinton, Dec. 21, 1776, Sir Henry Clinton MSS, William L. Clements Library. There is a host of other references to the incident in contemporary letters and newspapers, but these seem very generally unreliable. Howe's report is considered valuable because he had easy access to information. The writer has accepted no one account as entirely accurate. For example, he discounts tales that Lee begged for his life, related by Howe and others but not supported by evidence from Bradford, Tarleton, or Harcourt. He gives no weight to a preposterous story that Lee insisted he be regarded as giving himself up voluntarily so as to take advantage of a recent proclamation from Howe giving amnesty to all those Americans who would lay down their arms. For other detailed contemporary accounts see John K. Laughton (ed.), *The Naval Miscellany*, I, *Navy Records Society* (1902), 137; Theodore W. Tappert and John W. Doberstein (eds.), *The Journals of Henry Melchior Muhlenberg*, 2 vols. to date (Philadelphia, 1942—), II, 764; London *Lloyd's Evening Post*, Feb. 26-28, 1777.

Lee is reported to have said in the summer of 1776 that he would commit suicide rather than surrender to the British. Charleston *South-Carolina Gazette*, August 24, 1776.

24. Thomas Rodney's Diary, *Papers of the Historical Society of Delaware*, I (Wilmington, 1879), 46. Major Moyney has not been further identified.

25. Frank Moore (ed.), *The Diary of the Revolution* (Hartford, 1876), 361.

26. Tappert and Doberstein (eds.), *Journals of Henry Melchior Muhlenberg*, II, 765.

27. Fitzpatrick (ed.), *Writings of Washington*, VI, 378.

28. *Ibid.*, 347.

29. *Ibid.*, 398.

30. *Ibid.*, 396.

31. G. W. Greene, *Life of Nathanael Greene*, I, 281.

32. Force (ed.), *American Archives*, Fifth Series, III, 1247.

33. Thomas Rodney's Diary, *Papers of the Historical Society of Delaware*, I, 19.

34. *Warren-Adams Letters*, I, 283; II, 443; James Winthrop to Samuel Sherburne, Dec. 28, 1776, New Hampshire, Miscellaneous Collection, Library of Congress.

35. Tappert and Doberstein (eds.), *Journals of Henry Melchoir Muhlenberg*, II, 765.

36. Force (ed.), *American Archives*, Fifth Series, III, 1369.

37. E. W. Harcourt (ed.), *Harcourt Papers*, XI, 180-81.

38. W. H. Wilkin, *Some British Soldiers in America* (London, 1914), 219.

39. *Collections of the New-York Historical Society for the Year 1882* (New York, 1883), 321.

40. Winthrop Sargent (ed.), *The Loyalist Poetry of the Revolution* (Philadelphia, 1857), 85.

41. *Royal Historical Manuscripts Commission*, Fifteenth Report, Appendix, Part VI, 318.

42. *Transactions of the Historic Society of Lancashire and Cheshire*, New Series, XII (1897), 145-46. Mary Wortley Montagu wittily suggested another punishment for Lee. He should be condemned, taken to the gallows, then pardoned on condition he marry the republican historian Catharine Macaulay. Katharine C. Balderston (ed.), *Thraliana . . .*, 2 vols. (Oxford, 1942), I, 121.

43. Germain to Howe, March 3, 1777, Colonial Office, 5/94, Library of Congress transcripts.

44. E. W. Harcourt (ed.), *Harcourt Papers*, XI, 211, 214, 218-19. Harcourt later received many honors and succeeded to the Harcourt earldom.

45. *LP*, II, 337.

46. Thomas Rodney's Diary, *Papers of the Historical Society of Delaware*, I, 28-29.

47. Henkels, *Catalogue*, No. 1183, p. 148. The nickname "Naso" for Lee seems to have been Moylan's invention. It has not been found elsewhere.

48. *The Montresor Journals, Collections of the New-York Historical Society for the Year 1881* (New York, 1882), 420; Edward H. Tatum, Jr. (ed.), *The American Journal of Ambrose Serle Secretary to Lord Howe 1776-1778* (San Marino, Calif., 1940), 174.

49. Lafayette, *Memoires*, I, 24.

CHAPTER ELEVEN

1. James Hunter (ed.), *The Journal of Gen. Sir Martin Hunter . . .* (Edinburgh, 1894), 23. Many reports of Lee's capture assert that Lee was carried off without cloak or hat.

2. Wilkin, *Some British Soldiers in America*, 218. Lee is also reported to have declared the Americans would set fire to Philadelphia if they could not defend it. William S. Stryker, *The Battles of Trenton and Princeton* (Boston and New York, 1898), 52.

3. Stryker, *The Battles of Trenton and Princeton*, 190.

4. E. W. Harcourt (ed.), *Harcourt Papers*, XI, 211. Several second- and third-hand reports emanating from the British assert that Lee displayed cowardice both when he was taken and immediately afterward. Probably these arose from wishful thinking. His courage is amply proved by reliable and positive evidence.

5. Lee seems to exhibit a noble fortitude in a letter to Primrose Kennedy written immediately after his capture. See *LP*, II, 356. However, the letter is possibly a forgery. It seems to have appeared first in an English newspaper. Its authenticity was promptly challenged on the ground that it plagiarized a

speech by Caractacus. Kennedy was wounded in the battle of Long Island and was sent home on leave early in January, 1777. He could have carried this letter. However, the letter is suspect upon another ground, the formality of its phrasing. Since Lee and Kennedy were good friends, the document, if genuine, would probably be less stilted.

6. Sparks (ed.), *Correspondence of the American Revolution*, I, 322.

7. See *Royal Historical Manuscripts Commission*, Fourteenth Report, Appendix, Part I, III, 7.

8. James Robertson to Henry Clinton, Dec. 14, [1776], Sir Henry Clinton MSS, William L. Clements Library, University of Michigan.

9. Howe to Germain, Dec. 20, 1776, Colonial Office, 5/94, Library of Congress transcripts.

10. Henry Strachey to C. D'Oyly, Dec. 27, 1776, George Bancroft Transcripts, New York Public Library.

11. Ford *et al.* (eds.), *Journals of the Continental Congress*, VI, 1029. Robert Morris had already personally undertaken to furnish a supply of cash to Lee.

12. Force (ed.), *American Archives*, Fifth Series, III, 1369.

13. Ford *et al.* (eds.), *Journals of the Continental Congress*, VII, 8.

14. *Ibid.*, 16; Sparks (ed.), *Correspondence of the American Revolution*, I, 322-23.

15. Samuel Hazard (ed.), *Pennsylvania Archives* . . . , 10 vols. (Philadelphia, 1852-54), V, 172.

16. C. F. Adams (ed.), *Works of John Adams*, IX, 448.

17. Fitzpatrick (ed.), *Writings of Washington*, VII, 1-2.

18. Force (ed.), *American Archives*, Fifth Series, III, 1345.

19. Jones, *History of New York during the Revolutionary War*, I, 173, 175.

20. Charles H. Walcott, *Sir Archibald Campbell of Inverneil Sometime Prisoner in the Jail at Concord, Massachusetts* (Boston, 1898), 43.

21. Tatum (ed.), *American Journal of Ambrose Serle*, 195.

22. *Calendar of Historical Manuscripts, Relating to the War of the Revolution in the Office of the Secretary of State, Albany, N. Y.*, 2 vols. (Albany, 1868), I, 671.

23. Major Francis Hutchinson to Frederick Haldimand, Jan. 20, 1777, Haldimand Transcripts, B, 20.

24. Tatum (ed.), *American Journal of Ambrose Serle*, 186-87.

25. Lee himself testifies to this effect. Lee to James Robertson, [1778], Clinton MSS.

26. *LP*, II, 357-58.

27. *Ibid.*, 358-59.

28. Elias Boudinot, American commissary of prisoners, reports that in the following January he asked Lee the purpose of this proposed conference. According to Boudinot, Lee asserted that he had learned the British plan of campaign for 1777 and that it was his intention to inform the Americans about it so that they could withstand British attacks without fighting major engagements. Lee is supposed to have told Boudinot he believed the Americans could not win in the field. If such was Lee's purpose, he surely did not tell Howe it was. His explanation to Boudinot—assuming that the latter reported it correctly—was an effort to cover up his real purpose. The remarks Lee made to him must be considered in the light of the fact that the general was soon to rejoin the

American army. Lee could hardly say then he had intended to initiate peace negotiations. Elias Boudinot, *Journal or Historical Recollections of American Events during the Revolutionary War* (Philadelphia, 1894), 74-75. It should be added that this volume contains recollections based upon a diary, not the diary itself. Boudinot is therefore a doubtful authority, especially when he discusses Lee, whom he detested. The writer cannot accept a statement made to him that Boudinot is surely to be trusted because he was one of the founders of the American Bible Society.

29. Fitzpatrick (ed.), *Writings of Washington*, VII, 154-55.

30. Burnett (ed.), *Letters of Members of the Continental Congress*, II, 284.

31. Walter Clark (ed.), *The State Records of North Carolina*, 16 vols., numbered XI-XXVI (Winston and other cities, 1895-1905), XI, 382.

32. Ford *et al.* (eds.), *Journals of the Continental Congress*, VII, 135.

33. "Historical Notes of Dr. Benjamin Rush, 1777," *Pennsylvania Magazine of History and Biography*, XXVII (1903), 140-42; C. F. Adams (ed.), *Works of John Adams*, I, 261-63.

34. Ford *et al.* (eds.), *Journals of the Continental Congress*, VII, 140-41; Burnett (ed.), *Letters of Members of the Continental Congress*, II, 270-72.

35. Fitzpatrick (ed.), *Writings of Washington*, VII, 211-13.

36. *Ibid.*, 224-26.

37. *Collections of the New-York Historical Society for the Year 1878* (New York, 1879), 422-25.

38. G. W. Greene, *Life of Nathanael Greene*, I, 331-34.

39. Fitzpatrick (ed.), *Writings of Washington*, VII, 252-53.

40. Sparks (ed.), *Correspondence of the American Revolution*, I, 349-51.

41. C. F. Adams (ed.), *Works of John Adams*, I, 261-63.

42. Burnett (ed.), *Letters of Members of the Continental Congress*, II, 298-99.

43. Fitzpatrick (ed.), *Writings of Washington*, VII, 300.

44. G. W. Greene, *Life of Nathanael Greene*, I, 344.

45. Ford *et al.* (eds.), *Journals of the Continental Congress*, VII, 197.

46. Fitzpatrick (ed.), *Writings of Washington*, VII, 343-44.

47. *LP*, II, 360.

48. *Ibid.* The second request was voted down by Congress on March 29. See Ford *et al.* (eds.), *Journals of the Continental Congress*, VII, 207.

49. The famous document is printed in *LP*, II, 361-66, and in various other places. It was preserved among the papers of the Strachey family for over seventy years after Lee's death. Stolen from the family, it was finally purchased by the New York Public Library, where it is now preserved. Its authenticity was questioned in 1860 by Charles Carter Lee, who may have inherited an admiration of General Lee from his father, Light-Horse Harry Lee. Charles Carter Lee argued that the document contained bad grammar and a confusion of ideas, and that Lee could not have been guilty of such faults. He also contended that the plan was too stupid to emanate from Lee. If it were genuine, he asked, why did not Howe expose Lee and free his officers? He scoffed at the fact that the paper seemed to be in Lee's handwriting—a coincidence or forgery. Summary of address given before the Historical Society of Pennsylvania by Charles Carter Lee, December 11, 1860, *Historical Magazine*, V (1861), 52-53. But the paper is unquestionably authentic. It is in Lee's handwriting, though unsigned. There is a note upon it in Strachey's handwriting, "Mr. Lee's Plan—

29th March, 1777." Words misspelled in Lee's letters, "thoushands" and "perswaded," are misspelled in this paper. Charles Carter Lee's arguments are really trifling. Furthermore, Lee himself claimed authorship of the plan.

50. See Troyer S. Anderson, *The Command of the Howe Brothers during the American Revolution* (New York and London, 1936), 218-19, 221-27, 279-80.

51. See p. 286.

52. There is no reference to Lee's plan or opinions in Howe's reports to the cabinet. Howe's papers were apparently destroyed many years ago. Howe's attitude toward Lee's proposal therefore must largely be deduced from his behavior, which suggests rather definitely that he put no faith whatever in Lee. If Lee aligned himself with the British in March, 1777, the fact would probably appear in the papers of Howe's successor, Sir Henry Clinton. Nowhere in those papers or in Clinton's many writings on the War of Independence is there evidence that Clinton considered Lee a friend to Britain. There is ample evidence that Lee desired a cessation of hostilities and a peace giving America a very favorable position within the British Empire in 1778 and later.

53. *LP*, II, 368.

54. The phrase may be interpreted to mean not only that Lee tried to deceive the British but also that Washington knew of the attempt.

55. The writer's opinion, for what it is worth, is that Lee did sincerely desire to bring the war to a prompt conclusion, and that he wished the happiest possible fortune to the Americans. His guess, offered with many and serious misgivings, is that Lee was trying to mislead Sir William Howe. There can, however, be no assurance regarding his intention.

56. When Lee declared on April 5 he was "unfortunate in all things," he had just learned of Congress' firm intention to do all in its power to protect him. Did he mean he was unfortunate because he was not aware of the decision of Congress before March 29? *LP*, III, 368.

57. Lee's friends in Congress may have informed him through Jacob Morris of the attitude taken by Washington and Greene. Indeed, it is possible their attitude was generally known among American officers.

CHAPTER TWELVE

1. *Royal Historical Manuscripts Commission,* Fourteenth Report, Appendix, Part X, 433.

2. Germain to Howe, March 3, 1777, Colonial Office, 5/94, Library of Congress transcripts.

3. William Walcott to Washington, April 2, 1777, Washington MSS, Library of Congress; Howe to Germain, June 3, 1777, Colonial Office, 5/94, Library of Congress transcripts; *Royal Historical Manuscripts Commission*, Report on the Manuscripts of Mrs. Stopford-Sackville, II, 68; Fitzpatrick (ed.), *Writings of Washington*, VII, 378-79; VIII, 220-21.

4. Jones, *History of New York during the Revolutionary War*, I, 173-74.

5. Walcott, *Sir Archibald Campbell*, 31-32, 35; Sir Archibald Campbell to William Heath, May 16, 1777, *Collections of the Massachusetts Historical Society*, Seventh Series, IV, 96-98.

6. Fitzpatrick (ed.), *Writing of Washington*, VII, 235-36.

7. *Ibid.*, 207-209.

8. Walcott, *Sir Archibald Campbell*, 43-44.

9. Papers of the Continental Congress, No. 147, I, folio 195, Library of Congress; Fitzpatrick (ed.), *Writings of Washington*, VIII, 133; *LP*, II, 371; Ford *et al.* (eds.), *Journals of the Continental Congress*, VIII, 411-12.

10. Paul Leicester Ford (ed.), *The Journals of Hugh Gaine, Printer*, 2 vols. (New York, 1912), II, 35.

11. Examination of Thomas Bowman, [June 7, 1777], Washington MSS.

12. Ford *et al.* (eds.), *Journals of the Continental Congress*, VIII, 449-50.

13. Howe to Germain, July 8, 1777, Colonial Office, 5/94, Library of Congress transcripts.

14. Germain to Howe, Aug. 6, 1777, *ibid.*

15. *Id.* to *id.*, Sept. 3, 1777 (Separate), *ibid.*

16. *Diary of Frederick Mackenzie* . . . , 2 vols. (Cambridge, Mass., 1930), I, 152-53.

17. Fitzpatrick (ed.), *Writings of Washington*, VIII, 417.

18. *Ibid.*, 421.

19. Ford *et al.* (eds.), *Journals of the Continental Congress*, VIII, 621.

20. Burnett (ed.), *Letters of Members of the Continental Congress*, II, 438.

21. Howe to Germain, Aug. 30, 1777, Colonial Office, 5/94, Library of Congress transcripts.

22. Fitzpatrick (ed.), *Writings of Washington*, IX, 186; *Royal Historical Manuscripts Commission*, Report on American Manuscripts in the Royal Institution of Great Britain, I, 133.

23. *The Journal of Nicholas Cresswell* (London, 1925), 246.

24. Lee to Clinton, Aug. 22, 1777, Clinton MSS.

25. Clinton to Lee, [August, 1777], *ibid.*

26. *LP*, II, 376-77.

27. Thomas W. Balch (ed.), *Willing Letters and Papers* . . . (Philadelphia, 1922), 54. Lee won a $500 prize in a lottery early in 1778. New York *Royal Gazette*, Feb. 7, 1778.

28. *The Detail and Conduct of the American War* . . . (3d ed.; London, 1780), 105.

29. J. T. Headley, *Washington and His Generals*, 2 vols. in one (New York, 1875), II, 144.

30. *A Sketch of the Olden Time; or, General Lee's Farewell Dinner, at New-York, Founded on Fact. Being the First of a Series of Revolutionary Tales by an Antiquary* (New York, 1829). The dinner is reported to have taken place at the King's Arms Tavern, with Robertson presiding at the table. Baron von Riedesel, Harcourt, and the Earl of Balcarres are mentioned as other guests.

31. Howe to Germain, Jan. 16-17, 1778, Colonial Office, 5/95, Library of Congress transcripts.

32. Joseph Webb to Washington, Jan. 30, 1778, Washington MSS.

33. Fitzpatrick (ed.), *Writings of Washington*, XI, 55, 70-71; Howe to Washington, March 10, 1778, Colonial Office, 5/95, Library of Congress transcripts.

34. Lee to Clinton, March 16, 1778, Clinton MSS.

35. [Lee] to James Robertson, [1778], *ibid.* Lee's letter to Robertson was

certainly written before May 3, for a copy of it, which is cited here, was forwarded to Clinton with Lee's permission on that date. The original is not now available. The context suggests strongly that it was written before Lee left New York. Robertson apparently sent a copy of the letter in May to Clinton because Clinton, then about to replace General Howe, might find use for it.

36. Burnett (ed.), *Letters of Members of the Continental Congress*, III, 169.

37. *LP*, II, 397-99; Boudinot, *Historical Recollections of American Events*, 79-80; Tatum (ed.), *American Journal of Ambrose Serle*, 305-306. In the volume cited last, Lee is portrayed as sending a message to Lord Howe that he had kept his promise. It seems certain that the message was intended for Sir William. Lord Howe did not return from England until early in June.

38. *LP*, II, 382.

39. Duane (ed.), *Extracts from the Diary of Christopher Marshall*, 159.

40. The only contemporary evidence the writer finds cited is a letter from Washington to William Gordon of January 23, 1778, Fitzpatrick (ed.), *Writings of Washington*, X, 337. But in this letter Washington states clearly that Gates, not Lee, was the man set up against him in the winter of 1777-78. Washington's letter has been misconstrued even in one of the latest and most scholarly works on the War of Independence, Louis Gottschalk, *Lafayette Joins the American Army* (Chicago, 1937), 205. The misconception undoubtedly arises from the fact that Washington was responding to a letter from Gordon regarding a rumored attempt by Richard Henry Lee and others to replace him with Lee *just before Lee's capture in 1776*. See p. 147. The alleged drive against Washington of 1776 is confused with the alleged plot against him of 1777-78. On the Conway Cabal see Bernhard Knollenberg, *Washington and the Revolution: A Reappraisal* (New York, 1940), 65-77.

41. Boudinot, *Historical Recollections of American Events*, 77.

42. Fitzpatrick (ed.), *Writings of Washington*, XI, 213-14; William G. Simms (ed.), *Army Correspondence of Colonel John Laurens, in the Years 1777-8* (New York, 1867), 154; Boudinot, *Historical Recollections of American Events,* 78; "Extracts from the Journal of Mrs. Henry Drinker," *Pennsylvania Magazine of History and Biography*, XIII (1889), 304; Ebenezer Wild's journal, *Proceedings of the Massachusetts Historical Society*, Second Series, XI (1890-91), 107.

43. Boudinot, *Historical Recollections of American Events*, 78.

44. *Ibid.*, 79-80.

45. It should also be noted that Boudinot's memory was faulty. He says Washington at this time appointed Lee to the command of the right wing of the army. Obviously, Lee could not accept such a command while on parole. He was offered the post later, and he accepted.

46. "Items of History of York, Penna., during the Revolution," *Pennsylvania Magazine of History and Biography*, XLIV (1920), 314.

47. The plan is printed in *LP*, II, 383-89.

48. Timothy Pickering, Jr., to John Pickering, July 6, 1778, Massachusetts Historical Society; *LP*, II, 390.

49. Burnett (ed.), *Letters of Members of the Continental Congress*, III, 169.

50. *LP*, II, 390, 472-73. Boudinot states Lee actually urged before a committee of Congress, much to the disgust of its members, that the Americans gather their families and property at Pittsburgh so as to be ready to retire to the

Mississippi. Boudinot, *Historical Recollections of American Events*, 80-81. But no evidence to substantiate his story has been found. The writer has no faith in the story.

51. Ford *et al.* (eds.), *Journals of the Continental Congress*, X, 329-32; Burnett (ed.), *Letters of Members of the Continental Congress*, III, 161, 169.

52. *LP*, II, 389-90.

53. Fitzpatrick (ed.), *Writings of Washington*, XI, 295.

CHAPTER THIRTEEN

1. *LP*, II, 391-92.

2. *Ibid.*, 392-93; Ford *et al.* (eds.), *Journals of the Continental Congress*, XI, 492.

3. [Lee] to Robertson, [1778], Clinton MSS. The letter carries a forwarding note to Clinton by Robertson, dated May 3, on board the *Greyhound*. Moreover, the letter is initialed by Clinton.

4. Tatum (ed.), *American Journal of Ambrose Serle*, 305-306; Lee to Clinton, June 4, 1778, Clinton MSS. It is worth recording that the first document cited also contains a British report to the effect that both Alexander Hamilton and Daniel Morgan expressed a wish that reconciliation could be effected but that they believed it could not be.

5. See *LP*, II, 405-406, where a letter of June 17 from "George Johnson" to Lee is printed. The letter was apparently copied from Force (ed.), *American Archives*, Fifth Series, I, 99. "George Johnson" was James Robertson, whose signature so strongly resembles "George Johnson" that an editorial mistake resulted. A careful analysis of this letter together with the Lee letter cited in the preceding note has made possible the reconstruction, in part, of the two missing intervening letters. The original of the document of June 17 has not been found.

6. Evidence regarding any further activities by Lee should logically be found in the Clinton MSS. But there is no such evidence in those papers, although they contain many documents concerning negotiations and attempted negotiations with other American leaders.

7. Lloyd A. Brown and Howard Peckham (eds.), *Revolutionary War Journals of Henry Dearborn 1775-1783* (Chicago, 1939), 121.

8. G. W. Greene, *Life of Nathanael Greene*, II, 79.

9. Fitzpatrick (ed.), *Writings of Washington*, XI, 363-66.

10. *LP*, II, 394-95.

11. Frank Moore (ed.), *Diary of the Revolution*, 588.

12. *LP*, II, 399-402.

13. Fitzpatrick (ed.), *Writings of Washington*, XII, 60-63.

14. *LP*, II, 398-99.

15. George Lux to Greene, May 26, 1778, Nathanael Greene MSS, III.

16. Lafayette to Lee, [May, 1778], Alexander Hamilton MSS, Library of Congress, II; Lee to Washington, May 30, 1778, *ibid.*, I.

17. Jared Sparks MSS, XXXII, 184. Lafayette told the story of this incident to Jared Sparks in 1828. The writer is rather inclined to accept Lafayette's story, in spite of the fact that fifty years had passed, because it is perfectly consistent with the attitude of Lee at this time.

18. See Lee to Major Hunter, n. d., *LP*, IV, 44-47.

19. Lee's signed oath of allegiance, together with those of other high officers, is now preserved in the War Department. Photostatic copies of these documents are available in the United States, Revolution Collection, Library of Congress. Oaths of many minor officers are housed in the National Archives.

20. It will be recalled that Lee had insisted upon the withdrawal of the British forces before negotiations were undertaken.

21. His thinking is briefly outlined in a letter to Germain, June 5, 1778, Colonial Office, 5/96, Library of Congress transcripts.

22. Philemon Dickinson to Washington, June 27, 1778, Washington MSS.

23. G. W. Greene, *Life of Nathanael Greene*, II, 87.

24. It has been said that Greene's attitude was the same as that of Wayne and Cadwalader. William S. Stryker and William S. Myers, *The Battle of Monmouth* (Princeton, 1927), 58. But see Greene to Washington, June 18, 1778, Washington MSS.

25. The written opinions of the generals, dated June 18, are all in the Washington MSS. On Lee's views see also G. W. Greene, *Life of Nathanael Greene*, II, 385-86.

26. That is, southward of South Amboy.

27. Fitzpatrick (ed.), *Writings of Washington*, XII, 85. See also Washington's orders to Wayne, who commanded the advance guard. *Ibid.*, 86-87.

28. Minutes of council of war, Greene to Washington, Wayne to Washington, Lafayette to Washington, June 24, 1778, Washington MSS; *LP*, II, 468; Stryker and Myers, *Battle of Monmouth*, 75-77.

29. Fitzpatrick (ed.), *Writings of Washington*, XII, 117-18.

30. *LP*, II, 468.

31. See Alexander Hamilton's statement upon Lee's behavior in regard to this command of the advance force, *ibid.* Hamilton's statement is characterized by prejudice against Lee.

32. *Ibid.*, 417-19; Fitzpatrick (ed.), *Writings of Washington*, XII, 119, 120.

CHAPTER FOURTEEN

1. Stryker and Myers, *Battle of Monmouth*, 106-109.

2. *LP*, III, 7-8.

3. *Ibid.*, 231.

4. Note by Clinton, pp. 37-39, Langworthy, *Memoirs of the Life of the Late Charles Lee*, copy in Division of Manuscripts, Library of Congress. Clinton also stressed the fact that Washington's main body was advancing at twelve o'clock in column, not in battle formation. *Ibid.*, 34.

5. Fitzpatrick (ed.), *Writings of Washington*, XII, 127, 128.

6. The rains of preceding days had made the woods almost impassable. David Griffith to Hannah [Griffith], June 30, 1778, United States, Revolution Collection.

7. *LP*, III, 178-79.

8. *Ibid.*, 156.

9. Note by Clinton, pp. 37-39, Langworthy, *Memoirs of the Life of the Late*

Charles Lee, copy in Division of Manuscripts, Library of Congress; note by Clinton, Stevens' *Facsimiles,* V, No. 531.

10. Daniel Morgan to Washington, June 27, 1778, June 28, 1778, Washington MSS.

11. Clinton to Lord Howe, June 29, 1778, Clinton MSS; note by Clinton, Stevens' *Facsimiles,* V, No. 531.

12. Thomas Anburey, *Travels through the Interior Parts of America* . . . , 2 vols. (London, 1791), 339-40. It has been erroneously implied that Clinton's supposed remark meant that he was "on velvet" because Lee was secretly cooperating with him. Stryker and Myers, *The Battle of Monmouth,* 102. This volume contains a detailed study of the Monmouth engagement and of preceding and succeeding events. It is useful, but it contains many errors. Moreover, those who compiled it accept as gospel even hearsay evidence against Lee, give little or no credit to sound evidence in his favor, and continually ascribe to him without evidence the most sinister motives. It should be added that they and other writers on Monmouth engagement have made little use of Clinton's many statements regarding it. The writer believes that these statements make possible a more accurate account of the engagement than has hitherto appeared.

13. When Clinton turned about to face his pursuers his right flank became his left, and vice versa.

14. *LP,* III, 165-66.

15. *Ibid.,* 171.

16. Scott afterward claimed he retreated only after observing Lafayette falling back. He acted without orders. But Lee, Mercer, Edwards, and Lieutenant Colonel Brooks, Lee's adjutant, insisted that Scott began the retreat. *Ibid.,* 108-110, 118, 165-66, 171, 182-83. Scott may have erred by concluding that the two regiments moving to take position upon the knoll were retreating. Their line of march was to the right rather than forward.

17. *Ibid.,* 20.

18. *Ibid.,* 12, 14, 16-17, 134-35; Gottschalk, *Lafayette Joins the American Army,* 224-25. Professor Gottschalk's account of Lafayette's part in the engagement is scholarly and accurate. As he points out, Lafayette's behavior at Monmouth won him no laurels. *Ibid.,* 226, 229-30.

19. *LP,* III, 20-21.

20. The village was actually called Freehold then as now.

21. Note by Clinton, p. 33, Langworthy, *Memoirs of the Life of the Late Charles Lee,* copy in Division of Manuscripts, Library of Congress. Lee feared a cavalry attack. Clinton intended to use infantry. Wayne contended that the line behind the ravine and running to the village was defensible, but the judgment of Clinton and Lee was no doubt correct.

22. *LP,* III, 12, 23-24, 183-84, 193-96, 199-200.

23. *Ibid.,* 77-78, 129-30.

24. *Ibid.,* 52-53, 198-99. Washington's letter has not been found. It should be noted that the differing accounts of Laurens and Lee concerned a message received and read hurriedly under great pressure. There is no special reason to believe either account was dishonest. When Lee and Laurens gave their conflicting testimony, Lee was on trial before a court-martial, with Washington as his accuser. Laurens, on the other hand, was devoted to Washington. Neither account can be classified as coolly impartial.

25. *Ibid.*, 184-86.

26. *Ibid.*, 232. It is often stated that Lee never informed his superior of his predicament. Indeed, he himself later was not certain he had, in all likelihood because at the moment he thought the message of little importance. This conclusion fits in with Lee's belief that Washington could do nothing to help him. But see Clark's sworn statement just cited, the authenticity and accuracy of which can hardly be questioned.

27. It has been erroneously contended that Lee did not intend to occupy the hill. But see *ibid.*, 117-18, 172-73.

28. *Ibid.*, 232.

29. *Ibid.*, 78, 81, 112, 147, 191-92. There is a story, known to many Americans, that Washington on this occasion called Lee "a damned poltroon." Contemporary testimony under oath cited above and other contemporary accounts describing the incident contain no suggestion of profanity. The story that Washington swore at Lee began with Lafayette, who told it in 1812, over thirty years later; and Lafayette was not present at the meeting. It is certain Lee would never have permitted any man to use such language toward him without demanding an apology or satisfaction upon the dueling ground; and there is no record showing he demanded that Washington retract a personal insult. Two qualities which cannot possibly be denied to Lee are pride and fearlessness. It should be added that Lafayette violently took Washington's part against Lee after Monmouth. His recollections must always be taken with caution. Here is another myth of the War of Independence.

30. *Ibid.*, 112.

31. Note by Clinton, Stevens' *Facsimiles*, V, No. 531.

32. *LP*, III, 112-13, 159.

33. *Ibid.*, 75-76, 114, 200-201.

34. Washington's aides Fitzgerald and Hamilton later contended Lee did little or nothing toward carrying out Washington's orders to hold off the British. But see *ibid.*, 59-60, 62, 70-71, 113-14, 138, 157-58, 159, 188-90.

35. *Ibid.*, 78-79.

36. Clinton set the time of the withdrawal at ten o'clock, Washington, at midnight. Oddly enough, Clinton's reckoning of time on June 28 was consistently two hours behind Washington's.

37. Fitzpatrick (ed.), *Writings of Washington*, XII, 139-46.

38. *Ibid.*, 156-57.

39. *LP*, II, 472.

40. *Ibid.*, III, 255-65, especially 260-61.

41. Clinton was very touchy about his military reputation. During and after the War of Independence he wrote many notes defending his own conduct. Some of his notes were written as comments in the margins of books dealing with the war, such as the histories of Stedman and Gordon, and Langworthy's *Memoirs of the Life of the Late Charles Lee*, cited several times in this chapter. The notes consistently tell the same story. Clinton's view in retrospect is most clearly portrayed in his notes in the latter volume, in the Division of Manuscripts, Library of Congress. See also his account of Monmouth, n. d., prepared for the press but not printed, in the Clinton MSS; Stevens' *Facsimiles*, V, No. 531; and Clinton's unpublished account of his role in the War of Independence in the William L. Clements Library, "An Historical Detail of Seven Years

Campaigns in North America from 1775 to 1782 . . . ," I, 99-115. Clinton's "Historical Detail" consists of three volumes. It is to be hoped that it will soon be published.

42. Dispute about the Monmouth engagement extended even to the number of casualties. Clinton officially reported 65 slain, 59 dead from heat and fatigue, 170 wounded, and 64 missing. Washington set his losses at 69 killed, 161 wounded, and 122 missing, many of whom, as he says, later returned to duty. But Washington is reported to have received accounts from burying parties that they had interred 217 redcoats. *LP*, II, 447, 466-67. The figures are irreconcilable, and there is no sound reason to give full credit to one set of figures rather than to the other. In view of the nature of the action one would expect Clinton's losses to be a bit heavier than Washington's.

CHAPTER FIFTEEN

1. *LP*, III, 69.
2. *Ibid.*, 99.
3. Concerning the activities of Washington's aides see also *ibid.*, II, 430-35.
4. *Ibid.*, III, 79, 82-83. According to hearsay evidence, before Washington retired on June 27, he received Dr. Griffith on a strange errand. As the story goes, Griffith appeared from the darkness, was challenged by a sentry, and demanded that he be allowed to see the general upon important business. The sentinel called the officer of the guard. Griffith insisted to him that he had "secret and important" intelligence for Washington. The officer consulted the general, and Griffith was admitted to his quarters. The chaplain warned Washington to be on his guard the following day against the bad conduct of those upon whom he depended to execute his orders. Griffith gave this warning on the authority of persons whom he could not name but who were both honorable and attached to the American cause. In effect, Griffith supposedly warned Washington against treachery or something close to treachery on the part of Lee. The story is a fascinating one, but it should probably be placed among the many myths of the War of Independence. It was first told by George Washington Parke Custis many years after the war. Custis states he obtained it from a Colonel Nicholas, a Virginia officer. Where Nicholas got it is not stated. The story is therefore hearsay at least third-hand. On June 30, three days after this dramatic supposed interview, Griffith described the engagement at Monmouth in a letter to his wife. Lee's conduct at Monmouth was then under heavy fire. Griffith's description, cautiously worded, suggests that Griffith was then questioning Lee's behavior. George W. P. Custis, *Recollections and Private Memoirs of Washington* . . . , ed. by Benson J. Lossing (New York, 1860), 290-92; David Griffith to Hannah [Griffith], June 30, 1778, United States, Revolution Collection, Library of Congress. Griffith testified against Lee—according to Lee, unwillingly—at the latter's trial by court-martial. *LP*, III, 82-83, 203-204. It is an interesting fact that Griffith and Lee came close in death, if not in life. Both men were buried in the churchyard of Christ Church in Philadelphia.
5. *LP*, II, 430. No good reason appears for giving this letter the date June 29, as the editors have done.
6. *Ibid.*, III, 98-99.

7. The letter of Wayne and Scott is printed, *ibid.*, II, 438-40. It is possible this letter was received after Washington replied to Lee, but it seems likely that such was not the case. See John Marshall, *The Life of George Washington*, 2 vols. (Philadelphia, 1832), I, 257.

8. *LP*, III, 100.

9. *Ibid.* The letter is printed as if Lee had dated it June 27, an error.

10. *Ibid.*, 101.

11. Fitzpatrick (ed.), *Writings of Washington*, XII, 133.

12. *LP*, III, 2. The charges were based on Article V, Section 2, of the rules of war adopted by Congress on September 20, 1776, which called for the punishment of army personnel disobeying the lawful orders of the commander in chief; Article XIII, Section 13, which prescribed death or other penalty for one who should "misbehave himself before the enemy, and run away, or shamefully abandon any fort, post, or guard, which he . . . shall be commanded to defend"; and Article II, Section II, providing that any officer who behaved himself "with contempt or disrespect towards the general, or other commander-in-chief . . . or shall speak words tending to his hurt or dishonor" should be punished by court-martial.

13. No evidence appears that other officers behaved better after the letters were published and Lee was found guilty of disrespectful conduct.

14. Simms (ed.), *Army Correspondence of John Laurens*, 200; *LP*, II, 467-68. Several years later, after Lee's death, Hamilton made the charge publicly in a eulogy of Greene. Henry Cabot Lodge (ed.), *The Works of Alexander Hamilton*, 12 vols. (New York and London, 1904), VIII, 68. At least one British official rejoiced because of Lee's difficulties. They led his old acquaintance Sir Joseph Yorke to gloat and to laugh. He wrote to Amherst, who probably reacted similarly: "What has diverted me highly has been to see that fellow Lee, suspended for misbehavior and cowardice by those American heroes. They have paid old scores for us all with that intractable fellow who was to drive us out of America. I could not help laughing at this for an hour together. . . ." J. C. Long, *Lord Jeffery Amherst* . . . (New York, 1933), 250-51.

15. Lafayette to Henry Laurens, July 9, 1778, *South Carolina Historical and Genealogical Magazine*, IX (1908), 60. Long afterward, however, Lafayette told Jared Sparks that Lee could not be suspected of treachery at Monmouth. Sparks MSS, XXXII, 188.

16. Fitzpatrick (ed.), *Writings of Washington*, XII, 255.

17. Charles Campbell (ed.), *The Bland Papers* . . . , 2 vols. (Petersburg, Va., 1840-43), I, 96.

18. Lee to Stirling, July 2, 1778, Stirling to Lee, July 2, 1778, Stirling to Washington, July 2, 1778, Washington MSS.

19. See p. 166.

20. Lee left a colt to Grayson in remembrance of their friendship. *LP*, IV, 30.

21. Hamilton's own opinion of Washington at this time was a low one. It is possible that he was not too well pleased with Washington's management of the army before and at Monmouth. Nathan Schachner, *Alexander Hamilton* (New York, 1946), 120, 127-31. Hamilton, even as a young man, had a very high estimate of his own abilities and fancied himself as something of a military genius.

22. L'Enfant's name appears in the record of the court-martial as Langfrang.

23. Knox clearly though cautiously indicated in a letter of July 3 to his brother William that his sympathies lay with Lee. Francis S. Drake, *Life and Correspondence of Henry Knox . . .* (Boston, 1873), 58-59.

24. The proceedings of the court-martial are most conveniently available in *LP*, III, 1-208. The writer's description of the court-martial is based on careful study of this record. The record is fascinating reading. The testimony of individual witnesses may easily be found by consulting the entries under their names in the index, *ibid.*, IV.

25. *Ibid.*, III, 233.

26. Lee to Major John Clark, Sept. 3, [1778], Henkels, *Catalogue*, March 22, 1910.

27. *LP*, III, 208.

28. Lee afterward indicated the court was not unanimous in reaching judgment. *Ibid.*, 346.

29. At Cooperstown, New York, in 1823.

30. For examples, see Gordon, *History of the Independence of the United States*, II, 356-67; C. Stedman, *History of the Origin, Progress, and Termination of the American War*, 2 vols. (London, 1794), II, 14-24; Henry Lee, *Memoirs of the War in the Southern Department of the United States*, 2 vols. (Philadelphia and New York, 1812), I, 56-63; *Tyler's Quarterly Historical and Genealogical Magazine*, VII (1925), 39, for Timothy Pickering's opinion; Marshall, *Life of George Washington*, I, 250-58; *LP*, IV, 300-17, for Jared Sparks's account; Henry B. Carrington, *Battles of the American Revolution 1775-1781 . . .* (New York, Chicago, New Orleans, 1876), 422-45; Edwin Salter and George C. Beekman, *Old Times in Old Monmouth . . .* (Freehold, 1887), 43-50, under title "Monmouth's Centennial," for some astute comments by General J. W. De-Puyster; Stryker and Myers, *The Battle of Monmouth, passim*. The best testimony among these writers that the verdict was contrary to the facts is contained in the work last cited. Filled with praise of Washington and with innuendo against Lee, it ends with the same opinion as the others. See especially p. 250.

31. See account of the battle by Stedman, cited in the preceding note. In Clinton's copy of Stedman's history, now in the John Carter Brown Library, Providence, Rhode Island, there is no serious effort to controvert the thesis. Clinton ordinarily commented sharply in the margins of his books concerning the War of Independence when he found statements of which he did not approve. It should be added that Stedman had a very low opinion of Clinton's abilities.

32. It was believed that Lee joined the Conway Cabal after his release by the British. Graydon (Littell, ed.), *Memoirs of His Own Time*, 299.

33. Did the court reach its verdict long before the evidence was all taken and did the fact leak out? Or were Major Samuel Shaw and Wayne shrewd guessers? Shaw predicted on July 16 that Lee would be dismissed from the service. Quincy (ed.), *Journals of Major Samuel Shaw*, 63. On July 20, Wayne declared in a letter to Light-Horse Harry Lee that he believed Charles Lee would not be long in the American army. Anthony Wayne to Henry Lee, July 20, 1778, Anthony Wayne MSS, V, Historical Society of Pennsylvania.

34. Note by Clinton, n. d., Clinton MSS. The writer sees nothing Arnold could gain from deliberately giving Clinton misinformation.

35. Gershom Mott to Colonel John Lamb, July 25, 1778, John Lamb MSS,

New-York Historical Society. Conrad Alexandre Gerard, French ambassador to the United States, reported home on the Lee trial and verdict: *"Malheureusement cette affaire tient aux cabales qui divisoient le continent entre les Generaux Wasington et Gates. On assure que les chefs sont reconciliés; mais M. Lee est la seconde victime de leur division."* Gerard declared Conway was the first victim of the Washington-Gates rivalry, and predicted Thomas Mifflin would be a third. John J. Meng (ed.), *Dispatches and Instructions of Conrad Alexandre Gerard 1778-1780* ... (Baltimore, 1939), 231.

36. Dr. William Shippen, Jr., to Richard Henry Lee, September 12, 1778, *Historical Magazine*, IX (1865), 210.

37. John Penn to Governor Caswell, July 15, 1778, *State Records of North Carolina*, XIII, 197.

38. Quincy (ed.), *Journals of Major Samuel Shaw*, 63.

39. Samuel Holden Parsons to [Samuel Adams], July 9, 1778, Samuel Adams MSS.

CHAPTER SIXTEEN

1. Fitzpatrick (ed.), *Writings of Washington*, XII, 139-46.
2. *LP*, II, 453-57.
3. *Ibid.*, 452-53.
4. *Ibid.*, 457-59.
5. *Ibid.*, 475-80.
6. *Ibid.*, III, 249-50.
7. *Ibid.*, II, 430-35, 449-51.
8. *Ibid.*, 472-73. Laurens then believed that Lee plotted with the British to trap the American army and that Dr. Robert Wellford, mentioned above, was a go-between. He was of the opinion that Wellford merely pretended to be a convert to the American cause in order to deliver a message to Lee. However, long afterward, Washington himself testified to Wellford's loyalty to the United States. Fitzpatrick (ed.), *Writings of Washington*, XXXVII, 26. Washington had Wellford as a guest at dinner almost immediately after he crossed the British lines and knew him over a period of many years.
9. *LP*, II, 467-72.
10. *Ibid.*, 474-75. In his reminiscences Boudinot, still critical of Lee's behavior at Monmouth, ascribed it to "a partial lunacy" rather than to treachery. Boudinot, *Historical Recollections of American Events*, 81-82. Like Lafayette, he seems to have altered his opinion after the excitement died down.
11. *LP*, III, 229-30.
12. *Ibid.*, 228. Rush wrote several unsigned letters during the War of Independence, for similar reasons.
13. *Ibid.*, 237.
14. *Ibid.*, 228-29.
15. Lee to Major John Clark, Sept. 3, [1778], Henkels, *Catalogue*, March 22, 1910; *LP*, III, 230-33.
16. *Ibid.*, 236.
17. Fitzpatrick (ed.), *Writings of Washington*, XII, 459-60.

18. *LP*, III, 238; Dr. William Shippen, Jr., to Richard Henry Lee, September 12, 1778, *Historical Magazine*, IX (1865), 210.

19. Sparks (ed.), *Correspondence of the American Revolution*, II, 153-54.

20. John Penn to Governor Caswell, July 15, 1778, *State Records of North Carolina*, XIII, 197.

21. Lee afterward denounced Penn. See p. 269.

22. Arthur St. Clair to Washington, Nov. 15, 1778, Washington MSS.

23. Ford *et al.* (eds.), *Journals of the Continental Congress*, XII, 887.

24. Meng (ed.), *Dispatches of Conrad A. Gerard*, 351; Joseph Hewes to Governor Caswell, Nov. 24, 1778, *State Records of North Carolina*, XIII, 299. In October, Lee himself declared his fate would be settled as a party issue. *LP*, III, 238.

25. Jared Sparks, *The Life of Gouverneur Morris . . .* , 3 vols. (Boston, 1832), I, 177.

26. *LP*, IV, 152-53.

27. Dr. Benjamin Rush to John Adams, Oct. 27, 1778, *Pennsylvania Magazine of History and Biography*, XXIX (1905), 17-18. On November 6 Rush wrote to Dr. David Ramsay that Congress did not dare to approve, "for the proceedings of the court . . . not only shew that Lee is innocent of the charges . . . but that he saved the army & country on the 28th of June. They dare not reverse it, for this would impeach the veracity and candor of our commander in chief, & he possesses nearly as much influence over the resolutions of our Congress as the king of Britain does over the acts of the British parliament." *Ibid.*, 20.

28. *LP*, III, 244; Ford *et al.* (eds.), *Journals of the Continental Congress*, XII, 1082.

29. Burnett (ed.), *Letters of Members of the Continental Congress*, III, 475, 478.

30. Arthur St. Clair to Washington, Nov. 15, 1778, Washington MSS. The writer has been unable to discover whether the presence of Richard Henry Lee was really necessary in Virginia. Possibly he found the struggle against Washington unprofitable. In Virginia, however, he continued to support Lee. It is a curious fact that his brother, Francis Lightfoot Lee, voted in Congress to confirm the findings of the military court. The conduct of a third brother, Arthur Lee, a diplomat in Europe, was then under heavy fire from Silas Deane. If one were of a suspicious turn of mind, one might conjecture that Richard Henry and Francis Lightfoot sold out Charles Lee to win friends for Arthur Lee, whom, of course, they ardently defended. Henry Laurens gave his backing to Arthur Lee. There is no evidence to give strength to such a thesis.

31. Ford *et al.* (eds.), *Journals of the Continental Congress*, XII, 1184.

32. *Ibid.*, 1188.

33. *Ibid.*, 1195. Nathaniel Scudder of New Jersey also voted against Lee, but his ballot was not counted, because his state was represented by him alone. No delegate from Delaware was present.

34. Among the absentees, William Paca and Richard Hutson, who voted on December 2 to postpone the issue, were on the floor of Congress soon after December 5; Elbridge Gerry, William Ellery, and Daniel Roberdeau were present on November 28 and December 16; Thomas McKean on November 23 and December 16; Cyrus Griffin on October 29 and December 23; and John

Witherspoon on November 2 and December 16. Nine other delegates, including Richard Henry Lee and Robert Morris, left the Congress between October 16 and December 2 and did not return during the year 1778. It would be absurd, of course, to suggest that all these men believed in Lee's innocence or that they all absented themselves to avoid the issue. Paca, and probably Hutson, sided with Lee.

35. On December 17, Lee asked Congress to supply him with a copy of its proceedings in his case. Congress postponed answering until the journals could be examined, voted to refuse the request, and finally reversed itself, granting his wish. Ford *et al.* (eds.), *Journals of the Continental Congress,* XII, 1229-30, 1235, 1239. Even then Congress gave him no information which would indicate the attitude of individual delegates. *LP,* III, 276-77.

36. Thacher, *Military Journal of the American Revolution,* 462.

37. *LP,* III, 238-39.

38. *Ibid.,* 320.

39. Burnett (ed.), *Letters of Members of the Continental Congress,* III, 519.

40. *LP,* III, 255-65.

41. *Ibid.,* 265-69. Lee sent a copy of this essay to Gates on December 18, asking him, if possible, to secure its publication in Boston, and saying, "I know not who wrote it, tho' the world is pleas'd to lay it to me." *Ibid.,* 278. The essay is nevertheless unquestionably Lee's product. Style and content mark it as his production beyond doubt. In effect, Lee told Gates he had written it but did not wish to acknowledge the fact. It will be recalled that Conway's letter to Gates led to disaster for Conway.

42. Robert Honyman of Hanover County, Virginia, wrote in his diary: "General Lee's trial is published, & has wrought a great change in the minds of many in his favour. His great abilities were never so conspicuously distinguish'd as upon this occasion. . . ." Diary of Robert Honyman, 325-26, Division of Manuscripts, Library of Congress.

43. Fitzpatrick (ed.), *Writings of Washington,* XIII, 383-84.

44. *Ibid.*

45. *LP,* III, 273; Burnett (ed.), *Letters of Members of the Continental Congress,* III, 521.

CHAPTER SEVENTEEN

1. Ford *et al.* (eds.), *Journals of the Continental Congress,* XIII, 218, 253-55, 259-60. *LP,* III, 310, 312-15.

2. In March, Rush also advised Gates to resign, ironically declaring, "The war is nearly over, so that you cannot retrieve your *ill* fortune, nor atone for your crimes by loosing a province, or wasting an army hereafter—nothing but a resignation can save your reputation, or restore you again to the favor of the public." *LP,* III, 217-18, 316, 323.

3. *Ibid.,* 202.

4. *Ibid.,* 253.

5. Lee's letter to Steuben, dated December 2, is now in private hands and unavailable. The writer's description of its contents is based upon a portion of it, quoted in the catalogue of the William Randolph Hearst Collection sale,

November 16-17, 1938, and upon a summary of it in Friedrich Kapp, *The Life of Frederick William Von Steuben* . . . (New York, 1859), 164-65. There is no doubt about the nature of Lee's reply.

6. *LP*, III, 254.

7. Perhaps it was youth and. Gallic blood in Hamilton and Laurens which led them to indulge in gasconade. They could do nothing so foolish as did Lafayette. He was silly enough to challenge the Earl of Carlisle, head of the British peace commission, for making in an official capacity remarks Lafayette considered insulting to the king of France! Washington tried, but too late, to restrain the young Frenchman, pointing out gently that he would be ridiculed. Carlisle must have laughed heartily.

8. Quincy (ed.), *Journals of Major Samuel Shaw*, 54-55.

9. *LP*, III, 283, IV, 152.

10. Graydon, *Memoirs of His Own Time*, 323-24. Graydon obtained his information from Edwards.

11. *LP*, III, 283-85.

12. Quincy (ed.), *Journals of Major Samuel Shaw*, 55.

13. Alexander Garden, *Anecdotes of the American Revolution*, 3 vols. (Brooklyn, 1865), I, 73.

14. *LP*, III, 297-300.

15. *Ibid.*, 294-97. Boudinot was surely the perpetrator. Lee asserted he was, and Livingston, who was in close touch with Collins, had no doubt Boudinot was responsible. He writes as if there could be no question regarding the identity of Lee's assailant.

16. *Ibid.*, 300-301.

17. See p. 347, note 10.

18. *LP*, III, 291-94.

19. *Ibid.*, 356-57. Wayne may not have been on the best of terms with Laurens and Hamilton. In 1777, while asserting his loyalty to Washington, Wayne said he intended to be friendly with Lee and Gates.

20. See p. 288.

21. Most of these parallels were brought to the attention of the writer by Mr. Bernhard Knollenberg.

22. Hutson had supported Lee in Congress.

23. *LP*, III, 305-306.

24. *Ibid.*, 331.

25. *Ibid.*, 307-308.

26. *Ibid.*, 308-309.

27. Note his inclusion of the phrase, "a mere chief justice of South Carolina," which Lee had not used.

28. Drayton had refused to support those who actively resisted the execution of the Stamp Act in South Carolina.

29. *Ibid.*, 317-18.

30. See a note to this effect by Major Alexander Garden upon a manuscript version of Lee's last letter to Drayton, in Autograph Collection, Historical Society of Pennsylvania.

31. Graydon, *Memoirs of His Own Time*, 468-70.

32. A thrust at the heavy-drinking William Alexander, Earl of Stirling.

33. *LP*, III, 278-81.

34. *United States Magazine,* I (1779), 168.
35. *Ibid.,* 41-42.
36. *LP,* III, 302-303.
37. *United States Magazine,* I (1779), 163-65.
38. New York *Royal Gazette,* March 13, 1779, March 17, 1779.
39. *United States Magazine,* I (1779), 166-72.
40. Ths accusation probably should be linked with a remark made by Lee on April 4, when he informed Gates he had recently seen General Armstrong in the streets with a mulatto girl. *LP,* III, 322-23.
41. *Ibid.,* 333.
42. Ford *et al.* (eds.), *Journals of the Continental Congress,* XIII, 442.
43. Headley, *Washington and His Generals,* II, 168 n. The writer has been unable to trace the story of this incident to a contemporary source. James Thacher's *Military Journal* is given as authority for it by Headley. A search through several editions of Thacher's work failed to unearth it. Headley's account, however, tallies so well with what is known about Lee and Brackenridge that it is probably fundamentally accurate, though possibly in error as to details.
44. Horace W. Smith (ed.), *Nuts for Future Historians to Crack* (Philadelphia, 1856), 74. There is some doubt in the mind of the writer regarding the authenticity of the story. It appeared in a document published in an attempt to discredit both Reed and Reed's grandson, who was also his biographer. The original was not produced, and it has not been found. The Lee of the story certainly resembles the Lee of history.
45. Duane (ed.), *Extracts from the Diary of Christopher Marshall,* 215. The identity of the "doxey," if one existed, cannot now be established.
46. *LP,* III, 375.

CHAPTER EIGHTEEN

1. *LP,* III, 322.
2. *Ibid.,* 323-30.
3. *Ibid.,* 321, 322.
4. Dr. David Ramsay to Benjamin Rush, Feb. 3, 1779, Benjamin Rush MSS, Library Company of Philadelphia.
5. *LP,* III, 322. Lee tried to secure the republication of the extract in Boston through Gates.
6. The "Queries" may be inspected in J. Thomas Scharf, *The Chronicles of Baltimore . . .* (Baltimore, 1874), 172-75, and in *LP,* III, 341-45.
7. Scharf, *Chronicles of Baltimore,* 155-62.
8. *Ibid.,* 175-82. See also Lawrence C. Wroth, "William Goddard and Some of His Friends," *Rhode Island Historical Collections,* XVII (1924), 41-44.
9. *LP,* III, 348-50. Compare Reed's version of 1779 with the original letter, *ibid.,* II, 293-94.
10. Fitzpatrick (ed.), *Writings of Washington,* XVI, 7-9, 150-54. There is a copy of the printed "Queries" in Washington's papers.
11. *LP,* III, 362, 365, 373, 380.
12. *Ibid.,* 381-82, 384, 387-88, 391-98. Eustace gave Reed a certified copy of

the Reed letter of November 21, 1776, so often mentioned above. In 1798, seeking Hamilton's friendship and legal services, Eustace declared Hamilton had always possessed his "esteem," "good will," and "good wishes." He then told Hamilton he had deserted Lee from "motives of patriotic submission to the commander in chief." Eustace to Hamilton, Oct. 27, 1798, Alexander Hamilton MSS, XXXII. Eustace's shift of allegiance was dictated, at least in part, by self-interest. When Eustace was trying to irritate Hamilton and force him into a duel, Lee apparently wrote the following to Eustace: "Should the pedant Hamilton take notice of what you say and you should fall, depend upon it your life shall not pass unavenged." "Anecdotes of General Lee," in Lee to Nathanael Greene, Sept. 12, 1782, Nathanael Greene MSS.

13. On June 15, 1782, Oswald published a letter of May 25 from Lee to Richard Henry Lee in which Lee demanded restrictions upon the powers of American legislatures, particularly a guarantee of freedom of the press and protection of private property against arbitrary seizure. LP, IV, 407.

14. Joseph Nourse, formerly Lee's secretary, but a clerk in a government office in Philadelphia in 1779, may have been one of the persons to whom Lee made his claim. Lee does not specifically state in writing the nature of his claim, but there is no doubt that his "treason" plan was its basis. See ibid., III, 369, 374. See also ibid., 448, in which Lee hinted at his claim in a letter to the president of the Continental Congress, October 8, 1780. Wrote Lee, ". . . for Gods sake, Sir, if there is the least ground for suspecting my integrity let me be regularly called before Congress to clear up my character which I am confident I shall do without the least difficulty if I have committed any fault, been guilty of any treason it has been against myself alone, in not once from the beginning of the contest to this day consulting common prudence with respect to my own affairs—so far from bargaining for vile lucre with the English general to sell your lives and fortunes—but of this, gentlemen, I dare say you are yourselves convinc'd. . . ."

15. Ford et al. (eds.), Journals of the Continental Congress, XV, 1348-49.

16. LP, III, 405-409; Ford et al. (eds.), Journals of the Continental Congress, XVI, 33-34. It was said on January 25 by one of Lee's enemies that Lee was drawing provender for his horses from the Continental commissary at Winchester. The fact not being established, no conclusion can be drawn from it. Cf. LP, III, 407, 458.

17. LP, III, 407-409.

18. Ibid., 423-27.

19. Ibid., 372.

20. Ibid., 401.

21. Ibid., 447. The perpetrator of this canard cannot be identified. Elias Boudinot's name would be high on a list of the names of the persons who might have been responsible.

22. Ibid., 445-48.

23. Ford et al. (eds.), Journals of the Continental Congress, XVIII, 914, 1190.

24. Collections of New-York Historical Society for the Year 1878 (New York, 1879), 460. A wild rumor that Lee was engaged in a plot to help the British by freeing and leading some of Burgoyne's men still in Virginia reached New York early in July. It probably was derived from Gates's letter. See New York Royal Gazette, July 7, 1781.

25. *LP*, III, 370-73.
26. *Ibid.*, 400-401, 467-68.
27. *Ibid.*, 412-13.
28. *Ibid.*, 455-59.
29. *Ibid.*, 464-65.

CHAPTER NINETEEN

1. *LP*, III, 454.
2. According to an anecdote told at the time, and often since, Lee met Gates at Fredericksburg as Gates made his way southward and warned Gates not to exchange his "northern laurels" for "southern willows."
3. General Adam Stephen, who lived near Gates and Lee, had been cashiered from the army for drunkenness in the battle of Germantown. There is a tale of a remark which Lee is supposed to have made when the three generals came together: "You, Stephen, was broke for getting drunk when every man should be in his senses; I for not fighting when I was sure to be beat; and you Gates, for being beat, when you had no business to engage." "Anecdotes of the Late General Lee," *The Key* (Frederick, Md.), Feb. 3, 1798. Various other interesting versions of this tale which appeared later seem to be corrupt. Lee is also reported to have composed in retirement the following epigram, which appeared in the same publication, on April 28, 1798:

> Seduc'd by error, to misfortune born,
> Deceiv'd by Congress; made my country's scorn;
> While foes oppress me, friends I seek in vain;
> What hope is left?—I myself remain!

4. Lee seems to have claimed Mrs. Gates was trying to court Washington by abusing him. Wilkinson, *Memoirs of My Own Times*, I, 111 n.
5. Ellen Hart Smith, *Charles Carroll of Carrollton* (Cambridge, Mass., 1942), 182-83.
6. *LP*, III, 428-33. Lee predicted Monroe would be "one of the first characters of this country," if he could rid himself of his shyness. Monroe managed to succeed in spite of his diffidence.
7. For further light on Lincoln's attitude, see *ibid.*, IV, 8.
8. *Ibid.*, III, 386.
9. Lee to Greene, Sept. 12, 1782, *ibid.*, 34-35. On Greene's attitude see also *ibid.*, 1, and Lee to Greene, March 14, 1782, Nathanael Greene MSS, William L. Clements Library. Greene, of course, was familiar with the situation at Monmouth, since he had served there under Washington. He may have had access to peculiarly important information, for the Major John Clark, who carried messages between Washington and Lee, had formerly been his aide-de-camp. It may be significant that Greene was not one of the judges at Lee's court-martial.
10. *LP*, III, 375-76. In June, 1782, Lee sent his sister a list of officers whom he described as men of honor, friends, and his advocates. He named Wayne, Schuyler, Mifflin, Sullivan, Muhlenberg, Greene, Knox, Light-Horse Harry

Lee, General George Weedon, and his own aides-de-camp. John Cadwalader also seems to have esteemed Lee after the latter was in retirement. *Ibid.*, 464.

11. William Davies to Richard H. Harrison, March 20, 1780, Washington MSS.

12. *LP*, III, 427.

13. William Clajon to Horatio Gates, June 7, 1780, Gates MSS.

14. Lee to Nathanael Greene, March 14, 1782, Nathanael Greene MSS. In this letter Lee refers to the British surrender at Yorktown as "the whimsical affair of Cornwallis."

15. *LP*, III, 457, 461, 462, 465-66, 469-80.

16. The tradition cropped up most recently in Julia Davis, *The Shenandoah* (New York, 1945), 126, where it is said that Washington tried to see Lee *after* the War of Independence. The tradition could not possibly be based on fact because Washington was never near Lee's estate in the period 1779-82. It is a distortion of an incident which actually occurred at White Plains in 1776 and seems to have originated with John Esten Cooke.

17. *LP*, IV, 9-11.

18. *Ibid.*, 26-27.

19. Bill from John G. Fraser to Lee, Sept. 28, 1782, Autograph Collection, Historical Society of Pennsylvania.

20. On Lee's last illness and death see Oswald's account in the Philadelphia *Independent Gazetteer*, Oct. 5, 1782; Ebenezer Hazard to Dr. Jeremy Belknap, Jan. 29, 1783, *Collections of the Massachusetts Historical Society*, Fifth Series, II, 184; *Christian's, Scholar's, and Farmer's Magazine*, I (1790), 738; *LP*, IV, 161.

21. Philadelphia *Independent Gazetteer*, Oct. 5, 1782; Robert Morris' diary, Oct. 4, 1782, Library of Congress; John Vaughan to Benjamin Franklin, Oct. (?), 1782, Oct. 10, 1782, Benjamin Franklin Papers, Nos. 107 and 110. Robert Morris wrote in his official diary: "This morning Mr. G. Morris and myself attended the funeral of the late Major General Charles Lee who formerly rendered considerable services to America, but who by an excentricity of character had been latterly led into a conduct unworthy of his talents and abilities and by means whereof he had lost the esteem even of those who wished to be his friends." The Philadelphia *Freeman's Journal* of October 9 commented ungrammatically, "His early services in behalf of the United States deserves a grateful tear."

Horatio Gates may have been one of the mourners. He was in Philadelphia on September 28, and joined Washington's army in New Jersey on October 5. However, his name is nowhere specifically listed.

In 1861 Lee's remains were moved a few feet to a point beneath the south wall of the church. "Disinterment of the Remains of Major-General Charles Lee, at Christ Church, Philadelphia," *Historical Magazine*, V (1861), 370-71. There is no marker over his grave.

22. *LP*, IV, 29-32. William Goddard was separately given Lee's papers. Goddard's descendants preserved the bulk of these and permitted their publication by the New-York Historical Society. Lee's papers were largely lost or destroyed after their publication.

23. Memorial by Alexander White to Congress, read Dec. 2, 1784, Papers of the Continental Congress, No. 41, X, folio 605; Ford *et al.* (eds.), *Journals of*

the Continental Congress, XXVII, 708-709; Isaiah Thomas, *The History of Printing in America* . . . , 2 vols. (Worcester, Mass., 1810), II, 355.

24. W. P. Palmer, S. McRae, and W. H. Fleurnoy (eds.), *Calendar of Virginia State Papers, 1652-1869,* 11 vols. (Richmond, 1875-93), II, 624-26.

25. Sidney Lee to Washington, Jan. 14, 1783, July 3, 1783, Washington MSS.

26. Fitzpatrick (ed.), *Writings of Washington,* XXVI, 342.

27. *Ibid.,* XXVI, 353, 437, XXVII, 60, 329, 363, 392-93.

28. Sidney Lee to Washington, May 23, 1784, Washington MSS.

29. Fitzpatrick (ed.), *Writings of Washington,* XXVII, 481-82.

30. Sidney Lee to Washington, April 5, 1785, Washington MSS. Jacob Morris, Robert Morris, and Horatio Gates also lent their services to Miss Lee.

31. Fitzpatrick (ed.), *Writings of Washington,* XXIX, 97.

32. Edward Langworthy, *Memoirs of the Life of the Late Charles Lee, Esq.* (London, 1792). The sketch is readily available in *LP,* IV, 119-67. The virtual impossibility of avoiding all errors in the field of history is strikingly illustrated by the table of contents of this volume, which gives Langworthy's name as "Isaac."

33. "Memoir of Charles Lee, Major General in the Service of the U. S. of America," in Sir Henry Bunbury, Bart., *Life and Correspondence of Sir Thomas Hanmer* (London, 1838). A convenient reprint is to be found in *LP,* IV, 171-95.

34. Jared Sparks, *Life of Charles Lee, Major-General in the Army of the Revolution* (Boston, 1846, Vol. XVIII in Sparks's *American Biography* series), reprinted in *LP,* IV, 197-334.

35. George H. Moore, *The Treason of Charles Lee Major General Second in Command in the American Army of the Revolution* (New York, 1860), republished in *LP,* IV, 335-427.

36. John Fiske, *Essays Historical and Literary,* 2 vols. (New York, 1902), I, 55-98.

37. Edward Robins, "Charles Lee—Stormy Petrel of the Revolution," *Pennsylvania Magazine of History and Biography,* XLV (1921), 66-97.

38. *American Museum,* IV (1788), 189, copied from the London *St. James' Chronicle,* [?], 1783. The epitaph has been ascribed to Tom Paine. Foner (ed.), *The Complete Works of Thomas Paine,* II, 1099-1100. Paine could have written it, but his authorship does not seem to be established.

INDEX